CW01333897

UNIQUELY DANGEROUS

♘

A True Story
By Carreen Maloney

UNIQUELY DANGEROUS

A True Story
By Carreen Maloney

Copyright © 2018 by Carreen Maloney

All rights reserved. No part of this book may be reproduced, stored in a retrieval system, or transmitted by any means: electronic, mechanical, photocopying, recording or otherwise, without written permission from the author.

ISBN 978-1-7320654-0-6 (hard cover)
ISBN 978-1-7320654-1-3 (ebook)

First Hardcover Edition

Printed in Canada by Friesens in Altona, Manitoba

Interior and cover design by Chris Fettin of Hundred Acre Design in New Orleans

Cover silhouette of Doug Spink's profile drawn by Eve Axelrod

This book was typeset in Garamond, Helvetica Neue and City Stencil fonts

Author's Note

What follows contains spoken and written material from many sources. It has been attributed and retained in its original form, including grammar, spelling, style inconsistencies or errors. Any omissions for clarity or relevancy are indicated with ellipses. The primary style guide used was *Chicago Manual of Style*, and any deviations from it were mine alone, not the work of the precise and knowledgeable Frances Peck, who was the main editor of this book. Most sources have allowed me to use their real names. Where names have been changed to protect sources, aliases have been noted.

Author can be reached at:

3436 Magazine St., #136
New Orleans, LA 70115

uniquelydangerous.com

In Memory of Hiromi Monro

*This book is dedicated to the animals
who are killed by humans
when their secret lives with zoos are discovered.*

PART ONE

1. The Raid 2
2. Valuable Target 7
3. Inside Information 12
4. Blue Tarps 17
5. Stall Tactics 21
6. Former Fiancée 26
7. Sumo Wrestling 33
8. Quiver Killer 39
9. Silent Treatment 48
10. Dead Inside 55

PART TWO

11. Pony Boy 62
12. Bright Future 69
13. Stud Farm 75
14. Coming Out 80
15. Flying Phalluses 89
16. Lady Buble 97
17. Tech Seeds 101
18. Base Jumping 107
19. Last Ride 113
20. Blonde Ambition 120
21. Hockey Bags 124
22. Primate Drama 129
23. Frozen Timber 133
24. Mr. Hands 139
25. Legal Matters 143
26. Gift Horse 150
27. Stockpiling Semen 158
28. Disappearing Act 164
29. Checkmate Cunt 170

PHOTO ALBUM 175

PART THREE

30 Death Sentences 196
31 Bestiality Busting. 204
32 Morning Wood 208
33 Vaseline Mice 214
34 Cause Célèbre 220
35 Judgment Day 224
36 Star Witness 234
37 Connecting Dots. 240
38 Unmitigated Defiance 246
39 Ghosted Out 252
40 Scarlet F 256

PART FOUR

41 Zoo Community. 264
42 Selling Secrecy 274
43 Public Records 281
44 B Word. 285
45 Legal Beagle 290
46 Heavy Petting. 296
47 Cultural References 302
48 Donkey Love 309
49 Double Standards 312
50 Gag Order. 317
51 Dead Ringer 323
52 Déjà Vu 331
53 Double Trouble 338
54 Doorway Darkening. 346
55 Oh Canada 353
56 Northern Exposure 357
57 Night Terror 361
58 The Disappeared 367

BACK MATTER

Appendix. 373
Wet Goddess 397
Acknowledgments 403

PREAMBLE

Ever since this whole thing started, there's a question I get asked a lot.

Why did I pour time, energy and resources into *this* story? Of all the remarkable tales waiting to be told, why choose one that most people wouldn't be motivated or willing to write? Or perhaps even to read?

I don't have a complete answer yet. I hope it comes to me in time.

In part, my desire to write this book gathered momentum because no one else wanted to do it. Someone had to set words to a story practically begging to be told.

That probably still wouldn't have been enough to suck me in if it hadn't happened close to where I used to live. The animals who were seized landed at my local shelter, an organization I've written about extensively for more than a decade.

Sometimes you follow the story not knowing why. You follow it simply because it's there. You follow it because that's what a journalist is trained to do. You aren't supposed to worry about where it's going, or what you'll find when you get there. Just knowing it's leading somewhere should be enough to keep you on its trail.

PART ONE

Night is safe.
Normals own the day.

—Douglas Spink

1

THE RAID

The road was well paved but not well traveled.

Driving up Reese Hill was enchanting in a fairy-tale sort of way. The narrow blacktop curved up the gradual incline through dew-soaked forest. Occasionally large, newish houses appeared, built into clearings.

Doug Spink's old one-room cabin—the place that caused all the controversy—was right at the top of Reese Hill Road. A dead end.

The secluded twenty-two-acre property overlooked a patchwork quilt of farms in Washington's Sumas Valley. It was there, about five miles from the Canadian border, where Spink had settled with his family of horses and dogs.

For the thirty-nine-year-old, it made sense to live where the street stubbed out. It was the highest roost on the road. "There's no line of sight for sniper fire," he used to say. "That matters when you are someone like me."

Recently released from prison, the tech company owner, encryption service provider and former stud farm operator was on probation for his part in a cross-border drug-smuggling operation. But that's not what he meant by "someone like me." Spink was also a known zoophile, or "zoo"—an outspoken member of a mostly covert community of people worldwide who form their primary social and sexual bonds with animals.

Spink felt that being identified by authorities as a zoo was reason enough to be vigilant. Hypervigilant, even. But he also believed he had other reasons to be concerned for his safety, and for that of the horses and dogs he called family.

For one thing, there was the cross-border custody dispute over ownership of a champion show jumping horse. "My life and my barn were plundered," he said of this conflict. "It has been open season on my life and my home, and I'm not allowed to protect myself."

For another, there was his belief that the federal government considered him dangerous because of his encryption expertise. He backed up that claim by referring to a US Probation and Pretrial Services poster that was sent out by his probation officer and circulated among law enforcement officers before the raid. The poster included Spink's mug shot, a map and a list of items to search for. First on the list were:

> All electronics: computers*, storage devices, video equipment, thumb drives, CD, DVD, laptops, cell phones, blackberries, wireless devices, ipods, routers, servers
> *if a computer is found, contact me before you touch it. They **need** to be treated different.*

Spink's feelings of vulnerability led him to decorate his property in a style meant to deter trespassers. A plastic skeleton left over from Halloween hung from one tree. A grinning fake skull was affixed to another. If that wasn't enough, a typed two-page note in capital letters was laminated and nailed to a tree near the entry gate, which he always kept locked. Its warnings included this:

> THERE ARE SERIOUS PROTECTION DOGS PATROLLING THIS PROPERTY 24/7—NONE LESS THAN 100 POUNDS, ALL TRAINED IN OBEDIENCE AND SCHUTZHUND WORK. THEY LOVE AND RESPECT THEIR FRIENDS, BUT RARELY WELCOME STRANGERS. THEY ARE LICENSED, WORK AS A PACK, HAVE GOOD EARS, AND THEY RUN VERY FAST DURING A CHASE. HOW FAST CAN YOU RUN?
>
> IF YOU DO NOT HAVE AN INVITATION TO ENTER THIS PROPERTY, DON'T CROSS THIS LINE. ANYONE DOING SO IS AN ILLEGAL INTRUDER AND SUBJECT TO INTENSIVE PHYSICAL RESTRAINT AND EJECTION. ONLY THEN WILL WE CALL FOR YOUR AMBULANCE RIDE.

> **WELCOME, AND SMILE!** YOU ARE CURRENTLY BEING RECORDED BY 24/7, OFFSITE-STORED, REDUNDANTLY-LENSED, DAY/NIGHT VIDEO SURVEILLANCE. YOUR LICENSE PLATE HAS BEEN NOTED (FRONT AND REAR). CAMERAS ARE RECORDED, NOT MONITORED.
>
> DO YOU HAVE AN INVITATION TO ENTER THIS PRIVATELY-OWNED, POSTED-NO TRESPASSING PROPERTY? IF YOU DO, WELCOME – PLEASE CALL (866.966.7445) TO LET US KNOW YOU'VE ARRIVED & WE WILL MAKE YOU OUR GUESTS.
>
> THERE ARE SERIOUS PROTECTION DOGS PATROLLING THIS PROPERTY 24/7 – NONE LESS THAN 100 POUNDS, ALL TRAINED IN OBEDIENCE & SCHUTZHUND WORK. THEY LOVE & RESPECT THEIR FRIENDS, BUT RARELY WELCOME STRANGERS. THEY ARE LICENSED, WORK AS A PACK, HAVE GOOD EARS, AND THEY RUN VERY FAST DURING A CHASE. HOW FAST CAN YOU RUN?
>
> IF YOU DO **NOT** HAVE AN INVITATION TO ENTER THIS PROPERTY, DON'T CROSS THIS LINE. ANYONE DOING SO IS AN ILLEGAL INTRUDER & SUBJECT TO INTENSIVE PHYSICAL RESTRAINT + EJECTION. ONLY THEN WILL WE CALL FOR YOUR AMBULANCE RIDE.
>
> ✦
>
> IF YOU ARE A MEMBER OF LAW ENFORCEMENT WITH A VALID, COURT-ISSUED ORDER OR WARRANT – PLEASE CALL THE CARETAKER TO NOTIFY OF YOUR PRESENCE (800.909.3972; CALL WILL BE RECORDED) AND WE WILL ENSURE YOUR SAFE ENTRY AND WELCOME HERE. IF YOU DO NOT HAVE SUCH AN ORDER, DON'T CROSS THIS LINE; CONTACT OUR ATTORNEY @ 877.909.9988, x7.
>
> IF YOU ENTER WITHOUT REQUIRED WARRANT OR COURT ORDER, WE WILL TAKE EVERY LEGAL ACTION NECESSARY TO HOLD YOU ACCOUNTABLE FOR YOUR FLAGRANT DISREGARD OF THE U.S. CONSTITUTION (4ᵗʰ AMENDMENT), AS WELL AS YOUR OWN <u>SWORN OATH OF OFFICE</u> TO UPHOLD THE LAW. YOUR BADGE DOES NOT MAKE YOU ABOVE THE LAW, ANY MORE THAN OUR CITIZENSHIP MAKES US ABOVE THE LAW. WE RESPECT THE LAW. DO YOU?
>
> COME IN PEACE AND ENJOY OUR HOSPITALITY. COME TO DO HARM, AND FACE OUR LEGALLY-ENSHRINED RIGHT TO PROTECT OUR PROPERTY, OURSELVES, AND OUR FAMILY. Ὅπερ ἔδει δεῖξαι...
>
> *Old Blood remembers - forever*

Sign attached to a tree at the entry to Doug Spink's home in Sumas.

People called Spink paranoid, but he called it prudent.

Even with these elaborate security measures in place, Spink had grown reluctant to leave his property. He holed up there for weeks at a time. Periodically, he would venture out to pick up supplies for himself and his animals. He would wait until nightfall. Then, once neighboring houses were dark, he'd climb into his green 1992 Chevy Suburban and slowly drift down the hillside, headlights off. His truck was barely visible as it slid through the inky rural darkness.

He suspected that one day the authorities might come up the road for him. Which is why he added a warning meant specifically for law enforcement to the note nailed up near the property entrance. From the police, Spink demanded advance notice in the form of a telephone call, and a warrant: "If you do not have such an order, don't cross this line."

∩

Shortly before 10:00 a.m. on April 14, 2010, Douglas Spink was three hours into a sound sleep when nineteen federal SWAT team members arrived unannounced. It was the shouting and pounding at his door that startled him awake. When he opened the door, still groggy, he saw a stack of shiny automatic weapons pointed at him. There were officers from the United States Probation Department, Federal Bureau of Investigation, United States Marshals Service, Whatcom County Sheriff's Office and Whatcom Humane Society. In all, about thirty law enforcement officers went to the top of Reese Hill Road to take Spink in.

His seven large-breed dogs, some trained to protect him, scrambled out of the cabin through their own door, and were soon running loose along with the four horses.

Spink's protective instincts for his dogs were as quick as theirs were for him. He shouted commands, one dog at a time, to settle them down. "Wiskey, easy, Wando, easy, Ruben, easy, Rugi, easy, Buji, easy, Lazarus, easy, Jackson, easy…"

"It's a miracle they didn't get shot," he recalled later.

But there would be no shots fired. No dog attacks. Not even mild resistance from Spink. The authorities agreed he was polite and compliant. Police didn't even need to frisk him, because he was stark naked. The government may have considered him dangerous, but the only items officers found during their search that they tried to classify as weapons were a couple of pocket knives and a box cutter.

The media wasn't far behind law enforcement. On cue, news helicopters hovered above Spink's place like buzzards circling a fresh kill. Blue tarps attached to the cabin that sheltered a makeshift outdoor sitting area made the target easy to spot. That's what stood out from above: the rooftop of the little cabin, and the blue tarps attached like wings.

Paul Peterson, a former US Air Force fighter pilot and international investment banker, and one of Spink's former business partners, was watching television in Portland, Oregon, that day. "The news came on and it was a helicopter view of his home," recalled Peterson. "And you know it isn't good when the caption underneath calls it a 'compound.'"

News outlets in Washington State were the first to report on the raid, but the lurid details caused the story to go viral worldwide: former cocaine smuggler caught running a bestiality farm featuring horses, dogs and—most peculiarly—Vaseline-slathered mice.

The story stunned and transfixed the general public. It shook the line that divided man from beast.

Readers and viewers who lived in the area were repulsed by the case, but also curious and captivated at the same time. Despite their declarations of revulsion, they found a way to gossip through the "ick" factor, telling crass jokes and marveling at what had happened just up the road in sleepy Sumas, right there in Whatcom County.

The trading of rumors would linger much longer in the region than the breaking news. The event was too scandalous for prolonged coverage. News editors wouldn't assign investigative teams or pullout features. Reporters wouldn't even reply to the emails Spink sent them in an effort to have his say.

Yet the raid that morning, and the headlines it generated, were far from the end of the story. And even farther from the beginning.

For more documentation on the planning of the raid, see Exhibit 1, page 374, and Exhibit 2, page 376.

2

VALUABLE TARGET

The police allowed Spink to get dressed. He put on a sweatshirt, cargo pants and tennis shoes before being handcuffed and loaded into a black SUV driven by US marshals. He was whisked away to SeaTac, a federal detention center south of Seattle. It was a place he was familiar with—SeaTac was where he'd done his pre-sentencing time five years earlier, after the arrest that involved cocaine.

"On the way down to SeaTac, I was tired," he recalled to me later. "And I was worried for the dogs. I was not worried for the horses. All they needed was hay a few times a day, and they were fine on the property. They had water from the spring, self-refreshing. But I knew I had a great support network to make sure they were all okay."

During the 130-mile drive, Spink wasn't nearly as worried as he would have been had he known what was transpiring back on Reese Hill Road.

∩

Doug Spink wasn't the only person inside the tiny cabin on the morning it was raided. A British tourist named Stephen Clarke was there too.

Clarke was on the tail end of a three-day stay at Spink's, the last of several stops he'd make on a tour around Canada and the United States.

Spink had fallen asleep at seven that morning under the impression that his guest was leaving around ten. When the authorities descended at quarter to ten, they entered the property easily because Clarke had left the gate open—the gate that Spink was always diligent about locking. While Spink was dealing with the police swarming outside, Clarke hung back inside the cabin. Spink thought Clarke seemed unsurprised by this alarming turn of events.

Clarke had been taking vacations to the United States for ten years. Spink had never met the fifty-one-year-old UK citizen in person prior to this visit, but they weren't total strangers. They had friends in common. And for years, both had frequented the same internet chat forums for zoos, where Spink went by the nickname Fausty, and Clarke called himself KBE, short for Knot Big Enough. Spink found Clarke bland and boring, but conceded that he had a way with dogs.

For Clarke, the idea of visiting Spink had begun forming months earlier. Spink often posted photos on the chat forums, pictures of his dogs and horses lounging around the cabin and property. The animals looked calm and relaxed with each other, and that atmosphere piqued Clarke's interest.

Why travel so far to meet Spink? A report of a Whatcom County Sheriff's Office interview with Clarke on April 29, 2010, after the raid, provided a glimpse into his mindset:

> Clarke used to own 2 dogs. (Clarke very emotional discussing topic.) Fight between the dogs broke out in a public place. There were allegations that he used unnecessary force to separate them. The dogs taken away and put down.
> Clarke could see that Spink managed many dogs without them fighting. Clarke's goal was to see how this was possible. Spink had some unusual views. Spink believed it was possible for dogs to live together without a hierarchy—no alpha, superiors, inferiors, etc. Spink provided no real explanation on the forum. During the visit, Clarke learned more. Spink's claim was simplistic, but it did work. Didn't fully understand dynamics.

Clarke had many questions: Did Spink's dogs—all intact males—get along? Did they ever fight? How did Spink achieve harmony among them?

Spink enjoyed sharing his philosophies, and he liked people to observe the environment he'd created for his four-legged friends. He was proud of it. But he was a study in contrasts. Fiercely security conscious, he was cautious about allowing new people into his personal space. His beliefs about animals had inspired threats of injury and death in the past. Plus he was on probation for his role in a Canada-US drug-smuggling operation. But Clarke pushed all the right buttons. He challenged Spink, practically taunted him, and said he didn't believe Spink's claims were possible. Eventually Spink invited him to come and see for himself.

Before Clarke arrived, Spink informed him that living arrangements on his property were sparse. The modest cabin was cramped, chock full of books and dogs, and not set up to accommodate overnight guests. He gave Clarke two choices: camp outside, or sleep in the horse trailer with the hay. But when heavy rains dumped on Sumas that week and Clarke showed up without camping gear, Spink felt bad about making his visitor sleep outside in the wet, clammy cold. He offered to let Clarke squeeze into the heated cabin. That's where police found both men when they descended on the property.

"I thought next to nothing of Clarke," Spink said. "He was leaving that day. I figured he'd sneak out with his tail between his legs, not a peep more heard. That he'd whine about his visit being spoiled by a SWAT raid at the end."

That's not what happened. Rather than disappearing, Clarke actually helped authorities round up Spink's animals.

"Clarke had been told he was free to leave, but remained on the property due to his rental car being blocked in by patrol cars and Humane Society vehicles," said a Whatcom County Sheriff's Office polygraph report from May 5. "Clarke had apparently been given the choice to walk away from the property and chose not to."

That seemed unusual considering Clarke was a suspect too. How much of a suspect became clear when police saw his recordings.

Like Spink, Clarke had a lifelong interest in computers and technology. He was a computer programmer until 1990, when he went into business for himself installing alarms and closed-circuit video systems, and he was fanatical about encryption, a topic he talked about during his polygraph exam (which indicated no deception). He even had his own method for creating a password. "Clarke said he keeps all of his files encrypted," the polygraph report noted, "and rips a news article out of the newspaper and then picks a word or phrase for the password. Clarke stated this is his policy, so if he ever got arrested, he would not have or be able to reveal the password. Clarke said when he knew he was getting arrested at Spink's house he dropped the news article on to the ground."

Despite that, police were somehow able to view the recordings he made on Spink's property. Enforcement officers reported that they watched the tape from Clarke's camera right on site shortly after their arrival.

What they saw provided the most scandalous moments in the civil proceeding that would unfold two months later in a Whatcom County courthouse: Stephen Clarke having receptive anal sex with Doug Spink's dogs. Clarke's recordings landed the British visitor in handcuffs, and became the key piece of evidence federal prosecutors would later use against Spink.

∩

Spink used his camera too, but as a safety precaution. Up until a couple of days before the raid, he took thousands of photographs depicting his animals and their daily routines—playing, eating, sleeping. He took photos of the food he bought and served them. He wanted the treatment of his animals documented for legal protection. "Radical transparency," he called it.

Even as the raid was underway, his confidence didn't waver.

"I was ready to fight," he remembered, "to show that these thugs can't just break into our homes whenever they decide they don't like what we're saying. I was in the right. I was doing nothing wrong. I was scrupulous about ensuring nothing illegal was on my property, ever. I knew they had made a false jump on me, and I was ready and eager to turn the tables and show that this shit needs to end."

But he didn't turn the tables. "How horribly, tragically, comprehensively wrong I was. I could not imagine the horrors to come."

The events that followed the raid of April 14, 2010—a series of prosecutions, trials and incarcerations—stemmed from one key assessment: the federal government had labeled Spink uniquely dangerous, a significant threat worth spending massive sums of taxpayer dollars to track, raid and prosecute. For years after the raid, the government continued to pour resources into watching Spink's activities. For a while, they monitored his every step using an ankle bracelet.

"This is, in the Government's view, an extraordinary case—both in the nature of the violations as well as in the special concerns presented by the defendant, Douglas Spink," stated federal government lawyers Susan Roe and Steven Masada in a sentencing memorandum later that year.

What made Spink such a high-value target? Prosecutors and police weren't alleging that he was still involved in the drug trade. Were they going to these extreme efforts because he was a zoo? That seemed unlikely, because animal welfare is the bailiwick of the state government, not federal.

"I knew they had nothing on me, so I'd be out in a few days and ready to rip into them for this false start persecution," Spink recalled. "I was prepared for that: what to say, what tools to use to communicate, the counter-lawsuits to file. This was going to be the first time a zoo was able to stand up and say: back the fuck off. You can't arrest me for being who I am, and I will prove it. I thought I was prepared."

Spink believed he had done everything in his power to prevent his animals from being taken away or harmed. He had faith in the American court system. And he didn't see how he could lose given the safeguards he had put in place.

He couldn't have been more wrong.

"The last I saw of my life and family was out the rear window, and then it was gone."

Doug Spink would never return home to Reese Hill Road.

INSIDE INFORMATION

For me, the Spink story didn't start by reading salacious headlines. It began with BlackBerry pings.

The text messages were from staff at the Whatcom Humane Society, where I had volunteered as an animal rescue writer for a decade. They said that a collection of animals had been seized from a bestiality farm in Sumas. I lived less than a half-hour drive from WHS, and about the same distance in another direction from Spink's place.

I was dismayed by what I was hearing, and concerned for the animals. A bestiality farm was a concept I hadn't known to exist in real life. All the cruelty and torture people inflicted on animals, and now rescuers had to worry about them being used as sex slaves too? As an animal lover, I was appalled. As a journalist, I felt driven to find out the truth. I decided to start at the source of my information: the Whatcom Humane Society.

I had visited dozens of shelters in various cities over the years, interviewing staff and volunteers repeatedly on emotional topics such as overcrowding, euthanasia and the inevitable bouts of compassion fatigue that set in as a result of the challenging, difficult work of animal rescue. I watched in the euthanasia room as animals' lives were taken because there weren't enough kennels to house them, and I saw the psychological toll this took on staff. Many reported they never got over it, even years after leaving the job. Anger, depression, substance abuse, even suicide attempts (and sometimes completions) were the potential fallout. My stories about what I learned were published in shelter newsletters and in magazines such as *Modern Dog* and *Animal Sheltering*.

As my local shelter, WHS had special significance to me. I'd written for and about the society for ten years, and spent vastly more time there than I did at other shelters. It was my go-to destination when I found stray and injured animals, as I often did.

In this case, WHS had taken custody of Spink's seven large-breed dogs: two Great Danes, two German Shepherds, a Rottweiler, a Bernese Mountain Dog and a rare South African mastiff called a Boerboel. They also seized four stallions and thirteen field mice.

The dogs were split up between the two locations operated by WHS. Five went to the facility at Irongate Industrial Park, where workers settled them into the back kennels farthest away from public view. The other two were taken to the shelter's Williamson Way location near the Bellingham International Airport.

Three of the stallions were sent to a local farm. The fourth, the high-value show jumper Capone, was sequestered in a boarding facility in another community whose location was kept secret to deter potential horse snatchers.

The thirteen brown mice didn't survive the ordeal. The day after the raid, Laura Clark, executive director of the Whatcom Humane Society, requested permission from Whatcom County Sheriff Bill Elfo to euthanize them on the grounds that they were injured and suffering.

Spink, when he learned of this decision, disputed this claim. He said the mice were fine when he last saw them before the police rolled in. Since he couldn't do much to prove that from prison, one of his friends asked the authorities to conduct necropsies (animal autopsies) on the mice to show they hadn't been used for perverse purposes.

Permission was not granted.

∩

The news stories about Doug Spink were astonishing. But after the initial headlines fizzled, the media never investigated what was really going on, which made me want to do my own research. I wondered what was behind the headlines, especially because there was a major hole in all the stories—none of the reporters actually spoke to the man at the center of the controversy.

But before I was able to interview Spink, my research took me to the shelters. The first WHS shelter I visited after the raid was the run-down structure near Bellingham Airport. Everyone I encountered there was in a state of head-shaking disbelief. Like all shelter workers, the staff and volunteers had witnessed extreme neglect and unimaginable cruelty. Being jaded was not unusual in their line of work. But their reactions to this case were different from what I'd observed before. They were worked up. Angry, shocked, confused, repulsed.

The story dug especially deep into the psyches of those who'd actually met Doug Spink, the people who had regular contact with a man they thought cared so much about his animals. In the small intake area attached to the shelter's surgery bay, a worker named Joni Black pulled me aside to talk. She grew teary-eyed when she told me she had met Spink while working at Northwest Veterinary Clinic, in Blaine's Birch Bay Square, where he'd brought his dogs for vet care.

Three years earlier, Spink's Golden Retriever, Rion, had sustained life-threatening injuries during a fight with his other dogs over a package of sugar cookies. Black had driven Rion into Canada for specialized veterinary treatment as a favor to Spink, who couldn't cross the border because he had a felony on his record. Her efforts were in vain. Rion didn't make it. He died a few days later of a cardiac event while still at the hospital. Back in Washington, Black comforted Spink at the clinic as he sobbed over the loss.

Black shared with me an email in which Spink detailed his love for six-year-old Rion:

> Right now I can't even begin to envision a life without him by my side. I know that his time with me was a blessing, a genuine gift. I know that no matter how long we were together, it would never be enough. I know I'd lean on him for lessons in the graceful beauty

of life every day he was here, confident he'd be there tomorrow to lead me along yet again. I know I'd never be ready to go on without him, even if he were here forever. None of it makes me ready to face the mornings without him here. I loved him as deeply as any being can love another being, as he did me.

Now, however, Black was upset and angry that she'd held this man in her arms and consoled him, not knowing he would later be accused of operating a bestiality farm.

Joni Black wasn't the only staff member from the Birch Bay veterinary clinic who recounted these feelings. Another, who asked not to be named, said, "We really honestly believed he really, really loved those dogs. But he is really good at fooling you, because we were all one hundred percent convinced, and when this all came out we were entirely shocked and betrayed, you know, it's very sickening."

Over the next several weeks, I visited both Whatcom Humane Society shelters several times, and interviewed everyone who felt like talking. Among the people I spoke with was executive director Laura Clark. I had interviewed Clark many times before. We weren't friends, but we had a mutually beneficial working relationship. She was quotable and enjoyed being in the limelight, and I wrote stories in publications that showcased her work in animal welfare. Clark even nominated me for a WHS Act of Kindness Award, which I received in 2006, a few months after returning from rescuing animals in New Orleans following Hurricane Katrina.

But the civility that Clark and I had previously enjoyed was about to come to a halt. Many times she made appointments with me to do the interview about Spink, but when I arrived at the designated hour, she changed her mind and refused to participate. She'd see me heading her way, tripod and camera in tow, and that was her cue to start yelling at me from across the parking lot. "I don't have time to talk about bestiality today, Carreen!" she would bellow.

Perhaps she was trying to embarrass me out of conducting an interview because of the topic. Or maybe she thought I'd simply tire and give up after a while. Neither of those things happened. I kept scheduling appointments and showing up for them until finally one day she agreed to appear on camera. She refused to remove her baseball cap, which shadowed her face, but I went ahead with the interview anyway.

Clark said the shelter was getting up to fifty calls per day from individuals and groups that wanted to know what was going to happen to Spink's animals. Numerous people were coming forward with ownership claims. Her staff was in danger, Clark said, and needed protection.

I said that I believed it was important to take photos and get footage of the animals while they were at the shelter for purposes of historical documentation. There was significance to this federal case, and worldwide interest in the story. Clark assured me she would allow it, but not yet. The animals were stressed out from all they'd been through, she said, but promised the access would happen soon.

That was the only time I would get Clark on camera talking about Spink. After I turned it off, she told me a video seized during the raid contained a scene in which Ruben, the South African Boerboel, was tied down and gang-raped, penetrated anally by more than one man. She said she would arrange for me to view the tape. But she never did.

I eventually got the tape from another source. The scene described by Laura Clark was a fabrication. Instead, the video showed a man—who authorities confirmed was Stephen Clarke—receiving anal sex from three dogs. It was noteworthy that Clark had reversed the positions of the man and the dogs, as well as the ratio, and had added in the tied-down detail. But I wasn't sure yet what the inaccuracies meant.

BLUE TARPS

Once I learned of the raid on Doug Spink's cabin, the story began to gnaw at me. What had happened up there, and why? Who was this eccentric man linked to these activities? After more than a week of interviewing and wondering, I realized that to get to the bottom of this story, I had to go to the top of Reese Hill Road. I headed to the place the *Huffington Post* described as a "ramshackle, heavily-wooded compound" and the *Seattle Times* dubbed an "animal sex farm."

I told myself I would just do a drive-by, familiarize myself with the neighborhood. Maybe I was kidding myself, because I put a freshly charged battery in my camera and brought along a spare.

As I turned to go up the hill, I imagined what Spink's property would look like. I pictured a large, tall fence, fortified gates, high-tech security systems.

Although it was a pleasant, sunny spring day, the farther I drove, the more ominous it felt, as if I were being willingly lured into a trap. I was voluntarily headed for the snare. Straight into the lair of a man who many had labeled dangerous.

When I got to the end of the road, it curved into a short bib. Then it was gone.

At the entrance to the wooded, mostly undeveloped twenty-two-acre property, I knew I had the right place, because I recognized the blue tarps from the aerial footage taken by news choppers on the day of the raid. I expected to find yellow police tape stretched across the entrance to deter intruders, but there was nothing like that. There wasn't even a gate; I didn't know who had removed it, or why. For a few minutes I sat in my car, absorbing my surroundings and summoning my courage.

The property was peaceful, private and lush. Birds chirped sweetly. Just a few feet ahead, three deer bounded by and disappeared into the trees, startling me momentarily from thought.

Leaving my Honda at the edge of the paved road, I cautiously walked the rest of the way in, keenly aware that I was invading someone's home, and that other people could be staying there. Zoophiles? Drug smugglers? I had no idea what I would find.

The place felt eerie, as if the life had been sucked out of it. Which of course it had. It had been more than a week since the raid, but it felt as if Spink and the animals had just been there.

As I approached the blue tarps, I noticed an old couch positioned underneath them to form a seating area as if it was part of a regular living room. A mattress was on the ground. A shiny green street sign announced that this was Stallion Drive. Around the property, fences had been fashioned from tree branches. Enclosures for the horses had been created using red and blue twine left over from hay bales.

There were trashed remnants of efforts to create a homemade flower garden—pebbles, rocks and flowerpots made from old plastic food containers. A bucket half full of brussels sprouts lay in the dirt. I wondered whom they had been intended for. A hammock was precariously positioned over the edge of the bluff, suspended between trees high above the stream that wandered through the property. It was obvious that the man who lived here was comfortable being outdoors, and that he considered the land as much his home as any indoor structure.

Then, at the bottom of an incline, there it was: the infamous tiny cabin. I turned my video camera on and slowly made my way towards it.

The building was rustic, but everything required for survival was there. Clothes were suspended on hangers from the cabin's eaves, presumably hand-washed and hung there to dry. Plastic snap-together shelves were placed against the outer walls and protected by the roof overhang. They were laden with supplies: utensils, coffee mugs, vitamins, food.

Electricity ran to the cabin via orange extension cords plugged into the power box near the edge of the road. There was no running water. A camp shower hung on a tree.

The door was cracked open a sliver, not wide enough to see inside. I stopped and listened for a few moments. Slowly, tentatively, I pushed it open.

When I look back at my shaky amateur footage, what stands out on the audio track is my ragged, heavy breathing. Inhales and exhales. The soundtrack of my fear.

My hands were trembling. It took everything I had to keep myself focused on the camera's viewfinder. I had to keep reminding myself that the sounds of footsteps were my own.

The cabin was one cramped room. The doors looked salvaged from somewhere else because they didn't match the rest of the place. A table, a couch and a narrow bed filled most of the space. The place was a mess. Insulation was torn from the ceiling and hanging down. Papers and magazines were scattered about. Lying on the table was a large framed collage of different business cards, all printed with Spink's name and titles. As I stared at them, I realized they provided a history of the various companies he'd been involved with. I thought the cards might help me track his career path if I decided to go forward with telling this story, so I took a picture of them.

A whiteboard on one wall displayed a list of ideas for something called a "cross-species co-op." Animal-themed greeting cards were tacked up, along with a calendar featuring photos of wolves. A vase of withered flowers stood on the table against the back wall, a hint of order that looked out of place in the clutter.

Had Spink been living in chaos? Or had the police trashed his home during the five hours they reportedly spent on the property? The answer came two years later, when Spink got out of prison and produced numerous photographs he'd taken up to a couple of days before the raid. In the shots, books lined up neatly on shelves. Dogs napped peacefully on couches. Everything was in its place.

Surveying Spink's cabin, I was puzzled. This place didn't look like a bestiality farm, or whatever I imagined a sex-focused enterprise might look like. The little cabin could barely accommodate one person comfortably. To view it as some kind of Hôtel Haute Dog—an international tourist destination—took a significant stretch of the imagination.

When I eventually spoke with Spink years later, he was indignant about the way his modest home had been portrayed by prosecutors and the media. He believed his cabin was an ecologically responsible way to live, particularly fitting for a man who, in the 1990s, had been an activist for Earth First!, the self-described radical environmental group. He wanted to know: why were people so appalled that he was living simply? When did that become a crime? For Spink, it was a dream to live in a hand-built cedar cabin in the woods, crafted around 1930 by the original farmer, who cut and milled the cedar on the property. He "had running water 24/7" in the form of the freshwater stream that trickled through the property. "I was demonized because I was living this way," Spink told me. "How dare I go off the grid? Should I be living in an apartment or a condo?" He said he chose the location for the dogs and horses.

At the hearing later that summer into whether Spink had violated his probation—the official reason for his arrest on April 14—his attorney, Howard Phillips, submitted a memorandum to the court defending his client's sparse living arrangements. "Mr. Spink was released from prison with nothing and he did the best he could to live a quiet life in humble condition[s] such as his small cabin."

When I left Reese Hill Road, I was plagued by questions without answers. My journalist's antenna was up. And I was more determined than ever to meet Spink's animals and see what shape they were in.

5

STALL TACTICS

As the weeks following the raid ticked by, I began to suspect that Laura Clark had no intention of allowing me to film or photograph Spink's dogs and horses. It felt like she was slow-playing me, stalling for time until the animals were no longer at the shelters.

My suspicions were soon confirmed. A few weeks after Spink's arrest, Clark refused to talk to me anymore, and told Whatcom Humane Society staff that, for the first time in ten years, I was banned from both shelters. It was an interesting development. Whatcom County locals informed me she was also spreading false rumors that I was trying to help Spink get his animals back to be used for a bestiality ring. She ordered her staff and others to stop doing interviews with me, or else.

I wasn't too concerned about the rumors. They were so ridiculous that I figured people wouldn't believe them. What really bothered me was not being able to find out what had happened to the animals. When the raid first happened, I was relieved they were safe. But that relief soon gave way to concern.

Clark had told Susan Simmons, former president of the WHS board, that Spink's dogs were "deranged." Was it true? If so, would there be attempts to find homes for them, or would they be secretly euthanized because they were tainted by allegations of bestiality? I wanted to confirm the demeanor and condition of the dogs for myself.

Stalling a journalist might not seem like a difficult feat for a shelter director to accomplish, but Clark's mission was complicated by the fact that I had independent relationships with workers and volunteers.

Monty Apt was the employee who went furthest out on a limb to help. His courage didn't surprise me. I had known him for a long time, and he had a renegade spirit. Witty, compassionate and dedicated to helping animals, especially dogs, he wanted to help me get the dogs on film. It was an undertaking that was by no means risk-free. You could never be sure when people might be coming and going to check on the animals. All we could do was mitigate the risk.

Two of Spink's dogs—Rugi, the Bernese Mountain Dog, and Ruben, the South African Boerboel—were staying at the Williamson Way shelter near Bellingham Airport. That was also where the society's administrative offices were located. We considered trying to get footage of those dogs, but decided the chances of getting caught were too high. It would be nearly impossible for Apt to get me in and out of Williamson Way undetected.

Instead, we focused on the Irongate shelter, where the other five dogs were housed. There was one hour during the week that Apt thought was safer than other times, a momentary gap in the foot traffic of a busy shelter.

He would surely be fired if we were discovered.

It wasn't yet 5:00 a.m. when I pulled into the parking lot at Irongate. I had an hour max, and that was pushing the envelope. My vehicle had to be completely out of the area by the time staff started showing up.

Apt threw on the lights in the shelter and went about starting his work day. I set up quickly, powering up my freshly charged equipment as fast as I could, not wanting to waste a moment of precious time.

One by one, Apt brought the dogs out of their kennels and walked them by my camera so I could film them. He followed the typical morning routine, which included putting the animals in the outdoor runs for their morning constitution. I filmed Spink's two German Shepherds (Wando and Wiskey), two Great Danes (Lazarus and Bugi), and Jackson, the Rottweiler.

Spink's dogs were not deranged. I watched each dog for signs that they were demented or behaving unusually. I petted each one of them as Apt brought them out. They were curious, social and friendly, with healthy weights and shiny fur. They acted just like regular dogs.

As I filmed Apt caring for Spink's animals, I interviewed him about the case. By the time Spink's cabin was raided, Apt had worked at the shelter for four years, and had a lot of experience working with dogs. He was resigned that he was giving them the best he could, but caring for vibrant, athletic dogs in confinement wasn't an easy job. Frustration and kennel stress were setting in. One of Spink's Shepherds had bitten him in the knee, redirecting his frustration at Apt when they walked through the noisy kennel area. The other bite incident involved a different staff member, when the same Shepherd "scaled up and over the kennel door like it was nothing, and ran up and bit her in the stomach," Apt said. Neither bite broke the skin, but they did leave bruises.

One of the central questions on my mind for Apt was whether he believed Spink loved his animals.

"I'm sure he did," Apt answered. "I mean, they're all well cared for. But just not in the right way." Like others I'd spoken with at the shelter, he was upset. "For the first two days, I was completely angry and distraught and didn't know what to think of the whole thing. It's on the same level as molesting a child as far as I'm concerned. Just taking a dog's innocence and betraying it like that. It's not right."

One of the ways Apt dealt with his anger was to rename the animals. "Just because of what it's associated with," he explained. "You know, the names they had when they were with that guy, Mr. Spink."

The media had reported that the field mice brought in from Spink's property were slathered in Vaseline. Apt didn't know about the mice, but he said the two Great Danes had a substance on them when they came in. It wasn't Vaseline, because Vaseline is close to odorless, and the Great Danes smelled strongly of petroleum. "Some sort of petroleum product just came right off them," he recalled. "Dennis did the baths. I told him he should use gloves, but he didn't."

By the time my hour at the shelter was up, I'd seen no sign that Spink's dogs were "deranged," as Clark had suggested. However, they were clearly having a difficult time there, which isn't unusual for animals placed in that type of loud, crowded and confined environment. Large dogs used to freely roaming wooded acreage as a pack, they were now crammed into small kennels, alone. They were stressed out. One of the Shepherds was hoarse from barking so much. Another was trying to scratch his way out of his cage.

I was able to see the remaining two dogs over at the Williamson Way shelter while they were in kennels before Clark banned me from the WHS shelters, but it was during regular business hours, and it wasn't possible to film them under her watchful eye. Ruben, the South African Boerboel, was taking confinement the hardest, which was not surprising given his breed. Boerboels are livestock protection dogs. The males weigh in at 140 to 200 pounds on average, and they are powerful enough to kill a full-size male lion. The Boerboel wouldn't necessarily survive the fight, but neither would the lion.

Locked up in a small kennel, Ruben's mental state was starting to spiral. Photos I obtained later using Freedom of Information requests show Ruben with a shunt in his shoulder. According to staff, he sustained the injury during a fight with another dog while in the shelter's care.

After my hour was up, I quickly packed up my recording equipment and beat it out of the area before anyone spotted me.

At that point, I didn't know where Capone was being kept, but I knew about the Whatcom County farm where the other three stallions were staying. I tried to visit them on three separate occasions, but each time I made arrangements with staff members to drive out there, Clark found out about it, and instructed her staff not to allow me to see them.

∩

While Laura Clark was stalling my attempts to film the animals, I was doing my own stalling of a different sort.

I had planned to put together a magazine story about Spink. I contacted Carrie Allan, editor of *Animal Sheltering* magazine and senior editorial director of the Humane Society of United States, to see if she might be interested in running it. I had written other freelance stories for the magazine, which is published six times a year by HSUS, America's largest animal welfare organization.

Allan said yes, she would run the story. But each time her deadline approached and she would politely inquire as to whether I'd finished the piece, I'd say I needed more time. I was still trying to figure out what—if anything—to write. Finally she asked if I was ever going to get the story done, or should she just drop it from the schedule.

I never did write the article for *Animal Sheltering*. The story was too complex to commit to words early on, before I had figured out what I was dealing with.

At that point, I had no intention of writing a book, though that became the end result of my investigative efforts. In those early days, all I had were questions, interviews and documentation that I didn't know what to do with, and a gut feeling that what I was seeing on the surface was just a murky rendition of the truth that lurked underneath.

FORMER FIANCÉE

Putting together the puzzle of Doug Spink's life meant talking to everyone I could track down who was willing to speak about their time with him. Corinne Super was an important part of the picture.

Super had lived on the same property as Spink in Canada, before he was arrested for smuggling drugs and went to prison. At the time of the raid on Spink's cabin, she was fighting in British Columbia civil court to gain custody of Capone, the champion show jumping horse who was among the animals removed from Spink's place. What's more, she and Spink had been engaged—at least, that's how Spink described it.

Shortly after the raid, Laura Clark gave me Super's cell phone number. I called to arrange an interview at her farm in Langley, British Columbia. She was cautious and guarded. It took some convincing, but she eventually agreed to let me come out to meet her. Mysteriously, she refused to give me her address. Instead, she told me which road to take, and said I should call her when I got close.

The day of our meeting, I jumped in my car and headed inland towards the small and quiet Lynden-Aldergrove border crossing. After I entered BC, I got Super on the phone. She said to let her know as soon as I'd crossed a small bridge. Then she would guide me in.

"Turn! Turn right!" she instructed when the time came. I turned into a long driveway, and there she was, standing in the middle of it. She was tall, lean and long-legged, a cascading mane of blonde spiral curls pulled back into a ponytail, and dressed casually in jeans and work boots, typical attire for farm work.

It was sunny and warm that day, and we sat on a bench outside next to her indoor riding ring. She talked about how hard the situation with Spink had been on her.

That turned out to be a consistent theme in the many interviews I conducted with Corinne Super, both on camera and off. Over the next couple of months, we met numerous times at her farm. As she hauled straw, hay and grain, and fed and groomed her horses, I followed and watched and asked questions. Sometimes I took notes; other times I audiotaped or videotaped the meetings.

"He's shattered any kind of trust I would have for another person," she said. "I don't think I could ever leave myself open like that again. He's closed that. Which is too bad. It's taught me to be more careful."

As time went on and I learned more about the contentious, tangled relationship between Spink and Super, it became clear that these two people didn't agree on much. But they did share one resounding belief: that each had stolen away some of the other's ability to trust people.

∩

Corinne Super and Doug Spink met in 2003 at a stable in Pitt Meadows, a mixed urban, suburban and rural municipality in the lower Fraser Valley, just east of Vancouver, British Columbia. Super was a trainer at the facility, and both she and Spink rented stalls there for their horses.

Super, her then-husband, Mark, and their eight-year-old daughter lived in a log house in nearby Mission, but in 2004 they bought a farm farther east in Chilliwack. They rented the stallion barn to Spink, who moved into it with his dogs and horses, including the show jumper, Capone. Another tenant rented the farmhouse. In time, the house tenant left, and Corinne and her daughter moved in. Mark stayed behind in Mission.

During my interviews with her, Super repeatedly insisted that, contrary to Spink's statements, the two had never been romantically involved. Rather, they'd been friends and partners in the horse world. "We were very much connected through the horses and through our common love of the horses and riding, and just being barn crazy."

I asked why Spink would lie about being engaged to her.

"To try and make me look even more scandalous, I'm sure, because I was married. When Doug was in the barn and when we were friends with the horses, I was married."

Besides, she said, Spink was gay.

> Doug always made it very, very clear to me that he was gay. I certainly have it in letters, I have it written that he wanted to be very clear that he wasn't misleading me, that there would be no chance of any kind of a romantic thing with him. . . . That he enjoyed my friendship very much. I think he called me a beacon of light in a very tough time for him. And he welcomed my friendship and my enthusiasm with the horses, and he enjoyed my company, but that he was truly dedicated to his family, and that he was gay. He knew he'd been gay for a long time. That was the difficult part he had with his ex-wife. He went into long, lengthy discussions about it. I don't know what his concern was to make me crystal clear to understand that, I'm not truly quite sure why he would think that that was an issue.

During their life together on the Chilliwack farm, Super had ample time to observe the way Spink lived. She told me he was a "dog whisperer," and would work in the barn with a pack of canines surrounding him. "He'd be sitting in the middle with all the computers and stuff around, and the dogs would all be laying around him in a bit of a powwow, like a sleepover."

From what she saw, the dogs seemed fine, and they got along with each other. "They would just all be laying at his feet. I think it was a bit unusual that you could have seven or eight full-grown, oversized dogs living together, intact dogs. I don't think that's very common to be able to have that many dogs together like that."

Over time, Super learned about Spink's belief systems, which she found unusual. "He refers to people as two-leggers. He says that there is a four-legged world, and there is a two-legged world, and he only has use for the four-legged world. The two-leggers are nothing but an inconvenience. The mainstream, the rules and our society and our culture is based around the two-leggers, and that is not where he belongs, so those rules don't apply to him."

Spink was a night owl, and extremely private. He always lived in the barn, she said, "because he wanted to be with the dogs and the horses. He would always have a very private boundary, he calls it the boundaries. . . . If the barn doors are shut, you do not enter under any circumstances." Thinking back on it, Super said, this was ridiculous, because it wasn't Spink's barn. Still, if the doors were shut, "Do not enter. Period. If the barn doors are open, you are somewhat welcome, but you have to announce yourself."

Super was certain that Spink's intensely private side must have made the raid on Reese Hill Road a devastating, traumatic experience. "What just happened to him is his ultimate fear, that his animals, his privacy, his dark secrets, his life, his stuff, will disappear, will be taken from him. What just happened, I think, would be the ultimate hell, the ultimate demise."

The recent raid was not the first time Super had seen Spink's name connected with bestiality, she said. She told me about being a witness on a police report filed with the RCMP in Chilliwack regarding bestiality allegations against him. She said police came to her farm and took his computer tower, though she wouldn't give me documentation or an RCMP contact I could call to confirm this. She described an interview room at the police station where she was shown a stack of pictures that portrayed a man having sex with numerous animals. She identified the man (whose face wasn't shown) as Spink because she recognized the piercings on his genitals.

I asked her: how did she know he had piercings on his genitals if they hadn't been in a sexual relationship?

"He would go out to get the paper naked," she said.

∩

During our interviews, the subject Super spoke about most fervently was Capone, the prize-winning show jumper she was fighting to gain custody of. As her twenty-two horses whinnied, romped and nuzzled each other in the big barn and paddocks surrounding us, she talked about her dedication to Capone and her love for him, reiterating that she desperately wanted him back. Spink hadn't taken proper care of the celebrity stallion, she said. (Spink later accused her of the same thing.)

Spink had purchased Capone in 1998, years before he met Super. What, I asked, was her claim to the valuable horse?

She replied that she had paid Spink's debts for him during their relationship, and had spent upwards of $100,000 on Capone's care. She didn't produce receipts or other evidence of that assertion, even though I asked for them several times. She said repeatedly that she would get them to me later, but she never did. The only document she produced to back up her claims was an ownership agreement for Capone. There was a telephone number I didn't recognize written on one of the two signature lines, but no signatures.

Super said that she had to rescue Capone to protect him from Spink, who she insisted didn't treat animals or people properly. She described him as a cold, calculating character with no moral structure or empathy for any living being. "He cannot function in society safely, period. We are all at risk. Whether you're human, whether you're animal, whether you're a criminal, whether you're white collar, he is a threat to every aspect of life. He cannot function out here. He is a danger to all of us on every level."

What motivates him? I asked her.

She stared at me intently and responded without hesitation.

"He cannot function within a routine, normal, respectable, law-abiding environment. He has no respect for anybody, or regard for rules or authority. When you have absolutely no respect and no regard, you have no guilt."

She summed up her assessment with a layperson's diagnosis: "He is a psychopath."

Super had been searching for Capone for six months, and said she was about two weeks away from finding him when Spink was raided. That raised a question, one of several I mulled over in the coming months. How could someone know they were two weeks away from finding a horse if they didn't know the animal's whereabouts, or whether they would ever find him?

Super also told me she'd shown up at the Whatcom Humane Society with a horse trailer to collect Capone approximately an hour and a half after the raid on Spink's property. Much to her surprise and disappointment, Laura Clark wouldn't give her the stallion. This was a high-profile case involving a high-value horse, and Clark knew it. She wasn't about to release the animal without legal guidance.

The drive from Super's farm in Langley to the Whatcom County shelter was at least an hour in light traffic, plus there was an international border to cross. To reach the shelter in ninety minutes, Super would have had to jump in her vehicle at almost the exact moment the authorities had descended on Spink's cabin. I asked her: how did she know so quickly that Spink had been raided? Her answer: she saw it on the news.

If that was true, it was fortuitous timing. My hunch was that it was more likely someone had tipped her off.

∩

It was only later that I started to put the rest of the story together. In 2013, almost three years after my first meeting with Super, I interviewed horse breeder Charla Wilder, owner of Valley View Percherons (Percheron is a breed of draft horse). Wilder lived in Custer, Washington, less than four miles from my house, and had sold Spink a horse named Little Joe, or L.J.

A straightforward, no-nonsense horse person, Wilder worked at the livestock auction in nearby Everson, so I visited her there. In the main auction area, spectators sat on bleachers while animals were put in front of a crowd of bidders. There were cows, pigs, sheep, goats and chickens. I assumed many of these animals would be slaughtered for food. It was hard to watch their frightened faces and know they might be on the way to their deaths. I took photos of the animals in between talking to Wilder.

Wilder mentioned that Super had come to the auction house and filed a report of a missing horse—namely, Capone—at the end of March 2010, a couple of weeks before the raid on Spink's cabin. Those missing animal reports get submitted to the Department of Agriculture office in Olympia.

The timing didn't feel random. Had someone advised Super to file the missing horse report shortly before the raid? Was that why she was surprised when she showed up at the Whatcom Humane Society with a horse trailer, only to leave disappointed and empty-handed?

Whatever the circumstances, Super was resolved: she wasn't giving up on getting custody of Capone.

As she repaired fencing around her farm, she emphasized her determination in an interview that ended with her on the verge of tears.

> I've had very wise people ask me, why don't you just walk away? Is it really worth it? Is it really worth having that asshole in your life and on your tail? Why don't you just walk away? I said, you know what? Because I cannot get Capone's face out of my mind. I cannot stop thinking about him standing there and needing better. And I can't stop thinking about how I have to fight for him. He needs a voice and he needs help. And I can't walk away. I can't. And that's why you keep fighting.

She was glad that Spink had landed back in prison. "When Capone disappeared from my barn, every day I prayed that this would lead to Doug going back to jail somehow." To her, being stressed was a small price to pay. "It's worth living through this hell and this nightmare and this torture and this stress and everything else. It's worth it if it puts him back in jail. And it did. He's back in jail. So far the plan's going according to the way we were hoping, and this is the next hurdle, to get [Capone] home in the barn."

Otherwise, the ordeal wouldn't have ended, Super said.

> At least now it's ended. That's what I have to remember, that this is all going according to plan. Really, in a weird, twisted way, it's all going to plan. He was supposed to go back to jail. He did. And now I will just fight and get all the cards aligned the way they should be to get Capone. That's the way it's gonna go. It's the only way it can go. I don't care what kind of evil shit he pulls from the depths of the earth. I will battle it. No matter what he throws at me, I'll battle it. That's all I can do.

SUMO WRESTLING

Corinne Super was in a state of euphoria as she drove her pickup truck north towards the Canadian border on June 11, 2010. Reality was sinking in. A civil proceeding had just wrapped up in a Whatcom County courtroom—Superior Court Judge Ira Uhrig presiding—and she had won. The headiness of victory elated her; she was smiling and laughing almost the whole way, when she wasn't worrying about what she was going to do next.

Being towed in a horse trailer behind her was Capone, the champion show jumping stallion worth millions of dollars. The celebrity horse had been released to her custody that afternoon. After the decision came down, Super drove immediately to collect him from the secret location where he was stashed, a farm in Arlington about fifty miles south of Bellingham.

I was in the truck with her. I had interviewed her many times by now, so she agreed to let me come along for the ride to document what happened next.

Super had to get Capone over the border and to her farm in Langley, British Columbia, but it was near the end of the business day on a Friday, and she didn't have his veterinary paperwork ready for a border crossing.

Neither had she made arrangements for a safe place to keep the valuable stallion on the American side until she could secure the proper papers. Her lack of preparation surprised me.

As Super got closer to Canada, her glee about winning custody of Capone grew tinged with worry. She had no plan. I made a few calls to try to find somewhere to put the horse. The first was to my husband, Hiromi Monro. We had founded and ran a wholesale plush toy business together called Fuzzy Town, and stored our inventory in Ferndale, in a warehouse midway between Bellingham and the border. I asked Hiromi if he'd mind getting equine supplies from the feed store if we decided to keep Capone in the warehouse for the weekend. He happily agreed to help, and we said our goodbyes.

"I love you," I said.

"I love you too," he replied.

I couldn't have known then how important those last words would become. My marriage to Hiromi would become one of the factors that wound up drawing me into my investigation, and helped keep me there for almost eight long years.

♘

"You don't sound separated," Super remarked after the call ended.

She was right about that. But indeed we were. Hiromi had a name for us: "separatés." By now I had grown accustomed to sentiments like Super's, people questioning whether we really were separated, and whether we should be. Friends would see us out for meals together, laughing and talking, and wonder what happened, why we couldn't just work it out. We were rebuilding a strong friendship that had somehow gotten lost as we traveled the journey of our marriage.

I met Hiromi Monro in Tokyo at the end of November 1996. He was one of twin sons born in 1968 to a Japanese woman and an American man from Seattle. At home in both countries, Hiromi had grown up in Japan until he was twelve years old, when he and his twin brother were sent to boarding school in Massachusetts. After high school graduation, Hiromi attended the University of Southern California's School of International

Relations before returning to Tokyo as a man of twenty-two to begin a career in the film industry.

He was twenty-eight when I met him, just six months older than I was. It was sumo wrestling that brought us together.

At the time, I was working as a reporter for the weekly newspaper *Business in Vancouver*. I traveled to Japan for a two-week press trip organized to teach Canadian journalists about the sport. Media coverage was already being courted for the upcoming Sumo Canada Basho scheduled for June 1998 at Vancouver's Pacific Coliseum. Our host on the trip was Chiyonofuji, master of the Kokonoe stable and one of the most popular sumos of all time. "The Wolf" was known for his muscular stature and powerful throws. He was the fifty-eighth *yokozuna* (grand champion) of the sport, with the third most championship wins in modern sumo history.

Chiyonofuji commanded a darkly handsome, mighty presence as he ushered the media around the basho tournament and the grounds of his stable, which included a training ring and communal dining room for his team. The dining area was our last stop after the tour. The sumo wrestlers wore loincloths and sported topknots as they served us their traditional dish of *chankonabe*, a stew they eat in huge quantities to gain weight and prepare for battle. We sat cross-legged on the floor around a long, low table in front of steaming bowls of soup packed with meat, tofu and vegetables. I don't eat meat, so I didn't touch my sumo stew. I could tell it offended them, but I just couldn't do it.

On my last night in Tokyo, Hiromi attended the final press conference. He was working as an assistant producer for Takeshi Kitano, also known as Beat Takeshi, an acclaimed comedian, television personality, actor, author and film director.

When I spotted Hiromi across the room, I knew immediately he was going to have great significance in my life. It's hard to explain that feeling if you've never experienced it before. It just *is*.

I have a souvenir of the precise moment we connected. Heather Kirk, a friend from Tourism Vancouver who had arranged the press trip, was hiding behind a potted plant and snapped a picture that captured the first time we spoke. She knew it was a special moment. In the photo, it's clear from our faces that romance was already blooming.

Hiromi was quiet and reserved, but not shy. Although he didn't say much, when he did speak, everyone stopped and listened. He never wasted his air time with idle chatter; he spoke the sage words of an old soul. I still recite his adages when I'm searching for advice to give someone: "Never back a man into a corner. That's when he fights the hardest." And, "You can't ask a man with no legs to run."

After the press conference, our group had plans to go to a nightclub called Muse. Hiromi agreed to meet us there later, but we ended up in a VIP area at the back where he didn't think to check. It was only as I was walking through the club to find the restroom that I bumped into him as he was on his way out because he assumed our group had left. If not for that fortuitous timing, it's unlikely we would have ever crossed paths again.

We spent the evening talking at a bar that played movies all night, and the next day we walked around Tokyo until I had to go to the airport to catch my flight home. He asked if he could visit me in Vancouver two weeks later. I happily agreed, completely taken with this mysterious man from Japan.

Things moved quickly. In mid-December, he came to Vancouver for the weekend, and we decided he would pack up his life in Tokyo and move in with me at the beginning of February. Shortly after he arrived, he asked me to marry him. At first I wasn't sure if he meant it, because he started hyperventilating. I sat him down on the floor in our apartment, his back against the kitchen cabinets, and held a small paper bag to his face to breathe into while he calmed down. I offered not to take his proposal seriously if he wanted to take it back—no hard feelings—but he insisted he didn't want to take it back. A usually cautious man had decided to be spontaneous.

The next week, on a Friday afternoon that was Valentine's Day 1997, we were married by a justice of the peace. Hiromi wore a tuxedo, and I wore a poofy white wedding dress I bought off the sample rack because there was no time to order anything. I figured it was the only time I'd get to wear such an ornamental, impractical garment.

In the two and a half months since our first meeting, we'd spent just seventeen days in each other's presence, and exchanged a bunch of long emails and phone calls before agreeing to stay together until death do us part.

We had many wonderful years together, Hiromi and I. He taught me patience and the wisdom of biding time, and I taught him about spontaneity and taking chances. For a long time, it seemed like a fairy tale come true. There were challenges of course, as with all marriages, but they seemed surmountable and rewarding.

But then we began to drift apart. We didn't share common interests other than our business, and I could feel our friendship eroding little by little. We didn't have children to focus on (and the long list of family activities that comes with having kids), so the drift was even more noticeable. We were just two adults living in a house, who had begun to circle around, rather than connect with, each other. The disconnect was palpable.

At year twelve, I asked for a separation to see if we could bring ourselves closer together by taking some time apart. That sentence sounds ridiculous when I write it now, on another Valentine's Day exactly twenty years after our wedding. What was I thinking?

As long as I live, I can't imagine making a decision I'll regret more than the one to separate from Hiromi. If there is such a choice waiting in my future, I shudder to imagine what it could possibly be.

∩

Corinne Super decided not to bring Capone to our toy warehouse. She was concerned he might slip and break his legs on the concrete floor. Instead, a friend of mine got in touch with a family who had an enchanting old wooden barn on a small farm in Lynden, conveniently close to the border. They were happy to help. Being horse people, they were also pretty starstruck about having a celebrity jumper hanging out at their place.

After we set up Capone in the barn, the family parked a tractor across the driveway, and let it be known that they had guns and weren't afraid to use them. They were determined not to let Capone be stolen back for the purpose of bestiality.

Super couldn't stay the weekend because she had twenty-two horses to care for back at her farm in Langley. But she did cross the border to visit Capone both days. She also called several times to check how the stallion was doing. One of those times I didn't have my phone with me for about an hour. When I finally picked it up, it was blowing up with missed calls from her. She was in a complete panic that I couldn't be reached and had become convinced that I was working with Doug Spink. That I had taken off with Capone.

I calmed her down and assured her Capone was fine. I found it curious that she thought Spink had enlisted my help. What was it about him that she believed would be so convincing to me?

Capone loved the old barn in Lynden. He ate and drank and relaxed in the large stall. Other animals who lived on the farm stopped by to visit him—goats, sheep, ducks, chickens, a dog and a cat. I could tell he liked having them around. The visits were so touching to me that I videotaped them. What Capone loved most was when the farm people put a mare in a round pen nearby. They knew he would enjoy the smell, sound and sight of her, and did he ever. He would stick his head out a square hole in the side of the barn and whinny to her, and she'd whinny right back.

Until this story, I knew nothing about horses or how to care for them. Now I know a little bit more than nothing. Capone was fine with me entering his stall to clean it, and to give him fresh straw for bedding. I brought him hay to nibble on and refilled his grain and water bowls. At night, I slept on a lawn chair beside his stall to make sure he was safe.

Some people geld stallions because they claim they are dangerous and hard to handle. Capone didn't act that way, and neither did any of the other stallions I met while working on this book. He was gentle and sweet and affectionate, well socialized, and appeared to my eyes to be in excellent health.

If only I could interview a horse. If any witness could speak to what life was like in the care of Doug Spink, it was Capone.

On Monday, Super returned to load Capone into the horse trailer. I watched her truck and trailer disappear down the driveway, heading towards Canada.

QUIVER KILLER

Monty Apt couldn't risk meeting up with me to discuss the Spink case in public anymore. Laura Clark wouldn't appreciate finding out from her sources that he (or anyone else) was helping me with this story. It could cost him his job at the shelter. So instead, he sometimes came over to my house to talk after work.

There was a lot to discuss that summer. There was the civil proceeding to determine who got custody of Spink's dogs and horses, plus Spink's federal hearing in Seattle for alleged probation violations. I attended both. Apt had to work, but he was able to let me know how the dogs were doing at the shelters. We shared what we knew.

We were having one of these impromptu meetings sitting across from each other on barstools at my kitchen island late in the afternoon on Monday, June 21, when the doorbell rang. I wasn't expecting anyone. It was rare to get surprise visitors way out of town where I lived. Hiromi and I had built our house in the woods on acreage, down an old logging road.

People sometimes report an impending sense of doom before they are delivered bad news, a premonition that tragedy is about to strike.

That didn't happen to me. I wasn't even alarmed to find a police officer standing on my porch when I opened the door.

"Are you Hiromi Monro's wife?" he asked.

"Yes," I said, still unfazed.

"He's been in an accident."

"Is he okay?"

Looking back, I can't believe what a dumb question that was, especially with all my experience covering tragedy. Of course he wasn't okay, or a police officer wouldn't be standing there. Even the officer's next words didn't snap me into reality.

"No, he isn't. He died."

"No, he didn't."

"Yes, he did. He had an accident on his bicycle."

"No, that can't be him. He doesn't have a bicycle."

I was in total and utter denial. It couldn't be true. It had to be a case of mistaken identity.

Then the police officer handed me something. I looked down at the small bundle of metal. His keys.

I started to shake all over. It was true. Reality sank in. My first instinct was to go and be with him, but the officer stopped me. It would be too upsetting, he said, a gruesome scene. I invited him inside the house. When Monty saw the officer, his first instinct was to hide his beer, as if he was an underage kid drinking when he wasn't supposed to. Afterwards, he said he didn't know why he did that.

The police officer left, and Monty and I were both in shock. He wanted to stay with me so I wouldn't be alone, but I had to notify Hiromi's family of his death, and I wanted to do that by myself. I remember standing on the porch, watching Monty walk towards his vehicle parked in my circular driveway. He kept looking back, asking if I was sure. Did I really want him to leave? He didn't think I should be alone. I reassured him that being alone was what I needed.

The police officer had advised me to call Hiromi's twin brother to notify him first, then have him tell their mother. I don't know why he suggested that sequence of events, but it sounded like wise advice from someone who saw this kind of thing a lot, so I followed his suggestion. It was an awful phone call to make.

I had requested the police bring me the bicycle Hiromi had been riding so I could look it over. It wasn't long before a different police officer showed up at my house, and opened the trunk of his car to reveal a mountain bike. I didn't recognize it. Where had it come from?

I asked him to pull the bike out so I could examine it. There were a few scuff marks, but no blood that I could see.

∩

Three hours before Hiromi's dead body was discovered, I had gone to our toy warehouse looking for him to see if he wanted to go out for lunch. His SUV was parked in the lot. The back of it was open, so I knew he was nearby. I assumed he was out visiting friends at another business in the industrial park, which he often did. I didn't go inside our building. Since our separation, we had agreed on a mutual privacy rule of no unannounced visits. I had called a couple of times before coming over that day to see about lunch, but he hadn't answered the phone.

I walked over to his truck and placed a timer in the back, the kind you plug a lamp into when you go on vacation. He had been using a hot plate inside the building, and I didn't want him to burn the place down. The timer would be a fail-safe in case he accidentally left it turned on.

A timer.

The symbolism of that small plastic object was gut-wrenching, and heartbreaking to think about now.

As I set the timer down, Hiromi was lying just a few feet away from me in the pit of the loading dock, dead. He had been there since around five the previous evening.

I have reenacted at least a hundred times how I could have missed his dead body lying there. I've paced it out again and again. He missed hitting my range of vision by only a few inches. The dock pit slopes down, and he was lying in the deepest part, forty-six inches below parking lot level. It was just low enough to hide him from my sight line.

By the time an acquaintance of Hiromi's discovered him three hours later, approximately twenty-one hours had elapsed since his death. The man's panicked screams for help punctuated the quiet and otherwise uneventful summer afternoon in the sparsely populated business park, drawing others to the scene.

The next morning, I went to the warehouse to try to make sense of what had happened. His body had been taken away, and emergency workers had hosed the large pool of blood into the drain at the bottom of the pit.

The man who had found Hiromi came back again, drunk and mildly belligerent as he showed me graphic photos of the scene he had taken with his phone. The police hadn't exaggerated. It was gory and bloody.

White gravel dust had coated the bike's wheels as Hiromi rode around the parking lot, and his tires left tracks on the dock pad and in the pit. They revealed that he had made several successful jumps over the edge of the dock before something went fatally wrong. Cyclists I've spoken to tell me it's a deceptively difficult jump to make, to cycle off an edge and land into an incline, especially for a beginner. Hiromi was brand new to the sport. The temptation for an inexperienced rider is to try to pull out of the drop when it goes awry, but you can't defy gravity. He was thrown over the handlebars, and landed on his bare head. The jump was only forty-six inches. But he was six feet tall; if he was standing on the pedals, his six-foot-tall frame added up to a ten-foot impact of unprotected skull on concrete.

∩

In the midst of grief, shock and disbelief, another state of mind took root: a need to know what had happened to Hiromi. I was compelled to track down the facts.

Perhaps that sounds like a strange reaction for a new widow to have. But as a journalist, it's my default setting. Going after the 5Ws (plus H) felt like a way to create order in the chaos: who, what, where, when, why and how. The fact finding was an attempt to understand.

I learned from the police that Hiromi had borrowed the bicycle from Transition Bikes, a company run by Kyle Young and Kevin Menard. We were almost neighbors in the business park. There was just one warehouse that sat between Fuzzy Town and Transition Bikes. Hiromi had spent a lot of time at Transition, especially lately. The bike company had fashioned a practice track behind their warehouse made out of dirt, wood and other materials.

But Hiromi decided to try jumping a different location on that fateful day: our warehouse dock. The model he was riding was called the Quiver Killer, a high-end dual-suspension mountain bike worth about $6,000. The police were keeping it in their evidence locker while they investigated. Young and Menard asked the police to get it back for them. I agreed to relinquish the bicycle, but not until I could find a biking expert to examine it. I wanted to determine if the scuffs on it matched the theory of the accident. I also didn't want Transition promoting the bike or auctioning it as the one Hiromi had died on. I asked police to convey that wish to Transition's owners. The world of extreme sports sometimes has trophy reactions to souvenirs of death when people lose their lives in pursuit of their chosen sports.

I didn't know Young and Menard nearly as well as Hiromi did, but we'd spoken cordially a few times. While I was on the dock the morning after the accident, a Transition employee walked over and offered his condolences. He told me Hiromi's interest in mountain biking was recent, which explained why I hadn't known about it. Hiromi was a talented athlete in many sports, but not cycling. The employee said the more experienced riders "had been teasing him that he sucked at jumping."

He asked if he could give one of the eulogies at the memorial service. I said yes. He was the only person from Transition Bikes who spoke to me after Hiromi's death. I asked him to invite Young and Menard to the funeral in the business park, but they didn't show up, and they have never acknowledged his death, at least not to me.

I needed to confirm for my own peace of mind that this was indeed an accident. My thoughts went to the story I was working on. Hiromi had died at the warehouse where Corinne Super and I had considered stashing Capone, the multi-million-dollar horse at the center of a heated dispute over ownership. Could Hiromi's death have a connection to the Spink case?

I went to see the lead crime scene investigator at the Whatcom County Sheriff's Office. He said there was no doubt lingering in the investigators' minds that this was an accident, because none of the evidence contradicted the accident theory.

I also called the county medical examiner, Gary Goldfogel. An autopsy was standard procedure in deaths like this, when there were no witnesses. I asked him for the estimated time of death.

"You've been watching too many crime shows," he said gruffly. "There's no way I can know the exact time of death."

The medical uncertainty was compounded by the fact that Hiromi's body had been lying in the hot June sun for many hours.

Although medical science didn't have an answer for exactly when his heart had stopped beating, there are ways to figure out someone's approximate time of death just by going back to the web of people they connect with, and figuring out when the connecting stopped. I was able to determine that Hiromi had most likely died between five and six the previous evening, on June 20. I reconstructed the timeline according to the plans he missed and his phone log, which revealed the moment when outgoing calls and texts from his phone went quiet forever. The ambiguity means his death certificate doesn't include a date of death. It just says "found" on June 21, 2010, the day after he died. There is no official marker of his departure from this life, an indignity of paperwork purgatory that still causes a visceral reaction in me all these years later.

Goldfogel said that Hiromi died quickly, within two or three minutes, and suffered what was considered an "unsurvivable injury." Even if there had been a skilled medical team on site, it wouldn't have been enough to save him.

I expressed my concerns about possible foul play to Goldfogel and asked him to examine Hiromi closely, to do every conceivable test on his body. Hiromi and I had talked about death before, and I knew he wanted to be cremated and scattered at sea. The characters used to form his name Hiromi mean "Pacific Sea." A skilled sailor and windsurfer, he loved the water. This would be the last chance to gather information from his body before Hiromi set sail for the last time.

After the autopsy, I went to the funeral home to photograph every scratch and bruise on his dead body. I didn't know what else to do. As an investigator, keeping my own record of what had happened to him was the final act of love and support I could perform.

As I did all of this, I felt regret, and the typical guilt that comes with the what-ifs when someone we love dies: if the chain of events had unfolded differently, would he still be alive? He had lived his life cautiously in every way, except when it came to sports when he was a younger man. But he had started doing chancier things in sports again after we separated, such as snowboarding out of bounds. And now this: jumping off our loading dock.

At his memorial service, some people asked me if he had committed suicide. That was an absurd question. He didn't believe in suicide as an answer, and even if he had, no person would reasonably think they could engineer their own death from a drop of less than four feet.

One of the comments posted under the single brief *Bellingham Herald* news story about his death said it was natural selection that he had died, because he was dumb not to wear a helmet, and at least he wouldn't be contributing his stupidity to the gene pool.

The callous comment didn't upset me. But the thought of the unworn helmet did. To this day, I'm still bothered by why his helmet was sitting nearby in his open truck, waiting and ready to be placed on his fragile head. In my nightmares about it, which used to play frequently and vividly, I imagine how awful the impact must have sounded when his head hit the pavement. Goldfogel was upset by Hiromi's death too, and told me he was getting sick and tired of doing autopsies on people with their heads bashed in when they could have easily been saved with helmets. He said that if Hiromi had been wearing a helmet, he would have escaped the crash with nothing more than a few scratches.

Three weeks later, I held the funeral at the warehouse. The dock pit was turned into a shrine decorated with ribbons and flowers. I commissioned a small metal plaque inscribed with Hiromi's name and dates of birth and death. It proclaimed this was "His Last Ride On Earth." I had the plaque installed in a discreet location, low on the cement wall, closest to the spot where he had died. A friend who worked in the business park gathered wildflowers to blanket the pit and cover the bloodstain, an indelible mark outlining the shape of his body.

In the months to come, I would try to scrub the stain away several times to no avail. When the moon came out, the stain glowed a phosphorous green, a haunting lunar version of Luminol. One night under a full moon, I stopped by to check on the place. The body outline was lit up, conspicuous. It was more than I could bear. I crawled into the pit and curled up in a fetal position on top of the stain shaped like Hiromi. My face hovered over the drain as I sobbed into the metal grate that covered the hole, knowing his blood was down there somewhere.

∩

The first social event I attended after Hiromi's death wasn't until the summer was nearly over, in August. It was a fund-raiser for animal welfare. The setting was the Bachman-Turner Overdrive mansion in Lynden, Washington, the same community where Capone had spent the weekend before heading to Corinne Super's farm in Canada.

BTO, a rock band from my hometown of Winnipeg, Manitoba, had a series of hits in the 1970s, and sold more than thirty million albums worldwide. The 15,000-square-foot house in Lynden, which contains a bowling alley and a recording studio, was built in 1976 so the band could escape the overpowering notoriety they felt in their home country at the height of their popularity. Now the home belongs to Andy Clay, a woman who is active in the animal welfare community. Sometimes she hosts events to raise money for the Whatcom Humane Society and other groups.

BTO's catalog includes the hit song "You Ain't Seen Nothing Yet." As it turned out, I hadn't.

That night, I was placed at the same table as Laura Clark. As if that situation wasn't awkward enough, the tension was heightened when Clark told Clay that I was putting her family in danger by photographing the outside of the mansion. Clark didn't know that I'd gone to Clay beforehand to ask permission.

During the event, Clark first asked, then demanded, that I turn over to her any and all evidence I had collected on the Spink case. When I asked her if the dogs were alive and what had happened to them, she threatened to send the federal government after me to seize my notes and tapes.

I responded by asking again, "What happened to the dogs? Are they still alive?"

To date, I haven't been able to confirm whether Spink's dogs made it out of WHS alive. Clark claimed they were all adopted into good homes, but she won't supply proof. I'm not sure what's true. But at that fundraiser, seeing her reactions, I knew I had to find out more.

In addition to what had happened to the dogs, I was plagued by many other questions. As a lifelong animal welfare advocate and rescuer, I wanted to understand this secret world of people who claim to love their animals too, only in a much different way. Are they crazy? Immoral? I was concerned about the animals. Are they being exploited or harmed? And as a journalist, I was perplexed by the many unknowns. How big is the zoo community? Do they walk among us? Should we be concerned about them? Should we do what we can to stop them, to prosecute them as Doug Spink had been prosecuted?

9

SILENT TREATMENT

Doug Spink got a lot of media attention after the raid in Sumas. What he didn't get was the opportunity to be interviewed by the media. Although reporters covered his story extensively and sensationally, they didn't communicate with him—not even when he reached out to them from federal prison.

Spink, like other federal inmates, had no internet access while on the inside. Instead, he relied on CorrLinks, the prisoner email system. To connect with someone via CorrLinks, a prisoner sends an email request to link up, similar to a social media friend invitation. The receiver can accept, ignore or block the request. If the request is accepted, the receiver is added to the inmate's list of approved contacts, and the two can then email back and forth.

Usually reporters were curious enough to accept Spink's friend requests, but then didn't respond when he wrote to them. He grew so frustrated that he started to print out his emails and snail-mail them to journalists at their newsrooms using the US Postal Service. Still he was met with silence.

In fact, Spink's attempt to communicate with journalists was introduced as evidence against him in his federal probation revocation hearing. I couldn't determine whether his emails were forwarded to prosecutors by journalists, or pulled off CorrLinks by the authorities. Through Freedom of Information requests, I was able to find out that reporter Peter Jensen of the *Bellingham Herald* had forwarded emails written to him by Spink to Laura Clark.

The silent treatment is not standard practice in journalism. While it isn't unusual for journalists to write a story about someone who refuses to speak, it's unheard of for them to ignore the subject of a story en masse. Protocol is to interview dangerous characters, and that includes serial killers, pedophiles and rapists. If anything, journalists tend to be criticized for going after sources too relentlessly. In the Spink case, it was turnabout. The subject in the spotlight pursued the unwilling journalists instead of the other way around.

This raised a question: was it ethical for the media to ignore Spink, to refuse to interview him while simultaneously writing thousands of words about him in stories that drew many readers?

In this fast-paced, controversial and frequently subjective profession, which doesn't require a license to practice, questions about news ethics are debated ad nauseam by journalists and editors. Consensus can't always be achieved; there isn't necessarily a right and ethical answer every time. But *not* wanting to land an interview with the individual at the center of public speculation and attention—no matter who he or she is—runs counter to professional standards that encourage getting all sides of the story. Wouldn't all of us want the opportunity to speak in our own defense if we were being written about by the media?

Besides refusing to communicate with Spink after the raid, reporters didn't check details that seemed implausible, such as the Vaseline-slathered mice. There's a colloquial term for what Laura Clark and the police accused Spink of doing with the mice: "gerbiling," the purported practice of inserting live rodents such as gerbils, mice, rats and hamsters into the human rectum for sexual stimulation. Despite the public's morbid curiosity about the practice, and attempts by tabloid reporters and others to verify that it actually occurs, gerbiling has been debunked as an urban legend by Snopes.com and other myth busters. Not one case has ever been confirmed or corroborated with medical reports.

Yet the mice were presented by authorities as a clear-cut component of Spink's alleged bestiality farm. Reporters allowed themselves to be manipulated without applying scrutiny, and their imaginations ran wild. The mice were arguably the most damning allegation against Spink in the court of public opinion.

Newspapers took on a hardy-har-har tone, sometimes pretending they didn't want to cover the story even as they *were* covering it. "The week continues with a story we don't want to write and you don't want to read, and yet here we are," wrote David Schmader in *The Stranger* on April 22, 2010. "We're speaking of course of the Whatcom County drug smuggler suspected of running a bestiality whorehouse out of his barn."

Seattle Times columnist Nicole Brodeur didn't hold back. On July 19, 2010, she wrote a story titled "This guy really needs supervision," in which she demanded that Whatcom County prosecuting attorney David McEachran charge Spink with animal cruelty. "The Whatcom County Sheriff's Office found there was probable cause for first-degree animal-cruelty charges against Spink. Those charges could make it harder for Spink to adopt animals in the future and, it should be hoped, teach a lesson to other depraved freaks of nature." Then Brodeur suggested the public could help monitor Spink.

> Whatcom County Prosecutor David McEachran sees no reason to file charges.
> The federal charges "accomplished more than we could ever accomplish," McEachran told me, adding that state charges would put Spink in jail for only five to eight months.
> After that, "There's no way to monitor him," he said.
> Then why not get creative: Enlist the people from the animal shelter to keep watch on him, or ... McEachran laughed into the phone.
> "We have limited resources," he said. "If there was something we could really gain in order to protect the public, that would be something we would do."
> Isn't protecting animals protecting the public?
> "I think I have answered what I've answered," McEachran said, hanging up.

"I tried for months to contact [Brodeur] to offer factual corrections from prison," Spink later emailed me. "She dodged all emails, postal letters, and phone calls." I also contacted Brodeur for comment, but she didn't respond.

Two days after her column came out, Brodeur went on Seattle talk radio station KIRO-FM 97.3 along with Jenny Edwards from Hope for Horses. The 10:00 a.m. show was hosted by John Curley.

If you were to go back in history, Curley said, "this kind of weird, disgusting, abhorrent behavior has been going on for thousands and thousands of disgusting years. I would like to put them all in a big boat and send them away."

"Wouldn't we all," seconded Edwards.

There were moments of attempted comedy during the show, such as Brodeur singing a line from "People In Your Neighborhood," an old song from *Sesame Street*, before bursting into gales of laughter.

Bloggers had a field day too. One blog popped up specifically inspired by Spink's troubles. Called *The Spink Spot*, "the spot to discuss bestiality cases in the news," the site was still up at the time of writing, but the posts had been taken down. (The blog's author refused to do an interview with me, citing fear of Spink and his associates.)

If reporters' stories were unrestrained, the online comments by members of the public went all out. It wasn't uncommon for readers to suggest violent acts against Spink as a solution, such as castration, rape, beating and death. One *Huffington Post* story, titled "Douglas Spink Arrested In BESTIALITY Case: Mice In Vaseline, Dogs, Horses Found At Exitpoint Stallions Limitée," logged 967 comments before the news outlet finally stopped accepting new ones. A few examples:

SkreetGil1
3:11 pm
4/20/2010
He is damaged so he needs to be euthanized too.

vlsawyer
5:51 am
4/24/2010
Lynch mob mentality is what we need if the courts can't take care of these types of people.

roninroshi
10:42 pm
5/14/2010
In the joint he can be the horse...lock him up and throw away the key!

When Spink's federal probation hearing concluded in Seattle in June 2010, he asked his lawyer, Howard Phillips, for a tally: how many members of the media had requested interviews? The answer he got was disappointing.

Phillips handed him a single business card. Mine. I had passed it to the lawyer during a break in the court proceeding and asked that he give it to his client along with a message: if Spink wanted to tell his side of the story, I was willing to listen.

Spink had reached out to reporters often since his incarceration, anxious to correct errors in their stories and tell his version of events. Because I hadn't written anything about him yet, and wouldn't do so for years, there was nothing to correct so far as I was concerned.

Two days later, on June 16, he sent me an email through CorrLinks.

> Ms. Maloney—
>
> My lead attorney, Howard Phillips, passed along your contact information and suggested you'd been in touch with him in order to express an interest in talking directly with me. If that's the case, I'm comfortable talking and wanted to drop a note to open communications.
>
> If I've misread your interest—or Howard has—I offer my apologies in advance.
>
> Most sincerely,
> Douglas Bryan LeConte-Spink

Spink wasn't very optimistic about my interest in his story. He didn't trust my connections to the rescue world in general, and the Whatcom Humane Society in particular. He said he didn't need or want a "Kardashian-style" look at his life. He also made it clear that he wasn't willing to be a spokesman for other zoos.

His attorney had a similarly negative response. The media had already savaged Spink, and Phillips was being prudent about publicity. I arranged to talk to Spink's lawyer at a nondescript sports bar not far from the federal courthouse in Seattle.

Phillips had been appointed to Spink's case through the Criminal Justice Act Panel, which provides the federal equivalent of public defenders for people who don't have the financial means to retain counsel.

The somewhat random nature of Phillips' assignment didn't cause him to represent his client with any less vigilance.

He walked into the bar and headed over to the small corner table where I was waiting for him. He ordered a whiskey, so I did the same. Neat and trim, Phillips was a natty dresser who gave off a serene, quietly confident air. He didn't seem a bit phased by the furor and controversy surrounding his infamous client.

He bluntly stated that he classified me as "the enemy," and politely added that he would relay that exact message to his client. He said he'd be advising Spink not to speak to me under any circumstances. He had witnessed how the media portrayed the man, and he understandably thought nothing good could come of my project.

Phillips expressed empathy for the troubles his client had faced. He had witnessed how distraught Spink was over losing his four-legged family. "When he would talk about his dogs, his hands would start shaking," he said.

Phillips didn't stay at our meeting long. He drained his whiskey, picked up his boxy black leather satchel—which he called his bag of woes—and swept out of the joint just as swiftly as he had arrived.

∩

Despite Phillips' firm warning to Spink, our CorrLinks communications continued over the next two years, until Spink was released from prison on July 16, 2012. Spink sent me voluminous amounts of text, both by email and snail mail. A prolific and articulate writer, his messages to me were long, angry at times, and always detailed. Mine were sparse, cautious and stilted. I wasn't sure how dangerous this unusual man really was, so I was hesitant about writing much, other than asking him questions to draw out his story.

Even as I was corresponding with Spink, I still wasn't sure what I was going to do with this story, but I also wasn't ready to give up on it. Something kept pulling me in that prevented me from dropping it. The life I had built up over thirteen years with my husband was disintegrating around me, while this story was the one—albeit strange—constant.

The two years after his death passed by in a blur, a period of time spent recovering from grief and reconciling the loss. And there were logistical tasks that needed to be tackled too. We had built a life designed and suited for two people, not one, which meant that much of what we had created together had to be dismantled and scaled down. I was faced with the task of mapping a new future for myself, and it was too early to know what that would look like.

10

DEAD INSIDE

Although I still hadn't written publicly about the Spink case, that hadn't stopped me from continuing to gather information. The subject was complex, and I didn't know what to say yet. It also didn't seem fair to publish words about this man until I could interview him away from the prying eyes and ears of official monitoring. If I hoped to get the whole truth, I had to interview Spink in private, after he was freed.

In mid-July 2012, after weeks of Spink hinting about his imminent release, I received the first text from him: "In Seattle. Still of a mixed mind wrt [with regard to] a meeting. Not sure what more to say. -D.S."

For the next three weeks, we messaged back and forth until he agreed to an in-person interview on August 16.

I was nervous about meeting Spink. So many people had warned me to stay away from him—that he was uniquely dangerous—and now the day had arrived.

What I hadn't anticipated was how cautious he would be about meeting me.

> **Spink**: I'll confirm time & place Sunday am if that's ok. My intuition is still screaming a shrill warning at me.
> **Me**: Don't freak out, it will be a casual meeting. I am coming alone.
> **Spink**: It takes quite a bit to freak me out at this point in time, to be honest.

He wanted to meet in Seattle, about two hours' drive south of my home. I planned to send a note when I got close to the city. But when I arrived there, instead of selecting a meet location, Spink kept texting, moving me from place to place around the Central District for about an hour, concerned I was being followed. First he tried to send me to a particular intersection, but I got lost, so he instructed me to go to Café Flora, a popular vegetarian restaurant. I tried to persuade him to meet me there for breakfast, thinking it would provide a comfort zone for both of us. I was wrong.

He asked me to drive to Julia Lee's Park, a small green space on a street corner surrounded by high foliage. I did, and got out of my car. While I waited, I received a text from him asking if I knew the young couple seated on a park bench nearby. I didn't. He wasn't comfortable with their presence.

He wrote about a "team effort." He had other ex-cons from the halfway house where he'd been staying watching me.

"I'm not the one with eyes on the park at the moment," he texted.

He mentioned what I was wearing: a long denim coat.

"Ok for a little walk?" he asked.

I felt vulnerable and nervous being separated from my vehicle, but I followed his directions anyway, spurred on by curiosity rather than ruled by common sense. He led me around a few corners, and then told me to keep going straight down the road, towards the park by Lake Washington. "When we see you heading down Harrison towards the lane—alone—we'll go from there."

But the street was closed off, and because it was Sunday, the barricaded construction zone was deserted. Was it a trap?

He instructed me to walk through it anyway.

That didn't feel right, so I didn't. I circled the block instead, unsure what to do next. That seemed to satisfy his procedures, because he had me circle back again to Harrison Street.

And suddenly, there he was.

Directly across the street, he stood in a darkened doorway, blue baseball cap pulled down low over his eyes.

I approached him and we shook hands.

Doug Spink was broad-shouldered and muscular from years of rock climbing. He had olive-toned skin, a nod to his Indigenous heritage—Quebec Métis on his mother's side, Cree on his father's. His voice was deep and his eyes were so dark they looked black. I had never met anyone with black eyes like his before.

Spink's eyes saw things differently than most eyes too. He had a condition known as face blindness (prosopagnosia); he couldn't recognize facial features, not even of people he'd known for years. Instead, he distinguished people by other characteristics, such as their gaits. As I got to know him better, I wondered if that had anything to do with his tendency to frequently transform his own appearance by changing his facial hair and hairstyle—bare face, stubble, mustache, beard, goatee; thick braid, long wavy hair, shaved head, baseball cap pulled down low.

We walked a short distance, found a grassy spot next to a sidewalk and sat down, cross-legged. I rolled audiotape, and so did he. It was a pleasant sunny day in a residential city neighborhood. There were houses nearby, but not so close as to inhibit conversation.

I asked him: why was he doing all these intense security procedures with me?

He said it was because of who I associated with. He felt vilified by animal rescuers and others who he believed only claimed to care about his dogs and horses. "Most of you don't give a fuck what actually happened to the animals."

It was true that when I told people about the story I was working on, hardly anyone asked what became of his animals after the raid. And Spink wasn't wrong about the rage many felt towards him. There were horrific comments online, on blogs and news stories, about how Spink should be castrated, tortured, even killed. One animal rescuer, someone I'd always considered a gentle sort, offered to do a drive-by shooting if only I would tell her where we were meeting. Another person, a neighbor of mine, said I was inspiring him to stock up on ammunition.

That kind of pervasive hatred and persecution took its toll on Spink, and on other zoos he knew. "We are all damaged people," he said.

We talked for a couple of hours during that initial face-to-face interview. No human beings interrupted us, but in a moment that lightened the mood, a silver tabby cat sauntered up, rolled on her back and let out a loud "Meow."

I was surprised by Spink's candor and easy way with conversation. I had expected to encounter obfuscation and hostility, but there was none of that—until I asked him if he still wanted his animals back if they were neutered. That question he answered silently, with a withering glare from onyx black eyes that grew even darker.

Spink's four horses were alive, and he knew where they were, but he wasn't convinced his seven dogs had survived the shelter experience. Whatcom Humane Society executive director Laura Clark claimed they had all been adopted into good homes. He didn't believe her. Later, he asked me to put pressure on Clark to have photographs taken of each of his dogs alongside a daily newspaper so he could verify they were alive. I was never able to make that happen.

***

My in-person interview with Doug Spink that Sunday afternoon on the grass would be the first of many in various locations in Canada and the United States, from the Pacific Northwest to the Canadian Prairies. We also continued the correspondence we had begun two years earlier. I amassed huge amounts of information on Spink in particular, and zoos in general.

As I struggled to piece this book together, to accurately and thoroughly cover a topic that no one else was willing to touch, Spink spoke openly and frankly, although there were times when my questions aggravated wounds that hadn't healed, and probably never would.

A couple of weeks after our first meeting, he agreed to let me check his criminal record, giving me his social security number to make it easier. The federal government had portrayed Spink as a dangerous and depraved character, devoting a brigade of people and a mass of tax dollars to prosecuting him and tracking his movements. Maybe they knew something I hadn't discovered yet. My nationwide search for Spink's criminal records in September 2012 pulled up only one hit: the widely publicized 2005 drug charge, possession with intent to distribute, which Spink spoke about freely.

During our interviews, he talked about Corinne Super. He said her actions and words against his character had nothing to do with rescuing Capone from acts of bestiality. He insisted she knew he was a zoo from the start and had pursued him anyway. He was open about his sexuality, just as he was with his friends and on internet forums. There's no doubt he was proud of who he was.

Most of all, Spink talked about his non-human companions and how much he missed them. He struggled with guilt, a persistent nagging feeling that he might have done more to keep his family from being taken away.

Over the years, as I worked on this story, one of the questions people asked me repeatedly was "Did he love his animals?" When I told Spink I got asked this question, I expected him to be offended. But he wasn't. Just the opposite.

"That's the question they should be asking," he said.

One day, when the timing seemed right, I asked if we could review six hundred photographs of his dogs and horses taken during their time together. He took thousands of photos because he wanted undeniable proof of how he treated his family in case the authorities came for him.

We went through the pictures one at a time. He talked about the animals' personality traits. He spoke about the bonds they shared with him, and with each other. He referred to those who formed tight friendships, and those who didn't. I saw the big bowls of high-quality food he mixed for the dogs and horses at mealtime—"always a happy time"—meals that included vegetables he grew himself, potted in salvaged containers such as empty yogurt tubs. He pointed to their favorite toys, to the different colored bandannas he dressed them in day to day, and the seasonal ones for Christmas, Thanksgiving and St. Patrick's Day. I saw the fuzzy warm coats he bought them for the rain or cold, and the blankets he wrapped them in while they were sleeping.

Other than losing custody of the animals themselves, the most painful loss for Spink involved the urns that held his dead animals' ashes. After the authorities' five-hour raid on his property, the place was trashed. When he eventually got his belongings back, several items were missing: jumper cables, a $600 generator, books and magazines. And the ashes he had carried with him for years from home to home were gone. Someone had dumped them out.

"I knew that people hated me, of course," he said. "I have dealt with being 'who I am' all of my adult life, and I have been 'out' for almost a decade. But the level of violence and vitriol and outright hatred—it just went beyond anything I could have possibly imagined."

The most tender of his sore spots was Capone, the champion show jumper. I wanted to know more about the stallion, but whenever I asked about him, Spink would turn angry and upset. He referred to Capone as the love of his life. He likened the horse's being taken as a "captive hostage" to his own imprisonment after the raid.

After prison, getting back to life on the outside was particularly painful for Spink without his animals by his side. "I have always responded to horrific loss with love," he said. "But with nobody to love…? I feel dead inside."

PART TWO

We never see other people anyway,
only the monsters we make of them.

—Colson Whitehead, *Zone One*

11

PONY BOY

Doug Spink grew up in Mister Rogers' neighborhood. Not the enchanted Neighborhood of Make-Believe that North American children watched on television—it was the place where Fred Rogers actually lived.

The tony suburb of Fox Chapel is just six miles from downtown Pittsburgh, where the long-running PBS series *Mister Rogers' Neighborhood* was produced. Back in the '70s, when Doug was living in Fox Chapel as a child, it was Pennsylvania horse country, an enclave of expansive forests that gave way to rolling, manicured lawns. The lots were large, the houses tended towards grand, and property boundaries were an unobserved formality—residents rode their horses along trails that wound through the borough.

Young Doug rode there, too. He knew the trees and the trails, the shortcuts and the water bodies. To him, Mister Rogers' real neighborhood was more magical than the version as seen on TV. The boy would travel by foot or on horseback along Old Squaw Trail, which passed right near Fred Rogers' house on Old Mill Road. It was a picturesque setting on wooded acreage cut with creeks and a man-made lake. Doug played there by the water for hours, building dams in the creek and occasionally catching water snakes to bring home and observe in his terrarium.

"Fred Rogers' property was part of my terrain," he said. "He was exactly like he was on TV. He even wore the cardigans."

Rogers' residence wasn't the only noteworthy property that Doug and his older sister, Joy, grew up galloping through. Just half a mile down from their house on Squaw Mill Road was Rosemont Farm, a sprawling ninety-acre estate owned by the Heinz family and valued in the millions. The estate was home to Teresa Heinz Kerry, widow of US senator John Heinz and wife of former secretary of state John Kerry. Teresa Heinz raised three children in the colonial-style house with Senator Heinz until he died in a plane crash in 1991.

But perhaps not surprisingly, it was Rogers' property that endured as one of Doug's most cherished childhood haunts. He was an unusual boy, and Rogers' show encouraged children to accept others no matter what their differences. Rogers started each program with his comforting theme song, "Won't You Be My Neighbor?," which addressed the need to be included. "Way down deep, everybody wants to love, and everybody wants to have people love them," Rogers would say.

Douglas Bryan Spink was born on St. Patrick's Day 1971 in a Pittsburgh hospital to Claire and Jack Spink, a genius baby delivered into a family of moderate privilege. He was their second child, three years younger than his sister Joy. They brought him home to the house they had built for their young family after Joy was born. "I had Doug so Joy wouldn't be alone," explained Claire, who could not have predicted that her children would grow up to be mortal enemies.

Despite the affluence that surrounded them, the Spinks themselves weren't rich. Claire had inherited some old money from her grandfather, who had prospered selling the family business to DuPont many years back. And her husband, Jack, made new money as a salesman in a commercial construction company that built steel mills and power plants. The family purchased their seven-acre plot before Fox Chapel fully developed into a haven for Pittsburgh's opulent class. They had a comfortable but comparatively modest home that wasn't updated for twenty-seven years.

Beauty surrounded the Spinks, but their union wasn't picture-perfect. Jack and Claire Spink had a marriage of convenience.

When they met, Jack was handsome and charming, a company man near the outside edge of an age when it was expected he should settle down, find a wife and start a family. Claire seemed like an ideal choice. Cultured and intelligent, she was also well educated. After earning her bachelor's degree from the University of Vermont in 1958, she went off to Radcliffe College, Harvard's coordinate institute for women until the male-only school began awarding Harvard degrees to Radcliffe students in 1963. She completed a one-year Harvard-Radcliffe program in business administration, an experience that would later inspire her son to get his MBA.

"We were an experiment by Harvard to see if women had the capability to do an MBA," said Claire. "They didn't believe women could do it."

Jack thought Claire would be malleable and cater to his demands, but he was wrong about that.

"He thought he could easily manipulate her, but she's extremely strong-willed and smart," Joy recalled. "She's not a marshmallow. You can't break her."

That didn't stop Jack from trying. Claire recounted a defining incident in which they argued and he hit her. Her reaction was instantaneous. She wound up and walloped him right back.

He didn't try that again.

"He just wasn't tender to begin with, and he didn't know how to relate to us," Joy said. "He wasn't really a family person. He wasn't a huge part of our life. He just came and went." Jack wasn't about to let marriage and fatherhood affect his lifestyle. "He didn't really try to make the marriage work."

Joy, Doug and Claire all used the same word to describe Jack Spink: sociopath. He was also a slick salesman capable of master manipulation. Doug watched his father win over strangers with ease, turning his ability to connect quickly and easily with people into a party trick. The family would be at a restaurant having dinner, and Jack would ask the kids to pick someone out. Anyone. Then he'd approach them, always returning triumphantly to the table with a bunch of personal information given up voluntarily by his targets—names, telephone numbers, addresses, occupations.

Many little boys dream of growing up to be just like their fathers. Doug grew up determined to be anything but like his. Jack had enviable charm, but he was also a hard-core alcoholic, capable of the cruelty that flows readily with impaired judgment.

Then there was the womanizing.

Once, he swaggered up to a group of women chatting outside the church and introduced himself with a line. "Hello, I'm Jack Spink. I'm the great white hunter, and women are the big game."

Claire witnessed this exchange. She was well aware of her husband's dalliances. "His prey was females," she said.

Doug described his father's conquests more bluntly and graphically. "He would fuck anything that moved. And some things that didn't."

While Jack wandered, the rest of the family filled the void by bringing others into their fold who loved them in a way he couldn't—it was the animals.

The neighbors noticed they were unconventional. "A feral family" was how one former neighbor characterized the Spinks and their menagerie. "[Claire] had horses and a pack of rescued dogs when we met her. I used to think she was our lane's answer to St. Francis, she seemed so compassionate toward animals." Claire was president of the Animal Rescue League of Pittsburgh, and as adults, both Doug and Joy would work in animal rescue.

Hundreds of Spink family photos paint a vivid color portrait of what life was like in their household. Animals appeared in most of them, and not just species commonly considered human companions such as dogs, cats and horses. There were plenty of those, but the Spinks also welcomed rabbits, raccoons, birds, snakes and mice into their household.

A Christmas card from 1976 shows Doug and Joy on a red plaid sofa with Fluffy, an orphaned raccoon they'd adopted. "She was the best pet I ever had," said Joy in a phone interview. "She slept under the covers with her head on the pillow."

When Joy was in fourth grade, Jack accidentally ran over Fluffy as he backed his car out of the garage. "My dad had an appreciation for animals at a distance, but empathy wasn't his strong suit," Joy said. Despite that, Jack cried when he killed Fluffy.

Like many siblings who grow up under the same roof, Doug and Joy experienced different childhoods. Joy used the word "idyllic." Doug didn't. At times, he felt bullied by other children because of his differences. He felt that his older sister didn't offer any protection from the bullies, but rather added to his troubles with her derisive taunts of "pony boy."

"I'm very mouthy, so I would push and push and push," Joy told me. "The more he didn't react, the more I would push."

In 2008, in an online discussion forum called Bluelight that Spink moderated for a time and often posted to, he wrote that he eventually accepted being labeled as different from other kids:

> Having been picked on mercilessly for years in school, for obvious reasons (freak! dog boy! smells like horse shit! etc.), in middle school I just decided that I didn't care if people hated me. I'd carry on with life, do my thing, try to be nice to people around me, read books, and enjoy life as best I can. The strangest thing was that, once I made that choice, many of the people who used to torment me the most suddenly turned around to say 'oh, yeah, that dude's cool—he's a total freak, but he's our freak so don't mess with him or you're messin' with us.' I still really don't understand why that happens, but hey I was glad to at least not be the brunt of every school prank.

Throughout childhood, the Spink siblings struggled to relate to each other. Joy was social and enjoyed hobnobbing with the debutantes of Fox Chapel. She attended sports events and parties, typical teenage American pastimes. Doug had no use for that scene. He was a dedicated student and devoted the bulk of his energy towards reading and learning. From a tender age, he took life seriously.

"He wasn't really a traditional high school kid," Joy said. "He was quiet, he kept to himself."

Doug agreed with that assessment. "As a child, I was not good at socializing with other children of my own age. More often than not, I was at the barn, riding."

Riding—or reading. While kids who visited him played downstairs, he often cut out of the fun early and headed upstairs to do homework.

"He had these baby-blue footed pajamas, and he loved studying in them," Claire said fondly. "He was so self-motivated. He never had to be told to study."

He had been taught that being born into privilege brought duty and responsibility. "Find a way to apply your gifts, you have an obligation to improve the world" was the message he took from his upbringing.

He threw himself wholeheartedly into his interests: an early fascination with Legos, followed by dinosaurs, then on to scuba diving, rock climbing and BASE jumping. There was a pattern of intensity toward his pursuits that would continue into adulthood.

Despite his intelligence, Doug sometimes felt confused by humans and their motivations—the communication gap between what they said, and what they actually meant. He didn't find animals to be any less complicated than human beings, but he preferred their company.

While other boys were starting to entertain sexual feelings for human beings, Doug was having his first sexual experiences with a dog from the neighborhood, an event he wrote about on the Bluelight forum.

> My first true love was a Golden who lived a few miles away. We spent many, many cold nights together—I'd sneak out, go let him out of his kennel (he was locked up outside 24/7/364) and we'd get frisky and then just cuddle under a tree or bush for hours, until at last I had to return him to his kennel, walk back home, sneak into the house, and sleep for an hour or two before school.

Animals also gave Doug a way to cope with painful childhood trauma. When he was about eight years old, he was molested by an older man, a family friend. "I remember it as a very unsettling, conflicted experience—something about it didn't seem right, but also something about it felt good. After the first night, I refused to sleep in the house with him any more (we were visiting for a few days) and instead stayed outside in a tent."

His abuser kept a python in a cage in the house, and Doug rationalized that the snake had gotten out of the cage and come into his room at night. Rather than the man's touches, he wanted to believe that the snake had touched him instead. "Even then, I was trying to rationalize a sexual experience, in order to make it seem less traumatic, as involving a non-human."

Doug loved all animals when he was a kid, but horses were a particular passion. From the time he could walk, riding and caring for horses was a part of his routine. By age two, he was riding, and by age four, he was fox hunting in the main field. Before turning twelve, he had won two Pony Hunter championships.

He even incorporated horses into his Halloween costumes, sitting atop his pony like a proud brave year after year, his steed painted like a warhorse, a hint of his Indigenous heritage. It was said that painting one's pony helped honor and protect the man and his horse as they rode into battle together.

Doug's adoration for animals threaded through everything he did, including his earnest childhood artwork. A watercolor he painted of a horse was captioned, "Opon a misty feild a stallion arises through the faded fog. [*sic*]"

Doug Spink's childhood artwork.

12

BRIGHT FUTURE

There was a time when the man branded by the federal government as an unwaveringly defiant, uniquely dangerous character seemed to be destined to become anything but that.

Spink went to top-notch schools and excelled in all of them. For his high school graduation, he was chosen to write and deliver the scholar's speech. In it, he spoke about how precious education was to him. His mother, who saved the speech all these years, sent me a photocopy of it.

"Perhaps in life there is nothing more important than a person's education," Spink told his classmates. "All that he or she contributes to society can be traced back to values instilled upon him by those who have helped to shape his intellect."

Spink's young self couldn't have known that his next words would foreshadow the trouble that came his way later in life: "My most educational experiences have not come through the mastery of facts, but rather through an understanding of the importance of the ways in which those facts are perceived, for in the perception of facts lies their beauty."

And their ugliness, as he would find out.

Despite his success with school, on the inside, Spink was struggling to come to terms with the realization that he was sexually attracted to other species, not his own. As he wrote in 2008 on the Bluelight internet discussion forum:

> I tried as hard as anyone can try anything to be "Normal," for years. My secret zoo side was known by nobody, and I did everything possible to stamp it out so I could lead a good life. Needless to say, looking down the barrel of a lifetime spent as someone who is by definition despised, attacked, potentially prosecuted, and perhaps sent to a mental institution (in the old days) isn't exactly motivation to "bring out the zoo in anyone." <sighs> I really felt, if I couldn't "get it under control," that my life was worthless and why bother—hence the multiple suicide attempts in my teen years, heavy involvement in bleeding-edge soloing as a rock climber, etc.
>
> If, in fact, something in my childhood "flipped the switch" somehow—I'm nevertheless quite sure that the switch is essentially impossible to switch back.

After high school, Spink traveled to the west coast to study anthropology at Reed College, a small but renowned private liberal arts school situated in the lush greenery of Portland, Oregon. While not one of the Ivy League schools, Reed is an intensely academic institution whose reputation stands up to the best of them. Loren Pope, former education editor for the *New York Times*, wrote glowingly about Reed in her 2006 book *Colleges That Change Lives*. "If you're a genuine intellectual, live the life of the mind, and want to learn for the sake of learning, the place most likely to empower you is not Harvard, Yale, Princeton, Chicago, or Stanford. It is the most intellectual college in the country—Reed in Portland, Oregon."

With fewer than 1,500 undergraduates enrolled, Reed offered an impressive nine-to-one ratio of students per teacher. Doug Spink didn't attend classes alone. Most days he brought his Golden Retriever, Gifford, to the classroom with him. It was his style to be accompanied by dogs, horses, or a combination of both whenever possible.

While at Reed, Spink continued to succeed academically, becoming a Rhodes Scholar regional finalist. If he had won, he would have received what is commonly considered the world's most prestigious scholarship to England's Oxford University, a school famed for its academic excellence.

After earning his degree in cultural anthropology in 1993, Spink went on to the master of business administration program at the University of Chicago's Graduate School of Business (now Booth School of Business), the second-oldest business school in the United States and frequently ranked number one in the nation. He received his MBA in fourteen months.

He also had an opportunity to complete the JD/MBA, a dual degree program offered at the university, which would have earned him a doctor of law degree alongside his MBA. But the double degree wasn't to be.

While living in Chicago, Spink took a job working for a dog breeder twenty-two years his senior. They began dating in the summer of 1993 and married in the fall of 1994 at a justice of the peace in Portland. That decision nixed any plans for a combined degree. Now Spink needed an income. His new bride had four children from a previous marriage, plus thirty-two Golden Retrievers. That added up to thirty-eight mouths to feed.

"Had I completed the JD/MBA program, I'd likely have taken classes with Barack Obama—I finished my MBA in the summer of 1994, and would have been taking classes at the Law School from fall 1994 through fall 1996. He taught constitutional law, which of course was a focus of mine, and sort of still is, ironically."

Spink's interest in constitutional law wasn't by chance. He believed that the principles of the Constitution might help protect him someday.

∩

Fresh out of business school and armed with a prestigious MBA, Doug Spink stood on the brink of being set for life. Professionally speaking, at least.

In 1994, he landed a well-paid job at Boston Consulting Group. With a base salary of $135,000, plus an annual bonus of $35,000, he made enough to take care of his new family, both two- and four-legged.

Less than a year later, the ambitious young man took a step up the corporate ladder, landing an executive position at SafeCard Services/ Ideon Technology Group. Founded in 1969, SafeCard provided insurance to protect consumers whose credit cards were lost or stolen.

The company went public in 1977, and by 1992, it had grown to four hundred employees, thirteen million customers, and $158 million in annual revenues.

By the time Spink joined SafeCard as the director of financial controls in the information technology group, the company was facing financial troubles. To shore up falling profits, it pinned its corporate hopes on two products that didn't live up to projections. The first was a credit card that offered PGA perks geared to golfers. The second was the Family Protection Network (FPN) credit card. For $250 per year, parents could register information about their children with SafeCard. If a child was reported missing, the company would dispatch a SWAT team of ex-military and law enforcement experts to conduct a search.

According to financial filings and company records, SafeCard spent $100 million and hired three hundred employees to launch these ill-fated products. Despite the vast resources they devoted, within a few months it became obvious that the ventures were tanking. And Spink knew it, because he compiled the data. He warned the company's chief executive, which was noted in an article about SafeCard in the April 28, 1997, issue of Bloomberg's *Business Week*:

> Spink, who was responsible for compiling daily computer reports to senior management for the PGA Tour and FPN projects, says he talked to [SafeCard chief executive Paul] Kahn almost daily beginning on Apr. 20, 1995, and warned him FPN was bombing. By Apr. 25, only 286 people had sought enrollment information, and FPN didn't have a single paying customer, according to internal records.
>
> "It was a known, irrevocable certainty within the company at the time of the Apr. 27, 1995, annual meeting that the company would report massive losses for 1995 due to the complete failure of the PGA Tour and FPN business launches," says Spink.

By speaking out about what he saw happening at the company, Spink played a key role in the probe into SafeCard, as *Business Week* stated in its story.

> During a three-month investigation, *Business Week* has examined lawsuits and hundreds of other documents, including internal memos and notes, receipts, stock trading records, research reports, and Securities & Exchange Commission filings. *Business Week* also interviewed more than two dozen former employees, directors, and company consultants—most of whom spoke not for

attribution. In addition, *Business Week* has reviewed two 60-odd-page signed statements by Douglas Spink, 25, who was SafeCard's director of financial controls in its information technology group from September, 1994, to March, 1996. Spink, an MBA from the University of Chicago Graduate School of Business, has also provided his statements to [SafeCard Services Inc. founder Peter] Halmos and is expected to be a key witness in the shareholder litigation.

Becoming a corporate whistle-blower while he worked at SafeCard was a dramatic moment for Doug Spink, but it wouldn't come close to rivaling the controversy of his later life experiences.

∩

Following his stint at SafeCard, Spink decided to venture out on his own into territory still relatively uncharted in the 1990s: internet retailing. Under the company name Timberline Direct, he created a set of online catalogs that used the family of programming languages known as Perl. A November 1, 1998, article in *Aftermarket Business* described Spink's company:

> Timberline Direct, founded in 1996 as Merus Communications, manages three catalog brands serving customers across the United States and Canada. These catalogs are: Athletica Endurance, featuring name-brand sports nutrition supplies specifically designed for endurance athletes; Gravitygames, a series of catalogs carrying snowboarding, skateboarding, and in-line skating gear and supplies; and Tidewater Specialties, a catalog featuring duck hunting and retriever trainer equipment, home furnishings and accessories.

In 1998, Spink orchestrated a deal to sell the online catalogs for $5.4 million to G.I. Joe's, a popular Pacific Northwest sporting goods chain. Timberline's catalogs became G.I. Joe's turnkey online presence.

At twenty-seven, Spink had achieved what most people could only dream about: extraordinary financial success at a young age. Now it was time to make another dream come true. This one came in the form of a promising young black stallion with three white socks. On October 31, 1998, an agent acting for Spink purchased Capone I for 47,000 deutsche marks (about $27,000 US back then) from the Holsteiner Verband stallion auction in Neumünster, Germany.

The black horse with the white star on his forehead would become the star of Spink's stud farm, and the love of his life.

13

STUD FARM

As the calendar marched towards 2000 and the world obsessed over Y2K, it seemed like life was charmed for Doug Spink. He was a successful, wealthy high-tech businessman, and married to a woman he loved dearly. Their family had moved from bustling Chicago to the peaceful beauty of Oregon, where they bred Golden Retrievers and ran a Golden rescue organization. They settled into a lavish home on a vast piece of property. Eighty-two acres of paradise perched on a bluff overlooking the tiny town of Gaston, a small rural community, population 650, situated thirty miles west of Portland.

Spink's panache made him a darling of the Portland media set. A profile in the *Oregonian* newspaper affectionately referred to him as a "financial swashbuckler." In addition to reverential discussion of his business exploits, the article detailed his high-powered adventures in kickboxing, BASE jumping, backcountry exploring and rock climbing.

Besides his sporting pursuits, the newly minted millionaire had another endeavor he was passionate about: the elite stallion stud farm he had created a few miles west of Portland, in Beaverton. Timberline Farms, which became a limited liability company in 2000, was set up to import and breed Grand Prix show jumping horses.

The former manager of Timberline was willing to speak to me about her experiences with Spink, but only on condition of anonymity. Joanne (not her real name) feared reprisals from within the horse world, and the potential loss of career status that she and her husband had built over many years. Despite the risks, she felt compelled to speak out because she believed her former employer had been treated unfairly by the authorities, the media and the public. "I knew him from his horsemanship, and the guy loves his horses," she wrote to me in an email.

Working with Spink "was one of the most powerful things that has ever happened to me. It was just so much fun. I would get there in the morning and overnight he would have sent me 17 emails for things we could start working on." Spink was complex, she recollected:

> Doug is one of the most remarkable people on the face of the planet, but he's also really screwed up. A strong, brilliant, creative creature.
> When I described Doug as a badger—beautiful but best not held in close—it's because he's an adrenalin junky. I met him the day he was going for his first sky diving lesson, and he took that all the way to BASE jumping all over the world. He's that kind of a pathological risk taker. Brilliant! But not safe. And drawn to risk like the proverbial moth.

When Spink hired Joanne to manage Timberline Farms—her first job working with horses—she was tasked with caring for the animals, dealing with veterinarians and farriers, purchasing supplies, and making sure the horses traveled safely to and from competitions.

The business premise was this: as Timberline's stallions built their reputations in competitions, their semen would become sought after. Frozen stallion semen would be shipped to customers with mares, and those mares would be inseminated to create foals from exquisite bloodlines. The result: champions and beauties.

"My job was to bring the horses to where they were internationally known," Joanne said. "We had a huge fat budget."

It took $30,000 a month to cover the expenses for just a few stallions, she recalled. When she was growing up, "money was a rare commodity," so she was in awe of Spink's seemingly infinite ability to generate cash flow to cover the farm's substantial expenses. "For him there was just this river of money always there, and anytime he needed it, he just took a dip."

As Spink's supplies buyer, Joanne had prestige when she strolled into the tack shops. "I would go in and drop a few grand. Imagine how much they were kissing his ass."

After just one year, Timberline's horses were already receiving worldwide recognition for their talents. The farm's biggest star by far was Capone I. The charismatic, gentle black stallion, just a youngster at age two and a half when he arrived in America, grew up to be regarded as one of the world's top show jumpers.

In a May 24, 2008, post on the Horse Grooming Supplies website, Spink summarized his history with Capone:

> I rode Capone on his first trail ride, in his first schooling show, in his first Modified division championships, in his first Amateur Low championships, in his first Mini-Prix wins, in his first Grand Prix, and on his first fox hunts.
>
> That's pretty much the long and short of it—I've hardly been solely responsible for every piece of his training, but we've come up together from the first time he had a saddle on through today as a team.

But the successful development of Timberline's star athlete had a dark underbelly. Capone's notoriety presented a compelling financial motive for others to loot Spink's life later on, when the opportunity presented itself.

"The unfortunate thing for Doug is that he has this one remarkable horse," Joanne observed. "Everybody is juggling around to get their spot to grab him."

To Doug Spink, Capone's value wasn't as a money maker, although he was proud of the stallion's sporting achievements. Spink thought of Capone as the love of his life—a partner in every way.

He alluded to his unusual philosophies in the company backgrounder for Timberline.

> Are we unconventional in our approach to stallion care? Absolutely.
> We don't wall off sexual energy in our stallions as something dangerous or inappropriate, but rather channel that energy towards positive, safe, appropriate paths. There's a proper time and place for it, and we work towards those sorts of skills rather than fighting un-winnable fights against deeply-rooted instincts.

It is interesting to note that under laws designed to prohibit cross-species sexual activity, sexual contact with animals is only illegal if the acts aren't commercially motivated. It is considered perfectly legal and legitimate business activity to masturbate animals in order to breed them for profit. When it comes to horses, an artificial vagina (a tube-like device filled with warm water) is a more common collection method than masturbation. That's not the case for dogs; nearly every veterinarian I've interviewed has masturbated a dog at least once or twice for semen collection purposes.

The people who successfully collect semen from animals are sometimes zoos, many of them closeted. Zoos who engage in sexual contact with animals, whether for commercial or pleasure purposes, might participate in some or all of the behaviors humans practice when arousing each other. Sexual stimulation of both the human and nonhuman animal can include heavy petting, oral sex and penetration.

∩

Breeding horses and developing them for show can involve abusive practices. Soring, for example, does harm to the front feet of horses' legs and hooves to cause an unnatural, exaggerated gait. When horses who are subjected to soring touch down on the ground in pain, they pick up their feet faster and higher, fancy foot work that is desirable in horse shows. The pain is induced by coating the legs in caustic chemicals such as diesel fuel or kerosene, encasing the legs in plastic wrap, and leaving the horse in a stall to suffer in agony for days at a time. Other forms of soring include cutting the hoof down to the quick and tightly nailing on a shoe, or forcing a horse to stand for hours on a block.

Another painful procedure used on horses is rollkur, the hyperflexion of a horse's neck through force to bring the head down towards the chest.

Although Soring and rollkur are controversial practices banned by some equestrian bodies, they have not been eradicated. Yet these undeniably painful and abusive practices don't summon nearly the amount of societal outrage that zoophilia does. I wondered why.

Spink's ex-manager, who is not a zoophile, had her own theory about cross-species sexual interaction, and why people get so upset about it. "It's the deep, insatiable need to have something black and white and definite," Joanne said. "It's why people do all sorts of horrors to one another. In a horse world that tolerates soring and rollkur, but screams for guns and nooses when someone is having apparently uncoerced sex with an animal…one does have to look a little sideways at the minds involved."

14

COMING OUT

The new millennium was dawning when all that previously glittered in Doug Spink's life began to disintegrate to dust. A closely held secret was eating away at his marriage, a secret so deeply shrouded that even he tried to deny it to himself sometimes. As he matured, despite the turmoil and self-hatred that churned inside him, he could no longer mask his attractions. He was a zoo.

It was even more complicated than that. Despite having an imaginative, exploratory mind that often experienced vivid fantasies and dreams, he had dreamed of women in a sexual way only twice in his life. Once it involved an ex-girlfriend. The other time, the dream featured singer-songwriter Amy Winehouse. He did, however, occasionally have sexual thoughts about human males. He wasn't just a zoo; he was a gay zoo, with a preference for male dogs and horses, with some interest in male humans.

As Spink grew to accept the reality of his sexual orientation, the cracks in his marriage widened into fault lines. His six-year union was doomed.

Many zoos never reveal the truth of their sexuality, keeping it hidden for the course of their entire lives. Society doesn't accept them, and most zoos don't believe they can change that reality, so they keep quiet for fear of reprisals. Spink never had that choice. In the late 1990s, he was outed.

It was another zoo who did the deed, the fallout of a longstanding feud between them. I wasn't able to track down this man to get his side of the story, but according to Spink, he considered himself reformed of his zoo behavior, and set out to destroy others in the zoo community. He outed people—including Spink—by compiling huge dossiers on them, which he then sent out to everyone he could find who associated with the person. He set up a website to publish the names of zoos, and made sure Google searches would identify who they were. He only stopped doing this when he was doxed by other zoos who exposed personal identifying information about him on the internet to scare him into submission.

Being outed meant Spink had a decision to make. Would he finally release the secret he had protected since puberty, and risk reprisals in the process? Or would he try to keep his zoo identity partitioned off inside himself, only to have it bob up to the surface again at some point beyond his control?

He decided to embrace it.

Hiding his true self seemed to only delay the inevitable, anyway. His human relationships—both personal and professional—had a habit of dissolving into dead silence once people found out who he was, either by his own admission, or by someone doing a Google search on his name. And the suppression of his feelings was taking a toll on him in the form of pervasive self-hatred.

It was a struggle to find the right approach and timing. There wasn't a playbook for this. But as Spink slowly stopped hating himself and began to embrace and take pride in the person he was, he grew more comfortable revealing his secret to those around him.

In time, the truth-telling went beyond his inner circle. He reached out to the rest of the world too, using a medium he felt comfortable with: the written word, on internet forums and discussion boards. Years after being outed, on May 15, 2008, he wrote about it on the Bluelight forum:

> I suspect that all these ramblings by me sound very narcissistic to many readers, and perhaps at some level they are. If so, I beg pardon. For most of my life, until my mid-20s, this side of me was absolutely, totally, completely, entirely hidden. From everyone. Forever. I lived my life in utter and total fear that I'd be "found out."

Every sexual encounter was a potential disaster, every feeling I had for my partners had to be hidden and denied around others. That kind of life really, really fucks up your mind. I had major issues with suicide and depression and every other bad thing I can think of. I had all but a split personality, at some level—I was one person "inside" and a totally different person on the outside.

After I was first outed and my worst fear had come true, I slowly came to see it as a blessing and not a curse. If I wasn't doing anything horrible in my zoo life—and I really don't think I am, in an objective sense—then why was I so ashamed of it? Why did I hate that side of myself so much? It's been a long, slow, challenging process to un-peel those layers of denial and lies and dishonesty and instinctive hiding. A big part of it has involved forcing myself to answer questions honestly, in public, so I don't backslide into old, unhealthy habits of thought.

An academic to the core, the internet was a medium where Spink thrived. Flexing his active mind was pure joy to him, and had been since he was young. Intellectual debate—even when it was prompted by written and oral attacks against him—was challenging and stimulating. Much more satisfying than the silent treatment he often experienced. He felt comfortable and confident communicating with human beings this way: "My deepest emotional bonds are with partners outside of our species—most of my life is lived apart from human language and human interactions. Perhaps that's why I am so wordy online?"

But Spink's public proclamation of his zoo status and his ensuing notoriety continue to be the exception, not the norm. "I've survived coming to terms with a sexuality that is as unanimously reviled and persecuted by Normal society as anything in the world," he said. These days, he calls himself the "uppity zoo" because he refuses to be ashamed of who he is.

"You either find a way to accept it or you kill yourself."

∩

Zoophiles around the world live in fear of what could happen if they reveal who they really are. One man I interviewed by telephone told me he doesn't dare drink or use drugs because he might slip up while impaired and tell someone about his attraction to dogs. Stephen Clarke felt the same way and avoided alcohol as a result, according to his polygraph report.

Hiding in plain sight was a more difficult proposition for one sixty-eight-year-old man I interviewed by email. Bernard (not his real name), a veterinarian from Baton Rouge, Louisiana, worried about being exposed on the job. He wrote to me about "the awkward problem of becoming aroused when examining a female dog."

"I've always feared I might be discovered," he said in an email. "That I would lose my job, go to prison, or worse." He thought there were times when people came close to figuring out his secret. "I have had people look at me funny, and comment that I was gentler/the dogs took to me better, than their previous vet."

He only decided to take the risk of reaching out to me because he was near retirement.

Bernard, whose writing style resembles a Louisiana drawl, had to find a way to discourage women who were interested in him romantically, "ways a' tellin' would-be suitors I'm not interested without offendin them or outin' myself. I've usually gotten by with wearin a weddin ring, an' failin that, have tried claimin' t' be gay."

Like most of the other zoophiles I interviewed, Bernard realized he wasn't attracted to his own species when he reached puberty and found that animals caught his attention, not human beings. Specifically female dogs. "I began to feel 'funny' whenever one of the females came into estrus. I was too young t' know what the feelings meant, but I know now that was a sign about my sexuality. By puberty my family (except my brother who I told that I love dogs) all worried I might be homosexual, as I didn't go out and spend time chasing girls like the other boys, I kept to myself with the dogs."

Despite being comfortable with his zoo status, Bernard suffers physical side effects that he believes come from hiding his true self.

> Havin' t' live a double-life an' keep work an' my personal life seperate has probably contributed t' my havin stomach ulcers an' acid reflux disease, as well as my high blood pressure. It takes a toll on the mind an' body that's fer sure. Still, I feel good about myself, I'm proud a' who I am, I'm a well liked an' respected vet, an' the way I see it, my preference fer beagles is no different than someone who prefers blondes, brunettes, or redheads, everyone is different,

we cain't all like the same things. My zoosexuality in general is no different than someone bein' heterosexual or homosexual, jus' how my brain was wired at birth. Some're wired t' be hetero, some're wired t' be homosexual, an' some people, like me, 're wired t' be zoosexual. Specific chemicals an' neurotransmitter patterns in our brains determine at birth what our preferences'll be later in life.

Bernard said the hardest part of being a zoo is the dramatic difference in the life spans of humans versus nonhumans, a sentiment I heard often from zoos. People live an average of seventy-nine years, while a dog's average lifespan is ten to thirteen years. Horses live twenty-five to thirty years.

Bernard deals with the loss by always having dogs descended from the bloodlines of a lemon Beagle named Ashley who he refers to as his first girlfriend. He was sixteen and Ashley was two when he started having sex with her. When he turned eighteen, he left home with Ashley.

When Ashley died, Bernard nearly drank himself to death. Then he became involved with one of Ashley's daughters. "When that dog got old, she too had pups, and again I kept a girl for my new 'wife' and the same thing went on about every 13–15 years since."

His current "wife" is another Beagle that his brother's oldest son calls Aunt Chloe.

Bernard's brother continues to be supportive of him, something for which the veterinarian is grateful. "I feel sorry fer other zoos who have mentioned how their family shuns an' rejects them."

Despite the complications that being a zoo brings to his life, Bernard said he doesn't wish to be a Normal. "I am who I am, I cain't help that I was born a zoophile." If he had his life to live over again, he said, "I wouldn't change a thing." I discovered that many zoos feel this way. Even though they lament that the world doesn't accept them and they fear being outed, overall most are glad to be zoophiles. They believe they have a special bond with other species that the rest of us Normals could never understand, and that we are the worse off for it.

For Doug Spink, there might have been an element of relief in having been outed as a zoo, but it indisputably brought turmoil to his life too. Soon afterwards, he was stripped of his trial judge title with the American Kennel Club, and he had to shut down his Golden Retriever rescue and breeding operations.

Although he had already gone through publicly confessing he was a zoo on the internet, that didn't make it any easier to confess to his wife that whatever modicum of sexual attraction he felt for human beings was towards men, not women. She didn't take the disclosure well.

"It is so powerfully hurtful for me to know that you are pained and disappointed by who I am," he wrote to her in a 4,600-word letter a few days after his oral confession. "If this is what 'coming out' is like, I'll happily stay in the closet for the rest of my life with the rest of the world. It was like a nightmare unfolding in front of me, as bad as I had imagined in my deepest fears for all the years that I have fought to deceive myself."

In the letter, he lamented that he had become the portrait of the very men he had felt sorry for in the past:

> For a long time, I've had supreme pity for those men who were married and had families, and through whatever mysterious and alchemical process woke up one day realizing that they were gay. How could a man reconcile the vows of marriage and the responsibilities of a family with a part of them that is so supremely and unarguably unalterable? It is the proverbial rock and a hard place, an unwinnable game with all losing outcomes. How could a man care deeply enough about his wife to marry her and have children, and then come to the horrible realization that in his heart of hearts he wasn't physically attracted to her, or any woman for that matter?
>
> Little did I know then that at least a chunk of my pity was actually self-pity. I am that man.

Despite his wife's disappointing reaction to his revelation, there was some solace in knowing that he no longer had to hide who he was.

> I'd be lying if I didn't say that there is an incredible, profound, soul-deep sense of relief that has come from my own "coming out to myself." I've been gay for as long as I can remember, and fighting every day to keep that knowledge, somehow, buried so deep it

would just disappear. That's not how it works, and for years there has been a fundamental lie in my life, a lie to myself which is the worst kind of lie.

You've been complicit in this lie, and I don't blame you for that. For you, our physical relationship was very important and it is understandable that you, too, would deny the obvious in simply ignoring something that was really as plain as the noses on both of our faces. I haven't had the strength to face my coming out on my own, and I've used you as a crutch to deny myself to myself. I'm not sure whether either of us right or wrong, good or bad, in what we've done here. I think we've both just been trying to survive as best we can.

The relief that came from being honest with himself and his wife was mixed with pain. She was dear to him, the best friend he'd ever had. She understood and accepted his complex character when other human beings didn't, wouldn't or couldn't. But that understanding was no longer a strong enough bond to hold them together. "Your conception of how I should love you is out of sync with how I, as a person, can love you," he wrote. "This creates unhappiness in you, a perfectly natural response. I am well aware of this unhappiness, and it creates in me self loathing, for I feel as if I am bringing this unhappiness to you, someone I love. I then look at you, indirectly, as a source of unhappiness. This feeds on itself *ad nauseam*."

I would have liked to interview Spink's former wife to gain additional perspective on him, and insight into their marriage. But shortly after I first met Spink in Seattle, he agreed to cooperate with my research on one condition: that I not attempt to contact his ex-wife, or include her name in this book. In return, he would give me access (provided the sources agreed) to everyone else who had come in contact with him—friends and enemies, former and current business partners, and family members. Usually I avoid making any type of deal that puts limits on my investigation, but the wide-ranging access he was offering in return made it a reasonable request. Plus, I didn't sense his motivation was to cover up anything in his background. In the case of his ex-wife, he gave his reasoning as follows: "It just feels like the interactions we had and the friendship we had went through a trajectory. We came fully apart, and tangling her back into my story after she has already moved out of my life—it just seems mean-spirited, unnecessary and not fair."

Later, when I was introduced to Spink's boyfriend of nine years, he added him as another caveat: I couldn't use his name in this book, although he didn't try to prevent me from interviewing him as he had done with his ex-wife. I would speak with this man many times over the years by phone, met him once in person, and we also communicated through text and email.

On several occasions during the time I've spent working on this story, Spink brought up this agreement we made in order to confirm that I was still planning to keep my end of the bargain. He said his insistence was based on wanting to protect both the human partners he had loved from negative publicity because of their connection to him.

∩

In addition to the sprawling place in Gaston, Spink and his wife also owned a smaller, refurbished farmhouse about twenty-five miles away in North Plains. The second home helped them facilitate their separation. From September 1998 until 2001, the couple was "separated but still together-ish," Spink recalled, living apart in their houses, alternating who stayed where, but still spending ample time together as friends. I could relate to their situation—it was similar to the arrangement Hiromi and I had for the year and a half before his death. The Spinks' union didn't have the same bloody ending that ours did, although its finale was dramatic in its own way.

The Spinks' failing marriage came to its fiery conclusion in 2003, when Doug went to pick up his Golden Retriever, Rion, from his wife to take him to Canada, where he had decided to live. But Rion wasn't there—he was staying at a friend's place. His wife said Spink could visit the dog whenever he wanted, but she refused to give him back. They had a bitter, angry confrontation.

"I told her I would gut her like a fish and hang her from a tree by her intestines if she didn't get Rion back to me in twenty-four hours," he told me. "I'm not proud of that."

A friend of his wife's witnessed the dispute and called the police, but the officers who showed up didn't arrest Spink. There had been angry words exchanged in an emotional situation, but no physical violence. His wife heeded his warning, and returned Rion to him.

His wedding vows in tatters, Spink made a new vow, this time to himself: never again would he allow himself to get romantically entangled with a woman. But he would break that pledge with Corinne Super, and with devastating consequences.

To read an excerpt from Doug Spink's coming out letter to his wife, see Exhibit 3, page 377.

15

FLYING PHALLUSES

As I worked on this story and learned more about zoophilia, I delved into questions that had lingered in my mind since I first began communicating with Doug Spink while he was in prison. Is zoophilia a real phenomenon? And are there more zoophiles out there?

Zoophiles—also known as zoosexuals, or simply zoos—are people who form their primary emotional, social and sexual bonds with animals instead of human beings. When I started researching, I had two expectations that turned out to be grossly inaccurate. First, I expected to find recent statistics about the prevalence of zoophilia. Second, I expected the numbers would reveal that it isn't very common.

Wrong, and wrong again.

The most recent numbers are decades old and come from pioneer sex researcher Dr. Alfred Kinsey, who collected the data for his groundbreaking Kinsey reports. The controversial and widely quoted *Sexual Behavior in the Human Male* (1948) and *Sexual Behavior in the Human Female* (1953) together sold three-quarters of a million copies and were translated into thirteen languages.

Kinsey was thorough. He had an impressive number of participants. He studied roughly eleven thousand subjects (half males, half females), often interviewing them himself. His statistics revealed that sexual activity between humans and animals is common—shockingly common, to the uninitiated. Kinsey discovered that 8 percent of men and 3.6 percent of women have had at least one sexual experience with an animal during their lifetime. Some of these experiences occur during childhood, never to be examined or revisited again. For others, the attraction is hardwired into their psyche, a permanent, lifelong component of sexual desire. Sometimes even the main desire.

When it comes to rural areas—on farms, where reproduction happens out in the open—Kinsey found the figures to be much higher. Among rural males, 40 to 50 percent reported having had sexual experiences with animals. Kinsey noted those figures were likely lower than actual numbers: "These must be minimum data, for there has undoubtedly been some cover-up in the reports of these activities," he wrote.

Kinsey concluded that the factors that draw human beings into sexual activities with each other aren't all that different from what causes people to have sex with animals from other species:

> In any event, it is certain that human contacts with animals of other species have been known since the dawn of history, they are known among all races of people today, and they are not uncommon in our own culture. . . . Far from being a matter for surprise, the record simply substantiates our present understanding that the forces which bring individuals of the same species together in sexual relations may sometimes serve to bring individuals of different species together in the same types of sexual relations.

Shortly before completing his first report, Alfred Kinsey formed the Kinsey Institute. Now located at Indiana University, it is still America's preeminent research organization about sexuality, with a mission "to advance sexual health and knowledge worldwide." I called the institute's director of communications, hoping there might be a more recent study about zoophilia in the works. "There are no plans to study it at this time," said Jennifer Bass.

Next I wrote to Catherine Johnson-Roehr, curator of art, artifacts and photographs at the institute. In her reply, she said their gallery collection is voluminous—48,000 photos, plus another 7,000 pieces of art and artifacts. She also described a popular show held in the gallery a few years earlier, titled *Passionate Creatures*:

> It featured a wide variety of artworks from around the world that dealt with eroticism and animal imagery. We did not include photographs of humans in sexual situations with animals, but instead we focused more on sexual fantasies depicted by artists, often inspired by mythology (Leda and the Swan, Europa and the Bull). We were surprised to find a large number of artworks in our collection included depictions of animals—not just zoophilia, but also an animal couple might be shown engaged in intercourse near a human couple, or a human couple might be observed or interrupted by a cat or dog. We also included depictions of human genitalia as independent creatures, such as flying phalluses.

Before researching this subject, I had dismissed zoophilia as mainly a myth. A joke. Something that hardly ever happened in real life, unless it was making a lascivious appearance on the pornography scene. I wasn't prepared for how many zoos there are. Or for how many of them would want to tell their stories.

Looking back, my ignorance on the subject is surprising, particularly given the decades I've spent volunteering in animal welfare—nearly all the zoos I interviewed have worked or volunteered in the animal welfare movement. How could I have missed it?

Credible research about zoophilia is rare, most likely because of the stigma attached to the subject. Kinsey discussed people's contempt for the behavior: "All in all, there is probably no type of human sexual behavior which has been more severely condemned by that segment of the population which happens not to have had such experience, and which accepts the age-old judgment that animal intercourse must evidence as a mental abnormality, as well as an immorality."

Although there isn't much in the way of research on zoophilia, someone did tackle the topic more recently than Kinsey, albeit with a much smaller but more specific group of subjects. Maryland-based psychotherapist Hani Miletski extensively questioned ninety-three zoos for her 1999 doctoral dissertation, published in 2002 and titled *Understanding Bestiality and Zoophilia*. I sent her Kinsey's quote about society's widespread condemnation of cross-species sex, and asked for her reaction.

"The sentiment you quoted is very common, and is held by most people who are not into sex with animals," Miletski replied. "In my experience, people find the idea disgusting, and many worry about animal consent."

Miletski's book was among the possessions seized from Spink's cabin during the federal raid. Despite repeated efforts, he was never able to get the book back, which annoyed him. He didn't think the federal government had any right to seize and keep his academic materials on zoophilia. "It speaks for itself: idiotic, ignorant, fascistic, petty, indefensible, absurd," he said.

Understanding Bestiality and Zoophilia centers on Miletski's basic research question: can humans have a sexual orientation towards non-human animals?

I, for one, intended to find out.

In her book, Miletski explained that she got the idea to study this taboo subject as a result of treating a patient who felt conflicted about his sexual attraction towards dogs:

> It all started when my client, I'll call him Chris, told me he could not find any literature about bestiality/zoophilia. I had been seeing him, in my psychotherapy practice, because he could not stop having sex with dogs. He was a very religious man and believed it was wrong to have sexual relations with anything other than women, and even then, only when you are married to that woman. However, he could not control his urges to have sex with the dogs in his neighborhood.

When she looked into bestiality and zoophilia, she couldn't find reliable research on the psychology of the phenomenon. She asked a librarian at the Sexuality Information and Education Council of the United States (SIECUS) to do a literature search, which turned up disappointing findings. "The most important part of a literature review is the review of other studies on the related topic," Miletski wrote. "Research on bestiality or zoophilia is scarce, and out-dated."

The only material SIECUS tracked down was a 1994 autobiography by the late Mark Matthews called *The Horseman: Obsessions of a Zoophile*.

In her acknowledgments, Miletski wrote that Matthews' story and personal difficulties had touched her. "In this book, the author describes his struggles to accept the fact that he loved his horse more than he loved his wife."

Matthews and her conflicted client got Miletski thinking: if these two men felt this way about animals, surely there were others out there with similar urges. Given the scarcity of information, why not create her own study? "I was intrigued with the idea that there are people who may be sexually attracted to animals, and may even prefer animals as sex partner to humans," she wrote.

Although Miletski saw the need for a study, not everyone around her agreed.

> This was not an easy thing to do. Some of my colleagues and friends thought I was out of my mind: "You are going to study what?" Some concluded there was something wrong with me, that I needed therapy, and/or that I myself was having sex with animals. The man I was dating at that time could not even handle discussing the topic. But, there were others who encouraged me and my controversial investigation, and I was set to be one of the first researchers to study this virtually unknown phenomenon and to conduct a large scale, professional study on bestiality/zoophilia.

She pressed on despite the negativity, driven by a sense of responsibility to her profession and its patients. "I found the major void of knowledge regarding bestiality/zoophilia alarming. In my opinion, clinical sexologists and psychotherapists need to be equipped with a carefully researched base of knowledge in order to understand the phenomenon and the individuals involved."

Eventually Miletski rooted out some literature. But she wasn't impressed, concluding it was unscientific, inconsistent and unreliable.

> I ended up finding many books and articles whose authors mention and sometimes even discuss bestiality and zoophilia. Many authors suggest that human beings have had sexual relations with animals since the dawn of history and throughout the world (in some countries more than others). These authors assert that sexual relations with animals has been practiced, thought about, dreamed of, and has emerged in myth, fairytale, folklore, literature, painting and sculpture (Cauldwell, 1948; Dumont, 1970; Kinsey et al., 1948; Kullinger, 1969; Masters, 1962). None of them, however, provides an in-depth picture into the lives and behaviors of the

people who engage in sexual relations with animals. Many authors volunteer their opinions and discuss humans' sexual relations with animals as though they are an authority on the subject. Their opinions, however, are often conflicting and cause much confusion to the reader.

Miletski hoped her research would clear some of the tangled brush of misleading information to bring understanding to a subject she believed was badly understudied. "Hopefully, this work will help to demystify a topic which has long suffered ridicule and pseudo-scientific rhetoric, and will open the door to further, much needed research," she wrote.

Her study unearthed a dizzying array of historical examples of cross-species sex. "The literature review I conducted reveals that human sexual relations with animals existed forever and in almost every place and culture in the world."

The next step was a bigger challenge: she had to find actual zoos to study. She placed advertisements online and in publications calling for volunteers. Much to her surprise, when zoos found out what she was doing, her project gained momentum. Similar to what I experienced with this book, they spread the word about her project, and others came forward to tell their stories.

In total, Miletski was approached by 160 zoos. Some participants were eliminated from the study if they didn't follow the guidelines she set out, such as the requirement to disclose their home addresses so she could mail out questionnaires to help ensure they were legitimate, actual people. (For their privacy and protection, she destroyed the zoos' addresses once she completed the project.)

The final study included findings from 93 zoos (82 men, 11 women). Participants filled out 350 questions over 23 pages, ranging from basic demographic information to graphic details about their sexual experiences with animals. Among Miletski's subjects, the most common animals to have sex with were dogs, followed by horses.

But Miletski didn't rely only on questionnaires to study the minds of the zoos. She also interviewed them by phone, and met with a group virtually in an online chat room. It was the 1990s, when the internet was still in its nascency, and Miletski wasn't connected yet, so two zoos—a woman and her boyfriend—came to her house and used their laptop to connect her to the group.

> On a cold November night in 1995, I logged on the internet for the first time in my life, and into a chat room where a whole crowd of zoos was waiting to speak with me. I was amazed at the sense of friendship and closeness the zoos exhibited among themselves. Most had internet names of animals, and they acted as though they were animals playing with other animals, like a litter of cubs would play with each other. They were playful, friendly and respectful to one another.

She interacted online with the zoos for four hours. Miletski's communications soon went beyond virtual. She established so much trust with the zoo community that she was invited to attend an annual gathering in May 1996.

> I was very flattered. Now I knew they trusted me. But, I had mixed feelings. I did not want to get too close to them; people might think I am a zoo and/or their friend and not take my study seriously. At the same time how could I give up an opportunity like this? I decided to go. This turned out to be a profound weekend. It opened the doors to a secret world populated by entertaining, intelligent people, engaged in a sexual behavior that much of our contemporary society views with revulsion.

At the gathering, Miletski met more than fifty zoos from around the United States, and conducted two focus groups. The trust they extended to her was significant. "They talked about how difficult it was to be a zoo, to find other zoos, and to 'come out' to their family members and friends. They complained about the fact that the media made zoos look like perverts, pedophiles, and rapists, and cried about losing their animal sex partners whose life span is much shorter than humans." They confided in her that they were terrified of being outed or caught.

Currently, Miletski is a licensed clinical social worker with a private practice. She has a master's degree in social work from the Catholic University of America's National School of Social Service in Washington, DC, and a doctorate in human sexuality from the Institute for Advanced Study of Human Sexuality in San Francisco. I emailed her several times before this book went to press to ask some follow-up questions. For example, I wondered whether the results of her research had surprised her. "I was surprised by many things," she responded.

> When I had the opportunity to get to know some of the zoos, I was surprised to find out that they are "normal," nice, intelligent, friendly people. People you would never guess that they are zoos.

> I was surprised to witness how much they love their animal partners, and how much they love and care for animals in general.
>
> I was surprised to see that some of my participants had sexual relations with lots of animals, and lots of different kind of animals, some unbelievable such as: lions, tigers, wolves, porcupines, llamas, rhinoceros, etc.
>
> I was surprised to find out that, like the men, the most common sexual behavior engaged in by the women was masturbation of the male animal. In pornography, the most common sexual behavior is the animal penetrating the woman.
>
> Generally speaking, I found lots of surprises here and there when I was reading the completed questionnaires that were sent back to me. It was really fascinating to learn about each person, and to learn about their lives and stories.

Then I asked her the question that had been on my mind since I started learning more about zoos, a question I knew had the potential to cause significant controversy: in her opinion, speaking as a researcher, does she believe zoophilia is a sexual orientation?

"Yes, for some," she said.

Miletski feels sympathy for zoos trying to fit into society despite widespread opprobrium. "Over the years, I had several zoos who came to see me for therapy. They did not want to change their lifestyle or sexual orientation; they had other issues they wanted to work on, like other people have. But, they felt more comfortable talking with me because they knew I will not judge them, and will not try to get them to change their sexual orientation."

I asked Miletski if she had ever received threats from people angered by her writing about zoophiles.

"Oh, yes! I got letters, and emails, and when I gave a talk in Las Vegas, at the Erotic Heritage Museum, in June 2013, I was heckled by a group of people who came to hear me speak just to make a point about the 'poor animals.' They did apologize afterwards, but it was a very uncomfortable experience."

I wondered whether, after studying so many zoos, Miletski discovered characteristics in common that would form a typical profile of a zoophile.

"No, I did not," she said. "They come from all walks of life, and the only thing that united them is their love and attraction to animals."

16

LADY BUBLE

One of the starkest examples of society's hatred, revulsion and rejection of zoophiles is the story of what happened to Phillip Buble. The incident occurred in 1999, around the same time Doug Spink was grappling with the repercussions of being outed in his own life. Being a known zoophile had cost Spink dearly, including numerous threats of violence aimed in his direction. Spink survived the threats without being physically injured, but Buble wasn't so lucky.

Phillip was living with his father, Frank Buble, in the tiny town of Parkman, Maine, when he came out as a zoophile. This revelation was acutely upsetting to his seventy-year-old father, a pilot who had retired from the aerospace industry. The elder Buble was mortified when his forty-three-year-old son began to openly declare his sexual orientation in front of his pilot friends. Phillip considered his thirty-six-pound mixed breed dog, whom he called Lady Buble, to be his significant other, and referred to her as his wife.

Tensions between father and son about Phillip's zoophilia were exacerbated by disagreements about repairs to the family home. The conflict came to a head on September 13, 1999, when Frank Buble returned home to find Phillip French-kissing Lady Buble.

That was it. The breaking point for Frank Buble.

When Phillip stepped into the shower, his father grabbed a crowbar and lay in wait. As his son exited, Frank began smashing him repeatedly with the metal bar. He didn't succeed in killing his child as intended, but the injuries were significant. Phillip's arm was broken, and he required sixty-three stitches to his head and face. He was treated at the Mayo Regional Hospital in Dover-Foxcroft and released.

When the case went to court, Frank Buble testified in Piscataquis County Superior Court before Justice Andrew Mead that lack of sleep, combined with his son's behavior, had "pushed him over the edge."

Meanwhile, Phillip wrote a letter to Justice Mead requesting permission for Lady Buble to accompany him in court:

> I'd like my significant other to attend by my side if possible as she was present in the house during the attack, though not an eyewitness to it, thank goodness. I've been informed your personal permission is needed given that my wife is not human, being a dog of about 36 pounds weight and very well behaved. You can confirm this with just about anyone at the Dover courthouse, many there have already met her in "person."

Defense attorney Randy Day painted a picture of Frank Buble's mounting frustration with his son. He argued mitigating circumstances: that Frank Buble had no prior criminal record, and that his son's unusual lifestyle drove him to it.

R. Christopher Almy, Piscataquis County district attorney, told the court that "the horrendous nature of the attack should not be forgotten, because the injuries to Phillip Buble were significant."

Frank Buble pled guilty to attempted murder and elevated aggravated assault. He was sentenced to eight years, with all but nine months suspended, on each of the two counts. The sentences were to be served concurrently.

Despite the violent attack, Phillip didn't want his father to be imprisoned. Instead, he said, his father "needs serious therapy." Frank Buble was indeed ordered to get psychological counseling, a requirement that pleased his son.

Phillip Buble went on to use the publicity from the incident to try to win acceptance for zoophiles. He talked about zoophilia on regional radio shows, and a year and a half after the attack, he testified against

Maine bill LD 1283, which sought to criminalize sexual acts with animals (the bill may have been a response to his well-publicized story).

"In what surely must rank as one of the most bizarre moments in State House history," wrote Emmet Meara in the *Bangor Daily News*, on March 27, 2001, "Phillip Buble, 44, of Parkman defended his sexual love for his dog for more than 30 minutes before the squirming members of the Legislature's Criminal Justice Committee on Monday."

Buble told legislators the proposed law was an attempt "to force morality on a minority. It will be a disservice to zoo couples and would keep zoo couples from coming out of the closet and drive us deeper underground. This helps no one and would force me out of state."

He said he didn't feel safe as a zoophile. His home had been paintballed. He became homeless for about six months before moving in with a friend's parents in Ohio, one of the few remaining states that didn't have a law prohibiting sex with animals. He stayed there for about two years.

I tracked down the man whose parents housed Buble, who identified himself to me only as Adam. In a 2012 telephone interview, he spoke fondly of his friend. He talked about how Buble dreamed of becoming a veterinarian one day, and what he was like as a person. "He loved electronics. He was very smart, highly intelligent, friendly, personable."

Adam said the beating may have caused neurological problems, because Buble's personality changed after his father's attack on him. "He lost his filter. He would be out in the open talking about stuff in a restaurant with kids around. He broke the social contracts." Or, Adam speculated, perhaps it wasn't neurological damage, but "him being very resolute about not going back in the closet."

Perhaps Buble's bluntness came from a combination of both.

Buble was overweight, with high blood pressure, and he took insulin for type 2 diabetes. His illnesses would eventually end his life. He died at Riverside Hospital in Columbus, Ohio, on December 3, 2010, at the age of fifty-four.

Adam said the disgust that society feels towards zoos eventually ground down Buble's spirit, and he became frightened and paranoid. "Slowly over time, he started to think everybody was after him.

He thought that the legal system was coming for him. He felt like what was happening to the zoo society was a form of genocide."

Philip Buble with Lady outside the Main State House in Augusta, where he testified about zoophilia. (Associated Press photo)

To read the letter Phillip Buble wrote to Justice Mead requesting that Lady be allowed in the courtroom, see Exhibit 4, page 378.

17

TECH SEEDS

As the 1990s drew to a close, it was becoming apparent that Doug Spink's marriage wouldn't survive the disclosure about his sexual preferences. But his business pursuits still held great promise.

The 1998 sale of his online catalog company, Timberline Direct, had made Spink a wealthy man. It enabled him to fund his properties and his stallion stud farm, the star of which was the elite athlete named Capone.

Soon he would negotiate a far bigger deal than Timberline.

Besides the catalog company, in the late 1990s, Spink had a hand in various internet and other technology firms. According to a March 1, 2001, filing to the Securities and Exchange Commission, "During the past five years Mr. Spink has invested in, co-founded, or served as an advisor to several e-commerce companies, including webmodal.com (co-founder and board member), assetexchange.com (investor), Bidland.com (advisor) and matacat.com (founder, investor and board member)."

One of Spink's business pursuits was Strategicus Partners, a technology consultancy he founded in 1998 that was acquired by the Stonepath Group the following year. Spink stayed on as chief technical officer until 2000, when he resigned and started Seedling Technology

Ventures. The new company, co-founded with a business associate, Paul R. Peterson, invested in fledgling technology-oriented enterprises in exchange for ownership stakes in the businesses.

I interviewed Peterson numerous times by telephone about his dealings with Doug Spink. I also drove to Seattle to meet him in person for a few hours, and went to visit him for a day at his company, located at the McMinnville Municipal Airport in Oregon, forty miles from Portland. These days, Peterson is not in business with Spink anymore. In 2011, the former US Air Force fighter pilot combined his interests in aviation and high tech to found Volta Volaré Corporation, which manufactures high-performance electric aircraft, and also invests in other clean technology companies.

One of the first things Peterson wanted me to know is that he is not a zoophile.

Peterson first met Spink in the 1990s, when they both lived in Portland. Peterson was working at a bank where he created an innovative new financial instrument, a mortgage product designed to attract successful entrepreneurs who wanted to buy homes, but didn't meet traditional bank requirements. Peterson's brainchild enabled Spink to finance the purchase of his Gaston mansion. Eventually the two men forged a business partnership, and a friendship.

Peterson said that after Spink was arrested for drug smuggling in 2005, the federal government harassed him and his wife about their connection to Spink, a stress factor that contributed to the deterioration of their marriage. Back then, the couple worked in the field of financial services and international trade, and the feds accused the Petersons of money laundering for the drug industry, an allegation that Paul Peterson vigorously denies.

Despite the troubles that partnering with Spink brought to his life, the drug smuggling arrest didn't prevent Peterson from working with Spink again after he was released on probation in 2007. But trouble flared up once more when Spink's cabin was raided in 2010, and Peterson again fell under the scrutiny of the federal government because of his connection to Spink.

I asked Peterson why he continued doing business with Spink when it came with such turmoil. "Because he's the smartest motherfucker I ever met," he responded succinctly. After mulling it over for a couple of days, he called me to add an afterthought: "I thought he made a stupid mistake and was going to recover. I gave him the benefit of the doubt."

∩

Back in 2001, Spink and Peterson thought they had hit pay dirt. They struck a deal to sell Seedling for $40 million in stock to Brighton Technologies Corporation of Allendale, New Jersey. As part of the acquisition agreement, Brighton's board members resigned. The plan was to put majority ownership and control of the new company—to be called Seedling Technologies Corp.—in the hands of Seedling stockholders. Spink would become chairman and CEO, and Peterson would be named director and president.

But Seedling's seemingly bright future went awry. According to Spink and Peterson, the Chinese-born businessman who founded Brighton managed to fraudulently register additional stock certificates with securities transfer agents. Seedling's legitimate shareholders' equity was diluted by millions of dollars when investors unwittingly purchased the fraudulent stock from associates of the Chinese businessman. Peterson led an inquiry into the shareholder groups to determine which were legitimate. Lawsuits from these duped shareholders started popping up that targeted Seedling.

Seedling was down, but not out. Spink and Peterson rallied, finding investors who agreed to infuse funds into a tech company they had also invested in called NxGen. The deal would be enough to save Seedling, and Spink and Peterson expected to net $15 million each.

On September 10, 2001, the business partners boarded a private jet and flew to Vancouver, British Columbia, to sign documents into the night at the office of Canaccord Capital Corporation. The deal would close the next day, at 9:00 a.m. Eastern time. After the paperwork was completed, the partners partied into the wee hours in Vancouver to celebrate their good fortune before flying back to Oregon.

That morning—9:15 in the east, 6:15 in the west—Spink picked up the phone and called Peterson to verify that their deal was done.

But Peterson wouldn't answer the question, even when repeatedly pressed by Spink.

"Turn on your TV, dude," Peterson said. "Just turn on your TV. All hell has broken loose."

Minutes before their deal was scheduled to close, the World Trade Center came under attack by Al Qaeda terrorists who piloted two airplanes directly into the country's financial epicenter. At 8:46 a.m., the North Tower was hit. At 9:03, a second plane struck the South Tower. Both of the 110-storey buildings caught fire. By 10:30 a.m., the twin towers had collapsed in a thick gray cloud of smoke and dust. Thousands died, financial markets plunged into ruins, and so did the business deals that depended upon them. Spink's arrangement was just one of many that melted away into the chaos.

Years later, I asked him if he was upset that the terrorist attacks had robbed them of millions. "I could never really get upset because it was bigger than us," he said.

Once Spink's businesses went under, the costly stud farm soon followed. The former manager of the farm recalled how quickly things changed for her boss.

> There were about four weeks when people were perfectly willing to extend him credit, and then once they realized the money was gone, that was it.
>
> When he had the money, he was seen as being a visionary and an exciting person. Someone doing cutting-edge work with interesting new ideas. Overnight people who one day thought how cool he was, how groundbreaking he was, all of a sudden they started telling stories about what a horrible human being he was. It tore my guts out. It just made me angry to watch it happen.

In 2002, Spink filed for Chapter 7 bankruptcy.

⁂

After interviewing Paul Peterson at his company in McMinnville, I drove twenty miles to Gaston. I wanted to check out the last house Doug Spink had owned before his financial crash, the mansion where he and Peterson held epic rave parties that drew hundreds of people back in the heyday of their high tech success. Peterson recalled the parties lasting for days, and reminisced fondly about how they would instruct visitors to park their vehicles in a crosshatch pattern to slow down police officers attempting to make their way up to the house to break up the festivities.

But when tough economic times hit the entrepreneurs, the parties were over. Peterson told me that when Spink lapsed on the Gaston house payments, he bought the mortgage from the bank in an attempt to help his friend and business partner keep his home, with the agreement that Spink would help out financially. But "he didn't pay a nickel in rent, he avoided it and ignored it," Peterson said. After nearly a year, Peterson couldn't afford to keep paying anymore, so he stopped. The bank foreclosed, and the sheriff showed up and changed the locks. "I couldn't afford to maintain a palace for a friend," Peterson said, adding, "This time it affected my credit."

Spink was angry and resentful, Peterson said, and "convinced that I made him homeless on purpose."

Just like his one-room cabin in Sumas, Spink's former home in Gaston is at the dead end of a road, perched high on a hilltop that overlooks a sweeping parcel of land. The accommodations aren't similar, however—unlike the cabin, the Gaston house is large and luxurious. The property also features a sizable barn.

When I arrived, two little kids were splashing around in a swimming pool outside. I knocked on the front door and their grandmother answered.

"I'm writing a book about someone who used to live here," I said.

"Who?" she asked.

"Doug Spink."

Upon hearing his name, her body language instantly changed from relaxed and friendly, to tense and guarded. The door began to close shut on me.

"My husband won't want me talking to you," she said.

But I kept asking questions, and slowly, the door swung open again. The woman stepped outside and spoke with me for about an hour.

She and her husband had purchased the house after Spink had been forced out. Like many people who face foreclosure, he took his anger about the circumstances out on the house. The elaborate brickwork was marred by gallons of paint, she said. Windows were smashed.

There were gaping holes in the walls and ceilings, and by the shape, she guessed they'd been made by a bowling ball thrown against them. "Fuck you" was smeared on the walls in dog feces. The couple's adult children moved in with them for three years to help repair the place.

∩

The properties, the companies, the marriage, the stallion farm—Spink had lost it all. But he still had what mattered to him most: his four-legged family. Five horses (Capone, Cantour, Cotopaxi, Ace and Joseph) and five dogs (Frasier, Fritzy, Maxwell, Bruno and Rion). Caring for their needs gave him strength and purpose, and the motivation to keep going.

The menagerie headed north to Canada, where he hoped a fresh start would be waiting for them. A promising new life in a different country.

What Spink didn't know was that one of the most devastating losses he would face in his lifetime was still to come. It lurked around the corner, about to slam into him head on.

BASE JUMPING

It has been said that you must learn to walk before you can run. In BASE jumping, there are times when you must learn to climb before you can jump. Climbing is what first drew Doug Spink and Dwain Weston together.

Spink was still a successful businessman living in Oregon when Weston immigrated to Portland from Sydney in early 2000. Both men enjoyed jumping close to home, and they were also traveling the globe to experience the physical and mental thrill of extreme sports. Weston went on to win the world title in BASE jumping in 2002, but Spink—a novice—had something valuable to offer to Weston: he was an experienced and talented rock climber. Their combined talents enabled them to tackle exit points they couldn't have conquered alone.

"Dwain had reasonable climbing skills, but Doug was motivated in his climbing and BASE jumping," recalled Gary Cunningham, a close friend of Weston's and president of the Australian BASE Association. "It required some skill and raw guts to push that extra bit further into the unknown."

Spink considered Weston to be his best human friend, someone who accepted him for who he was. Weston wasn't a zoo, but he knew Spink was, and he didn't care.

"Dwain seemed to strike up a great friendship with him some time after he moved to the USA," Cunningham said. "I remember Dwain telling me about him once and it sounded like he had great admiration for Doug. It was not only for his physical abilities but for his business achievements too."

Weston, a tall, lean Australian with longish blonde hair and a genuine smile, was friendly and funny. His easygoing nature belied the intense power and fearlessness that emanated from him when he leapt from unthinkable heights, performing acrobatics as he dropped from the sky.

Weston wasn't just loved by Doug; he was beloved in the BASE community as well, viewed as one of the most inspiring people in the sport. Cool and calculating under pressure, he jumped with grace, strength and precision. He survived many death-defying feats. The very nature of the sport is death defying. A BASE jumper free-falls from a site, employing a parachute just seconds before landing. According to Cunningham, it has taken a decade for BASE jumping to catch up to the skill level exhibited by Weston in his era. Weston earned additional admiration because of the energy he put back into the sport, dedicating his time and talent to teaching others. He championed safe competition and helped people stay alive doing what they loved.

In a YouTube video, Weston talked about why he did it. "In spite of all the danger, there comes a time when the animal inside says let me be free, and you must roll the dice and throw yourself into the unknown and see what happens because that is truly living."

∩

The BASE community is tiny. Only about 2,200 people have been issued BASE numbers worldwide since the activity grew beyond stunt status in the early 1980s to become a recognized recreational sport. A person earns a BASE number by jumping off at least one fixed object from each of the four categories that form the sport's acronym: building, antenna, span and earth. If the jumps are performed at night, participants receive a Night BASE number. Even fewer people hold Night BASE numbers, reportedly less than 1,000.

BASE jumping is widely viewed as the most dangerous recreational activity on the planet. The death rate is high: about 220 people have died since the sport's inception, a significant statistic because of the small number of people involved. Even basejumper.com, the website created to promote the sport, doesn't recommend it: "BASE jumping is a highly dangerous sport that can easily injure and kill participants. Think long and hard before making a BASE jump. We do not recommend BASE jumping to anybody. You, and you alone, are responsible for your safety."

The people drawn to BASE are thrill seekers and rebels. Outlaws, to an extent. Many are experienced skydivers seeking more daring challenges than jumping out of airplanes. The margin of error is much smaller for BASE jumping than skydiving, because the jumps tend to be from lower altitudes. BASE jumping parachutes are designed for quick deployment. Usually a jumper has just a few seconds to spare before ground impact.

"Most of the people who have really pushed in the sport had their own particular demons," said Spink (BASE715, Night BASE122). "There's an intensity of expression here. Terrible things will happen if you roll the dice enough times."

On top of the physical risks, BASE jumping is illegal in most places. Criminal charges against the jumpers—and possibly the ground crew—can include trespassing, breaking and entering, reckless endangerment and vandalism. Private property owners and government entities such as parks departments frequently push for criminal charges against renegade jumpers to discourage others from following suit.

Although he cautioned others about safety, Weston's own jumps were among the most daring. He noted that stark contradiction in an article called "Go Long Not Hard."

> I realize that it is wrong to say "Do as I say, not as I do", but the fact remains: if people begin to emulate some of these jumps then the death rate will increase. Admiration and recognition in BASE should not be given to those existing on the cutting edge, but to those with high amounts of knowledge, those who advance the technology we use, and those who demonstrate rock solid ability and sound judgment.

Weston had earned the right to be contradictory. The computer analyst was meticulous, executing his jumps with flawless precision. Twelve hundred jumps in ten countries, and he didn't just survive them; he barely suffered a scratch. No significant injuries. Not even the token broken ankle or two that is the common battle scar among BASE jumpers. It was an impressive personal safety record.

Besides the physical risks that come with BASE, there is an emotional cost. Losing friends is inevitable. Spink wrote about that grim reality on an internet forum: "BASE has brought me together with truly the most amazing, beautiful, interesting, complex, frustrating, intellectual, spiritual, courageous, ridiculous, hare-brained, brilliant people in the world. It has then taken them from me, one after another. If you join our sport, this will happen to you—it is wonderful, and it absolutely sucks."

The losses never got easier to bear. Just the opposite—they piled up. Once, during a long car ride, Weston confided to Spink about the deaths of eighteen people he had personally witnessed during his years in the sport, experiences for which it was impossible to mentally prepare.

"We're not really designed to watch that kind of violent death, people hitting the ground at a hundred and fifty miles an hour," Spink said.

Routine exposure to the death of friends and fellow athletes had taken a toll on Weston, losses that cast a dark shadow inside him. It didn't help that family members of dead BASE jumpers frequently blamed Weston because he was the most experienced person on the jump. "They would say, 'You killed my son,' and he just took it," Spink recalled.

∩

One of the most painful casualties for Weston and Spink occurred in August 2002 in Lauterbrunnen, Switzerland, a well-known BASE jumping site. Spink wasn't along for the trip, but Weston was there with one of their close friends, a charismatic and brilliant doctor named Nikolas Hartshorne.

In his professional life, Hartshorne was a Seattle medical examiner. His most famous autopsy was performed on the iconic musician Kurt Cobain, the lead singer, songwriter and guitarist for the grunge rock band Nirvana. After Cobain was found dead in his Seattle home in 1994 at age twenty-seven, Hartshorne concluded that Cobain had taken his own life by injecting himself with a massive dose of heroin and shooting himself in the head. Yet the theory has persisted that Cobain's death was murder, not suicide. The controversy thickened when it was revealed that Hartshorne had mingled socially with Cobain's wife, Courtney Love.

Spink and Weston spoke several times by telephone during the Switzerland trip. Weston was bickering with Hartshorne, dismayed that the doctor was jumping Lauterbrunnen in the first place. Strong tracking skills were a must to survive a jump in that location, and Hartshorne's tracking skills were weak.

Weston's concerns were amplified when Hartshorne pulled out a canopy he'd promised not to bring, one that Weston thought was a piece of junk. Weston begged, he argued, he cajoled. But it was to no avail. Hartshorne was determined to jump with the dodgy canopy that a manufacturer had given him for testing purposes. Over the years, Hartshorne had watched enviously as Weston was gifted truckloads of free equipment in return for testing and suggesting improvements. For once it was his turn to get free stuff.

Hartshorne's jump started out badly, and only got worse as his flight progressed. He launched off the cliff positioned awkwardly with his head down, and opened his canopy before his body position stabilized. The canopy opened towards the cliff. Hartshorne landed briefly on a cliff ledge before the canopy collapsed, throwing him off balance. He stumbled backwards and fell off that ledge onto another, where he sustained what is believed to be the fatal injury: a blow to the head. The canopy inflated again, flew back into the cliff wall, and dropped below Hartshorne, scooping him up as he collapsed into it.

The doctor tumbled several hundred feet down the rest of the wall enveloped in his canopy. Jumpers refer to that state as being "gift wrapped." Hartshorne slammed into the cliff six to eight more times before finally coming to rest at the bottom. Weston immediately jumped off the cliff after him in an effort to save his friend. He called Spink from his cell phone while he was at Hartshorne's side. "He said, 'Nik's gone. His guts and heart are all over my hands. I put my hands onto his chest to do CPR and they went right through to his backbone.'"

The loss of Nik Hartshorne was devastating to both men.

For Weston, the body count was piling up. He told Spink, "I've seen too much. There's no way I will ever unsee it. When I close my eyes that's what I see, and I don't know how long I can keep living with that."

19

LAST RIDE

BASE jumpers can face criminal charges just for participating in the sport they love, so even winning legal custody of a jump site temporarily is considered a victory for athletes in a sport that has long struggled to gain a sanctioned foothold.

That's what drew jumpers to Cañon City, Colorado, in 2003 when the first annual Go Fast Games was held. Sponsored by Denver's Go Fast Sports and Beverage Company, the event showcased three days of extreme sports. The final day featured six hours of jumpers hurling themselves off the Royal Gorge Bridge, an impressive span known for most of its lifetime as the tallest suspension bridge in the world.

Only experienced jumpers were invited to participate. Hundreds of jumps were performed from the span in the allotted time slot. Daredevils steered their airborne bodies through a steep rocky canyon above the rushing Arkansas River to touch down on a small landing area 955 feet below.

Doug Spink didn't make plans to attend the inaugural Go Fast Games. The then-thirty-two-year-old knew it wouldn't be the type of scene he enjoyed. Some disturbing moments in the preceding days had almost caused him to change his mind, but he had five dogs and nine horses at home to care for. If not for them, he would have been there.

Not going would end up being one of the biggest regrets of his life. A decade later, he would still suffer unyielding guilt and sorrow as a result of the decision.

∩

By the time the Go Fast Games rolled around, Spink hadn't seen Dwain Weston for a few months, not since Weston had left Portland to move in with his girlfriend in Los Angeles. On his last day in town, Weston stopped by to visit Spink. As the two men hugged and said their goodbyes, Spink had a feeling of foreboding that he would never see Weston again. The feeling was so strong that he spoke it out loud.

Lately Weston had been depressed. Spink said Weston confided in him that his relationship wasn't working, and that he felt trapped and wanted to move out. The week of the event, Weston called Spink to say, "that he woke up and couldn't think of a single reason to keep living," Spink wrote to me in an email. "That he wanted to 'quit while he was ahead' and that he'd accomplished all his life goals already, at 30. Survived it all. Why stumble on, then? Go out in a spectacular fashion. I argued against, predictably."

Spink, who had recently moved to British Columbia, reassured Weston. He promised to fly down to Los Angeles the following week, rent a truck, and help him pack up his belongings.

As the bridge event approached, their telephone conversations focused on the final stunt, Weston's exhibition jump from an airplane while wearing a wingsuit. He would be jumping with fellow daredevil Jeb Corliss.

Spink and Weston had a rapport that sometimes featured black humor, a coping mechanism common among people who encounter death on a regular basis—cops, coroners, journalists. As per their usual banter, Spink joked about what would happen if Weston missed his buzz above the bridge and slammed into it while hundreds of spectators stood watching on the span.

"It would be like setting off a hand grenade in a shopping mall," Spink said.

"Man, that's not cool," Weston answered.

"If you impact it right, you could take that whole thing down," Spink continued.

Weston speculated about the engineering of the bridge, commenting that it would be an evil act to kill hundreds of looky-loos.

But as the conversation progressed, Weston's voice began to change. It lost the tone of black humor Spink knew so well. Now Weston was in another mode, one that Spink recognized just as clearly: he was planning the jump. He began to discuss the idea of flying into the bridge as a form of spectacular suicide.

"There's gotta be a place on that bridge where I wouldn't take it down," Weston said. "I've done everything I want to do in my life, but the one thing I've never done is die. You only get one chance to do it and I want to do it right. I want to watch death with my eyes open."

The hairs on the back of Spink's neck stood up.

"You know what," Spink said, "I'm coming this weekend. I'm going to Colorado because I don't trust you to go."

But Weston brushed him off, said he was being silly, and asked him not to come along. He asked Spink to trust that he was just joking, and posed a question: "Do you respect me as a friend?"

Still, Weston's state of mind nagged at Spink, particularly because Weston said he was the sole person he had confided in. "He knew I could empathize being trapped in a failed relationship—he'd watched me survive it," Spink wrote to me. "He was terrified of his girlfriend killing herself if he made their separation public, which she was threatening. That's why he first called me that week: was she serious? I called bullshit on her, said it was a last gasp attempt to manipulate him. But he was not convinced."

To this day, Spink remains certain that he was the one who first planted the dreadful idea about the bridge in Weston's head. He believes that maybe if he hadn't joked darkly about the possibilities, what followed might never have happened.

October 5, 2003, initially unfolded as event organizers had planned. The athletes executed their jumps safely, and when the six-hour window had nearly closed, it was time to end the show with a special exhibition jump by Dwain Weston, 2002 world BASE champion, along with up-and-comer Jeb Corliss.

An airplane carrying the jumpers was to fly near the bridge, and the pair would exit the plane wearing wingsuits. The outfits have vents and pockets that inflate with air to enable the wearers to glide along at high speed. The resulting silhouette looks like a flying squirrel. It is the closest equivalent to human flight that a person can experience.

In *Daredevils: The Human Bird*, a 2009 British television documentary, Corliss talked about the last moments he spent in the plane with Weston:

> He was genuinely scared which I thought was a little bit strange because to me, this jump really wasn't that complicated. And as we're flying over the bridge, Dwain grabs me by my hand and he looks me in the eyes and says, "You know Jeb, whatever happens, happens."
> Yeah, ok. It kind of struck me as a bizarre thing for him to say.

At 1:50 p.m. that Sunday afternoon, Weston jumped out of the plane with Corliss, and hurtled towards the bridge in his black wingsuit. "We jump out," Corliss recalled, "I start flying, and I don't really see Dwain during the flight that much, I just sort of see him out of my peripheral a little bit because he was above me."

Videos widely circulated on the internet reveal what happened next. Weston suddenly popped out of the clouds heading straight towards the bridge. He didn't waver. He didn't cover his face with his hands, a natural self-preservation reaction, and an instinct that's nearly impossible to override.

As Weston got closer and closer to the bridge, screams of panic and confusion began to emanate from two hundred horrified spectators. Within seconds, his body had slammed into the metal bridge railing at approximately 120 miles per hour, and the screams were accompanied by the sickening crash of flesh against metal.

Weston's neck broke on impact. His hip was sheared off by the metal bridge railing. The force of the impact caused his parachute to open, and it carried his torso towards the rocks, leaving some onlookers to initially believe Weston had survived and pulled his own chute cord. The torso drifted to land on a ledge three hundred feet below the canyon rim.

His death was violent, but almost instantaneous.

Corliss was still in flight, and didn't know what had happened until he touched down.

> As I'm coming up underneath the bridge, all of a sudden I see Dwain's parachute deploying in my face. So I actually swerve sideways, miss him by maybe five feet, and as I go by him, all of a sudden I start seeing all this other stuff floating in the sky, I don't know what it is, I don't know what's going on. I'm thinking are other people throwing stuff over the bridge? What's going on? I mean I didn't understand why there was all this other stuff in the air.
>
> I open, I turn, I land. And a woman who was actually sitting right near where I landed said, "Dwain hit the bridge, he's dead." My first thought was that's impossible, you can't hit that bridge, you just can't hit that bridge.

When Corliss landed, he was covered with Dwain Weston's blood. Cleanup of the Royal Gorge Bridge took two days. Not all parts of Weston were recovered.

It became one of the most high-profile deaths in skydiving and BASE jumping history, even though it wasn't even a BASE jump. It was also instantly mired in controversy when the medical examiner ruled the death accidental. Spink didn't believe it.

"He wanted to experience it on the full spectrum, all channels, all systems go," Spink said. "No crying, no wincing, he's guiding his final angle in. The mastery that he showed in doing that—the commitment."

When Spink went public with his thoughts on what really happened, he didn't get support. Quite the opposite. Other BASE jumpers attacked him on the internet forums. His belief about Weston's death didn't make anyone look good—the supporters of BASE, the organizers of the event, even Weston himself. So why go there?

And many disagreed with Spink's assessment. Weston's friend Gary Cunningham, the BASE jumper from Sydney who has done two thousand jumps, is not convinced Weston committed suicide.

Instead, he theorized that Weston might have been trying to fly between the vertical wires that flanked either side of the bridge as a show-stopping trick.

"If he was trying to commit suicide he didn't do the best job of it. He was so close to making it," Cunningham wrote. "I like to think any talk he had with Doug about what would happen if he failed was just Dwain's very dark humor mixed in with emotional stresses at the time. While it all could have made him more determined to try his stunt, I like to think when he was actually flying that he was trying hard to make it and he came very close to succeeding."

Cunningham did agree with Spink on one thing—the style in which Weston wanted to die. He even used the same word: spectacular. "He wanted to go out in a spectacular way," Cunningham said. He wasn't in touch with Weston nearly as frequently since his friend had left Australia for America, so he wasn't privy to his state of mind at the time.

> Whatever he talked about or discussed with Doug before the jump, there is no conclusive evidence on what his precise goal was during the jump. Raw emotions seconds before or even during any jump can change what someone plans to do. From his comments to Jeb before they left the plane, whatever his plan was he was fully committed to try, knowing that it was high risk and he could possibly die. But that was Dwain throughout his jumping career, setting out to achieve what others would not risk, and he did that over and over again for many years finely calculating out everything.

On November 10, 2013, I sent a message to Jeb Corliss: "I know there was some controversy surrounding Dwain Weston's death and I'd like to write about the events of that day as accurately and respectfully as possible. As the one who was jumping with Dwain, you are the living authority on what happened up there. Would you consider talking to me?"

It took just a few minutes for an email to bounce back from Matt Meyerson, Corliss's public relations handler. "This is not something Jeb wishes to discuss. Thank you for the inquiry."

Fourteen years later, Spink still felt unrelenting guilt that he didn't prevent Weston's death. "I made a mistake. I failed him."

"What could you have done if Dwain was that determined to die?" I asked.

Spink said he could have duct-taped Weston into submission, thrown him into his vehicle and held him captive until the event was over. He was also furious that I refused to write the phrase "Dwain committed suicide" as an uncontested conclusion. For a week he sent me angry texts and emails about it.

Finally I asked him—why was it important? If Dwain Weston had in fact taken his own life, what was so wrong with allowing people who loved him to cling to a whitewashed version that made everybody feel better?

"Stories like this are extraordinary," he said. "We're never going to learn the wisdom of what happened if we don't look at the truth of this. This was an exhibition. He did something extraordinary, something horrible. He splattered his guts all over the people watching. It took an artistry to do it the way he did."

Perhaps it was not the *how* but the *why* that mattered most.

"He wanted to show people what he saw when he closed his eyes at night."

To read comments made on a BASE jumping forum by Doug Spink about Dwain Weston's death, see Exhibit 5, page 379.

20

BLONDE AMBITION

By late 2003, Douglas Spink was in a state of financial and emotional bankruptcy. The pillars that had held up his previous life—the high-tech businesses, the stud farm, the marriage—had all crumbled and collapsed around him. Even his relationship with his family had suffered in recent years. He never got along that well with his sister or his father to begin with, but his previously close relationship with his mother had become strained and distant because Claire Spink and his wife, a woman twenty-two years his senior, didn't get along.

All this turmoil prompted his relocation to Canada, where he hoped to build a new life in a new country. The change of scenery also meant a fresh start as far as relationships were concerned.

Spink met Corinne Super at a stable in Pitt Meadows, British Columbia. The owner of the facility introduced them. Super was a trainer there, and both had rented stalls for their horses. Doug's expertise was show jumping, while Corinne had a background in dressage. Their relationship began as a friendship based on a mutual love of horses, and it might have stayed that way if it weren't for Dwain Weston's grisly departure shortly after they met.

Spink was suffocating in a dark cloud of grief. His best friend's demise—a tragedy he was convinced he could have prevented—had occurred on the heels of his marriage dissolving and his business closing. "I was crushed after that," Spink said. "She stepped in after Dwain. It left me open to exploitation. I was vulnerable and needy. My guards came down. It was an awful burden he left me with."

Super remembered it differently. She believed she was the victim, not Spink, and that he had zeroed in on her because she was "horse crazy" and had the means to help him out financially. "I was the perfect mark," she said. "He was very smart. I was a good victim and he's pretty smart at picking them out."

Loss paved the way for Spink and Super to form a bond. She listened and consoled, and took him to Tim Hortons restaurants for coffee to raise his spirits. "I was hanging around, I was asking the right questions, I was showing interest, I was helping him financially, so all of that made sense to be the one to lead along," Super said.

Paying thousands of dollars a month each to stable their horses in Pitt Meadows, they began to think it made financial sense to pool their funds towards a mortgage. While most couples dream of creating a family together, Spink and Super dreamed of starting a horse farm.

Corinne Super and her husband, Mark, had the financial means to purchase a property. The couple bought a former cranberry farm in Chilliwack, east of Pitt Meadows. The large piece of cleared land came with two barns, a guest cottage and a farmhouse. Spink moved in as a tenant, renting the stallion barn, where he lived with his horses and dogs. Another man, a racehorse trainer, rented the farmhouse.

Vancouver is just sixty miles west on the Trans-Canada Highway, but the bustle and rush of the city seems worlds away from the quiet country pace of Chilliwack. The picturesque Fraser Valley farm community is surrounded by tall mountains, hemmed in by the Fraser River to the north and the US border to the south.

Initially, the Supers and their eight-year-old daughter continued living in their log house in Mission, a twenty-five-mile drive west of Chilliwack. But Corinne didn't remain there for long. Her opportunity to move to the farm came in the form of the racehorse trainer tenant, who wasn't taking proper care of his animals. "I watched the horses out in the paddock without a blade of grass, starving to death," Spink recalled. Spink and Super decided it was time to ask him to leave.

Once the trainer left the farmhouse, Corinne and her daughter moved in. Mark stayed behind in Mission. "Mark made it clear he wasn't moving to the farm, that he wouldn't ever move to the farm," Corinne said. Her relocation to Chilliwack marked the beginning of the end of the Supers' marriage.

As for Spink, after his marriage fell apart, he'd vowed to never get involved with a woman again. But his relationship with Super began to tread past friendship one small step at a time. More and more, he was invited to join Corinne and her daughter in the main house, although he felt more comfortable staying in the stallion barn with his horses and dogs.

No question Super was a beautiful woman. But Spink didn't take much notice of her looks. He wasn't physically attracted to women. Instead, he was impressed with her gifts. He often felt socially awkward, and he watched with envy as she easily talked people into doing all sorts of things. Her confidence reminded him of his father's slick salesmanship. "She is a brilliant and gifted con woman," he told me, with an ability to "bend reality around herself."

But at times, he also resented her for this, and once expressed that sentiment to her by email. "For the record, and despite the hours of wasted time sharing the pieces of my soul with you, you apparently have no fucking clue what it is like to go through life outside of the charmed bubble where the world falls at your feet because you are a blonde chick and all doors swing open automatically."

"It is not my fault that I was born blonde," Corinne wrote back. "It is a gift. It lays in my hands how I wish to use the gift. I wish it to be a positive gift, not a weapon. I wish to share it with people like you. If I can open some doors that are a struggle for you I wish to do that. Help you on your path because I believe in you."

It would cost a bundle to create a horse farm in Chilliwack like the one Spink had founded and operated in Oregon. To that end, Super had a job opportunity for Spink. She introduced him to her longtime friend Ove Jensen, otherwise known as O.J.

Fruits, vegetables and dairy products weren't the only consumables being produced in the Fraser Valley. It was also a popular place to grow marijuana, and a number of otherwise law-abiding folks ran small grow-ops to help pay the bills. Soon Spink was working for O.J. as a courier in the drug trade.

O.J. and Super went way back, but that alone wouldn't have been enough to secure this new career opportunity for Spink. He was an excellent candidate for other reasons. Besides his interest in logistics, security, technology and the law, he had no criminal record, and could crisscross the border unencumbered by a rap sheet.

The lives of Super and Spink were now wound together through horses, business and their shared domicile. Spink later described their courtship to me unromantically, calling it "a slow boa constrictor thing." He remembered when their platonic friendship turned physical. They were on their way to a show jumping competition at the Spruce Meadows equestrian facility in Calgary, in a pickup truck towing Capone's horse trailer. On the ten-hour journey from Chilliwack, Super made her case for a more intimate relationship. She said it wasn't fair for Spink to penalize her because of his negative experiences with women in the past.

He motioned to Capone in the trailer behind them, and explained that he was already in a relationship. His stallion would always come first, he said.

She said she understood. That it was fine with her.

Spink took her word for it, a lapse in judgment that would eventually cost him the love of his life.

When they arrived at Spruce Meadows, Super watched Spink collect sperm from Capone for artificial insemination. That night, they had sex in their hotel room.

When it was over, he regretted the act immediately. He knew it had been a mistake. But he was on this road now, and it would be years before he found the off-ramp.

21

HOCKEY BAGS

For a time, it seemed like the drug world provided the opportunity Spink needed to pull himself out of his tailspin—financial and otherwise. He'd been hired to work for a business used by organized crime to ship illicit drugs, essentially a courier service for the underworld. Federal agents described these businesses as "independent aerial smuggling cells."

It was an era that provided financial incentive for drug smugglers, just like Prohibition had done for bootleggers. Laws against marijuana (both medical and recreational) had relaxed in Canada, and British Columbia was producing some of the best bud in the world, triple-A connoisseur cannabis that was coveted by pot smokers. Meanwhile, US authorities were determined to resist legalization of the popular plant, and continued to include the battle against weed in their war on drugs. The Canadian cannabis trade was generating billions of dollars annually, Quentin Hardy estimated in the 2003 *Forbes* magazine story "Inside Dope":

> This illicit industry has emerged as Canada's most valuable agricultural product—bigger than wheat, cattle or timber. Canadian dope, boosted by custom nutrients, high-intensity metal halide

light and 20 years of breeding, is five times as potent as what America smoked in the 1970s. With prices reaching $2,700 a pound wholesale, the trade takes in somewhere between $4 billion (in U.S. dollars) nationwide and $7 billion just in the province of British Columbia, depending on which side of the law you believe.

Years later, business opportunities for drug runners would taper off as America eased its cannabis laws. When Washington and Colorado legalized the plant, the US market was suddenly flooded with high-quality pot grown domestically, and demand for Canadian product dwindled. But back when Spink got into the industry, there was real money to be made in exporting. The sparsely patrolled five-thousand-mile border dividing Canada from the United States was the only significant obstacle, and the smugglers hurdled that with helicopters.

The choppers took off from private farms on the Canadian side. Across the border, the landing and staging sites were selected with brazen irony. Smugglers carved small landing spots into northern Washington's federally operated parklands, such as the massive North Cascades National Park run by the US National Park Service. Half a million acres of mountains, glaciers and ancient forest provided ideal terrain for evading detection. Pockets of land were cleared into natural depressions in the mountains to hamper police surveillance. The chosen spot was revealed only an hour before meet time to reduce the risk of police tip-offs, and pilots located the target using GPS coordinates. Helicopters would head across the border at dawn's first light when rangers and park visitors were less likely to be watching. Duct tape obscured the aircraft tail numbers. The choppers buzzed along just above the tree line before dropping into one of the previously cleared spots with impressive accuracy.

Spink's role was as a catcher. He met the helicopters at the drop site in a rented truck or SUV and unloaded the skids, pulling off hockey bags filled with hundreds of pounds of drugs. A single load could be worth $2 million. Then he transported the bags to distributors in Seattle, who shipped the cannabis to customers around the United States. The payments collected for loads were in the form of cash or cocaine, which he drove back to another waiting helicopter.

Spink described himself as being on the "low end of the food chain" in the drug world. Nonetheless, his income as a courier was substantial, from $60,000 to $80,000 a month in "fly money."

Although his new career was lucrative, it exacted a price. Riddled with risk and stress, this path towards riches had the potential to end in a jail cell. Still, during the six months he worked as a catcher, Spink was relieved to be earning money again. Taking care of his four-legged family members was what mattered to him most, and he was able to afford the best for them again. He had ample funds to pay veterinarians and farriers, and to buy warm winter coats, top-quality foods and vitamin supplements.

∩

While being a catcher carried risk in terms of law enforcement penalties, it was the helicopter pilots who faced the most physical danger. American journalist Robert Sabbag filed a bold piece about the smuggling business titled "High in the Canadian Rockies" for the July 2005 issue of *Playboy*. In his gripping tell-all, Sabbag's sources were candid about the chances they took flying through the mountains, where distinct weather patterns can throw curves to even the most skilled pilots.

One pilot referred to only as "J.R." told Sabbag, "It's not for the faint of heart. With the wind through the canyons blowing 80 miles an hour, it's like hitting a wall. Sometimes the turbulence is so bad it pops the doors on the machine." Another source, nicknamed "the Prez," said the pilots pushed the odds, even on a good day. "On a helicopter at any one time there are 20,000 pieces trying to blow themselves apart."

Some pilots operating out of British Columbia paid the ultimate price. In March 2005, Dustin Haugen of Chilliwack was believed to be at the controls of a Bell Jet Ranger when it crashed in Abbotsford. He survived, but his girlfriend, twenty-two-year-old Christina Alexander, was killed. And in September 2005, Richard Long and Ove Jensen—the same O.J. who had hired Spink—crashed another Bell Jet Ranger, this time in Hope, British Columbia. Both men died. They were believed to be returning home from a smuggling flight.

Yet Spink and his cohorts carried on undeterred. For some, the payoffs were enormous. The drug runners Sabbag interviewed boasted about making $20 million the previous year, and proudly proclaimed that they were "better than Fed Ex."

I emailed Sabbag, and asked him why his sources would risk police retaliation by telling their story so publicly.

"I have been writing about drug smuggling for years, and I am always surprised when sources such as these—the smugglers themselves—agree to talk to me," Sabbag said. "But inevitably they do. Unlike people legitimately employed, outlaws, by definition, cannot brag about their success—maybe they see this as the one opportunity to do so."

Sabbag's high-profile article only intensified the resolve of law enforcement agents. They were being publicly taunted in print. Leigh Winchell, special agent in charge of US Immigration and Customs Enforcement in Seattle, told the *Seattle Times*, "I'd be lying if I said we didn't take it as affront. It takes a certain amount of bravado to be in this industry."

Weren't the traffickers worried that federal agents might be on their trail? Didn't they fear getting caught? Sabbag thought not.

"Smugglers, in my experience—outlaws in general—see the possibility of arrest as part of the cost of doing business," he wrote. "At the same time, I think it is safe to assume that they operate in the belief that they are never going to be caught. It is a kind of wishful thinking that is necessary to their work. If they *really* thought they were going to spend time in prison, they probably would not break the law. Not until the handcuffs are biting their wrists do they really believe it will happen."

∩

Wishful thinking wouldn't be enough to keep handcuffs off the wrists of the drug runners. Park rangers had started to notice the loaded choppers dropping into the trees. By the time Sabbag's story ran in *Playboy*, the US government had already committed significant resources to a multi-agency law enforcement investigation aimed at shutting down the aerial smuggling cells for good.

The police project, code-named Operation Frozen Timber, was developed and led by Peter Ostrovsky, a supervisory special agent for Homeland Security Investigations who worked out of Bellingham, Washington. The project involved finding the numerous clearings carved into federal forest lands, and embedding hidden cameras. The montage of images released by US Immigration and Customs Enforcement showed the details frame by frame: helicopters dropping into the clearings, their skids laden with drug-stuffed hockey bags; catchers quickly removing the bags and tossing them into a waiting vehicle; and within minutes, their departure with millions of dollars in contraband product.

Ostrovsky described Operation Frozen Timber in his LinkedIn social media profile as follows: "The operation involved first of its kind technical surveillance, high-altitude surveillance aircraft, electro-optical surveillance systems and interdictions of helicopters which resulted in 46 arrests, high profile extraditions and federal prosecutions."

When the eighteen-month operation was over, six Canadians and forty Americans were arrested. Authorities seized eight thousand pounds of marijuana, eight hundred pounds of cocaine, three aircraft and $1.5 million in US currency. The job opportunity Corinne Super had set up for Doug Spink had come to a dramatic end.

22

PRIMATE DRAMA

An affair between a gay male zoo and a female non-zoo was a union doomed to fail, a disastrous combination. Super and Spink shared a love of horses and life on the farm in Chilliwack, but that wasn't enough to sustain the couple. One Sunday, after yet another bitter argument, Spink stormed off the farm. A series of emails between Spink and Super followed, written over a couple of days in February 2005, including these excerpts:

> **Spink**: I had hopes and dreams that I could truly trust you to understand my emotional plumbing. . . . But you've shown interest only in pulling pipes off the wall and trying to turn the system into something it isn't instead of appreciating it for what it is. Maybe because I love and mate with other species, I KNOW what [it] is to love someone for their difference and for who they truly are—beyond words and lies. I wish you had done the same with me, but I've seen you choose not to do that too many times to pretend that it can be any other way.
> **Super**: I have always tried hard to understand your emotional plumbing. If it seems like I have been trying to re-plumb you with my advances I did not mean it. I am a sexual creature that likes to be touched and touch. It is part of the attraction. I am sorry that it makes you so uncomfortable. I think it is healthy. It leaves you feeling weak and vulnerable, open to attack. This is my first try at

loving a different creature perhaps if I had had your experience I would not have failed. I have never lied to you nor said anything about who or what you are except that I am attracted to it and want to learn more.

Their differences had eroded an already tenuous bond. Spink began to feel deeply dissatisfied with the relationship.

Spink: At the most basic level, I'm not of the species you and the other Normals belong to. I am a mutant that is wired up strangely enough that I don't fit in your world. It makes me vulnerable and it makes life a maze of funhouse mirrors for me in two-legged encounters, but it also gives me an outsider's perspective on your species that allows me to see the cowardly attacks before they come. And, as with 99% of two-legger aggression, most of those attacks come under the flag of Love and Embrace right before the knife flashes.

Tension between the two intensified after one of Spink's drug runs to the United States turned tragic. Long hours on the road and the stress of smuggling were wearing him out, and he made a stop along the way. His Rottweiler, Fritzy, was along for the ride, and went out to play in the snow. Spink didn't notice him wander away and onto the highway. The dog was hit by a truck and killed.

Spink held Super partly responsible for the loss, because his fatigue was fueled by the need to work long hours to pay for her spending.

Spink: Do you have ANY IDEA what it is to lose a mate as I have, not a "mate" like you know who abused you and hurt you when it seemed fun to him, but a mate who loved me for who I am and who I could be, who would have given his life to shield me from pain and died with a smile on his face? To lose him because I was too tired and exhausted and strung out emotionally to watch an old man with failing eyesight who was playing in the snow and who got lost just long enough to wander onto the highway to be smashed by a truck? To call his name and search frantically for 2 hours, knowing already he was dead when a bolt of pain shot through my heart? To find him dead on the road, to hold him and scream and pound the asphalt and scream and scream so long the voice gives out and the hands are bloodied? To be covered in his blood and spittle and fur, to carry him to my truck and put him in the backseat, arranging him to be comfortable even though he is dead? To sleep with my head resting on him, willing with every molecule of my being that my life force would transfer to him and I would be dead in his place?

Spink felt that Super was taking advantage of him financially. "I am so fucking sick of being dragged through the same goddamned melodrama by every woman who spouts the word 'love' but acts out control obsessions, mistaken identity, psychological guerilla warfare, and sooner or later pathological insecurity regarding any and all things financial which—apparently—it is my job to support forever any female that bumps into me and is nearby when a bit of money heads my way."

He grew increasingly angry that Super was dipping into his "fly money," as he called the income he earned as a catcher, and accused her of commandeering thousands of dollars at a time from his wages. "By even the most conservative estimates, you have ended up with more than half of every dollar I've earned in the last three months. How that happened, exactly, I have no idea—but I do know that I've been less than aggressive about fighting for control of my own funds."

Besides the money that Super allegedly took from him, Spink felt their relationship carried an emotional cost too, particularly because of the drama of the Supers' divorce. "I've done nothing but be supportive way above and beyond a level that is healthy and sane for me. I don't know how I signed up to be virtual partner in your own divorce adventure."

In his emails to Super, Spink made it clear that the romantic side of their relationship was over. She had ignored who he really was in favor of trying to turn him into a character from a Disney romance, he contended. But he was still interested in maintaining their friendship and business partnership, and to continue raising horses together. "I have always enjoyed working on horse stuff with you, and it would be a shame to lose that in the primate drama. I do hope that doesn't happen, but at the same time I cannot allow myself to be pulled back into the waters too deep if I am unable to maintain a healthy self-separation in the process."

He conceded to Super that he had always found it challenging to cohabitate with people, and took some of the onus for their rift upon himself for allowing the situation to happen. "I have been remiss in allowing myself to slide back into a situation that I know is terrible for me. I do horribly living with other humans of any flavor, and it is my responsibility to ensure I don't put myself and others into a situation that I know will turn out badly for everyone."

Once talk turned from their personal relationship back to business affairs, the emails became less emotional. Spink declared he wanted to split off a land title for himself that would include the stallion barn, where he planned to build living quarters. He'd always felt more comfortable being in the barn with his horses and dogs than staying in the farmhouse with Super.

For her part, Super was concerned how the new arrangement would affect life on the farm. "I understand where I went wrong is that a start? Without forgiveness, understanding, and discussion, I do not see a future, do you? Spewing hate and anger at me from your side of the farm does not a happy environment make."

As it happened, she wouldn't have to worry about how he would treat her from his side of the farm. Two weeks after their blowout, Doug Spink was arrested in Monroe, Washington, transporting hockey bags filled with cocaine.

23

FROZEN TIMBER

The traffic stop that put Spink into custody for the first time in his life was anything but routine. It was past 7:00 p.m. on February 28, 2005, when police pulled him over. He was driving on Highway 2 through the small city of Monroe, thirty miles northeast of Seattle, on his way to deliver a massive load of cocaine to a helicopter waiting in the expansive wilderness of North Cascades National Park. Police stopped him for driving five miles per hour over the speed limit.

When I asked Spink if he'd been speeding that night, he rolled his eyes in a gesture that indicated "as if." Admittedly, it didn't seem plausible that an intelligent, logistics-obsessed man carrying hundreds of pounds of drugs had sped through a quiet community on his way to deliver the contraband to a waiting chopper. The more logical explanation was that he'd been stopped because of intelligence provided by a CI, or confidential informant, who might have led federal agents to Spink. Spink believed the informant was Wesley Cornett, the man who had just handed him the cocaine.

After being pulled over, Spink was detained at Traveler's Park, a one-acre state park leased to the city of Monroe as a rest stop. For an hour and eight minutes, he sat handcuffed in a puddle on the pavement. His SUV was locked, and he did not consent to a search.

Spink knew that under the Fourth Amendment of the US Constitution, the police needed grounds to search his vehicle. Otherwise, they had no reason to search or to detain him longer than reasonably expected for a routine traffic stop—unless they outed the identity of their CI. That was something police were often reluctant to do, particularly if they hoped to continue using the informant to ensnare other targets.

What's more, probable cause had to exist *before* the search was conducted and any arrest made. It couldn't be retroactively justified by whatever was discovered in the vehicle.

The Fourth Amendment mattered. If it was trampled to obtain evidence, that evidence wouldn't be admissible in a criminal trial, a rule that was meant to encourage the authorities to respect the amendment.

When Spink was stopped, FBI agents quickly appeared on the scene and begun questioning him. But a crucial member of their team was missing: Susie the drug-sniffing dog. If Susie smelled drugs in Spink's vehicle, police would have the grounds they needed for a search and seizure.

Spink, whom no one had ever accused of not doing his research, happened to know that a few weeks earlier, on January 24, a case on this very issue had been decided in US Supreme Court. In *Illinois v. Roy Caballes,* justices had determined that the Fourth Amendment is not violated if a drug-sniffing dog is used during a routine traffic stop, as long as use of the dog doesn't unreasonably prolong the length of the stop.

The yellow Lab's absence posed a timeline problem. The average traffic stop lasted ten to twenty minutes. Agents rushed to retrieve Susie from another location. The clock was ticking.

Spink thought about security and logistics like some people think about what's for dinner. At the last minute, he had strategically changed the meet location, requesting that Wesley Cornett come to the Vertical World climbing gym in Everett instead. Had that precaution placed Susie farther away than police planned?

Spink also knew that voluntary compliance with police falls outside the protection of the Fourth Amendment. If a citizen cooperates voluntarily, no matter how prolonged the stop, then evidence collection is lawful, and the evidence gathered is admissible. Spink had to prove beyond any doubt that he was being detained, that his freedom of movement was being restrained involuntarily, to ensure that voluntary compliance wouldn't be considered. That inspired a repetitive patter that lasted for the duration of the stop while Spink sat handcuffed in a puddle on the ground, where the police had placed him.

"Am I under arrest?" Spink would ask.

"No," an officer answered.

"Then am I free to go?"

"No."

"Am I under arrest?" he would ask again.

"No," the officer said.

"Then am I free to go?"

This went on for an hour and eight minutes, as Spink laid the groundwork for what would eventually become a bargaining chip with federal authorities to get his potentially lengthy sentence reduced. He told me he refused to answer questions from police, and wouldn't reveal the meet location of the helicopter scheduled to fly his load back to British Columbia. Instead, he asked for a lawyer. When Susie finally arrived, she indicated drugs were in his vehicle, and he was booked into Federal Detention Center Seatac.

He was angry but not surprised when newspaper stories and government attorneys branded him a snitch anyway, an allegation he strongly denied.

"No one in our organization was caught or arrested or even questioned after I went down," he said. "It is because I said 'I want my lawyer,' and went to prison. Later in 2005 and into 2006, they did catch people in Operation Frozen Timber...but nobody caught was working for O.J., and of course O.J. himself died in September."

As proof that Wesley Cornett was the snitch, not him, Spink pointed to Cornett's Federal Bureau of Prisons registration number (35044-086). Assigned in the Western District of Washington, just like Spink's number (35132-086), Cornett's was issued eighty-eight inmates before Spink's. That had to mean Cornett was picked up first.

Spink speculated that Cornett was already working as a CI for the feds by the time he picked up the drugs from him that night.

Spink eventually pled guilty to one count of possession of a controlled substance with intent to distribute. He was sentenced to thirty-six months plus five years of supervised release, a relatively short sentence for such a large load of cocaine. He struck his plea agreement with federal prosecutor Ron Friedman.

I called up Friedman, who has since gone into private practice, to ask about Spink's case. He allowed me only eight minutes on the phone, but it was enough time to ask if it was true there was a problem with the legality of the seizure, and whether that had led to Spink's relatively short sentence. Had Friedman been concerned the seizure would be ruled unconstitutional? He denied that this was true, saying a judge wouldn't kick out a seizure of that size on a Fourth Amendment violation.

The size of the seizure itself was another question. The original weight cited by the feds was 349 pounds, Spink said. "It mysteriously jumped up to 374 pounds shortly thereafter, no explanation. There was a sentencing range jump at exactly 350 pounds...so that jump was highly suspicious. As we were fighting suppression anyway, we did not dig in and battle the mysterious change in weight."

Regardless of the exact weight, Spink had managed to distinguish himself from others once again. The seizure from his SUV that night was one of the largest for cocaine in the state of Washington. Years later, a 2011 federal government brief put it this way: "Spink's underlying drug conviction was itself extraordinary. As Spink gloated, it was one of the largest in Washington State's history—so large that the Attorney General of the United States knew Spink's name."

Operation Frozen Timber snared bigger targets than Spink and Cornett. One of them was Cornett's associate Robert Kesling, sentenced to seventeen years later that same year, in December. Spink again pointed the finger at Cornett. "Kesling went down because, even after my arrest, he kept Cornett working for him. I raised the flag that Cornett was obviously dirty, after I was arrested and went to prison—where I stayed for several years."

Despite the government's portrayal of Spink as a snitch, I wasn't able to uncover any evidence that he had betrayed his smuggling associates.

He insisted to me on multiple occasions that he never supplied information to the authorities about anyone in his smuggling ring.

"Once I was in prison and O.J. knew I was 'hit' and all the procedures were put in place to cycle phones, meet locations, computers, drop points, landing zones, and the rest, I couldn't do anything to O.J. even if I wanted to. I should know: I helped set up those procedures in the first place."

There was one person Spink said he provided information to the feds about: Seattle attorney Jeffrey Steinborn, the first lawyer hired by Spink after his arrest. Spink said that after he was taken into custody, Corinne Super drove to Seattle to give Steinborn $25,000 cash as a retainer. The choice made sense: Steinborn's clientele was mainly derived from drug-related offenses. As his website stated, "Most of my career has involved legal issues arising from the war on drugs—which for the last 40 years has been largely a war on marijuana."

Spink asked Steinborn to draft a motion to suppress the evidence—the load of cocaine obtained during the stop—on the grounds that he'd been detained without probable cause. Spink believed he could get the evidence booted because Susie the drug dog was way across town when he was pulled over. In his estimation, he'd been detained longer than was constitutionally allowed for search and seizure.

Steinborn is an outgoing, outspoken character. During an interview I did with him in 2010, he said that from the beginning, he was cautious in his interactions with Spink. "I tried to keep a distance from him. All of us defense attorneys know that for a desperate client, we are nothing but a chip to play. You've got to be really careful, and I always am."

Steinborn didn't trust Spink, and Spink didn't trust Steinborn. Spink didn't believe his lawyer was working on his behalf to suppress the evidence as requested, and he wondered if Steinborn was protecting the interests of another client, a larger entity. "He was trying to sell me down the river," Spink said.

So he fired his lawyer and hired another. But not before leaving Steinborn with a parting gift.

"I'll never know what really happened," Steinborn said. "All I know is that after I met with Super, within a few weeks I was forced to be taken off the case, and [Spink] made some statement that I was interfering with his snitching. And the next thing I know I got a phone call from [attorney] Susie Roe and a guy named Ron Friedman saying they were going to indict me, based on either what Corinne had said or what Spink had said, I never really knew."

This time, the seasoned attorney was the one in trouble instead of his clients, and he didn't like the role reversal. "It was pretty scary and it really pissed me off, and I always wondered, what the fuck happened?"

The lawyer found himself having to hire his own lawyer. "I turned over all my financial records and when they were done looking at them, they realized I hadn't committed any crimes. But they dangled me for about six months under threat of indictment."

The stress took a physical toll on him. "I needed to lose that twenty pounds but it was a hard way to lose it! It scared the shit out of me. I stopped eating, you know."

∩

Susie the yellow Lab wasn't the only canine who attended Spink's roadside drug arrest in Washington. Spink had two of his own dogs with him that night: his German Shepherd, Bruno, and his Golden Retriever, Rion.

Five years later, a Monroe police commander recalled the night of the drug arrest for Associated Press reporter Gene Johnson, whose story "Wash. drug smuggler suspected of bestiality" was published a week after the 2010 raid on Spink's home.

"It struck us all as very odd," said Cmdr. Steve Clopp, referring to how protective Spink was of his German Shepherd. "We really hadn't ever dealt with it before. I mean, you're driving around with 169 kilos of cocaine, you might be concerned with yourself or the predicament you're in. But he was just really concerned with the dog."

MR. HANDS

The nature of Spink's relationship with the German Shepherd who was with him on the night of his arrest wouldn't have broken any Washington laws back then. It took a high-profile case four months later to change that.

No matter the timing, it would be incomplete to discuss cross-species sex in Washington State without at least a passing reference to Kenneth Pinyan, a Boeing engineer better known to the zoo community as "Mr. Hands." Pinyan made worldwide news when he died near Enumclaw, just sixty miles from where Spink had been arrested driving an SUV full of cocaine.

Pinyan's notorious passing was officially marked in the "In Memoriam" section of the September 2005 issue of *Boeing Frontiers*, the employee newsletter for the aerospace company formerly based in Seattle:

> The Boeing Company offers condolences to the families and friends of the following employees, whose deaths recently have been reported to the company:
> Kenneth Pinyan, engineer; service date Aug. 19, 1997; died July 2, 2005.

The short, dignified mention was in sharp contrast to the firestorm of sensational media attention and public curiosity that swirled around the shocking manner of Pinyan's death. That summer evening, he had engaged in receptive anal sex with an Arabian stallion during a visit to a forty-acre farm northwest of Enumclaw. According to a King County medical examiner's report, the forty-five-year-old died of "acute peritonitis," the result of "perforation of the sigmoid colon during anal intercourse with a horse." The death was ruled accidental.

Pinyan knew immediately that he'd been seriously injured during the act; his colon had ruptured when the stallion reached orgasm. But he delayed seeking medical attention for reasons that aren't entirely clear. It's been suggested that he refused help because he didn't want to risk losing his high security clearance at Boeing. Or perhaps he feared public humiliation.

Zoos who knew him allude to other motivations. Pinyan's attitude that night was said to be self-destructive, as though he knew he was pushing the bounds of reason.

James Michael Tait, a friend of Pinyan's, was present during the fatal encounter with the horse. He sat with Pinyan for several hours as his body went septic, poisoning itself from the inside out. He begged Pinyan to go to the hospital with him, but his friend refused. It was only when he finally lost consciousness that Tait was able to load Pinyan into his vehicle. He drove him to Enumclaw Community Hospital, dropped him off at the emergency room, and fled. Police would later track Tait down using hospital surveillance video.

The act with the horse was also captured on video. Eventually it would be seen by untold numbers of people around the world via the internet.

After sorting through stacks of videotapes that Tait turned over in an effort to prove he wasn't doing anything wrong, police could find nothing to charge him with, because none of the animals featured on the tapes had been physically injured. Instead, he was charged with criminal trespassing in the first degree.

But that charge might not have accurately reflected what happened that night. Media reports claimed that Tait and Pinyan trespassed on a neighbor's farm for the purpose of having sex with the landowner's horses. After Tait was arrested in Tennessee in 2009 and accused of having sex with animals again, he called Doug Spink from jail multiple times, and discussed the earlier arrest in Washington. According to Spink, Tait told him he had rented the barn near Enumclaw from those same neighbors. And Tait insisted they were his horses, that they hadn't been "fence hopping"—going onto other people's property to have sex with animals that didn't belong to them. (Some zoos think fence hopping is unethical and risky and disavow the practice, believing a person should only have sex with their own animals.) Years later, Tait was still upset that he'd been charged with trespassing in Washington back in 2005.

Despite that, in an effort to end the ordeal, Tait reluctantly entered an Alford plea in King County district court on November 29, 2005, for the trespassing charge. That meant he could plead guilty while continuing to assert his innocence; an Alford plea doesn't admit guilt of the criminal act. He received a suspended one-year sentence and a $300 fine.

∩

Pinyan's high-profile demise was portrayed in a 2007 docudrama that drew widespread public interest and controversy. *Zoo* was directed by Robinson Devor and written by Charles Mudede, a columnist for the Seattle weekly alternative newspaper *The Stranger*. *Zoo* debuted at the Sundance Film Festival, competing against 856 films to emerge as one of sixteen winners. That same year, it was selected as one of the top five American films at the Cannes Film Festival.

Zoos had mixed reactions to the film (and expressed similar trepidation over the prospect of this book). One zoo summed up his conflicting thoughts in a note to me:

> It is a dangerous thing, for me, the book. The movie "Zoo," while walking a very careful line between the two sides of the story, raised awareness, which always makes me and others like me nervous. We are in the shadows, the horse and dog breeders, the doctors and lawyers, the laborers hiding in plain sight. Many of us don't really want extra attention. I don't want to walk in a parade. I just want to live. I don't want my family to be killed or taken away from me in spite. Attention leads to stings and witch hunts and such, vaguely legal persecution as prosecution, and only my increasing lack of concern for my aging self and my concern for the next generation motivates me into standing up and saying

anything …dangerous… while there is still breath in my lungs. I still say so with great apprehension, as we have learned from the story of the likes of Douglas Spink, those who have these "dangerous ideas" of inclusion are not allowed to go unpunished. Note that legally speaking he didn't even do anything except accept others— and look what price he and his family pays.

It wasn't just motion pictures that took notice of the Pinyan incident. In his year-end 2005 wrap-up, *Seattle Times* columnist Danny Westneat reported that a story about the Enumclaw horse sex incident was by far the most popular article on the newspaper's website. And four more stories about the same topic had landed in the top twenty.

"We don't publish our Web-traffic numbers, but take it from me— the total readership on these stories was huge," Westneat wrote. "So much so, a case can be made the articles on horse sex are the most widely read material this paper has published in its 109-year history. I don't know whether to ignore this alarming factoid or embrace it."

In time, there would be more to the sensational story of Pinyan's death than the *Seattle Times* or any other media outlet could have known back then. Five years after Pinyan's passing, the friend who tried to save him would inadvertently lead the federal government right to Doug Spink's cabin at the top of Reese Hill Road.

25

LEGAL MATTERS

Before Kenneth Pinyan's high-profile death by horse penis, Washington State didn't have a law against humans having sex with animals, unless the animals were physically injured during the sex acts. In those cases, criminal punishment fell under existing animal cruelty laws.

After Pinyan died in 2005, animal rights activists approached Senator Pam Roach to sponsor a bill expressly prohibiting bestiality. She was not selected randomly for the task. A senator since 1990, Roach is a devout Christian, a member of the Church of Jesus Christ of Latter-day Saints, and a graduate of Utah's Brigham Young University, the largest religious university in the United States (excluding online students).

The mission to make the new law was covered for *The Stranger* by Charles Mudede, the same writer who wrote the movie *Zoo*. His article, "The Animal in You," ran in the February 23, 2006, issue. "It was an almost comically easy law to pass: When Senator Pam Roach (R-Auburn) introduced Senate Bill 6417 to make bestiality a Class C felony, it instantly gained bipartisan support in Olympia. The bill passed on February 11, 2006, without one state senator voting against it (36-0)."

One of Spink's lawyers, Jim Turner, researched how the Washington law was made after he took him on as a client in 2012. "I have a friend in legislature, and he voted for it, and when I pointed out the flaws in it, he was sheepish and said if he had known that, he wouldn't have voted for it."

Turner thought the animal welfare community took an over-zealous approach to his client and other zoophiles. He contended that existing animal cruelty laws should have been enough to address animal abuse.

"This has nothing to do with the abuse on the animal, it's about the act and it's assumed that it would have an impact on the animal. It's about a dog's ability to consent. That is specious, to suggest that they are just dumb animals. Yet we consider them property. We kill them and eat them and do all kinds of other things to them. Yet having sex is cruel?"

∩

Laws pertaining to bestiality and zoophilia vary by country, and within the United States, they also vary by state. As of this book's publication, five US states (Hawaii, Kentucky, New Mexico, West Virginia and Wyoming) and the District of Columbia had no laws on the books specifically prohibiting sex acts with animals.

North of the border, the Supreme Court of Canada made a controversial decision in June 2016. By a vote of six to one, the justices ruled that bestiality is a crime only if penetration is achieved.

The case in question involved a Prince George, British Columbia, man who used peanut butter to entice the family dog to perform oral sex on his sixteen-year-old stepdaughter. After the man's conviction was overturned by the BC Supreme Court of Appeal, lawyers for the province took the case to the Supreme Court, which upheld his acquittal on the bestiality charge because there was no penetration.

"Penetration has always been understood to be an essential element of bestiality," wrote Justice Thomas Cromwell for the majority. "Parliament adopted that term without adding a definition of it, and the legislative history and evolution of the relevant provisions show no intent to depart from the well-understood legal meaning of the term."

Canada's laws concerning crimes against animals haven't significantly changed since 1892. If the laws were to be modified, Cromwell said, they would have to be addressed by the government, not the Supreme

Court. "The term bestiality has a well-established legal meaning and refers to sexual intercourse between a human and an animal. . . . It is manifestly not the role of the courts to expand that definition. Any expansion of criminal liability for this offence is within Parliament's exclusive domain."

One member of parliament took the June 2016 ruling as his cue to do something. The following fall, Nathaniel Erskine-Smith, Liberal MP for Beaches–East York, introduced a private member's bill known as the Modernizing Animal Protections Act. But the bill was viewed as a potential threat to hunting, farming and fishing. The politicians realized that protecting animals against sexual acts meant protecting them against all abuses, or the laws would be inconsistent. Prime Minister Justin Trudeau and his cabinet voted against it, and the bill was defeated.

☊

In 2009, Rutgers law student Michael Roberts decided to address the inconsistencies and discrepancies in the laws designed to stamp out bestiality and zoophilia. He chose to take on the topic because he couldn't find much written about it, and he thought it would earn him a good grade. Indeed it did. He got an A+ on his forty-page term paper, titled "The Unjustified Prohibition Against Bestiality: Why the laws in opposition can find no support in the harm principle."

"My professor was the one who encouraged me to publish," said Roberts, now a criminal defense attorney in private practice in New Jersey. "First with the social science research network where it was leading in downloads in its class for a while. I submitted the paper to colleagues for peer review, rewrote it a number of times and then tried to get it published with law journals." But despite the paper's top mark, the major law journals refused to publish it. "Most journals said great paper but too controversial of a topic."

Roberts' essay, which ran in 2010 in the *Journal of Animal and Environmental Law*, maintained that anti-bestiality laws as written are inconsistent with other ways in which animals are legally mistreated.

> The laws prohibiting bestiality as they stand today are not justified. Their very existence undermines the legitimacy of our legal system. To be justifiable, I suggest rewriting the statutes in clear, precise

language geared toward preserving animal rights. But before we can justify legislating animal rights we must agree as a society that animals do have rights and interests, and then stop subjugating those rights in unjustifiable ways.

Roberts noted that laws against bestiality have evolved over time.

The early twentieth century saw a period of increased tolerance, effectively decriminalizing the act by the end of World War II. In fact, it was more likely that an offending person would be arrested for breach of the peace or offending public order than any formal bestiality charge. This trend reached its apex by 1990 when no state had a law specifically opposing bestiality. The tide reversed by 2001, when twenty-four states made bestiality a felony. The reason for this shift was an increase in religious fundamentalism, a rise in animal rights activism, and greater social control being exercised by state governments. Following the landmark Supreme Court decision in Lawrence v. Texas, states had a difficult time regulating sexual acts, so they sought to prohibit bestiality by adhering to the animal rights doctrine.

Not surprisingly, as he noted in an email to me, Roberts has received telephone calls over the years from zoos being prosecuted on bestiality charges.

Why they think I am a champion to their cause I couldn't say. But I've found that many people have interpreted my paper different. Animal rights activists think my paper supports their position. Libertarians think my paper supports theirs. And I guess Zoophiles or whatever they are called now, think I am defending them. Really none of the above are true. The purpose of the paper is simply to point out that the laws as they exist in the super majority of our states are not justifiable under any recognized system of criminal justice. I do suggest ways states could rewrite their laws to prohibit certain sexual acts with animals without being overly broad, vague or ambiguous, but I don't think I take much of a position as to whether they ought to.

Interestingly, anti-zoo laws that are on the books do not prohibit touching animals' genitals for commercial breeding purposes. For example, people are legally permitted to masturbate male animals if they are selling the sperm for artificial insemination, or to impregnate female animals manually (and sometimes traumatically) if it's done for financial motives. Such practices are called "animal husbandry" and are perfectly legal. And it isn't unusual for the people who proficiently perform these acts to be zoophiles. These "freaks in the barn," as one zoo phrased it during an interview, are called upon when their expertise is required to collect semen from a valuable stallion or dog.

So if sexual practices with animals are done for money in pursuit of animal breeding, they are legal, no matter how traumatic the procedures are. If they turn you on, they are illegal. As I pondered this, I wondered: does that mean that in the eyes of the law, zoophilia is considered a thought crime?

In Washington, Pasado's Safe Haven, an animal welfare organization that happens to be based in Monroe (coincidentally the same small city where Spink was arrested with the load of cocaine) lobbied for the enactment of the anti-bestiality law in that state after Pinyan's death. Pasado's volunteer Rita Morgan, who worked on the project, said "animals don't have the evolved consciousness to say yes. They will never be able to say unequivocally that they consent to us. This is something that is part of the dark nature of humans."

Mark Steinway, one of the founders of Pasado's Safe Haven, also worked on the law, which included researching what other states were doing, and presenting the case to legislators that zoophilia should be criminalized.

"Everybody's immediate reaction to it is that it's so sick, but to me, it's a mental illness," said Steinway, who now works in management at the St. Tammany Humane Society in Louisiana. "It's about targeting those that are weaker than you, being in control over them. It's victimizing. Whether or not animals are okay with it, it's just wrong. It's putting them in a position where they don't have a choice."

The opinions Morgan and Steinway hold when it comes to zoophilia are shared by many other animal rescuers I spoke to, although most weren't willing to put their thoughts on the record. I found this reluctance unusual; animal welfare advocates are notoriously and publicly vocal about their beliefs. But they were uneasy about their names being in a book about zoophilia. Some also feared reprisals from the zoos whose behavior they condemned.

There was another person I thought would have the courage to speak on the record, someone I'd written about before: Corinne Dowling, founder of Give a Dog a Bone. This San Francisco–based nonprofit, which Dowling started in 2000, enriches the lives of dogs in shelters by setting up programs that provide physical activity and stimulate natural behaviors. As the organization's website states, "Any novel stimulus which evokes an animal's interest can be considered enriching, including natural and artificial objects, scents, novel foods and different methods of preparing foods, and new activities of all kinds."

I visited Dowling at San Francisco Animal Care and Control, where she interacted with dogs who spent months in caged custody awaiting the disposition of court cases. Using tennis balls attached to plastic sticks, she played with the dogs who weren't allowed out from the other side of the bars. To engage their prey drive, she gave them rubber Kong toys she stuffed with treats, cream cheese and peanut butter. For the dogs who were approved for yard time, she assembled makeshift agility courses using modest salvaged materials such as hula hoops, lawn chairs, broomsticks and mop handles. I was impressed to see how much good she accomplished with so little.

Keeping the dogs engaged, she explained, improved both their mental and physical well-being, and reduced behaviors such as repetitive circling, pacing, tail chasing and licking. And it didn't just improve their days at the shelter—it also dramatically increased their chances of getting adopted before their frustrations devolved into undesirable behaviors that reduced, or even destroyed, their chances of ever finding a permanent home.

I asked Dowling if an animal is capable of consenting to sexual activity with a human being.

"An animal cannot," she said. "They don't have the ability to consent. Consent implies an ability to understand what's being asked. So when you're saying, do you consent, you are asking for the person to acquiesce, to say yes to what you are saying, and if that being does not have an ability to say no, then there's not a question. You can't ask an animal a question like that, because an animal isn't capable of answering that question."

What about zoos who say that animals signal consent with their body language and responses?

"Again, that's a justification for their actions, because the dog is not consenting by his actions. The dog is responding to the stimuli. It's a biological response, rather than an overt yes. That dog at that point would respond to any stimuli. The animal is simply responding to stimuli, which is a basic animal instinct."

Is it animal abuse?

"There's no question that it's animal abuse," she replied.

Dowling said she was heartened by the fact that someone was investigating zoophilia and bringing it into the light. "I'm hoping that our society is ready to tackle this issue, because if we can't address this issue—if we can't even look at it—we can't begin to understand it if we hope to change it."

26

GIFT HORSE

Possession of cocaine with intent to distribute is a Class A felony, and for that crime, Spink was sentenced to thirty-six months in federal prison, plus another five years of supervised release. After sentencing, he was sent from FDC SeaTac to FCI Sheridan, a medium-security facility in Oregon operated by the Bureau of Prisons.

He was determined to make the best of his predicament. He wanted his prison time to count for something; he didn't want that segment of his life to be about wasted time. An academic at heart and a voracious reader, he devoured 206 books in 636 days.

He took on a prison job too, working as a horticulture instructor in Sheridan's education department in the field of greenhouse management. It wasn't surprising that he gravitated towards horticulture—he was passionate about nature and enjoyed growing flowers, fruits and vegetables. When we spoke about his time inside, he fondly recalled good times with other inmates, such as when they managed to grow a pineapple from a discarded leaf top salvaged off a fruit plate left by prison staff.

He also spent time rebuilding his fractured relationships with his parents. Claire and Jack Spink, who were divorced, came to visit him separately while he was incarcerated. During that time, his closeness with Claire was restored. They had lost touch during his marriage because his mother and his wife hadn't gotten along. As the years wore on and Spink's troubles mounted, his mother would become his biggest supporter and savior.

The prison visit was the last time Doug would see his father, who died on December 11, 2006, at the age of seventy-three, just a few months before his son's release.

☊

Spink couldn't care for his animals while he was incarcerated, so in March 2005, shortly after his arrest, he struck a deal with Corinne Super when she came to visit him in prison. She would look after his dogs and horses, and in exchange, he would lease his stallions—Capone I, Aquilan Calypso (aka Ace) and Neuville—to her, and she would be entitled to keep their prize money and stud fees until September 10, 2007.

It was Capone I, the most famous and remarkable horse Spink owned, who would bring in most of the revenue. Capone began his Grand Prix career when he was six years old. By age eight, he was jumping internationally. He earned more than ten Grand Prix wins in his illustrious career. In 2006 and 2007, he was ranked one of the top two hundred show jumpers in the world by the Fédération Équestre Internationale. His relatives jumped too. He was descended from a star-studded bloodline that included legendary show jumpers Contender, Ramiro Z and Ladykiller.

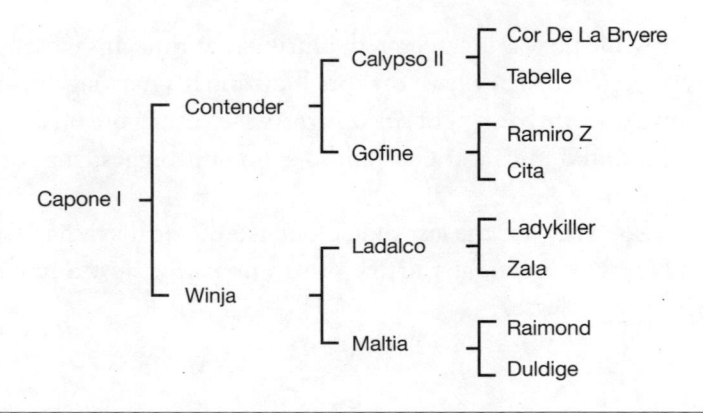

```
                                    ┌─ Cor De La Bryere
                      ┌─ Calypso II ─┤
                      │              └─ Tabelle
           ┌─ Contender ─┤
           │          │              ┌─ Ramiro Z
           │          └─ Gofine ─────┤
           │                         └─ Cita
Capone I ──┤
           │                         ┌─ Ladykiller
           │          ┌─ Ladalco ────┤
           │          │              └─ Zala
           └─ Winja ──┤
                      │              ┌─ Raimond
                      └─ Maltia ─────┤
                                     └─ Duldige
```

Star-studded bloodlines: Capone's family tree.

A horse's economic value is difficult to determine. Capone's worth has been estimated as between one million and several million dollars because of his successful career, as well as his ability to consistently produce offspring who are natural jumpers. Capone's semen earned $2,500 per emission, and was shipped frozen worldwide to create Capone babies.

But Capone's value to Spink wasn't based on economics. Although Spink had formed meaningful bonds with people in his life (his mother, his ex-wife, some friends), he didn't feel as connected and comfortable with humans as he did with dogs and horses. Especially Capone.

I tried numerous times to talk to Spink about what Capone meant to him without much success. He made it clear to me that the relationship wasn't platonic, but he didn't want the graphic details published here, figuring that would only get him into more legal trouble. Every time we spoke about the black stallion, Spink quickly became agitated and brought the interview to a standstill, wracked with guilt, pain, anger and grief. Even a passing mention of the horse took his mind to a dark place.

He explained these reactions in an email to me: "Writing about Capone, and my work with him, has brought forth the festering wounds of his own imprisonment and status as a captive hostage. As a result, I have no more to write. Hopefully this has served some use, in some way. The damage it brings to recall his absence consistently escalates, over time."

Spink and Super had struck a deal as far as the horses were concerned, but Super wanted more. Less than three weeks after Spink's arrest, she submitted a dubious letter to Equine Canada in which she claimed a change of Capone's ownership.

It seems implausible that such an unofficial letter—without even a signature from Spink or his former business partner, Paul Peterson—could convince Equine Canada to change its records regarding ownership of such a valuable horse. But it did. All Super had to do was mention bestiality when she spoke about Spink, and she got the desired results.

March 17, 2005

To whom it may concern;

Due to the current incarceration of the previous manager of the Holsteiner stallion Capone 1, Wolf Advisors has made the collective decision to transfer ownership of said stallion over to Corinne Super of Exitpoint Farm located in Chilliwack B.C. Canada. Wolf Advisors is no longer associated with said stallion. Wolf Advisors is of now dissolved. Further inquiries involving this matter may be directed to Paul Peterson representative for the previous Wolf Advisors or Corinne Super. Paul can be reached at 503.███████ Corinne at 604.███████.

Sincerely;
Corinne Super
Exitpoint Farm Inc.

Paul Peterson;
Representing Wolf Advisors

Corinne Super's letter stating that Capone's ownership had been transferred to her.

By May 25, 2005, Super had a new Fédération Équestre Internationale passport issued for Capone which named her as his sole owner. Horse passports are required to ease movement across international borders, and to ensure health regulations are being followed. They are also required to compete.

Meanwhile, Corinne Super's split from her husband, Mark, was in full progress. Like most divorces, the battle to divide the family didn't happen amicably. The couple fought over who got what and argued over their only child, who had been born in British Columbia on March 27, 1996, about a month before Capone was born in Germany on April 30.

The Supers even argued about Capone. If he and the other stallions belonged to Corinne, Mark maintained, then they should be considered marital assets and he should be entitled to half their value. But Corinne categorically denied in her divorce affidavits that Capone and the other stallions belonged to her. She insisted that they were to be returned to Spink upon his release from prison. "The marketable horses on my property are not undervalued," she stated in her affidavit. "I do not own the stallions. They are to be returned to Mr. Spink."

Things also got ugly between Corinne and her lawyer, Kathleen Walker. After a court hearing, Super confessed to Walker that she hadn't been honest with her. She hadn't disclosed the true nature of her relationship with Spink. Nor had she told Walker the complete truth about the Supers' marital assets. Walker was not pleased. Realizing that her client wasn't what she'd bargained for, she followed up the next day with a tersely worded letter:

> I told you from the outset that you had to be scrupulously honest with me. You have not been in a very material way which affects every claim that you have made and you have not only jeopardized the outcome of your case, you have placed at great risk any ability that I may have to obtain my fees from the sale of property, which may well be subject to charges and seizure by the Canadian government.

Walker was worried that receiving payment for her fees was at risk because of what was happening on the Supers' properties. "When we first met you told me that the Barr Street property was bare and without structures because Mr. Super tore the old building on it down in preparation for building," Walker wrote. "For the first time you told me yesterday, on March 22, 2007 that the building on the Barr Street property burned down as a result of a grow operation owned and operated by Mr. Super."

Under federal proceeds of crime legislation, assets obtained through criminal activity can be legally seized. That includes money, cars, boats, planes and houses. Walker demanded $11,000 (Canadian) for legal fees already incurred and a $50,000 retainer to continue with the divorce.

She also expressed concern that the Supers' daughter could be apprehended by child protective services because of visits to her father at the log house in Mission, which Corinne confessed to Walker was the site of another marijuana grow-op. "You also told me that Mr. Super owned and operated many marijuana grow operations, including one on the site of the Log House in Mission, a building where he exercises access to your young daughter," Walker continued in her letter to Super. "It is my understanding of the policy of the police and the Director of Child Protection in British Columbia that any children found on marijuana grow operations are automatically apprehended, without exception."

∩

As the Supers' marriage disintegrated, the relationship between Doug Spink and Corinne Super improved slightly. Contrary to the customary divisive effect prison tends to have on couples, Spink's time at FCI Sheridan brought them back together.

Both told me they discussed marriage during one of Super's prison visits, although they described two different conclusions to the conversation. She said she did not agree to marry him. He said she did.

I asked Spink why he agreed to marry another woman given his earlier pledge to never do that again.

"The marriage wouldn't have been a typical configuration," he said.

Was it because Corinne allowed him to blend in, to appear like a family of Normals?

He thought about it for a few moments. "Maybe," he said.

Super repeatedly and adamantly denied to me that she and Spink had ever been romantically involved. She said they were friends who conducted horse business together, and that was all there was to their relationship.

Evidence presented to me by Spink revealed otherwise.

He sent me a photo taken during visiting day at Sheridan, which portrayed him with his hands in his pockets while Super cuddled up to him, her hand laid affectionately across his stomach.

He also showed me a card she sent dated June 2005. Printed on the front was the phrase: "We must have loved each other long before this life, for when I first saw you, my heart leapt for joy." She had added her own handwritten note inside:

> I could not describe it in a better way. Wow it leapt! I carry on the best I can. I miss you. I cannot help but think about the fact that we would not be together if circumstances had carried on. Where would it all have lead? Where would we be now? What do you really want to happen?

Another card from her, dated December 19, 2005, was inscribed:

> Wow what a year. The hole here is beyond description. We are holding on the best we can. Looking ahead keeps us going. Merry Christmas. You are with us every moment. Love you — All of us. xoxo

Yet another card mailed to Spink in October 2005 revealed Super's struggle to understand this unusual man:

> In the barn when you told me you hoped one day I would understand I finally get it—I truely do. I understand. It still hurts but it feels good to understand it.
> Understanding you has been a challenge and a growth that I thank-you for. Painful and exhausting but full of love. It is strangely painful and comforting to learn that it is me as a species and a female but it is not me as a person. Serious self doubt and reflecting.

Given her comment about learning that "it is me as a species and a female" that caused the problems in their relationship, it seems implausible that Super didn't know (as she insisted to me) that Spink was a zoo.

Besides the cards, letters and emails that Spink shared with me as proof of their romantic relationship, his mother, Claire, sent me a copy of his approved visitor list from Sheridan. It had five names on it, each with a word to describe the visitor's relationship to the inmate.

The names included Spink's father and three friends. And there it was, listed plainly in a federal prison database: Douglas Spink's fiancée, Corinne Super. Unless Super had lied to federal agents about the nature of their relationship, the couple had agreed to be married.

Super's letters while Spink was in prison were filled with reassurances that she was taking good care of his four-legged family, that they would all be there waiting for him when he got out. But despite her professed love and understanding for who Spink was and where his heart belonged, she was simultaneously plotting to get Capone—the love of his life—for her own.

∩

Spink's time in prison was reduced because he was a well-behaved inmate. He was released after twenty-one months of his thirty-six-month sentence. He spent a few months in a Seattle halfway house, after which his supervision by US Probation and Pretrial Services officially began on May 25, 2007. It was scheduled to terminate on May 24, 2012.

Spink then headed north to the tiny rural community of Custer, Washington (population 360), near the Canadian border, where he rented a barn with a small apartment inside. I was living in Custer then too, yet we never crossed paths until after the raid and his arrest in 2010.

Spink got his dogs back from Super, but she refused to return his horses despite the lease agreement the two had struck. Show jumpers generally peak around twelve years old. Capone was just hitting his stride at age eleven when the battle for custody of him began.

Super said she fought for Capone out of love. Spink said she did it for the money.

For more background on how Doug Spink and his stallions featured in the Supers' divorce proceedings, see Exhibit 6, page 380.

27

STOCKPILING SEMEN

Spink and Super's custody battle over Capone was intense and bitter.

During a particularly heated argument the first summer after he was released from prison, Spink accused Super of mistreating Capone, of handling the stallion with cruel mouth bits in a quest to maximize him as her money maker. Leaving his dogs inside his apartment, he stepped out onto the porch and shouted at her into his cell phone, distracted. He'd just come home from getting groceries and had forgotten to put away a package of sugar cookies that sat on the kitchen counter.

He didn't hear the fight break out inside.

"Mentally I was not there. I was yelling on the phone."

His six-year-old Golden Retriever, Rion, was mauled in the brawl over the cookies that involved multiple dogs. The rest of the dogs were okay, but Rion was critically injured. Spink rushed him to the nearby Northwest Veterinary Clinic, in Blaine's Birch Bay Square, but the dog's condition was too serious to be handled there. He was transferred to Canada West, a specialized veterinary center and critical care hospital in Burnaby, British Columbia.

Spink couldn't cross the border because of his criminal record, so Blaine clinic employee Joni Black drove Rion to Canada West. Rion wasn't without visitors, though—Corinne Super and her daughter visited him while he was there.

A Canada West veterinarian sent Spink a fax outlining Rion's situation on August 25, 2007:

> As I have said, Rion is in critical but somewhat stable condition with cardiac (heart) problem, borderline renal (kidney) failure secondary to his severe bite wounds. He will need extensive skin and muscle surgery in the next few days if he is stable—I will keep you informed. He will need multiple blood transfusions tonight, I will speak with you tomorrow. The estimate as we discussed is $10,000–$15,000. Please initial the hospital form and sign. Thank you.
>
> Dr. Karlyn Bland

Rion didn't survive. He lived for five days before he suffered a fatal cardiac event at the Canadian clinic. Spink was devastated. He blamed himself for leaving the groceries unattended while the dogs were in the apartment. Animal welfare experts I interviewed contended that human error caused the incident. Spink said the same thing. Mark Steinway, founder of Pasado's Safe Haven in Washington, maintained that lack of supervision could cause otherwise gentle dogs to turn on each other and attack.

"Dogs are pack animals, there's a hierarchy," Steinway said. "If there's a weak one, they get picked on. That's just the nature of the beast. Ordinary good dogs could do that, especially when you have seven big dogs with a trigger."

In this case, the trigger was the sugar cookies. Steinway used an analogy involving another kind of trigger—kids and guns—to explain what happened. "Would you walk out of the room with three toddlers in there and leave a loaded revolver on the table? If one of them shoots the other, that's just toddler behavior."

The death of Spink's beloved Retriever didn't dampen his resolve to get Capone back. If anything, it strengthened his determination. That summer, he made hundreds of phone calls to Super demanding she return the stallion. He also threatened legal action. And on September 20, he wrote a letter that accused her of stealing Capone's semen:

> There is a rumor circulating that you are attempting to stockpile frozen semen on Capone prior to his return. If this is the case, I can only stand in disbelief that you have acted as a petty thief in trying to steal this magnificent creature merely to squeeze one last little bit of money out of your association with him. Given that you are neither owner of him, nor at present rightful lessee of him, you have no authority whatsoever to be collecting him. If this is in fact happening, know that I will soon track down whoever is storing the semen and obtain court warrant to seize it on behalf of its rightful owner: ESL. [Exitpoint Stallions Limitée was a company managed and partly owned by Spink.] Any clients who contract with you to buy this stolen semen will surely look to you alone for recompense when their foals are shown illegitimate.

But none of Spink's efforts worked. Super wouldn't budge.

That September, the two spent a long night negotiating in the parking lot of a seedy motel in Blaine, not far from Spink's place in Custer. According to Spink, the talk included the promise of an attempt at reconciliation. Super was finally convinced. She returned Capone to Spink's barn in Custer on September 28, 2007.

The custody battle, however, wasn't even close to being over.

Spink had no passport for Capone. Without one, he couldn't enter the stallion into competitions, even though the horse was talented enough to be considered a contender for prestigious events such as the Olympics. In an attempt to resolve the situation, on September 30 he wrote the Fédération Équestre Internationale (FEI) care of Equine Canada's Jennifer Mahoney. He expressed his disappointment and dismay that Capone's passport had been issued in Super's name without his consent. Capone was an asset of his company, Wolf Advisors Limited, whose assets were later acquired by Exitpoint Stallions Limitée (ESL). Both companies were run by Spink. They were also owned by him, along with other investors whose names he would not reveal.

> It has been brought to our attention that Ms. Super unilaterally transferred the listed ownership in the FEI passport issued by Equine Canada for Capone to her name. This neither reflects an economic transaction through which Ms. Super came to own this horse, nor does it reflect assent on the part of any representative of the owners of this horse—neither Wolf Advisors nor ESL. Optimistically, we hypothesize that Ms. Super felt that the status of

her lease of this stallion could be codified in this manner... though it is not our understanding that such is the proper procedure for recording a temporary lease arrangement.

In any event, despite repeated efforts both through myself and through ESL's corporate attorney, Ms. Super has not returned Capone's FEI passport to us. Consequently, I must at this time report this document as lost/stolen, and ask that a replacement be issued.

But FEI never issued a replacement.

Spink also had to secure his own permission to travel, because he was still under the supervision of the federal probation department. Back then, his relationship with them was amicable. He filed his reports on time, and got along well with his probation officer, Jerrod Akins.

On January 4, 2008, Spink faxed Akins, laying the groundwork to potentially seek permission to travel outside his parole jurisdiction if Capone secured a spot on the 2008 Summer Olympics team.

> There is a 50/50 chance that one of the stallions I train, Capone, is going to be headed to the Olympic selection trials in Florida in late January—the trials themselves are in late February/early March. If that happens, it will be critical that I am there for schooling, grooming, etc.—I don't know if this will all come together yet, it depends on the degree to which the owners [ESL] are willing to take the financial risk of going for a spot on the Team. If he did make the Team, then he'd be in Europe over the summer and to Hong Kong in August for the Beijing Olympics. That's a bridge I suppose we'll cross if we come to it—many steps between now and then yet to accomplish.

Capone never made it to the Olympic trials. Spink had custody of the stallion, but Super never gave up custody of the horse's passport. It was an insurmountable obstacle.

∩

Letters from Spink to his probation officer about his goings-on were friendly, informative and chatty. He was enthusiastic about restarting life on the outside, and making plans for the future. He wasn't tempted to go back to transporting drugs; he had learned his lesson on that front.

After some consideration, Spink decided to pursue another one of his dreams: becoming a veterinarian. He applied to a prestigious new neurology program at Washington State University's College of Veterinary Medicine, in Pullman. In his January 4 fax to Jerrod Akins, he mentioned this latest development.

> Over the holidays, I completed my application for the PhD program in Veterinary Neuroscience at Washington State University, in Pullman. My GRE scores came in at 720/720 which I believe puts me at the top of their applicant pool, and based on my discussions with my planned dissertation advisor and the head of the Admissions Committee for the program, I feel I have a very good shot at acceptance. They will mail letters to their chosen candidates by the end of January. I think I've mentioned my interest in this program to you before, but it occurs to me that I should be more explicit as this will require a move to a new judicial district. The program begins in September. I will let you know when I have an official acceptance letter in hand. It is an exceptional program, and I believe I can extend it into a dual DVM/PhD program as well.

As anticipated, Spink received his acceptance letter from Washington State University that January. But a few weeks later, it was rescinded. The rejection came in the form of a terse email from Steve Simasko, director of the neuroscience program at the Pullman campus.

Spink called up Simasko and demanded an explanation. "He said members of the admissions committee had been made aware of certain facets of my personal life."

He complained to the dean of the department and the dean of the school. But by then, the official reason given for the rejection had changed. Spink was told his educational background wasn't strong enough, that it was in the hands of the school's lawyers, and that they weren't changing their minds.

Spink couldn't prove why he'd been denied entry into the program, but he believed he knew the reason. It was a reaction he recognized and a pattern he had faced ever since he'd been outed as a zoo. People would start out being interested in his intellect, his achievements, his gifts across many disciplines. But when they inevitably figured out who he was—and what he believed—it was common for them to fall silent, to refuse to communicate with him ever again. He even had a phrase for it. He called it "going dark."

This time he decided to fight back. He contacted Lambda Legal, the American Civil Liberties Union and the Washington State Human

Rights Commission to report that he was the subject of discrimination on the basis of sexual orientation. At first these organizations were interested in taking on his case, he said, until they realized the sexual orientation he was referring to wasn't homosexuality, but something else entirely. Once that became clear, none would take his complaint forward. "They said it wasn't politically palatable," he said.

Spink was deeply disappointed, but decided not to let the rejection stop him from rebuilding his career. He went back to his roots—high tech—and started a promising new business.

He got the idea while in prison, from a *Wall Street Journal* article about the emergence of virtual private networks. A VPN increases privacy and security for its users by extending a private network across the public network of the internet. VPN users, by securely accessing this private network, can share data with others without compromising security. The virtual point-to-point connection is established using a variety of methods, such as dedicated connections, virtual tunneling protocols or traffic encryption.

VPNs kept users' online activities free from surveillance by governments and other invested parties. Potential customers included corporations with trade secrets, journalists in war-torn countries, lawyers protecting clients, and anyone else who didn't want the government or other nosy entities spying on their business.

Spink thought the idea of VPNs was solid, but that the way the entrepreneurs in the *Wall Street Journal* article were going about it was flawed. It inspired him to start his own version of a privacy and encryption company. After all, who better to understand the need for security and privacy than him? He had faced persecution because of who he was for many years. He had learned how to avoid detection for the sake of survival. Add his technical knowledge into the equation, and the business of privacy and encryption seemed a perfect fit for his skills, life experiences and goals.

And so it was that Baneki Privacy Computing Inc. was born.

He was out of prison, he had custody of Capone again, and he had a promising new business. But the life Spink was building for himself wouldn't last. And neither would his relatively peaceful relationship with law enforcement.

28

DISAPPEARING ACT

Corinne Super was determined to get Capone back, and she didn't care how much trouble she caused Spink to do it. Banking on the bestiality card to work its magic again, she appeared at the police station in Whatcom County, Washington, to ask for help. Perhaps it wasn't a coincidence that her visit occurred in May, just as the 2008 summer show jumping season was about to kick off.

The nature of her inquiry was captured in a police report by Whatcom County Sheriff's Deputy Steve Roff:

> In early May of 2008, Corrine [sic] goes to the Whatcom County Sheriff's Office and speaks with deputy. Corrine requests assistance in getting Capone back. The deputy reviewed Corrine's paperwork and tells her this is a civil issue. The deputy explained to Corrine the only way the Sheriff's Office would get involved was if she tried to get Capone back and there was a problem at the property. The deputy also told Corrine the Sheriff's Office would not force Douglas to give her Capone.

At the time, Spink didn't know about Super's visit to the local police, but he was taking precautions anyway. His horses and dogs were hardly ever out of his sight. He lived with them inside the barn he was leasing from a Custer family who also lived on the premises. From that vantage point, he kept a close eye on Capone's stall. On the door of each stall, he posted bright green laminated signs stating, in large block letters, that he and only he owned the horses, and that he was the sole person authorized to remove them.

He rarely left the property except to run errands occasionally. And when he did go somewhere, he made sure one of the family members who owned the land was on site to watch over Capone. They shared a common driveway, and the front gate stayed securely closed at all times.

His dogs assisted with matters of security. The pack included Schutzhund-trained German Shepherds who took their protection duties seriously.

After Spink's relationship with Super ended, he started seeing a man who would become his boyfriend for the next nine years. The man, who he met and initially got to know through zoo internet forums, flew in to visit him mid-May, and Spink decided it was safe to slip away for a short trip. They spent the weekend with two of Spink's dogs hiking in the Pacific Northwest wilderness, enjoying its pristine forests and water bodies.

He would live to regret that seemingly innocuous decision. When he left his barn on Friday, May 16, 2008, Capone was alone—and the property unattended—for only about three hours. It was just long enough.

A barren scene awaited him when he returned home from his weekend in the woods. The front gate to the Custer property was unlatched. The barn door was open, and so was Capone's stall door. The halter and lead rope were gone. Capone had vanished.

∩

Spink reported Capone's disappearance to the Whatcom County Sheriff's Office on May 18, 2008. Deputy Steve Roff reported on his exchange with Spink.

> I asked him if he had any idea who may have taken Capone and he said Corine [sic] Super may be involved with Capone being taken. He said Corine used to lease Capone from Exitpoint and they are currently suing her for prize money and stud fees that she collected and did not give to Exitpoint. I was later given a copy of the lawsuit with Corine. Douglas said Corine's lease ran [out] on Capone right

away and she did not return him right away. He said Corine kept Capone and was collecting as much semen as she could before returning him. Douglas went on to explain that Capone's semen is worth $2500.00 a unit and believed that Corine was collecting the semen to sell later.

In his typical outspoken manner, Spink didn't hesitate to supply explicit details about his past as a drug smuggler, as Deputy Roff outlined in his report:

During my interview of Douglas, he was very forthcoming about his criminal history. Douglas informed me he had been arrested by United States Federal Agents as part of a very large drug operation. Douglas described himself as a mule for the drug operation and was on the low end of the "food chain." Douglas also informed me at the time of his arrest he was in possession of a large amount of cocaine.

Douglas told me the following regarding the drug operation: Corrine and her husband owned a large farm in Chilliwack, British Columbia. Corrine was associated with the Hells Angels Motorcycle Gang. Corrine was married and was having an affair with a Hells Angel member. Douglas was also having an affair with Corrine while she was married and dating the Hells Angels Member.

The Hells Angels and Corrine started smuggling drugs between Canada and the United States. Douglas was approached and selected to be part of the operation because he was an American Citizen and had a clean record. Douglas would pick up the drugs in the United States and transport them to various locations. Douglas was arrested with a large quantity of cocaine and went to prison. When Douglas went to prison he did not involve anyone else.

Following up on Spink's accusation, Roff called Super to question her at 3:30 p.m. on May 22. She admitted she took Capone, and mentioned bestiality again.

Corinne told me she was responsible in the removal of Capone from Douglas' care. Corrine told me she was Capone's owner and that she had just taken back her property. Corrine said the reason for the removal of Capone was because Douglas was not taking proper care of Capone. Corrine then started to discuss how Douglas was not training Capone properly. Corrine also made allegations that Douglas was involved with Bestiality with Capone and other animals. Corrine told me the Royal Canadian Mounted Police was investigating Douglas for Bestiality Charges.

Roff asked her: why did she wait all these months to act? She said she was afraid of Spink. "Corinne discussed Douglas's criminal history and described him as very violent person," Roff wrote. "Corrine was afraid Douglas would assault her if she tried to get Capone back."

But in a taped interview with me, Super said she wasn't scared of Spink. "A lot of people are afraid of him and I don't know why. But I think there's a lot of people that think I have pretty big balls."

Spink later insisted that Super's actions and words against his character had nothing to do with rescuing Capone from acts of bestiality. She knew he was a zoo from the start, he said. He had told her who he was and she had pursued him anyway. "She got hundreds of thousands of dollars into her slimy little hands because of his talent," he said. "She has no incentive to trash me. She just wants the horse for free."

Spink told Whatcom County authorities that he had documents proving he was Capone's rightful owner. He produced Super's divorce affidavit in which she asserted that she didn't own Capone. Roff questioned her about that too.

> I asked Corrine if that was her signature on the affidavit and she stated, "Yes." I then asked Corrine to explain to me if she was the owner of Capone, why she would make those statements in her affidavit. Corrine told me she and Mark were dividing and disclosing their assets for the divorce. Corrine also told me Douglas asked her to lie and disclose that Capone and the other horses were his. Douglas was afraid Corrine's husband, Mark, would try to force Capone and the other horses to be sold as assets from the marriage.

Super had bestiality allegations working to her advantage in this battle, but Spink wasn't without his own supporters. One of them was his landlord, Sheryn Munro, who contacted Whatcom County police to complain that nothing was being done about the theft of Capone. Roff related the contents of Munro's salty voice mail message in his police report:

> On 6-12-08 I received a vulgar message from Sheryn Munro. Sheryn is yelling and screaming profanities at me. The following is what Sheryn screamed and yelled on her voice message left for me at the Sheriff's Office:
> "Look asshole, this is the fourth time I have called, somebody broke onto my fucking property, it was Shelly DeBoer, I have some fucking witnesses, I am sick and tired of you not arresting the cunt, will you call me the fuck back."

Shelly DeBoer was a neighbor of Munro's. Spink believed she had helped Super take Capone. He suspected DeBoer had spied on him until she saw him leave for the weekend.

At first, Spink hoped for assistance from the police. But that hope soon dissolved into frustration when the case went nowhere. On September 2, more than three months after Capone's disappearance and with his stall still sitting empty, Spink wrote a five-page letter to Whatcom County prosecuting attorney David McEachran demanding action.

> Unquestionably, tight surveillance was placed on my farm prior to Capone's abduction. I lease the barn here from a local family, with several teenage children. We share a common driveway, and front gate which is always closed. My barn interior is not visible from the main road. I live upstairs, in the barn, and thus I am on the property essentially 24/7. The lessors of this barn, themselves, are always here when I must go to run errands in Bellingham. The only time in 2008 that someone was not on this property—and watching the driveway and barn, was approximately three hours on the 16th of May. I left, to go hiking for the weekend, in the afternoon in a rented car, with a friend. My van was in the driveway—nobody would know I was not there without active surveillance. This was not serendipitous timing; it was pre-meditated criminal intent.

Spink went on to outline to McEachran why he believed his case was clear-cut, which included mention of his security detail.

> Anyone walking onto the property is immediately confronted with highly-motivated, highly-trained, specially-bred protection dogs who have earned titles in competitive Schutzhund events. There is no way someone doing so would be of the false impression that their entrance on the property was authorized, or indeed even safe from a physical perspective. Only someone knowing the dogs already would be able to do so without significant risk/injury. There is no ambiguity.

Spink expanded his airing of grievances past the police and prosecutors. He also spoke to the press. Both the *Bellingham Herald* and Canada's national *Globe and Mail* published stories about the disappearance and subsequent custody battle over the spectacular star stallion known as Capone I. The journalists didn't know—or chose not to report—the real story behind the relationship between Capone and Spink.

He also printed up a wanted poster offering a $5,000 reward "For Safe Return of Stolen Horse + Beloved Friend." The poster featured a map that pointed out Super's farm in Chilliwack. It also featured photos of Super and the stallion barn where Capone was being kept.

Spink also sued Super in British Columbia civil court, submitting as evidence the affidavits she'd made during her divorce in which she stated she didn't own his stallions. Super handled that inconvenient truth the same way she did with the Whatcom County Sheriff's Office. In an affidavit on September 6, 2008, Super submitted to the court that Spink had helped her with her divorce and told her to lie, to pretend she didn't own Capone when really she did. "Mr. Spink advised me to swear affidavits claiming that he was homosexual and that Capone 1 was being held on his behalf—neither of which is true."

∩

Spink grew frustrated with writing letters to lawyers, police and prosecutors. It was futile. He'd had enough of waiting around. In June, he made a bold telephone call to Deputy Roff, who noted the conversation in his report:

> On 06-18-08 at approximately 1400 hrs, I received a phone call from Douglas regarding Capone. Douglas asked me if it would affect his case if he had someone go to Canada and get Capone back. I advised Douglas not to do that. I tried to explain to Douglas his case was on going and the report was going to be forwarded to the Prosecutor's Office for review. I also explained to Douglas it would not look good in any civil or criminal case if he had someone go to Canada and take Capone back.
>
> Douglas attitude was that if Corrine did it, then why can't he. I told Douglas I was not familiar with Canadian laws and someone could get arrested if he or she tried to take Capone back and brought him back into the United States. Douglas tried to tell me he was just asking a question and did not plan to have anyone take Capone.

But Spink wasn't "just asking a question," as the events that transpired next would illustrate.

"Hope is not a plan," he told me, many times. And hope wasn't going to bring Capone home to him.

So instead, he made a plan.

29

CHECKMATE CUNT

Spink wasn't about to let an international border stand in the way of getting Capone back. If one method didn't work, he would simply try another one until success was achieved.

He found an ally in his Custer landlord, Sheryn Munro, who drove over the border to visit Corinne Super at her farm in Chilliwack.

"She came to me sort of pleading a case," Super recalled, "like she was having problems with Doug, and could I help her out with that, could I give her advice on how to deal with him, that kind of stuff."

At first, Super obliged Munro. She didn't realize the supposedly friendly visit was actually a ruse orchestrated by an enemy: her former fiancé. "She wanted to have a cup of tea, an afternoon chat, could I show her the horses, she would love to see my horses."

By late afternoon, Super had to leave to pick up her daughter from school, so she bid farewell to Munro. "She left, and then I left to get [my daughter], and she came back after I was gone," Super said. "My staff at the farm called me and said you need to get back here right now, she's in the barn trying to take the horses."

Super called the police for help and raced back to her farm. Munro left empty-handed. But a month later, she showed up again. This time, she meant business.

Super was driving through Chilliwack in her pickup truck, towing a horse trailer with Capone inside, when she realized she was being followed by Munro, who was also towing a trailer. Munro's trailer was empty, presumably to accommodate the intended cargo for the ride back to the United States.

The chase was on. For an hour or two, the pursuit between two women and one valuable horse continued unabated down the highway and through the city of Chilliwack. Super called the local RCMP detachment for help. "I said listen, I'm being pursued down the highway, I've got my horse in my trailer and I'm being pursued by another truck and trailer," she told me.

It was June 19, 2008, the same day that Whatcom County Deputy Steve Roff was scheduled to meet Super at the Sumas-Abbotsford border crossing "for a follow-up interview and to obtain some documents regarding the case," Roff noted in his report. Super reached Roff by cell phone while the chase was in progress.

> At approximately 1300 hrs, I talked to Corrine on the telephone and she advised Sheryn Munro was up in Canada and was trying to get Capone. Corrine told me she had Capone in a trailer and was taking him or coming back from veterinarian appointment. Corrine also told me Sheryn was following her in a truck towing a horse trailer. I told Corrine to contact call 911 and have the police meet her at her farm. Corrine advised she had already called 911 and the police were on the way to her farm.

After he finished speaking with Super, Roff called Spink.

> At approximately 1315 hrs, I spoke to Douglas on the telephone and informed him I was aware Sheryn was up in Canada trying to take Capone. Douglas told me Sheryn was just watching to make sure Capone was not taken to a different location. Douglas tried to explain to me that he had received information that Corrine was transporting Capone to a different location. I told Douglas I did not believe him and that I was aware Sheryn had taken a horse trailer with her to Canada. I explained to Douglas this case was still under investigation and I still had interviews to do before it was submitted to the Prosecutor's Office. I explained to Douglas,

due to his actions he had jeopardized the integrity of the case and there was no reason to conduct the rest of the interviews.

Super ended up in the parking lot at the RCMP detachment with Sheryn Munro still in hot pursuit. The 911 operator talked her through. "She said, 'Come in, I'll have officers waiting for you in the parking lot,'" Super said. But Munro wasn't about to give up on her mission that easily. "I pulled into the parking lot and she jumped out of her truck and started screeching, 'You've got my horse, you've got my horse, you stole my horse.'"

Police officers came out to mediate and, according to Super, advised the women to settle their differences in civil court.

It didn't end there, however. "She followed me home," Super remembered. "Chased me home, and got out, she was screaming and yelling, and tried to grab the horse, trying to get into my barn. The RCMP came, they were there, there were three or four police cars at the farm, and they told her they were going to charge her with trespassing if she came on my property."

Munro stationed herself on the road outside Super's farm, informing her that she was going to sit out front and Super couldn't stop her. "And [police] came to me and said, she's right, they can't stop her from sitting out front, it's a public road."

Munro hung out for a while before she tired of the waiting game. "She sat there for three hours and then she drove away," Super said. "That's the last I saw of her. I never saw her again."

Deputy Roff's report reflected the confusion that went along with being the investigator assigned to the Capone caper.

> The investigation of this incident has been very convoluted and difficult to investigate. As of this time it is not known who [is] the owner of Capone. Douglas has provided numerous documents, on the behalf of Exitpoint Stallions Limitée, to try to prove ownership. None of the documents were sufficient evidence to establish ownership of Capone. Corrine also submitted numerous documents to try to prove ownership. None of the documents were sufficient evidence to establish ownership of Capone.
>
> Through out the course of the investigation I have suspected both Douglas and Corrine have not been totally honest regarding the information they have provided. I also suspected Douglas and Corrine have each put their own spin on the information provided in an effort to prove ownership of Capone.

> It is not known if the dispute over Capone is from a failed business or romantic relationship between Douglas and Corrine.

And so the criminal investigation into Capone's disappearance petered out to nothing. Spink still had his civil suit in British Columbia, but after biding his time for a year and a half of frustrating, fruitless delays, he grew impatient with that route too.

It was time for a new plan.

He chose the date for his next course of action thoughtfully. By now it was autumn of 2009. Canadian Thanksgiving fell on the second weekend of October. Spink speculated that the watchful eyes on Capone at Super's farm might be distracted by the holiday.

He was right. Super went out of town with her daughter to spend Thanksgiving weekend with a friend. There was an on-site caretaker at the farm, but he was fast asleep and didn't hear anyone creep onto the property in the middle of the night and slip into the barn. Early the next morning, he found the door of Capone's empty stall hanging open.

The front entrance to the farm had a locked gate, so the horse had been taken out through the back fields. "You could see hoof marks had gone down and through the field," Super said. "Also the fencing at the back of the property was cut. At the very back of the property there's a gate on the road. The gate had been taken down. Chains had been cut. The gate was lying down in the ditch."

She could conjure up only one suspect.

"I just don't think that anybody is trained or skilled to walk a stallion out of the barn and past the other horses and through the neighbor's field and cut gates and cut chains and cut locks. It would only be something that he would do. I'm confident about that."

To date, Spink hasn't revealed whether it was he or someone else who made off with Capone, or whether the stallion was ridden or driven over the border back to the United States.

But where Capone ended up that night is certain: back at Spink's place. By now Spink had moved into a new home, the rustic cabin at the top of Reese Hill Road. Super would have no idea where to start looking for Capone.

Spink couldn't resist letting Super know that he had prevailed. She was enjoying the relaxing holiday weekend when his text landed in her phone around six o'clock Monday morning.

The message was short, but not sweet.

"Checkmate cunt."

To read Spink's posting on a horse forum about Capone's return to him, see Exhibit 7, page 383.

PHOTO ALBUM

Top: Even as a child, Doug Spink was fascinated by mice.
Bottom: Doug and Joy Spink with their pet raccoon, Fluffy.

Top left: Doug Spink cradles a chick.
Top right: Spink family Christmas card from 1975. Clockwise from left: Claire, Jack, Joy and Doug.
Bottom: Claire Spink with Doug.

UNIQUELY DANGEROUS   177

Top: Spink family home in Fox Chapel, Pennsylvania.
Bottom: Pony Boy on his Halloween horse.

All: Doug Spink riding horses when he was a youngster.

Top: Kyle King riding Capone to win Grand Prix in the 2011 Rocky Mountain Classic at Anderson Ranch in Calgary, Alberta.
Bottom: Doug Spink jumping with Capone in Oregon.

Top: Attorney Jim Turner waiting with Doug Spink in the federal courthouse in Seattle, the same building he BASE jumped off.
Bottom left: Spink clears the bar riding Cantour.
Bottom right: Spink BASE jumping from the Kuala Lumpur Tower in Malaysia.

Top: Most of Spink's dogs at his Sumas home shortly before the raid.
Bottom left: Spink with Bafana, who was later beaten to death by an unknown assailant.
Bottom right: Spink's dogs relaxing at his place in Custer.

182   Uniquely Dangerous

Top left: Spink with Accord at the Holsteiner Verband stallion auction in Neumünster, Germany.
Top right: Spink with Gifford, who attended classes with him at Reed College.
Bottom: Spink's dogs hanging out in his van.

Top: Spink's dogs playing.
Bottom: Spink hiking with his dogs on the same weekend Capone disappeared from his barn in May 2008.

Top: Spink in the Sheridan prison greenhouse.
Bottom left: Spink and Corinne Super share a moment in the Sheridan visiting room.
Bottom right: Screenshot of police surveillance video for Operation Frozen Timber.

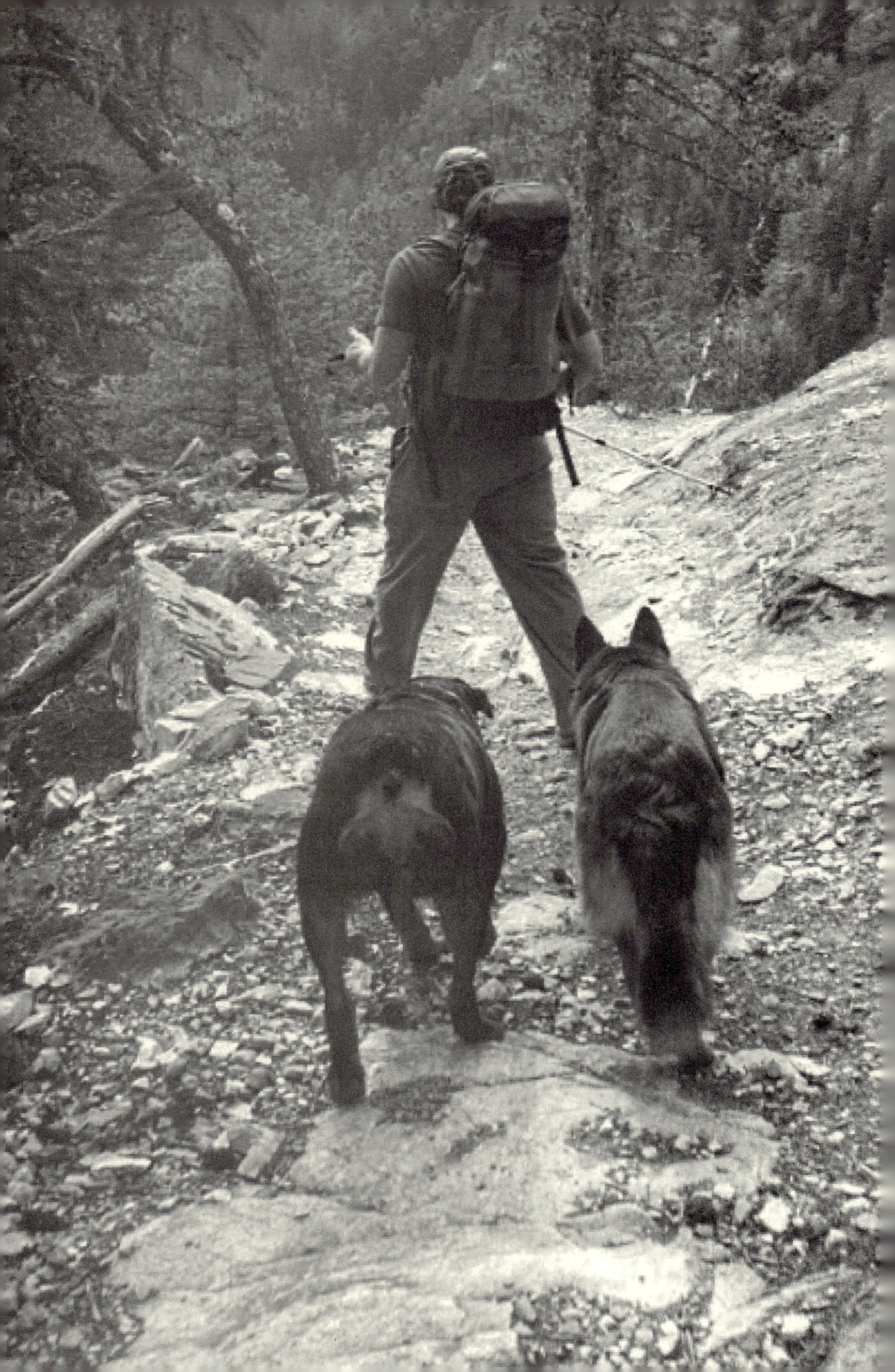

Left: Spink hiking with his dogs on the same weekend Capone disappeared from his barn.
Top: A street sign decorates Spink's property.
Bottom: Spink's cabin at the top of Reese Hill Road in Sumas, Washington.

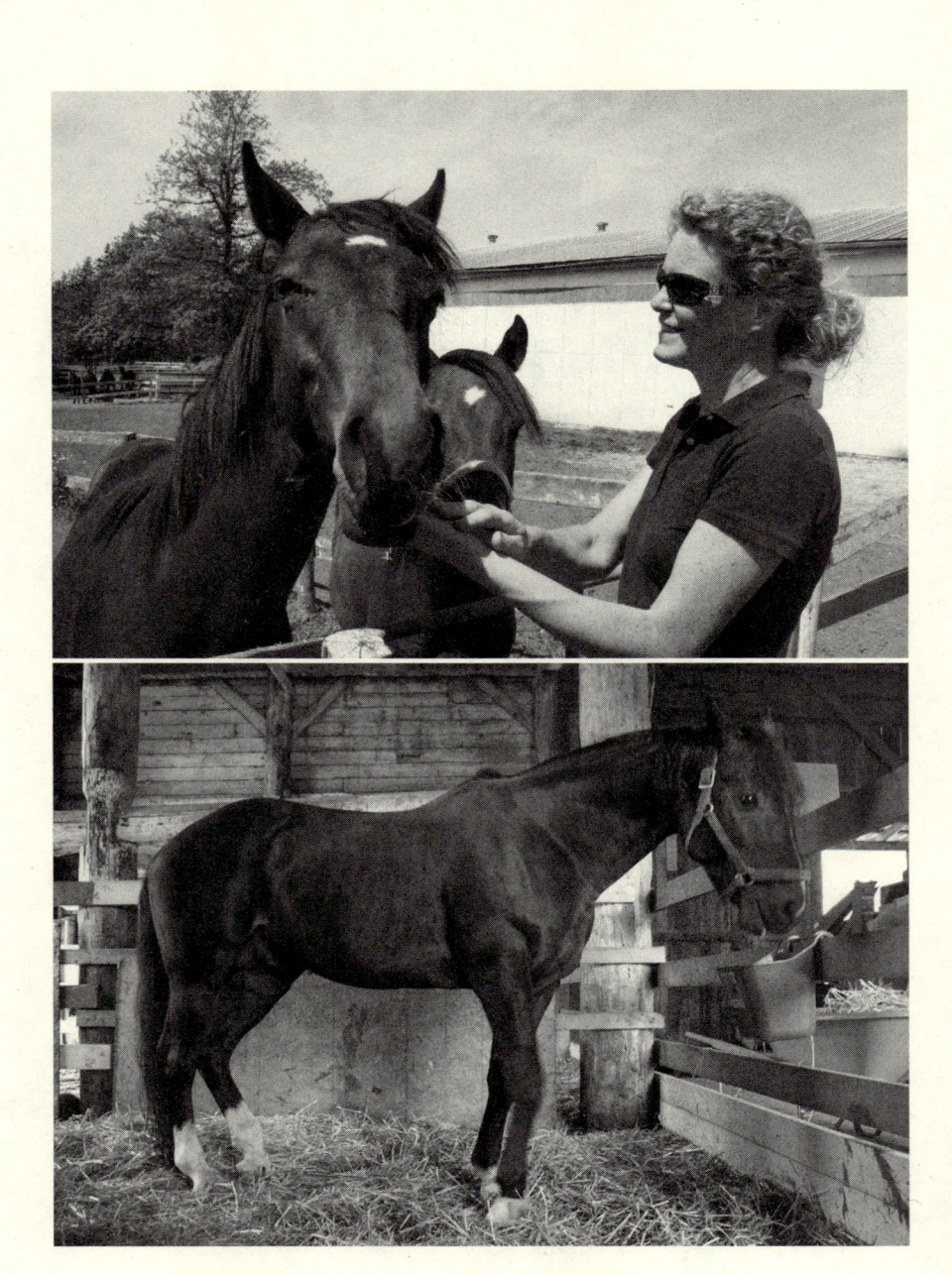

Top: Corinne Super with her horses at her Langley, British Columbia farm. Bottom and right: Capone spends the weekend in an old wooden barn in Lynden, Washington, while waiting for his border paperwork to come through after Super won custody of him.

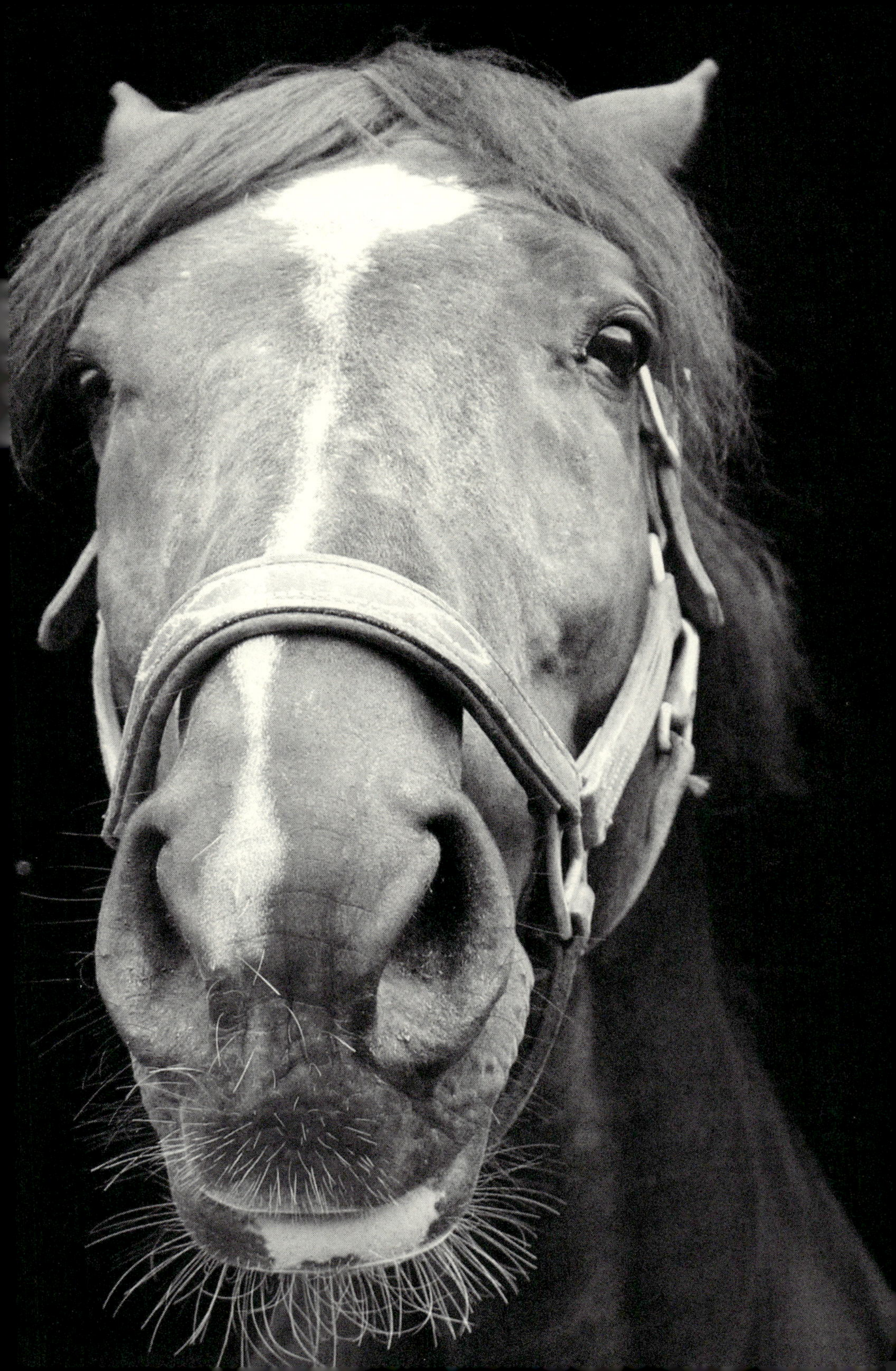

Doug Spink contemplates his future standing on a boulder in Port Townsend.

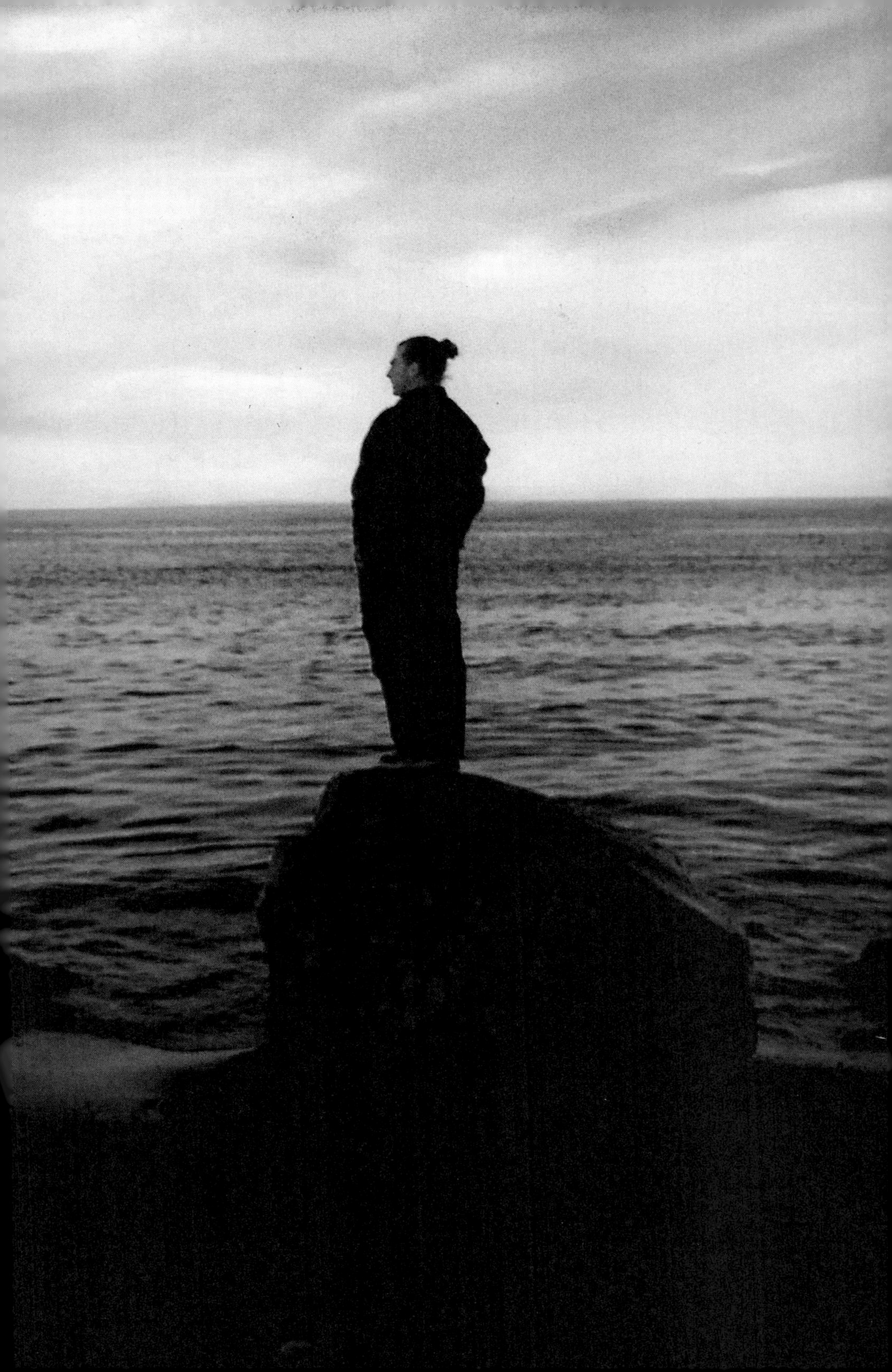

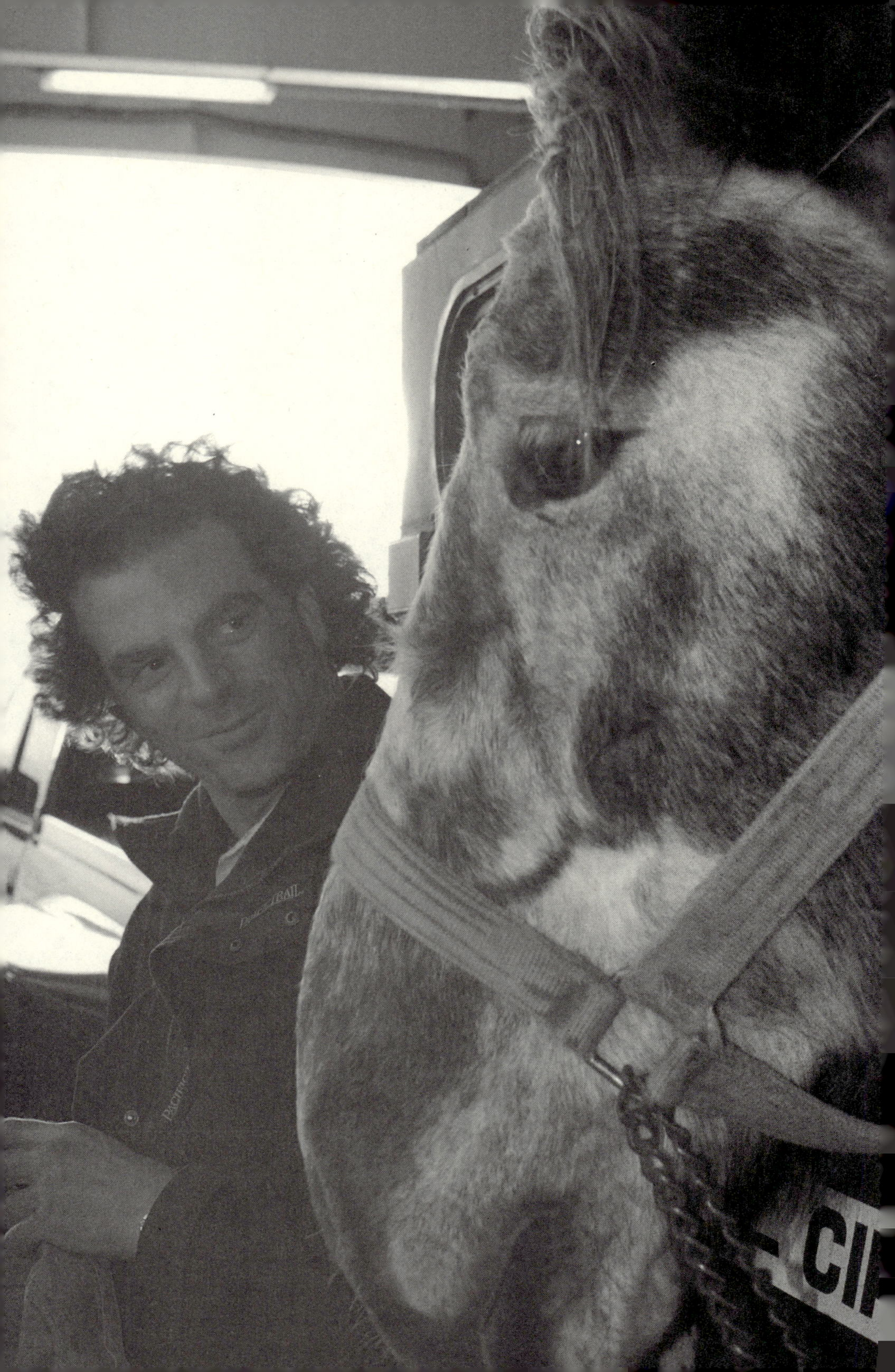

Left: Doug Spink with L.J., the only animal he got back after the 2010 raid of his Sumas cabin.
Top: Chain holding the tags of Spink's dogs who died, which he wore often in memory of them.
Bottom: Kateen Fenter examines a hole in the fence that divides her farm from Andrew Johnston's after Ghengis went missing.

Top: Introductory conversation between Carreen Maloney and Hiromi Monro in Tokyo.
Bottom left: Hiromi with Takeshi "Beat" Kitano.
Bottom right: Carreen and Hiromi's wedding day.

PART THREE

Turning and turning in the widening gyre
The falcon cannot hear the falconer;
Things fall apart; the centre cannot hold.

—William Butler Yeats, *The Second Coming*

30

DEATH SENTENCES

Spink distinctly remembers the unease that crept over him when the form letter arrived from US Probation. It announced that as of May 5, 2009, his file had been transferred from senior probation officer Jerrod Akins to assistant probation officer Jeff Robson.

It's not clear why Robson, who had seven years of service with US Probation, got the file. Spink thought it strange that a low-ranking officer was assigned to his case, given that he'd been arrested in a high-profile bust carrying a significant quantity of drugs. It also bothered him that thirty-year-old Robson was based in the Tukwila office, a different jurisdiction from the one Spink lived in. That seemed out of order to him.

Later in federal court, Robson testified that the transfer had happened because Spink's status had changed to low risk. It was true that for two years, Spink had been considered a model supervisee by US Probation.

Robson's relationship with Spink was very different than Akins' had been. Akins and Spink had kept in touch regularly through telephone calls and faxes. Occasionally the probation officer drove up to Whatcom County and visited Spink at his place, where they had coffee together and talked about horses.

In contrast, Robson, by his own account, never once called or visited Spink during the year he was assigned to supervise him. Instead, Spink's new probation officer researched him extensively on the internet. When Robson provided evidence to the court after the raid on Reese Hill Road, he supplemented his words with printouts from various websites.

Spink's writings are all over the internet. He's extraordinarily prolific, particularly online, and isn't content to fade quietly into the background. He is confrontational and refuses to back down or shrink away in shame when people attack him for being a zoophile, whether that happens online or in person.

One such confrontation occurred during his time as a volunteer moderator on Bluelight, a popular internet discussion forum that describes itself as a harm reduction community for drug users. In 2008, a participant with the screen name "Chicago66" posted a message accusing "Fausty" (a nickname given to Spink by his ex-wife) of raping animals.

> I would like to reiterate my desire for the permanent banishment of the s&t mod "Fausty". Having sex with animals is similar to rape as far as I'm concerned. An animal can't say no.

Others might have been tempted to try to get a post like that removed, but not Fausty. Instead, he used his position as moderator to spin the unflattering comment off into its own separate thread, and began to answer the flood of comments that rolled in. A few people were curious and asked questions. Others were angry and appalled.

One poster asked: How would the local animal shelter react if they knew his beliefs about animals? Spink replied bluntly:

> Animal shelter? Umm, ok—I know the folks over there pretty well, they stop by to visit the boys when they are out in our neck of the woods. Paraphrasing, they've told me before that it's nice to visit a farm where the well-being and happiness of the critters is clearly top priority—after all, they deal with horrors every day such as starved horses, dogs beaten to death by drunkards, etc. And of course they see Normal people drop off dogs at the shelter every day because they aren't convenient, or they shed too much, or whatever. They've been very kind to me when my Rottie boy [Fritzy], with whom I've shared life for more than ten years, died last month. They sent a wonderful card and listened to me as I blathered on for hours telling stories about our life together.

> So I suppose their concerns about whether I touch my boys' wee-wees or not are. . . zero.

The online kerfuffle went on for a couple of weeks as forum visitors posted their hatred and rage towards Spink. He kept responding until Bluelight asked him to tone down the frankness of his replies. He refused. Instead of censoring himself, he knocked the entire thread down, but not before preserving it for posterity on his hard drive.

Until his late twenties, Doug Spink had done everything he could to hide his secret, but after that, something inside him shifted. Stepping up to publicly defend zoophilia and other zoophiles had grown important to him.

But being outspoken would have dire consequences.

☊

In autumn 2009, James Tait was arrested in Tennessee. He's the zoo who took Kenneth Pinyan to the hospital after he was injured while having sex with a stallion in 2005. Spink, though barely out of trouble with the law himself, reached out to help. He didn't know Tait personally, but he knew about Tait from what had happened in Enumclaw.

After Pinyan's death, Tait left Washington State for Maury County, Tennessee, where he lived quietly and undetected for four years, until authorities were somehow alerted to his presence. On October 15, 2009, police arrested the fifty-eight-year-old along with his roommate, forty-four-year-old Kenny Thomason. Horses, ponies, goats and dogs had been living on the farm with Tait and Thomason.

Shortly after Tait's arrest, Spink wrote a letter to him in jail offering help. Tait responded promptly on October 31, 2009, with gratitude for this unexpected kindness from a stranger.

> D. Spink, Sir:
>
> I was quite pleasantly surprised by your letter offering help, when it arrived last night. NO—things have not yet been resolved—things are just slowly picking up steam—as someone is feeding the media little tidbits of meat—until the vultures can dine on the main course—US.
>
> As far as the farm, no one is watching it—being that they've confiscated everything with four legs from the property.

> They euthanized it for Kenny—but it still means the same thing as far as the disposition of all of the animals. They've murdered them—with the claim; all of those animals were too dangerous to be around people now. Bullshit. They received the death penalty: their crime—just being our close friends. Friends that both cared and loved each other. (How true, that they're all dead is real or not—it is what the officials told Kenny).

Tait's fears about what had happened to the animals weren't unfounded. Threats of vigilante violence against outed zoos are commonplace, including promises to kill, castrate and rape. But the most effective way to punish zoos is not with threats to their physical safety or freedom. It's not with criminal charges, jail time or violence against them. It is the killing of their animals to correct the perceived offense to human dignity that is overwhelmingly their greatest fear. I heard this from zoos over and over again. Spink raised it often, as in this September 9, 2012, text to me:

> There is no 911 we can call—DO YOU GET THAT YET? Us, our families, we are FAIR GAME. Forever. We have no protection, no defense but ourselves and our battered, hunted, persecuted community.
> And if we raise a FINGER to defend our families we will be killed or sent to prison for life—and our partners killed anyway—HOW DO YOU THINK THAT FEELS? TO HAVE THE MURDERERS WALKING FREE, FUCKING GIVING EACH OTHER AWARDS FOR FUCK'S SAKE? That is where we live, every second of every day.

And in another text ten minutes later:

> It's not just some "story," not to us. It's real. It is ongoing: the hate, the threats, the persecution, the risk to loved ones. Real. My "rapist" isn't safely behind bars. My loved ones can be murdered AGAIN—tonite, tomorrow, next week…you cannot possibly understand that, and good that you cannot. It is a horror.

Perhaps the officials had lied about killing the animals to hurt Jim Tait and Kenny Thomason. This was a tactic I'd heard about—one designed to torture the zoophile, perhaps conveyed in the interview room of a police station along with graphic details of the animal's death, such as "She didn't go down easy."

In researching this book, I discovered that it's not unusual for animals to be killed by the authorities once they are discovered to have had sexual encounters with human beings. Cross-species sexual contact is considered an offense to human dignity, and many people believe that the animals involved should be snuffed out to restore proper order and decorum to humanity. Some also fear that the animals who've had these experiences with people will start raping human beings.

This practice of taking animals' lives raises many questions. Why is society's revulsion with zoo behavior so intense that people want to destroy their animals? Is it not fundamentally wrong to kill these beings who are caught in the middle? If we call ourselves animal lovers, how can rescuers justify ending their lives? There's something 'scorched earth' about this perspective. It's as if we loathe zoophiles so much that we need to burn down their world. People are afraid of them, creeped out by who they are and what they do. And they fear zoos have contaminated and corrupted their animals, too.

As far as I know, there are no statistics on how many animals have been killed in cases where sexual contact with human beings is suspected or known. But what happens to zoos' animals is common knowledge in the zoo community.

It isn't just the authorities who might pose a life-threatening danger to the animals belonging to zoos—even family members might react violently once the secret is revealed. One British writer I interviewed by phone told me about something that happened around 1970 in Brazil, an incident that involved a family he knew of through a mutual friend. He didn't want to be named, because he was concerned that if they saw this book with his name in it, they would know their confidence had been broken.

The family's teenage daughter, who was about eighteen years old at the time, would always get up and excuse herself from the table right after lunch, the main meal of the day in Brazil, an occasion attended by all family members whenever possible. The family dog, an Alsatian, would follow the girl to her bedroom, and she would lock the door behind them. Her father began to suspect something was odd about her behavior.

"One day he tampered with the lock to make it appear as if the door was locked when in fact it wasn't," the writer from London said, adding the father waited a few minutes before he walked in and caught his daughter having sex with the dog. "He immediately killed the dog

(I think he got his gun and shot it) and said he would deal with her when he got home that evening."

The girl convinced her mother to let her take a nap. But instead of sleeping, she jumped from her bedroom window of the apartment, several storeys high, and died when she hit the ground. Did the teenager take her own life because of her shame at being caught by her father while engaging in zoophilia? Or was it heartbreak over the traumatic loss of her dog and lover?

Society's negative feelings about the animals belonging to zoos caused Spink to worry incessantly. He had good reason. During his time living in Custer, he was horrified and heartbroken when he came home one day and found that someone had broken into his home and beaten one of his dogs to death. Bafana was the most protective of his dogs, a Boerboel imported from South Africa, a rare breed of canine used to guard livestock and hardly ever found in North America.

Spink blamed Corinne Super for Bafana's death. He couldn't prove she was involved, but he believed strongly that she was wrapped up in the killing because of their volatile battle over Capone, although he readily admitted to me that he'd had many threats of death and injury from numerous parties over the years.

Spink tried to help Jim Tait because he thought Tait wasn't being treated fairly by the justice system. He let those feelings of dissatisfaction be known to Michelle VanDeRee, the Maury County assistant public defender assigned to Tait's case. Here's a portion of his letter of complaint to her on November 12, 2009:

> Mr. Tait has also informed me that he, personally, has no documentation from you or anyone else relating to his case, the charges under which he is being held, or anything else. Apparently, in the sole meeting you've ever had with him—several weeks ago— you flashed a copy of several "warrants" at him but refused to give him copies of same. He sits in jail with no reliable explanation for why he is being imprisoned.
> Either behave as a professional and an officer of this court, or expect to face any and all sanctions appropriate for such failures—both with the judge (if there even is a judge) in this

current case, and with your state Bar association. I don't have time to play games with you—Mr. Tait rots in jail while you dither, and his possessions and nonhuman companions are scattered to the winds. If you think I speak lightly in promising to ensure you are held accountable for your failures as an officer of this court, I suggest you find a few minutes in your busy schedule to validate that assumption on your part.

Spink's impassioned advocacy would come back to haunt him. It wouldn't be long before the authorities, infuriated that one zoophile was trying to help another, came calling on Spink himself. But even later, after all that happened, he unapologetically stood by his actions. "I got sent to prison for helping an American who was illegally sent to prison," he said. "I interfered with their program because I was asking questions."

Meanwhile, Tait continued to reach out to Spink, sending letters and placing collect phone calls from jail. Being separated from his animals was taking a heavy toll.

Nov. 23, 2009

This whole mess is tearing me apart, day after day. Every day, I think of what they've done to all of the animals, it sends me into deep emotional pain. All they ever did was to be our friends— to connect with us and bond—for that, they received death! I just wish this would all just stop, to go away, leave us in peace— instead, they inflict suffering.

With a very heavy heart,
Jim

> groups — and that's the only time I can attempt such calls.
>
> I hope we can get the fuck out of this crazy shithole — as we're both losing a lot of weight and if I don't get to the right kind of dentist soon — I'm going to lose most of my back teeth [the dentist the county has contracted doesn't fix just pull]. They had to put Kenny in a isolation/suicide watch cell because of the harassment we're getting; IE: "hey horse fucker" and the silly horse noises.
>
> All we're hoping for right now, is that this gets handled quietly — as we're told the trial is supposed to be a party of media and protesters.

Excerpt from one of Jim Tait's letters to Doug Spink.

BESTIALITY BUSTING

Tennessee authorities never revealed publicly how they found out Jim Tait had been living quietly in their midst. But *Zoo*, a docudrama film about Kenneth Pinyan's death, might contain a clue.

After Pinyan died in 2005, the horses on the farm he'd visited were taken in by Hope for Horses, a Washington State organization run by Jenny Edwards. She and her husband John Edwards appeared in the *Zoo* movie.

Hope for Horses' reputation wasn't pristine in Washington State—not everyone was a fan of Edwards' rescue efforts. One woman I interviewed (who didn't want to be named for fear of reprisals) had rented out stall space for horses in the care of Edwards and her organization. She said Jenny's husband, John, brandished sticks at the young stallions, causing them to cower into the corners of their stalls. She said Hope for Horses didn't give the animals in their care enough bedding, even though there were pallets of donated material on site to pull from. They didn't put enough time into caring for the horses either, the woman said, so eventually she asked the organization to leave her facility.

Another person made her concerns more publicly known in a speech to Pierce County Council on December 9, 2008: Linda Hagerman, an equine veterinarian and owner of Tacoma Equine Hospital. The case Hagerman referenced in her presentation involved the seizure of fifteen neglected horses from a farm on Waller Road in Summit, Washington. From December 2007 through January 2008, Hope for Horses removed the animals from the farm.

> There are many people who are dismayed and angry about the role Hope for Horses plays in the Pierce County Animal Control department, including myself. I saw for myself the neglect that the two horses I initially cared for suffered through while in Miss Edwards' care. Their medical needs were ignored, and they were not fed enough food. No matter what good intentions Miss Edwards has or spouts, the results are not seen. She is not a good choice as a rescue provider, and her overbearing role with the county needs to be stopped. As outlined in my letter, her participation in Pierce County Animal Control brings up issues of wasteful spending, conflict of interest, and the competitive bid process.

Jenny Edwards' connection to Pinyan and her appearance in *Zoo* did not end her interest in animals suspected of having sex with humans. Capitalizing on the publicity from the Pinyan case, she founded a company called Chandler Edwards. According to the company's website (chandleredwards.org), "Chandler Edwards was formed after a complicated and high profile bestiality case in 2005, that led to the realization of just how little we understood human sexual attraction to animals, or its impact on our communities."

The mission of the nonprofit corporation, which billed itself as "the only organization of its kind," was to track down—out—and bust the zoos. Edwards planned to inform law enforcement about zoophiles in their jurisdictions in an attempt to put an end to cross-species sexual contact. "The Chandler Edwards investigative team is experienced in discovering bestiality cases before the offender is caught, assistance during the investigative and arrest phase, and expert witness testimony," stated the website, which at the time of this writing was redirecting to mjennyedwards.com. The site also outlined its writer's impressions of bestiality.

> Bestiality (sometimes incorrectly referred to as zoophilia) is the intentional sexual conduct or contact between a human and an animal. Penetration may or may not occur. Semen emission may or may not occur. Physical injury may or may not occur.

What's important is the sexual motivation or intent of the human toward the animal and how the act is defined by the jurisdiction in which it occurs.

According to a database of registered Tennessee corporations, Chandler Edwards was incorporated on May 23, 2011, and became "inactive-dissolved as of August 9, 2012." But the organization's website alluded to an earlier year—2009—as the date of inception: "Since 2009, we have trained hundreds of enforcement officers, prosecutors, veterinarians, and social workers on how to spot signs of sexual abuse in animals, and how to get the help they need to successfully manage a case." The website added ominously: "Some involve people you know and would never suspect."

Jenny Edwards formed her bestiality-busting organization with Terry Chandler, a detective sergeant from Tennessee who worked for the Maury County Sheriff's Department from 2001 until 2013. That's the same Tennessee county where Jim Tait was arrested in October 2009. Did Edwards tip Chandler off to a suspected zoophile living in his county? Or did Chandler get in touch with Edwards when he figured out her connection to Tait? Was this an instance of Chandler Edwards "discovering bestiality cases before the offender is caught"?

Chandler sparked trouble for Doug Spink with US Probation. He contacted Spink's new probation officer, Jeff Robson, in Washington State to let him know Spink was trying to help Tait in Tennessee, something Robson confirmed in federal court on June 14, 2010, following the raid on Spink's property. Robson was being questioned by Assistant US District Attorney Steven Masada:

> **Masada**: Now, how did your investigation with Mr. Spink begin?
> **Robson**: Initially, I received a call from Detective Terry Chandler in Maury County, Tennessee. Detective Chandler informed me that Mr. Spink was calling the jail incessantly and bugging his staff, and he was also supposedly calling the public defender's office, and they were interested in filing a no-contact order, he was calling that much.

It should be noted that Spink could not have called the jail. People can't call prisoners in jail; prisoners can only call out.

Robson also wrote a memo to Judge Ricardo Martinez about Terry Chandler's involvement in Spink's case. Martinez had been the judge for Spink's drug case and continued to be the judge assigned to Spink for the duration of his interactions with the federal government. Robson's memo, headed "Violations," stated:

> On or about December 1, 2009, the U.S. Probation Office was contacted by Detective Terry Chandler with the Maury County Tennessee Sheriffs' Department. Detective Chandler reported during the course of an investigation of James Michael Tate for bestiality charges, it was discovered that Mr. Spink was associating with Mr. Tate and was on federal supervision in the Western District of Washington. According to Detective Chandler, numerous phone conversations were recorded between Mr. Tate and Mr. Spink discussing their activities involving bestiality.

James Tait's case became a catalyst. It inspired law enforcement to shut Doug Spink down for good. In the eyes of the authorities, he was a dangerous deviant who protected others who were into the same perverse activities, and they weren't about to let that go unaddressed. Government attorneys worded it this way: "Once alerted to Spink's conduct, the Probation Office made a series of startling discoveries regarding this seemingly compliant supervisee, which culminated in his arrest on April 14, 2010."

32

MORNING WOOD

Spink was sound asleep in his cabin at seven o'clock in the morning on April 14, 2010, when police from several agencies began to gather in a conference room at the Whatcom County Sheriff's Office to discuss the surprise invasion of his home.

Attending the meeting were federal personnel from the SWAT team, FBI, US Marshals Service and US Probation and Pretrial Services. Local officers from the Whatcom County Sheriff's Office and Whatcom Humane Society were there too. About thirty people in total were getting ready to take down the bizarre man living atop Reese Hill.

Freedom of Information requests reveal that the raid was originally supposed to go down April 7. But just as the April 6 business day was winding down, the plan mysteriously changed to a week later, on April 14.

The reason for the date change may not be publicly known, but the reason the authorities decided to raid Spink wasn't a secret. Later, in court, federal government attorneys would speak openly about it.

> Mr. Spink had done a pretty good job of staying below the radar for several years, and it wasn't until the last few months, when Agent Robson got this case and heard from Tennessee that he

wasn't behaving well, that Mr. Spink was engaged in calling jails and talking to people who have been charged with crimes and people who have convictions, that there was really more scrutiny of Mr. Spink.

Jeff Robson, who had never visited or called Spink since becoming his probation officer one year earlier, emailed other law enforcement personnel in preparation for the April 14 meeting, suggesting they carpool from Tukwila. He included notes on his impressions of Doug Spink. They didn't paint a flattering portrait.

> SAFETY ISSUES
> - Mr. Spink has 6+ large aggressive trained dogs.
> - He is extremely intelligent and paranoid.
> - He has a history of mental health issues: paranoia, suicidal, very unstable, OCD, and Asperger (form of autism where to struggle socially and lack empathy).
> - In a recorded jail phone conversation, Mr. Spink stated, "he was preparing for Law Enforcement to kick down his door."
> - Preparing could mean being armed and or setting traps.

In Bellingham, Laura Clark wasn't yet a year into her new position as executive director of the Whatcom Humane Society when her organization's officers were called upon to participate in the raid. WHS was the local agency with jurisdiction over matters of animal welfare in that community.

Clark testified about what happened that morning during the civil hearing that took place in a Whatcom County courtroom later that summer. Questioned by Spink's lawyer, Tom Seguine, on June 16, she stated that the FBI had been in contact with WHS for some time before the raid.

> **Seguine**: Do you remember when you first received a phone call from Mr. [Paul] Evans [WHS lead animal control officer] about what was going on out there?
> **Clark**: I had been in contact with Mr. Evans starting at approximately 7:00 a.m. the morning of April 14th when law enforcement agencies from both federal and state originations met at the sheriff's office that morning.
> **Seguine**: When you say you were aware of the case, what do you mean?
> **Clark**: Well, Officer Evans had been in contact with federal agents for weeks, um, before April 14th.
> **Seguine**: Uh-huh.

Clark: And we were aware that our role was to stand by and provide care for the animals, if necessary, once Mr. Spink was taken into custody.

Seguine also questioned Paul Evans about the assistance British tourist Stephen Clarke gave to the police after Spink was taken to prison by US marshals.

Seguine: And tell us what happened if you will, please.
Evans: We were able to secure two, three of the dogs.
Seguine: How?
Evans: With the leashes. We actually had leashes on us as well. Um, there was somebody who was down by the residence who was able to secure one of the German Shepherds.
Seguine: Okay.
Evans: I don't know who it was. And, then, the other dogs were secured by Mr. Clarke.
Seguine: How so, if you remember?
Evans: Just he used some of our leashes and got permission from one of the federal agents to secure the animals in the Suburban that was on the property.

The decision to take Spink's animals, it seemed, was made by the Whatcom Humane Society. Whatcom County Deputy Steve Roff—the officer who'd been in charge of the Capone custody case in 2008, when the stallion went missing from Spink's barn in Custer—was among the large group that conducted the raid. In a detail that Seguine would home in on during the civil proceeding, Roff noted in his report of April 16, 2010, that "the Whatcom County Sheriff's Office did not request the Humane Society to seize any animals."

⌒

It was approximately ten o'clock that morning when police swooped in and pounded on the door of the cabin. Spink was naked when he answered it. He had an erection, a detail noted by police—and later, prosecutors. The erection, they implied, was proof of wrongdoing, and used in an attempt to pressure him into a plea deal. "They said, 'If you don't plead guilty, we're going to examine your penis. We're going to bring up your erection,'" Spink recalled.

Howard Phillips, Spink's lawyer for the federal hearing on alleged probation violations, argued in a pre-hearing memorandum on June 10, 2010, that prosecutors should not be allowed to enter into evidence that Spink was naked at the time of the raid.

> Law enforcement agents reported that when they executed the warrant for Mr. Spink's arrest, that he was unclothed, 'naked'. There is a perfectly innocuous reason for one who sleeps without clothes to be naked when law enforcement unexpectedly executes an arrest warrant. Given the nature of the allegation of animal abuse, and the videos of Mr. Clarke being partially naked while engaging in sexual activity with dogs, any testimony that Mr. Spink was naked at the time the agents arrived gives rise to undue and unfair speculation that he was somehow engaged in sexual activity as was Clarke. This testimony is irrelevant, and unduly prejudicial, therefore should be excluded.

But the government pushed back, arguing in response to the defendant's memorandum that the naked detail should be kept in play: "Spink reportedly has a distinctive piercing, observed by arresting agents only because he was naked. The Government reserves the right to offer such evidence if it proves necessary at the hearing."

The plea deal Spink was offered by Assistant US Attorney Susan Roe was one year in prison, in exchange for which he would plead guilty and agree to identify other zoophiles. He would also be required to relinquish his animals to the Whatcom Humane Society, which would be authorized to decide their fates, possibly including death sentences if that was deemed appropriate by WHS. If he didn't accept the deal, Roe warned, she would ask the judge for five years, the longest sentence that could be imposed for probation revocation.

Most people would likely cave under such intense pressure, no matter how much they love their animals. Freedom is cherished.

Not Spink. He sent his lawyer, Howard Phillips, back to Roe with a curt response.

"Go fuck yourself."

⌒

Spink's refusal to barter with his animals—to exchange their lives for his own freedom—triggered two legal proceedings: a federal hearing in Seattle to determine the fate of Doug Spink, and a civil proceeding in Whatcom County to determine the fate of Spink's horses and dogs. Would the animals go back to Spink? Or become wards of WHS to be adopted out to others? Or possibly to be killed if that was deemed appropriate?

As I tracked the aftermath of the raid, interviewing anyone willing to talk, I was growing increasingly concerned that the animals might not make it out alive. That worry was exacerbated by an informal meeting I had with Whatcom County Sheriff Bill Elfo, the highest ranking local law enforcement officer in Whatcom County, and a big supporter of the Whatcom Humane Society. While the two of us talked in his office, I expressed my fears that Spink's dogs might be killed. He looked at me across his desk for a moment before he responded: Didn't they have to be killed? What if they went around raping people?

That wasn't possible, I replied. Animals couldn't restrain people to rape them even if they wanted to.

Still, his concerns haunted my thoughts. He was clearly not the only person in the community who felt this way. I began to realize there was a real and present danger facing these animals. It was upsetting to imagine killings that would be classified as rescues.

Doug's mother, Claire Spink, was also concerned about what was going to happen to her son and his animals. She stepped in to help the moment she heard about the raid. She didn't have a computer, so she wrote letters in longhand, going to an office supply store in her community to fax them to anyone she could find who might help: lawyers, probation officers, police officers, prison officials. She wrote to Laura Clark too. Smart, persistent and tough, Claire fought hard in an effort to help her son.

The Whatcom Humane Society, not wanting to make custody decisions that could result in expensive litigation later on, asked the federal government for guidance on the matter of ownership. Susan Roe suggested that WHS attorneys file an interpleader in Whatcom County civil court. An interpleader is a procedure designed to compel two or more parties to litigate an outstanding dispute. The parties included in the suit would be Doug Spink and WHS, as well as Corinne Super, who was still trying to gain ownership of Capone, and local horse breeder Charla Wilder, who had sold one of her Percheron draft horses to Spink.

The battle was on. Spink was determined to get his animals back, and the Whatcom Humane Society was just as determined to stop him.

33

VASELINE MICE

Of all the information presented by the media about Doug Spink after the raid, by far the most damaging and lewd factoid was the alleged presence of Vaseline-slathered mice at his home. The idea of depraved sex acts being performed with mice stuck in people's minds as one of the vilest things they'd ever heard.

There was just one hitch. The story of the mice appeared to be a fabrication spun by authorities, conjured up by the imagination of what people imagined a bestiality farm to be.

I spent a lot of time researching the mice and what might have happened to them, but there are still unknowns.

I did find out it wasn't Vaseline slathered on the mice. Vaseline is odorless. According to shelter workers, the substance on the mice and at least two of the dogs when they arrived smelled strongly of petroleum.

When I asked Spink by text why the animals had landed at the shelter that way, he became enraged. "Are you telling me Laura and her thugs SMEARED OIL ON OUR DOGS TO MAKE THEIR BULLSHIT LIES SEEM MORE CREDIBLE? God this nightmare just gets darker and darker."

Spink showed me hundreds of photos taken up until a couple of days before the raid that showed the dogs and horses hanging around the

Reese Hill Road property. They had no substances on them that I could see.

I asked Spink repeatedly about the mice—how and why he was keeping them. He said mice gravitated to his cabin to pilfer the food he kept there for the horses and dogs. He placed two humane box traps under the cabin to capture them. His German Shepherd, Wiskey, also liked to catch the mice. He was surprisingly gentle when he played with them, often carrying them in his mouth through the dog door into the cabin, but sometimes they got injured.

Spink needed a safe place to keep the mice between trips to release them, so he bought a cage complete with an exercise wheel. First he went to Petco, but the cages they carried were too big for his desk. Fred Meyer had a cage that was more suitable for his space, so he bought it. He would collect about a dozen mice in it at a time, then drive them down to the fields in the valley below his property for release.

"Having the mice in the little habitat on the desk was soothing to me," he said. "I like them. They're fascinating, really. Quick and clever and quiet and social and intense, in their own ways."

He had learned that if a mouse had even minor injuries, the others would attack the injured one. He had an aversion to putting them in solitary confinement because of his own prison experiences, so he used small cords to secure an occasional hurt mouse.

"I did use cords on their tails to keep the lightly-injured ones out of 'general population' until release," Spink wrote to me. "The other option was more cages, and solitary confinement—I really don't like that, personally, for obvious reasons. It seemed more 'humane' to keep them with me, on the desk or on the bookshelf, than have them in a jar or tiny little cage alone."

Spink recalled the mice that were in his cabin at the time of the raid.

> One had a slightly shortened tail—he was the one on the desk, in the t-shirt nest, with a little cord wrapped around his tail. That was tied to my computer monitor, and he slept there at night. During the day he was on the desk when I was working, and could hang out. He'd actually sit on my hand, sometimes, while I was talking on the phone or whatever. Not exactly "tame"—these are field mice, after all, but not freaked out. I learned the hard way that even with a minor injury like the tail, if he was in with the other guys they'd tear into him.

I'd say, total guess, I remember a dozen mice in the cage. And one on the desk/bookshelf with me. Two? Could have been two out of general population, just not sure. But I think one. I know at least one. Obviously they weren't unhappy with being out of GP—they could chew through the cord trivially easily—it was just thread, basically. Scavenged from an old rock climbing setup, or some camera lanyard, or something like that. Thin, fragile stuff. A mouse can chew through plastic and wood and even metal if given the time. These tiny little strings? Give him 5 minutes and he could be gone. So, I dunno, the fact that they stayed with me for a few days, before going down with the rest of them for release—I'd carry them in my hand, or in the pocket of my shirt—seemed to suggest to me they were ok with things.

Spink's solution for the injured mice only stoked public speculation about a bestiality farm. A cord tied to a mouse's tail, not to mention reports of Vaseline-coated mice, led police and the media to suggest perverted activities. Curiously, even though the media highlighted the Vaseline-slathered mice frequently (one article even claimed the mice were shaved), no photographs of the rodents were presented as evidence against Spink in either federal or civil court proceedings in 2010.

Spink wasn't surprised that the Normals, as he called those who didn't share his sexual attraction to animals, would automatically classify all cross-species sex as the product of a bestiality farm. He believed Normals couldn't fathom the idea of humans and animals connecting for what he considered to be loving relationships. Instead, he said, the go-to explanation for Normals was to believe his home was a for-profit commercial endeavor that catered to people seeking deviant sex acts.

∩

Laura Clark, executive director of the Whatcom Humane Society, had her own ideas about what was going on with the rodents up at Spink's place. She spelled them out during the Whatcom County interpleader proceeding on June 16, 2010, while being questioned by WHS attorney Larry Daugert.

> **Daugert**: "Do you have any experience in what mice covered with petroleum jelly are used for?"
> **Clark**: "I do."
> **Daugert**: "What is that?"

Clark: "It's a common practice in the bestiality community that mice and small rodents are used for what the slang expression is called felching and felching is when a subject will take a small animal, um, lubricate it, tie something to its tail and inject it into their rectum. The string or twine is used to remove the animal."

If Clark had experience with rodents being inserted into people's orifices, it would have been interesting to learn what those experiences were. Not a single medical case of the activity she described, also known as gerbiling, has ever been recorded. Not one incident, despite repeated and dogged attempts by many—including tabloid writers—to validate the existence of the outlandish sexual practice. Surely at least one medical report would exist if this practice really did. The consequences to humans would be inevitable and catastrophic.

A simple Google search reveals that the practice of gerbiling likely doesn't exist, and if it does, it is extremely rare. It has been debunked by the myth-busting, oft-quoted website Snopes.com:

> Contrary to widespread public belief, "gerbil-stuffing" is unknown as an actual sexual practice, nor are we aware of a verified medical case of a gerbil having been extracted from a patient's rectum. Despite the assiduousness with which doctors record unusual items removed from patients' rectums in order to write them up as illustrative cases, we haven't yet found a medical journal article involving a gerbil removal.
>
> The notion of gerbiling (not necessarily restricted to homosexuals—the insertion of items into the rectum for purposes of autoeroticism is practiced by heterosexuals as well) appears to be pure invention, a tale fabricated to demonstrate the depravity with which 'faggots' allegedly pursue sexual pleasure."

The *Encyclopedia of Urban Legends* by Jan Harold Brunvand voices similar opinions: "Misinformation is rife in the accounts of gerbiling. Not only is there the usual vagueness about hospital treatment of the supposed perpetrators; some writers have implied that published medical records support the claim that gerbiling is an actual practice. Searches of medical databases have found no such reports."

Wikipedia weighs in with its own categorical dismissal: "This is simply an unverified and persistent urban legend that is pure fiction."

Spink told me he has loved mice ever since he was a small child. In one of the childhood photographs that his mother, Claire Spink, sent me as background for this book, a young Doug smiles with delight as a white mouse with black spots rests on his arm.

For years, Spink became upset every time I mentioned the mice. He never stopped being angry that they were destroyed by WHS staff the morning after the raid.

"They killed all those field mice," he said. "That's as concise a descriptor of those hate-engorged monsters as anything I could ever say. What a horror. They disgust me more than words convey. At least factory farm killers are honest about their destructive choices; to hide murder behind a fetid patina of sanctimonious crap is doubly evil."

∩

If the lack of a single case of gerbiling on record isn't enough to exonerate Spink of accusations about the mice, the polygraph exam performed on Stephen Clarke further supports Spink's claim that he was doing nothing nefarious with the rodents.

Clarke, the British visitor who helped authorities round up Spink's animals during the raid, was arrested and charged with animal cruelty. He took the polygraph on May 5, 2010, as a condition of his plea bargain with prosecutors. This exam was preceded by a proffer on April 29. (A proffer is an interview with police to go over the material to be covered during a polygraph.) Clarke's statements during the proffer are consistent with Spink's.

> Clarke was surprised that Spink had mice. On the second day he was there, he noticed mice on Spink's desk. Spink said he had caught them in the hay and didn't want to release them. Clarke didn't ask further about the mice, because he's not interested in mice.
>
> The day before the raid, Clarke was awoken by a dog. One of the mice was hanging from the edge of the table by the tail. He had a look—its tail was attached to cord connected to cloth loop, in turn connected to a table mat. He lifted the mouse up and put it back in middle of table. He later asked 'Fausty' why the mouse was tied up. Spink said the mouse was ill and it was separated from other mice because they would attack it. The mouse seemed fine, but know nothing about mice. Didn't see any other mice with ties on tail. No knowledge of using mice for anal penetration.

The mice were covered again in Stephen Clarke's polygraph exam. "No deception indicated," the examiner noted on the report.

> Clarke stated he noticed some mice in a cage on the second day of his visit and Spink told him he had caught the mice in the hay and did not want to release them. Clarke said one of the mice was tied by its tail, and Spink said he was keeping it away from the others for it was sick. Clarke reported he did not have any sexual contact with the mice.

Clarke's proffer also covered whether Spink was operating a commercial enterprise. "Clarke did not pay for services," the examiner wrote. "He brought treats for dogs, but that's it. Spink never asked for compensation."

In the end, it didn't matter whether the idea of the commercial bestiality farm—complete with lubricated mice—was truth or fiction. The factoids were simply accepted as facts, adding fuel to the fires of hatred that intensified into a roar against Spink. His reputation was blackened, the life he had built for himself and his four-legged family summarily reduced to ashes.

To read a more detailed description emailed to me by Doug Spink about what he was doing with the mice, see Exhibit 8, page 385.

34

CAUSE CÉLÈBRE

Spink believed he was being persecuted and prosecuted because of who he was, not because of what he'd been caught doing. He had expressed remorse for his involvement in the drug business, but refused to apologize for his beliefs about animals. He felt he was in the right, and began calling himself a political prisoner after he was incarcerated the second time. "I've done time with terrorists and they haven't been treated like this," he complained to me.

Stephen Clarke, for example, videotaped himself committing sexual acts with dogs. He got thirty days in county jail. Spink wasn't shown on the tape, yet in the end he was punished much more severely, given three years in federal prison and two years of probation, seemingly because he wouldn't repent and admit wrongdoing.

I would come to find that the truth of what was going on at Spink's place—in my opinion—was more surprising than the societal aberration of a bestiality farm. The property in question was Spink's home, not a bestiality business. And his lifestyle was being lived by many other people around the world, just not as openly as Spink, who proudly called himself the "uppity zoo." He refused to apologize for his sexual attraction to animals. But he was unusual; the community of people drawn to develop physical connections with animals not of their own species is mostly underground. While zoos number nowhere near a majority, I was learning that their existence isn't rare, either.

Spink's philosophy was this: if his dogs wanted to have sex with someone, they should be allowed to. It wasn't his business to stop it. In the case of Stephen Clarke, the human was the receptive partner, which Spink believed made his own role pretty clear-cut. "I do not exercise choices over the nonhumans in my life unless there is a legitimate reason," he said.

∩

Animal cruelty is a state crime, not a federal one. But Spink wasn't charged with animal cruelty; he was charged with federal probation violations. Technically, he could face punishment at both the state and federal levels. He didn't even have to be convicted at the state level to be punished federally—it could be decided by a preponderance of evidence that he'd breached probation by committing a crime, which required him to adhere to all laws in all jurisdictions.

But animal welfare advocates were still outraged. A probation violation wasn't the same as a criminal charge, and they believed it was important to get an animal cruelty charge on Spink's record.

The same week as the civil hearing in Whatcom to determine who would get custody of Spink's animals, Whatcom County prosecuting attorney David McEachran sent out form letters to disgruntled animal welfare advocates to explain why he wasn't charging Spink with animal cruelty.

> Mr. Spink had his probation hearing in federal court this week and was found to have broken the terms of his probation by being involved in bestiality. He is facing a sentence of up to five years in federal prison. He will be sentenced in mid-July. If he receives a sentence from federal court I will not be prosecuting him in Whatcom County, for the same offense. The penalty we can achieve here would be minimal compared to the federal penalty above-mentioned.

McEachran added that "we do not have the resources to repetitively prosecute people for the same crimes that they have been held responsible for in different jurisdictions."

In a surprising twist, Spink told me that he *wanted* to be charged with animal cruelty. He wanted to fight the charge rather than have the implication hovering over him unresolved during his probation violation hearing. The burden of proof in that type of hearing is lower than what's required to convict in a criminal trial, and having a jury isn't an option. A federal judge needs only to be convinced by the preponderance of evidence, not beyond a reasonable doubt. The rules of evidence are also more relaxed. If Spink could be cleared of animal cruelty in the more exacting state court, he thought, it would be harder for the probation department to find him in violation based on the same offense.

He was also wary of the three-year statute of limitations looming ahead for the potential animal cruelty charge. If McEachran changed his mind later on and decided to pursue charges, Spink could conceivably be punished a second time for the same offense after serving his federal time. That remote possibility would later become a frustrating reality.

Spink had bigger goals too. He was outspoken about wanting to overturn the Washington state law that banned humans from having sex with animals, on the grounds that it discriminated against him because of his sexual orientation, and that it was unconstitutional.

Spink had studied the success of other movements—civil rights, women's rights, gay rights—to devise a strategy that might eventually improve life for zoos. He refused to back down or be ashamed. "I've broken the spell," he said, referring to his refusal to give up and show contrition even after his cabin was raided, his probation revoked, and his animals seized. "The dynamic has changed. Until you break the spell and stand up for our community, nobody's going to listen."

Spink thought that *Lawrence v. Texas*, a US Supreme Court case that resulted in a landmark 2003 decision, could be applied to protect zoos. The decision, which affirmed American citizens' rights to privacy, essentially made same-gender sex acts legal in every US state and territory, superseding antiquated anti-gay laws that had languished on the books in some states. The ruling asserted people's right to do what they wanted behind closed doors, the argument being that to make it illegal for people to have sex with the same gender intrudes into the bedrooms of consenting adults.

Spink's unrepentant attitude accelerated his unpopularity with authority figures, said his lawyer, Jim Turner. "They knew Doug was looking for a cause célèbre."

I asked Turner if his client's fight was winnable.

"Not now," he replied. "It's all politics. It's the argument that a lot of groups have struggled hard to get some semblance of equality in our society and they would really resent it. They would go out and scream bloody murder. They would say how dare you equate us to that."

JUDGMENT DAY

The day had arrived for the civil proceeding to begin in Whatcom County to determine the fate of Doug Spink's animals. The gallery of the modest Bellingham courtroom was filled to capacity with interested parties and curious spectators. This unusual man's story had rocked the small community's sensibilities, and onlookers spilled over into the standing room behind and beside the courtroom seats.

The hearing, presided over by Whatcom County Superior Court Judge Ira Uhrig, took place over three days: June 11, 16 and 18.

At the same time as the civil case was progressing through the system, Spink's probation violation case was moving through federal court. Spink couldn't be in Whatcom County for the civil hearing because he was still in FDC SeaTac, where he'd been held without bail since the raid on his cabin.

Laura Clark, from the Whatcom Humane Society, and Jenny Edwards, of Hope for Horses, showed up in court. They attended all of the hearings that involved Spink in Whatcom and Seattle. Both inside and outside the courtrooms, they always sat together.

Whatcom County Sheriff Bill Elfo stopped by the Bellingham courtroom from time to time, always taking a seat beside me. He'd ask for an update on what he had missed, and I'd fill him in on the latest details.

Attorney Larry Daugert, from the Bellingham law firm Barron Smith Daugert, represented the Whatcom Humane Society. Mount Vernon lawyer Tom Seguine appeared on behalf of Exitpoint Stallions Limitée, the corporation managed and partly owned by Spink.

Seguine didn't have an easy job ahead of him. He was defending the rights of an unpopular man.

∩

The first day of the Whatcom County hearing focused on two of Spink's horses, Little Joe and Capone. Local Percheron breeder Charla Wilder was quickly awarded custody of Little Joe, a horse she had sold to Spink, because no one contested her claim.

Next came Corinne Super, represented by Bellingham animal rights attorney Adam Karp. She and Spink had been battling over Capone since 2007, when Spink was released from federal prison, and she still held Capone's equine passport.

Judge Uhrig made his decision about the most valuable of Spink's animals before the rest of the hearing got underway. The Whatcom Humane Society didn't oppose Super taking Capone. The judge deferred to the pending case in BC Supreme Court to decide who should ultimately have custody of Capone, and awarded the stallion to Super in the interim.

After the first two horses were dealt with, the hearing finished for the day. It picked up again five days later, on June 16, to decide the fates of the other two horses and seven dogs.

At the outset of day two, Judge Uhrig made it clear that he had reservations about the animals ever going back to Exitpoint's care and control. He referred to the Bible, specifically the book of Leviticus, which contains passages about humans having sex with animals, translated as: "Do not have sexual relations with an animal and defile yourself with it."

> Could some other responsible person be found that has no connection whatsoever to ESL [Exitpoint Stallions Limitée] or anyone involved with ESL. Because the very connection with ESL would, I think, cause any reasonable person to have some concern, even though there may not be specific evidence of abuse of these particular horses, there is still an abiding concern that I think any reasonable person would have. I am not making any findings here. But, the mere allegations in the criminal case that was resolved by way of a guilty plea, I believe a while back, um, that I think causes concerns and you can find those concerns articulated back in the book of Leviticus and prior.

The guilty plea Uhrig referred to was Stephen Clarke's, on animal cruelty charges. Uhrig lamented the lack of criminal charges being pressed against Spink. "The legal issues at hand would, frankly, be much more easily resolved had criminal charges been filed. I do not know if criminal charges will be filed. That's not my concern right now, because I have to deal with the situation as it is presented, not how it could have been presented."

The second day of the hearing focused largely on whether Spink had been running a commercial bestiality farm, as the media had called it.

Accustomed to being hated for being a zoo, Spink had long since taken precautions to protect his family from being removed from him. One such provision was to have his animals become assets of his corporation, Exitpoint Stallions Limitée. Spink was officer, chairman and shareholder of the British Columbia corporation, which registered to do business in Washington State also on February 19, 2010. Spink thought the corporate structure would provide an extra layer of protection. On the contrary, the fact that the dogs and horses were owned by his corporation worked against him. It only furthered the perception that his home was a commercial enterprise designed for sex tourism.

Seguine, representing Spink, called to the stand John Livingston, a Bellingham real estate lawyer. Seguine's aim was to establish that Spink's real estate contract for the property was still in place at the time of the raid. This could help reinforce his client's position that these animals were assets owned by a corporation doing business on that property.

When Spink moved into the cabin in the fall of 2008, he had made a deal to purchase the Reese Hill Road property, on behalf of Exitpoint, from the Washington company MGV Enterprises, Inc. But he got behind in payments, according to the seller. Livingston testified that he met with Spink in February 2010. He was hired by him to stave off the forfeiture, but he wasn't successful, a failure probably accelerated by the worldwide attention to the property when it was raided on April 14. Nine days later, on April 23, the seller filed a notice of intent to forfeit on the real estate contract.

Daugert, attorney for the Whatcom Humane Society, focused in on Exitpoint's ownership of the animals. He didn't mince words:

> Um, I believe that title to the animals is in Exitpoint Stallions Limitée, a British Columbia corporation doing business in the State of Washington as Exitpoint Stallions, Incorporated. That's what the testimony is. Title to these animals owned by this corporation. I believe the evidence has shown that this corporation is a criminal organization.

The most salacious moments of day two involved the videotape of British tourist Stephen Clarke having sex with Spink's dogs inside the cabin. Even though it wasn't shown in court, the existence of this inflammatory piece of evidence set a lewd tone, and created a difficult obstacle for Seguine to overcome.

The videotaped sex acts were the centerpiece of Daugert's evidence against Spink. The lawyer was not deterred by the fact that Spink's animals were found to be healthy at the time of the raid:

> The evidence will show when we took custody of these seven animals now, which I think are the subject of this debate, that they were in the main in good physical condition. I mean, we can debate minor matters, but we cannot show that these were abused animals in the sense that they were starving or lacerated or whatever. The issues that we have as to abuse will be talking sexuality with seven dogs.

Daugert asked the judge to seal the tape and the transcript of its spoken contents from public view. "Now, this videotape I am told, because I have never seen it, but I have heard from people who have, it's one of the most disgusting things that they have ever seen," Daugert told the judge. "It doesn't deserve to be seen by anybody. But it is our evidence of the abuse of the seven dogs. I don't think it should be made a public record."

The judge admitted the video recordings and transcript into evidence and obliged Daugert's request to seal both exhibits from public view. "It is described as depicting acts of sexual contact between humans and animals," said Judge Uhrig. "Or described acts of depravity and acts that, which in some cultures are even to this day punishable by death. Acts which would be deemed disagreeable and offensive by I think most any right-thinking person in our society with perhaps some exceptions that I cannot think of. So I believe there is good cause to seal the exhibit for now."

The videotape evidence, Daugert said, "is the cornerstone of why we believe these animals have been abused. Not because they haven't been fed, not because they have been whipped or beaten or something like that, but because of what happens to these dogs and the transcript."

When I interviewed Spink two years later, he had a very different opinion on what should happen with the recordings. He thought they should be uploaded to the internet to be viewed worldwide, so that people could see what had actually occurred between Stephen Clarke and Spink's dogs. Spink wasn't ashamed. He didn't think there was anything wrong with it.

"If I could get away with doing it and not go back to prison for it, I would publish it on the internet right now," he told me. "The dogs engaged in proactive behavior with him. Dogs aren't allowed to have sex with people—okay, why? Because it's bad for the dog? Fucks up his psyche or gives him bad dreams? Show me the literature. It's not about the dog. It's because it's degrading to the people. It's our issues, not his issues."

During the hearing, Daugert emphasized that Spink had filmed Stephen Clarke's actions. But Spink told me that he didn't, that Clarke had used his own tripod. The image was consistent with having been filmed with a tripod—the picture was steady and fixed in place.

Deputy Steve Roff, from the Whatcom County Sheriff's Office, also viewed the tape. He testified that an unseen male entered the cabin and commented on the dog's sexual prowess to Clarke, who was having receptive anal sex with the canine at the time. The voice commenting in the background was Spink's, said Roff. When Seguine asked how Roff knew this, the deputy (who had handled the 2008 case of Capone going missing from Spink's barn) replied, "From my past dealings with him. He has a deep voice and he is fairly well spoken."

Roff described the contents of the tape in more graphic detail in his April 16 incident report:

> Deputy Gum and I took custody of a video camera from the United States Probation Department that had been seized during their search of Spink's residence. Deputy Gum and I viewed the footage which showed Clarke engaged in sexual conduct with what appeared to be at least three different dogs. Two of the dogs resembled German Shepherds and one resembled a Great Dane.
>
> Clarke engaged in the same type of sexual conduct with each dog. The sexual conduct consisted of Clarke being on his hands and knees and having each dog mount him from behind. Clarke was not wearing any pants or underwear. Clarke would allow or assist the dog(s) with inserting their penises into his rectum and engage in sexual intercourse/mating type behavior.

During the Whatcom County proceeding, Spink's mother, Claire, was called to the witness stand. The scrappy seventy-three-year-old had traveled from Pennsylvania to testify that she'd found adoptive homes for all the animals whose custody was being decided. She didn't seem to be nervous or feel intimidated about appearing before a packed courtroom of people who were there to watch as her son was accused of something most people would find embarrassing. Her dark intelligent eyes, which I found out later were always keenly observing, flashed in defiance as she took the stand.

Her appearance did not go well. Judge Uhrig wasn't satisfied with her answers. He seemed to view her with suspicion and distrust after she answered questions about Exitpoint. "Neither she nor anyone else offered any credible evidence whatsoever as to who is in charge of the corporation, moreover her testimony is inconsistent, vague, or perhaps deliberately evasive, and as a finder of fact I do not find her to be a credible witness."

In fact, he didn't seem to be convinced by any aspect of Claire Spink's testimony. "Mrs. Spink has demonstrated throughout her testimony what I would deem to be a remarkable ability to answer only such portions of any given question as she chooses and her answers are quite frequently quite uninformative."

The most uncomfortable moment came when he confronted her with an awkward question about the sealed exhibit: "Do you want to see the video?"

"No," Claire replied.

"Would that help answer the question that you have if at some point you saw the video?"

She again refused. "I don't know why I would want to see something like that, would you?"

"I don't know either. I am just asking. It's not your place to ask me questions. I'm asking you questions."

"Sorry," she said.

After her testimony concluded, Claire was visibly upset. Her features, which sharply resembled her son's, wore an expression that was a mixture of anger, hurt and frustration. Despite her failing health, she had traveled across the country in an effort to make sure her son's animals would be safely placed into new homes she had found for them, and it wasn't looking like the judge was even going to consider her suggestions for placements.

Meeting her for the first time, I approached her in the courtroom during a break to offer my business card. I told her I was sorry for what she was going through as a mother, and let her know I wanted to tell all sides of the story. I offered to interview her if she was willing. She said she wasn't sure, but would think about it.

∩

If Stephen Clarke's actions on Spink's property weren't damning enough, the distasteful idea of mice being used for sex acts further eroded Judge Uhrig's already unfavorable impression of Spink and Exitpoint. "I do not even know whether its very name is nothing more than a crude joke based upon the activities that took place on the ESL property," Uhrig said of Exitpoint. Spink told me later the company had actually been named as a tribute to his love of BASE jumping (the jump-off spot is called the exit point).

"I understand we can all pooh-pooh mice," Daugert said, "but what did ESL do with mice? There is only one conclusion . . . one can come to with the evidence of what they did with mice. We have a new word, 'felch.'"

Seguine also addressed the issue of the mice, and questioned WHS animal control officer Paul Evans about them.

> **Seguine**: My question is did you recall Mr. Robson coming to you with an item, do you recall him coming to you with an item?
> **Evans**: An item? I—no.
> **Seguine**: Okay. So after you read that report, you are unable to refresh your recollection?
> **Evans**: Mr. Robson I believe was the probation officer that did come out of the residence with a mouse with a string tied to its tail.
> **Seguine**: Did he have any other items with him that you recall?
> **Evans**: Not that I recall.

Laura Clark testified too, telling the court that the shelter was getting as many as fifty calls a day about Spink's animals "from concerned members of the community, from animal welfare organizations, some local, some national, from US probation, from Whatcom County sheriffs, from Mrs. Spink, from people claiming to be business associates of Mr. Spink, the list goes on and on."

Clark had nothing positive to say about Spink's dogs. "When we first took custody of these animals, it became very apparent very quickly that they suffered from severe temperament issues. Those issues included acting aggressively towards our staff and volunteers, with our veterinarian and towards volunteer dog trainers that volunteer at our shelter."

The dogs wouldn't be easy to place, Clark said, if they could be placed at all. "None of the seven dogs we have, I feel, could be safely placed into homes with any type of children, any type of inexperienced dog owner, anyone not very, very experienced in dealing with animals that have been abused and traumatized." She added that she didn't know if the two German Shepherds—Wisky and Wando—could be saved because of their Schutzhund protection training.

Seguine mainly focused on whether the seizure of Spink's animals was legal in the first place, given that the Whatcom Humane Society didn't have a warrant.

> Not only did they not try to get a warrant—and I should say here, Your Honor, there is no attempt to say they didn't have the ability to get a warrant. They can't say that because the record shows that the testimony was 25 to 30 people on the site. The testimony

is that Mr. Spink surrendered immediately. The testimony was that Mr. Clarke was docile the whole time. There is no indication that he was doing anything which would have prevented anybody from trying to get a warrant.

Under chapter 16.52 of the Washington State laws pertaining to the prevention of cruelty to animals, WHS could have brought a veterinarian to the site to evaluate Exitpoint's animals before seizing them, Seguine argued.

> That veterinarian can look at the animals and make a decision about whether they need to be taken off the property. Did they have the ability to do that? There is no question, whatsoever, they had the ability to do that. Officers Evans testified they had a veterinarian on staff. I also elicited testimony that the state veterinarian—I don't know if he was immediately available, but he was within five miles probably of this site. So there was certainly an opportunity for them to follow the statute, and if they had done so, the veterinarian may well have concluded some of the things that you are being asked to accept now.
>
> But they didn't do it. And why didn't they do it? Your Honor, I think there is really two reasons; one, was the shock and awe of the situation. The—I think these people are—the folks in the Humane Society have the best of intention. They believe very deeply in what they are doing and they felt they needed to make a decision. I understand that, but so there was a certain amount of zeal involved in this.

Daugert contended that the matter of the warrant wasn't as important as getting the animals away from Exitpoint. "So my case is, ultimately, to stand with the technical argument about warrants pales to what will happen to these animals if you do not give them back to the Society."

Still, Seguine argued, Spink's property (the animals) couldn't be seized from Exitpoint without cause, because that was against the law.

> And so how is it that they can come in here, on one hand say you got to show us that you are entitled to get these animals back, but on the other hand, don't worry about section one and, by the way, don't worry about the Constitution of the United States of America, not to mention the Washington State Constitution. Just put that aside, and as soon as you do that, and as soon as you start talking about fetching or felching or whatever, oh, my God, nobody wants to look at it in an equity or some other novel theory here which nobody articulated, you are supposed to just disregard all this other stuff.

It didn't end up mattering to the court what condition Spink's animals were in, or whether he faced criminal charges from the state, or whether the animals were seized legally. Judge Uhrig decreed that the Whatcom Humane Society was granted custody of Spink's seven dogs to do with what they saw fit. Practically speaking, that could mean death for the animals if that's what the shelter staff deemed appropriate. He awarded the stallions Cantour and Sigi to Hope for Horses, Jenny Edwards' organization.

Spink thought about appealing. But faced with the prospect of losing, he ended up agreeing not to appeal if Laura Clark would promise to try to spare the lives of his dogs. "Laura agreed to try to save the dogs but she wouldn't put it in writing," he told me.

Douglas Spink's worst fears—the most dismal contents of his deepest nightmares—had come true, fully and completely.

STAR WITNESS

It was early morning on June 14, 2010, when Doug Spink and Stephen Clarke were loaded onto the same bus to be transported from SeaTac prison to the federal courthouse on Stewart Street in downtown Seattle, each man headed to attend their respective hearings. It was an awkward trip. Clarke was the linchpin of the federal case against Spink, and now here they were, sharing uncomfortably close quarters.

One hundred miles north, the Whatcom County civil court hearings were on hiatus for a few days between the first and second days of testimony.

Spink was appearing in federal court for alleged probation violations. Clarke was going there to answer to an immigration charge. On his application to get a ninety-day visa, he had lied about having criminal convictions. He had also dropped the "e" from his surname when filling out the application so his criminal record would go undetected by agents of the US Immigration and Naturalization Services. That deception constituted a federal crime.

By the time his federal hearing happened, Clarke's state charges had already been resolved. He had appeared before Whatcom County Superior Court Judge Charles Snyder on May 11, and pled guilty to animal cruelty in the first degree. Sentencing guidelines for that crime range from thirty to ninety days in jail. The office of lead prosecutor David McEachran joined Clarke's attorney in recommending the minimum. Clarke was sentenced to thirty days in the Whatcom County jail, with consideration given for time already served. He had started serving time from the date of his arrest on April 14, so he was only three days away from finishing his days in custody owed to the state. Judge Snyder also ordered Clarke to pay a fine of $1,000 to the Whatcom Humane Society.

"I just wanted to get rid of him," the *Bellingham Herald* quoted McEachran as saying in a story headlined, "Video shows man sexually abusing dogs," from May 12, 2010. "I didn't want to clog up our jail with this guy. This is a problem that is born of another country."

After completing his sentence in Whatcom County, Clarke was transferred into federal custody. On May 14, he was charged by the U.S. Attorney's Office in Seattle with falsifying his visa application.

∩

The man known as Stephen Clarke was born Stephen Barrett in England, where he grew up with two sisters and a brother. A self-described loner, he struggled with forming close relationships with human beings, including his siblings. That disconnect might have been rooted in the dynamics of his early family life, as described in his polygraph report performed at the Whatcom County Sheriff's Office on May 5, 2010.

> Clarke said as he was [growing] up his parents were very strict and his father used to beat him, and he would often make lots of noise (scream, yell and cry) to either make the beating stop or shorten its duration. Clarke did not describe it as child abuse saying that he understands now why his parents where [sic] so hard on him. Clarke said he got into a lot of trouble shoplifting and burglary, which in combination with arguments about how much he was going to pay for rent, resulted in him moving out of his parents house in the middle of the night. Clarke said this has caused him to have no contact with his siblings to the point he could not provide any information about them.

The beatings inflicted by his father took a toll on Clarke. In response, he withdrew into himself.

> Clarke described his childhood as being a loner not having many friends and no relationships with girls or women. Clarke said he became sexually attracted to his male friends, but never had any homosexual relationships. Clarke said he would just visualize his friends and masturbate to the image of them. Clarke said this continued on into his adult life.

Clarke told his polygraph examiner that he had problems with stealing, particularly shoplifting, even going so far as to take items he didn't need. His behavior resulted in theft charges in 1980, 1988, 1990 and 1993. He also had sex offenses on his record.

"Clarke said, as he got older, he would take pictures of kids at a park or in various locations and then masturbate to the pictures," noted the polygraph report. "Clarke said he would at times also 'Rough House' with kids touching them in the area of their genital. Clarke said that this behavior alerted the authorities and he was arrested in 1995."

In January 1996, "Clarke was convicted to buggery with an animal and possession of a homemade film of himself indulging in buggery and oral sex with young children whilst on holiday in Thailand. Clarke also had films of himself being buggered by his own dogs and performing oral sex on his own dog."

Those charges led to Clarke being placed in a residential center for pedophiles for six months. Later that year, he was also convicted of grievous bodily harm after a store detective attempted to restrain him when he tried to get away.

In an effort to avoid being identified with his criminal past, Stephen changed his surname in 2005 from Barrett to Clarke. He made the decision because his neighbors knew about his sex offenses and his interest in zoophilia. "Clarke said his hope as new people moved into the neighborhood and the older ones moved out, there would be fewer individuals who knew about his secret."

According to his police statement, while his neighbors knew about his criminal record, Spink wasn't aware of it: "Spink never knew name change, full name, or criminal history." When I asked Spink later what he thought about Clarke's charges, especially the matter of sexual abuse against children, Spink responded, "He would not have been welcome on my property with that charge."

But it didn't matter to the probation department whether Spink knew about his guest's past or not. As far as they were concerned, his interaction with Clarke (and with Jim Tait, the zoophile jailed in Tennessee) constituted associating with criminals, and that was a violation.

⌒

A lie to the American federal government on a visa application potentially carries harsher penalties than a state conviction for animal cruelty. The threat of more time in custody was used by prosecutors to elicit Clarke's cooperation in the Spink case. Clarke pled guilty to making false statements on his application in exchange for time served in federal prison. Clarke would only stay in the USA long enough to testify against Spink before being deported, a deal he made with prosecutors to allow him to go home.

That's why Stephen Clarke was on the bus to Seattle, in the event he was called upon to be a witness during Spink's hearing. Clarke had given authorities the most inflammatory evidence used to take Spink down: his own behavior with Spink's dogs while he'd stayed at Reese Hill Road, his videotaping of that behavior, and the information he provided about Spink's zoo status in the days following the raid. "It gave them the tools to persecute me," Spink said. "Without Clarke, they had nothing. How reckless would it have been for them to do all this if Clarke wasn't there?"

Spink said that Clarke was contrite and apologetic on the bus about his role in the debacle.

"He said he was sorry, that he didn't realize they were going to do that to me," Spink recalled later, adding that given the pair's recent history, transporting them together was a faux pas by the legal system.

They reached the downtown Seattle courthouse. Clarke's hearing—in contrast to Spink's—was short and perfunctory. He appeared in the prisoner's box looking scared and wild-eyed, his straight gray hair disheveled and sticking out as if he had been electrified. The trip to the United States that he'd anticipated with such excitement had morphed into a total nightmare.

Spink's lawyer, Howard Phillips, decided not to call on Clarke to testify during Spink's hearing. Clarke's four-page affidavit, provided to Assistant US Attorney Susan Roe that same day in exchange for leniency, was accepted in lieu of live testimony.

In the affidavit, Clarke described sex acts that were captured on his videotape, which were in addition to the scenes of him receiving anal sex from three of Spink's dogs. One of those acts was measuring the dogs' penises with calipers. Police had discovered a list of the measurements among Clarke's belongings; in his affidavit, Clarke said the list was a "trophy or remembrance" of the dogs. "Exhibit 16 recorded me measuring Spink's dogs' erect penises as Spink and I talked about the length and girth of the penises. It also recorded a sexual act I performed on one of the dogs during this event." That act was oral sex.

Clarke's statement was also explicit about Spink's involvement. "To my knowledge, Spink did not engage in any sexual activity with the animals while I was there," he said. "He did, however, give me free rein to engage in any sexual activity with his dogs so long as the dogs did not resist, talked to me about his dogs and my sexual activities, and even saw me engage in sexual activity with some of his dogs."

Almost one year later, Clarke would recant some of his earlier statements in a declaration he prepared and signed March 21, 2011 in the United Kingdom, which he submitted to Spink's lawyer, Howard Phillips. In the document, Clarke stated that he "felt coerced and pressured to satisfy law enforcement and US Attorneys desire for information about Mr. Spink and my activities on his property."

The declaration of 2011 contradicted his affidavit of 2010. "It is not true that he gave free rein to engage in any sexual activity with his dogs as stated in the affidavit I signed. Specifically, Mr. Spink did not give me permission of any kind to engage in sexual activity with his animals."

Despite Clarke's efforts, his follow-up statements came too late to help Spink. Clarke declared that his motive for his earlier affidavit provided in 2010 was simply self-preservation.

"I signed the affidavit also to satisfy the demands of Ms. Roe and the Prosecution so that they would allow me to leave the USA, rather than keep me in custody there for many more months. They had made it very clear that this would be the consequence if they were not entirely satisfied with my level of cooperation."

He claimed the purposes for his visit to Spink's place were distorted by prosecutors intent on getting Spink. "My planned investigations into Pack Behaviour, Feeding, Socialisation—and various other completely non-sexual discussions—were deliberately disregarded to misrepresent my visit as purely sexual tourism."

A list that police found among Clarke's belongings.
Numbers in the left column are penis measurements of Spink's dogs.
Numbers 302–305 in the right column appear beside names of Spink's dogs.

37

CONNECTING DOTS

Doug Spink had more intimate knowledge of Seattle's federal courthouse than most defendants who appeared there. He had BASE jumped off the structure before its official opening in 2004.

His federal hearing on June 14, 2010, didn't draw nearly the crowd the Whatcom County civil proceeding had attracted, which wasn't surprising, because the story had been bigger news for the smaller community. And as it happened, the large federal courtroom had much more space to accommodate the smaller crowd of spectators than the cramped Whatcom County gallery offered.

Presenting for the federal government were attorneys Susan (Susie) Roe and Steven Masada. (Coincidentally, Roe was not the first Susie to play a prosecutorial role in Spink's life. The dog who sniffed out his load of cocaine that February night in 2005 was also named Susie.)

Spink was there in green prisoner garb, his hair buzzed short. He didn't look at the observers, but instead kept his eyes trained on his lawyer, Howard Phillips, and Judge Ricardo Martinez, who had also presided over his drug case.

Spink was accused of four probation violations:

1. Committing the crime of animal cruelty
2. Failing to submit truthful monthly reports
3. Leaving the jurisdiction without permission
4. Associating with persons engaged in criminal activities

Spink disputed three of the accusations, but he did admit to one—he had traveled outside his approved jurisdiction of Washington State twice without permission from his probation officer. It wasn't just that he left without permission that rankled the probation department, federal attorneys and Judge Martinez. It was what he said when he got there.

The search of his home on Reese Hill Road had yielded a boarding pass that revealed he'd flown to Las Vegas to see a business partner (not Paul Peterson) the month before the raid. But it was a trip in 2008 that played much more prominently in the hearing.

Spink had been invited to New York City that year to do a presentation on corporate jurisprudence at The Last HOPE, a conference held at Hotel Pennsylvania. HOPE stood for Hackers on Planet Earth. All the world could confirm he was there, because his presentation was posted online as a YouTube video split into five parts. The video, which was entered into evidence, showed him wearing a tie-dyed T-shirt emblazoned with "Sex Dogs & Rock and Roll" while standing at a podium where a sign prominently announced the conference dates: July 18–20, 2008.

In the video, Spink talked about his life, his beliefs about animals, corporate structures, and the law.

> I have kind of an unusual lifestyle in that my primary physical, emotional and social bonds are with horses and dogs. So my family is really mostly composed of dogs and horses. My life partner, who I've been with for ten years, is a famous athlete and very successful, has his own fan club. Pays a lot of the bills around the farm actually with his work.

He was of course referring to Capone. He spoke candidly about what it was like to be asked about having a partner who is a horse.

> It's actually cool because I can always say that my boyfriend really is hung like a horse. People usually blush like you can't say that and I did I say it. I'm not really sorry about it. So I have kind of a different life. I live in the barn with the guys and have for a long time. I think the fact that I grew up in kind of an unusual personal space colors the way I look at corporate law and a lot of other things.

UNIQUELY DANGEROUS   241

He openly discussed his prior involvement in drug smuggling, seemingly more enamored with the high-stakes excitement of the job than focused on the drugs themselves. He'd given me the same impression when he spoke to me at length about his time in the business. "It was really fun at a certain level if you ignore the rest of it—helicopters, cloak and daggers, sat phones, encrypted communications. Like, we did all that stuff. It was like being in a movie but it's you, and it's real."

At the conference, he also made statements about rules, words that came back to haunt him now in federal court. "That's always why you learn the rules, so you can learn how to get around them," Spink told his New York City audience. "It's way more fun to work around the rules, I think, than just to break them. You don't really need to be all that creative to just break the rules. It's not as much fun to just ignore the rules but to follow them and do creative stuff within that context." These statements irked Judge Martinez, as his words to Spink at the end of the hearing later revealed.

Deputy Steve Roff, from the Whatcom County Sheriff's Office, drove down to testify about the videotape police had seized at Spink's place. As would be the case two days later in the Whatcom County courthouse, the videotaped recordings were admitted into evidence, but not shown in open court. Susan Roe questioned Roff, who had viewed the tape.

> **Roe**: Was there anyone else on those recordings, other than Mr. Clarke or the dogs?
> **Roff**: Yes.
> **Roe**: Who?
> **Roff**: Mr. Spink's voice can be heard on the recordings.
> **Roe**: What's going on at the different times when Mr. Spink's voice is heard?
> **Roff**: Mr. Clarke is engaged in sexual conduct with the dogs, which includes the dogs having anal penetration into Mr. Spink's anus as well as Mr. Clarke.
> **Phillips**: Objection, Your Honor. That was not Mr. Spink's anus.
> **Roff**: I'm sorry. Mr. Clarke. I apologize.

Roff described what was happening on the tape as he read the transcript of the two voices. The speakers were engaged in conversation while Clarke had sex with a dog. Roff believed he recognized Spink's voice from past dealings with him.

Roff: *It would be 11 minutes and 31 seconds into the video, the front door of the cabin opens. You can't see who enters, but a male engages Mr. Clarke in conversation. I recognize that male's voice as being Mr. Spink. And the conversation goes:*
Spink: *Aha, caught in the act. I shouldn't be surprised.*
Clarke: *He feels a lot bigger than those shepherds.*
Spink: *Yeah. I have warned people about that. Not you. You don't need to be warned. But you could imagine people used to shepherds stumble into him thinking, wow, he is not a big dog. Only one person, yipping, tied with him before. I'm never doing this again.*

Roff stated to the court that there was a noise of someone opening the door and leaving the cabin. Two minutes later, the door opened again.

Roff: *13 minutes and 27 seconds into the video, the door opened again. You can't see who enters the door. . . . 15 minutes and 37 seconds into the video, Mr. Clarke is still engaged in sexual conduct with the mastiff, and Mr. Spink and Mr. Clarke have a second conversation.*
Clarke: *Well, in terms of sexual performance, he is certainly on par.*
Spink: *No doubt. That has never been a weak spot for him.*
Roff: *15 minutes and 50 seconds into the video, the mastiff disengaged with Mr. Clarke.*
Clarke: *Oh, damn. I didn't know it. I just made a lot of mess.*
Spink: *The good news is, in the context of the existing muddy, filthy mess that is my cabin right now, it is not even.*

Stephen Clarke, in his affidavit to the court, also said the voice was Spink's. "During the tape another man is heard on the tape talking saying, for instance, that he 'caught' me 'in the act' and making other related conversation with me. That man is Doug Spink. He walked in on the dog and me and I both recognize his voice and the incident."

∩

Initially, Spink thought Clarke was incidental to the trouble he faced during and after the raid. But then he began to wonder: could Clarke have started working with the federal government before arriving at his cabin? Had law enforcement cast a net around the Reese Hill Road property before the raid—a net that would capture anyone who happened to wander into it?

And when did Clarke begin his relationship with the police? Spink began to suspect that his visitor had been detained at the border on his way to visit his cabin from Canada, where the British tourist had been traveling before he got to Spink's. Perhaps Clarke was already working for the feds by the time he arrived at Spink's. If that were true, would the events that followed be considered entrapment?

I had no idea what Stephen Clarke's full involvement was. I put the word out to zoos that I would like to interview him, but he didn't oblige. That left me attempting to connect the dots without his input.

Here's what I did know:

- Clarke was scheduled to leave Spink's place fifteen minutes before the raid happened.
- The raid date was mysteriously bumped to a week later than its original date, which then coincided with Clarke's three-day visit.
- Clarke left Spink's gate open, which allowed police to breeze in unimpeded. Spink had lent him the key to make sure he locked up judiciously.
- According to Spink, Clarke didn't seem surprised when the police raided.
- Clarke was initially told he was free to go, but he stayed to help the authorities round up Spink's animals.
- Clarke had two cell phones with him, one of them with a Washington, DC, area code.
- Clarke was fanatical about encrypting his computer files because he didn't want to get caught. He would use a phrase from a newspaper clipping that contained the file password. He told his polygraph examiner that he dropped the article containing the password for the videotape on the ground when police raided. Yet somehow police viewed the video without obstacles or delay right there on Spink's property.

Had prosecutors wanted Spink so badly that they worked with Clarke to entrap the man who seemed too smart to catch any other way? If that was true, did the authorities consider the consequences of their actions?

In their drive to get Spink—a defiant, remorseless zoophile—they had released a convicted pedophile who had filmed himself having sex with Spink's dogs.

☊

On the first day of Spink's federal hearing, a man sat down beside me in the courtroom's spectator area. Sporting a crop of curly white hair and a full white mustache, he wore a suit set off with a colorful shirt. He struck up a conversation, curious about who I was and what I was doing there. Then he offered me his business card, which folded open to reveal a tiny pocket cradling a thin sheaf of rolling papers.

That was my introduction to Seattle attorney Jeffrey Steinborn.

Steinborn, who specializes in drug-related offenses, was the first lawyer hired by Spink after his 2005 arrest for smuggling cocaine. Back then, Spink didn't think Steinborn was pursuing what he believed was a viable motion to suppress the evidence in his case. Spink not only fired Steinborn, he also provided information about him to the feds because he was dissatisfied with how his case was being handled.

Steinborn never found out exactly what happened, but for six months afterwards, he lived under threat of indictment. "It was pretty scary," he said.

Now Steinborn was attending Spink's probation hearing, but only as a spectator. He wanted the satisfaction of seeing his former client in trouble again. "I just came to enjoy watching him get fucked, basically. He ruined my life for so long."

At the hearing and in a follow-up phone call I made to him, Steinborn warned me emphatically against writing about Spink. He urged me to carefully consider whether I should publish this book. His caution was dark and foreboding; he said that to continue interacting with Spink would destroy my quality of life forever, and that I would live to regret it.

UNMITIGATED DEFIANCE

In arguing that Spink had violated his probation, the federal government went beyond portraying him as an unapologetic zoophile. They characterized him as a menace to society, a brilliant and defiant deviant who was up to no good. His intelligence was viewed as a problem.

At Spink's sentencing hearing on July 16, 2010, federal attorney Steven Masada said:

> Now, there's no question Mr. Spink is extremely intelligent, a driven individual. And it's unfortunate, but these qualities contribute to the government's concern here, since Mr. Spink does not want to comply with supervision. He has in the past been a productive member of society, the hope is he will be again. But that is going to require a volitional decision on his part to alter his attitude toward the authority of this court, the probation office, and the laws of the United States of America. From what I've seen, we expect that may be a long journey.

Prosecutors were uneasy about his technical abilities too. "Spink's sophistication presents a particularly problematic situation," read the government's sentencing memorandum. "He has demonstrated his ability and willingness to hide conduct and deceive others. As stated above, he implements high-level encryption software. In fact, his tech company, Baneki Privacy Computing, is in the business of selling secrecy."

This accusation of "selling secrecy" annoyed Spink. He firmly believed that helping people and companies avoid government surveillance with "network-based tools that enable dramatically enhanced privacy and security," as the Baneki website phrased it, was a legitimate and noble business model, something he was meant to do. He wasn't going to back down from that position no matter what the feds did or said.

One of the four violations Spink was accused of was related to Baneki: his alleged failure to submit truthful monthly reports to the probation office. He underestimated his income on those reports, claimed the government, and misrepresented his role at Baneki as "tech lead." Government attorneys maintained that this title was deliberately misleading, meant to obscure his ownership of the business. On Baneki's corporate documents, Spink was listed as founder and chairman.

The government suggested that the existence of Spink's high-tech business rendered him almost impossible to supervise effectively. "As explored on cross-examination of the probation officer, it is indeed difficult to track the outer extent of Spink's influence given the sophistication of the operation and the nature of the internet itself."

Government attorneys also didn't like the ideas Spink was spreading via the internet, which centered on his belief that zoophilia isn't wrong: "The nature of Spink's known violations is shocking. As the evidence revealed, Spink is a prominent figure in the underground zoophilia community."

Howard Phillips, lawyer for the defense, argued that his client had a right to his own thoughts, no matter how offensive people might find them: "Mr. Spink's academic consideration of cross-species sexuality is not a crime and this court should not consider any evidence from the government that is designed to punish him for this non-crime."

Phillips also took issue with the government's suggestion that Spink's mental health contributed to the challenge of supervising him.

> The Government alleges that "Spink's current 'mental state' makes his supervision unproductive…if not impossible."
>
> It is defamation for the government to present in a pleading available to the public that questions Mr. Spink's mental state without one iota of evidence that he has a mental health problem.

> He has never been evaluated as such and for lay-prosecutors to make this statement in this forum should not be allowed.

The lawyers spoke about Spink so disparately that at times, it sounded like they were describing two different people. Phillips portrayed his client as a nice guy who was merely misunderstood, a congenial man who helped fellow prisoners with their court cases and business questions. Phillips had developed empathy for his high-profile client since he began representing him. "He's got eccentrics, there's no question about it. And when I took this case I definitely had the 'ewww' factor, when I was told what it was. But over the course of time I've gotten to know Mr. Spink."

The federal lawyers were not similarly enamored. Spink's recalcitrant attitude was defined by them interchangeably as "unwavering defiance" and "unmitigated defiance." His lack of atonement was a persistent theme throughout the violation hearing. They said he viewed supervision as "a shell game of deception, evasion, and misdirection." His lack of contrition was galling to the government.

> What drives the government's sentencing recommendation is the egregious breach of trust that occurred here and Mr. Spink's unmitigated defiance regarding supervision and his denial of responsibility.
>
> It is his unwillingness to cooperate with the United States Probation Office that exemplifies why the government and probation office believe Mr. Spink is unsuperviseable at this current time. Not even after the court found violations had occurred, we see no expression of remorse, no contrition and not even so much as an acknowledgment of the severe misconduct that occurred here.

Despite immense pressure on Spink to repent for his beliefs, he steadfastly refused to cave. "Spink has expressed no remorse, contrition, or acceptance of responsibility," noted the federal sentencing memorandum. "Instead, he decries animal cruelty laws that criminalize bestiality. While he is entitled to that opinion, engaging in criminal conduct carries consequences, his personal viewpoint notwithstanding. Without even a modest acknowledgment of wrongdoing, Spink lashes out in retaliation against those he perceives as his enemies."

The memorandum went on to say that the probation office wasn't effectively able to supervise him. "Spink's current mental state makes supervision unproductive and extremely difficult, if not impossible. His actions reveal an improper view of the Probation Office—i.e., as a hindrance to his preferred lifestyle and an obstacle to be avoided, if possible."

Federal lawyers asked for close to the maximum time allowed by law because, "This is, in the Government's view, an extraordinary case—both in the nature of the violations as well as in the special concerns presented by the defendant, Douglas Spink. The Government respectfully requests a disposition determination that reflects these unique considerations." They asked for almost the maximum sentence allowed by law.

> The maximum term of imprisonment that may be imposed upon revocation is five years. Having considered the totality of the circumstances here, the Government recommends that this Court revoke Spink's supervised release and impose a term of imprisonment of 48 months, to be followed by a 12-month term of supervision subject to the terms and conditions proposed by the Probation Office. This recommendation reflects Spink's complete lack of compliance and candor with the United States Probation Office as well as the serious and wide-spread nature of his violations. It is the Government's hope that the severity of this sentence will cause Spink to reflect upon his life, reform his outlook toward the Probation Office and the criminal justice system, and realize that purposeful and calculated misconduct carries correspondingly harsh consequences.

Government attorneys argued that because Spink had not complied with the parameters set out by the probation department, the benefits he received on his original sentence should be clawed back, an action known as "upward departure."

On the original drug charge, Spink had been given "downward departure"—a lowering of the mandatory minimum sentence—because a 5K1.1 motion was filed on his behalf. According to the US Sentencing Commission, a 5K1.1 motion can be filed when a defendant provides "substantial assistance to authorities" if the testimony supplied is significant, useful, complete, reliable and timely. Also considered is "any injury suffered, or any danger or risk of injury to the family resulting from his assistance." I wasn't able to gain access to Spink's 5K1.1 deal because it was sealed. That's not unusual, according to the Sentencing Commission, "for the safety of the defendant or to avoid disclosure of an ongoing investigation."

Now, government lawyers argued that Spink no longer qualified for special treatment. Given the "sizable downward departure Mr. Spink received for the underlying conviction and other circumstances present here," they said, "this upward departure from the advisory guideline range is more than justified."

But Phillips argued that Spink's original sentence should not be considered a gift bestowed under downward departure.

> No upward departure is necessary in the case merely because Mr. Spink received a downward departure in the underlying offense... the government did not agree to a downward departure as an "award" for substantial assistance. Instead, the agreed recommendation was the result of plea bargaining where the defense deferred pursuing a viable suppression motion in which the government would be compelled to disclose a confidential source, in consideration of the government recommending a lesser sentence of three years. Because the reduced sentence was not a "reward" but the result of plea bargaining, an upward departure is not warranted.

But the government wouldn't back down from its position that Spink deserved to be punished severely. During the proceeding, government lawyers persistently portrayed him as a snitch intent on saving his own skin.

> Spink's underlying drug crime was a serious offense. Facing significant criminal penalties, he struck a deal with the Government. In exchange for leniency, Spink agreed to cooperate fully with law enforcement authorities investigating narcotics trafficking and other crimes, to fully and truthfully answer any and all questions asked of him concerning his knowledge of such criminal activity. He promised to be candid, adjust his behavior, and adopt a law-abiding lifestyle. In return, he received a significantly lower term of imprisonment than other cooperating defendants similarly situated. It is now apparent that Spink misled the Probation Office thereafter, and reaped the benefit of a bargain he did not fully deserve.

Spink and his lawyers denied the accusation that he was a snitch, but in his remarks, Judge Ricardo Martinez agreed with prosecutors. Martinez also made it known that he wasn't impressed with Spink's comments on YouTube about rules.

> These restrictions on your behavior are mandated by the court. They are not something that you can choose to ignore regardless of whether you agree with them or not. And here my belief is that

you have blatantly done everything possible to circumvent those conditions. You've used, what everyone acknowledges, is your substantial intelligence to find a way to, "Get around the rules."

I believe you understood the rules, you just disagreed with them, do not believe that those rules apply. As with other rules of society, I can only imagine you agree those rules should not apply to you.

Let me quote, 2008 July presentation, New York City. "It's not as much fun to simply break the rules as it is to find creative ways to get around them." Do you remember saying that?

Spink replied, "I don't remember that specifically, but I do remember it in the context of always following rules."

The judge added a personal note in his words to Spink:

> I grew up on a farm. I have always had tremendous respect for the role that animals play in our lives. You and I have completely different beliefs when it comes to animals. You're not being punished, and the court does not punish you for your beliefs, you're free to believe anything you want. But the court will punish you for your actions and your conduct. Because while you're on supervised release of this court you will follow these conditions or else the consequences will be imposed.

Just as government attorneys had asserted, Martinez was also skeptical about Spink being effectively supervised. "I have serious doubt as to whether that is possible or not. And I seriously considered imposing the maximum five-year period of imprisonment with no supervised release to follow. But I decided not to do that."

Instead, Martinez revoked Spink's supervised release and sentenced him to thirty-six months in custody, followed by twenty-four months of supervised release.

It wouldn't be the last time Spink would appear in Judge Martinez's courtroom. But for now, he was headed back to prison.

To read Doug Spink's oral statement made to Judge Ricardo Martinez at his sentencing hearing, see Exhibit 9, page 387.

GHOSTED OUT

There was a time when Doug Spink had status in the horse world. He was eclectic and unusual, but also successful. He owned one of the top show jumping horses in the world, plus several other horses with stellar jumping ability from prestigious bloodlines.

He put the same devotion into learning about horses as he did with all pursuits he was passionate about. His equine skills didn't go unnoticed. Before the 2010 raid, he'd been hired to teach veterinarians how to successfully collect sperm from stallions, and how to impregnate mares with less trauma caused to the animals.

All that changed after the raid, when his beliefs about cross-species sex became widely known to anyone who searched his name online. In a distinct shift, he became a pariah in the horse world.

One of the many valued contacts he felt had abandoned him in his time of need was Dr. Christine King, an Australian-schooled veterinarian who had relocated to the United States. King wrote extensively about horses; her body of work includes several books and numerous scientific papers published in veterinary journals and textbooks. King had consulted with Spink about Capone's health, and had been so impressed that she went on to write a flattering question-and-answer style article about Spink for the January 2008 issue of *Horses Incorporated* magazine. Two years later, he wanted her to appear as a witness for him at his probation violations hearing in the hopes that she would testify about the care of his horses. She refused.

When King published her article, titled "Managing the Stallion Athlete," she praised Spink's equine skills. But by the time I got in touch with her, she wanted nothing to do with him. I contacted her by email on September 30, 2013, to see if she wanted to add any follow-up comments to her article, which I mentioned I'd be quoting in this book. She responded quickly, but it wasn't friendly communication.

> **King**: It's Dr. King, and I am sure that I want nothing to do with anything even remotely connected with Mr. Spink. Please leave my name out of anything you write. Enough damage has been done already. I will consider it a personal and professional affront if you involve me in any way.
> Now that you know that I am the owner of its copyright, I will consider it a copyright infringement if you reproduce it in your book.
> **Me**: I am not reproducing your entire article, I am quoting the article. My understanding of "fair use" is that quoting from the article is not an infringement of your copyright. My book is a work of journalism, and as such, I am allowed to quote published work.
> **King**: Yes, you are right; you are legally entitled to quote from the article (although there are limits). But PLEASE do not attribute me as the author.
> PLEASE! Let me live in peace, without the stink of having had Doug Spink as a client following me across the country!
> Please. If I say anything about that man and my dealings with him, it will be on my own terms, and in my own time.

I didn't think the time would ever come when King would give her blessing, and by the time of writing, she still hadn't. But I believe her statements are important. King is a knowledgeable equine professional who had a glimpse into the life Spink shared with his horses before his world was turned upside down by the raid—a glimpse I didn't have. So here is an excerpt from her article:

> To walk into Doug's barn is quite a mind-altering experience. Despite being inhabited by several large stallions, there is a sense of peace and equanimity that I found both surprising and delightful. There was even a sense of camaraderie and fun. I have absolutely no qualms about stepping into the stall with any of Doug's stallions, because regardless of their early histories (some of which are quite traumatic) and strong presence, each stallion knows he

is expected to behave like a gentleman. I've been tremendously impressed with Doug's approach to the stallions in his care, so I thought we should hear directly from him.

What follows are two excerpts of Doug Spink's words from the same *Horses Incorporated* article:

> Today, I focus my work with horses almost exclusively on stallions. As is true of the dogs with whom I share my life, the stallions in my life aren't economic assets or means to some other end: they are family, first and foremost. I resonate with them on the deepest of levels, and I always have: while all horses matter to me, stallions are central to my world—truly, my entire life is organized around their happiness and well-being. . . .
>
> Like any friend, a stallion is a mirror of our own selves. Those with peace, equanimity, and harmony in their heart tend to generate the same feelings in the stallions who share their lives. In that vein, we can all work to create positive environments around us so that our horses can benefit from those environments, and in turn echo back those gifts to us, creating a virtuous cycle of friendship and love. Not everyone is going to share their life with stallions as I do—for me, they are family, friends and partners combined. But we can all open ourselves to our equine associates in a way that expands our human worldview into the equine space, even as we ask them to expand their equine worldview just a little bit into the land of the primates. It is a wondrous journey, to cross the species barrier and see the world through alien eyes: to feel the world through non-human sense. Perhaps, in their intensity and (occasional) focus, stallions are the epitome of such transformative experiences—truly, sharing deep intimacy with a stallion is a big step away from the human world.

Dr. King wasn't alone in her feelings of revulsion and betrayal when Spink's sexual preferences became known. She was one of many people who refused to stand up for him when the truth of who he really was came to light.

Not even Spink's former stud farm manager, who still spoke glowingly of his positive attributes, wanted her name used here. At first, Joanne (not her real name), who used to manage Spink's Timberline Farms west of Portland, agreed to let me visit her current facility to conduct an in-person interview for this book. But it wasn't long before she withdrew her consent to meet me.

She informed Spink of her decision by email on February 8, 2013:

> You've kind of put your hand into the cultural cuisinart here, and though I find culture twisted and hypocritical and stupid ... I can't ask [my partner] to lose his career over this aspect of it, or me to lose mine.
>
> We're about to publish several books, and have a big new change coming in our business...and I can't derail all of that by risking being perceived as a person with whatever qualities culture slaps onto zoos and their friends.
>
> We're working on the culture our way—which is far less confrontational than yours. And I don't want to lose the decades we've both put into this...
>
> So I'll answer her questions but at a safer distance. And, felt I should tell you so.

It might seem as though support offered by a former employee would comfort Spink, even if she did ask to remain anonymous. But it didn't. Just the opposite: he was hurt and angry. After the raid, he felt deserted and abandoned by those who had worked alongside him. No one from the animal world had stepped forward to support him publicly when the shit hit the fan, out of fear the shit might stick to them, too.

"It does feel like a form of betrayal...because it's a form of betrayal," he wrote back to Joanne. "But I'm really used to those betrayals by this point in time, so the sting is mostly gone."

In the same email to her, he wrote:

> The good news is that you're in fine company. Everyone else in the "horse world" and "dog world"—people who I've mentored, supported, encouraged, trained, and helped to become successful across a wide swath of professional fields—is also saying nothing in public. And telling me in private how *won-derful* it was to benefit from my gifts... in private. How much they appreciate it, how disgusted they are by the lies and persecution, how "horrible" it all is. In private. In public, nothing. So you've all spoken, through silence. You've let me and my life and my skills and my career in horses and dogs be smashed, turned to lies, erased. That is what's happened, across the board. I swing in the wind, alone. Everyone's sorry.

To read more of Doug Spink's words from the *Horses, Incorporated* article, see Exhibit 10, page 390.

40

SCARLET F

Most of Spink's prison sentence after his drug charge in 2005 was spent at FCI Sheridan in Oregon, a relatively bearable institution compared to where he was placed after the bestiality farm allegations. FCI Beaumont in Texas has the reputation of being one of the roughest federal prisons in the United States, earning it the chilling nickname "Bloody Beaumont."

Spink viewed his second stint in custody much differently than the first. In 2005, he thought his prison time was deserved, because he'd been caught with an SUV full of cocaine. But when he was sent back in 2010 for another thirty-six-month sentence, he felt unjustly persecuted, and considered himself a political prisoner. The feds were right. He felt no contrition. He would not back down from his belief that zoophilia isn't wrong. But sticking to his convictions didn't make things any easier for him.

No matter what the reasons for his incarceration, he used the same coping mechanisms for getting through the time inside. His love of learning—both reading and teaching—was a lifeline. During Spink's second stay in prison, he spent another 824 days in custody and read 226 more books. "I was a little bit 'slower' because I tackled a bunch of 1000+ page books this time 'round," he wrote to me later when I inquired about how he spent his days there. "I also had far more access to research journals, magazines (*New Yorker, Science, Harpers, SciAm, Discover, Wired*, etc., . . .), the daily *New York Times* (a friend received it)—and all the stuff colleagues emailed in to me every day to keep me current technologically."

He had done a little teaching during his first prison stay, but this time he decided to take it to the next level. He sent me an email about what teaching meant to him: "Teaching is a revolutionary act, when done right. It has the ability to structurally subvert existing social frameworks, if done with passion and insight. It's an art, not a science. One invests one's soul in the real work of teaching."

At Beaumont, he was given the job of inmate tutor. He told me that he taught classes to prisoners who didn't have high school diplomas and helped them earn their general equivalency degrees, or GEDs. After his release, he described to me what his prison schedule had been like:

> GED classes are taught five days per week. I tutored full-time, which means three classes per day—two hours per class—with 24 students in each class. It's quite a workload, as any teacher can attest—despite the fact that I had little paperwork load to handle (that was all handled by the excellent COs who were my supervisors in my teaching career). It left me somewhat exhausted many days—in a good way. I do a great deal of outside-of-classroom, one-on-one tutoring as well... although I did have to put some boundaries up so that, when I'm back in the housing units in my bunk reading or listening to the radio, students wouldn't come up and ask for ad-hoc tutoring (usually math); famously, I ended up posting a "scheduled hours" note on my bunk at Beaumont, saying when it was ok to stop in my cube and ask advice and when it was "personal time" that I didn't want to be tutoring (generally, after 9pm and before 7am, and most weekends were off-limit to random tutoring questions... although exceptions always came up).

The challenges of tutoring in prison included the power dynamics of the situation—many of Spink's students weren't in class by choice.

> Per congressional mandate, all inmates who don't have their degree MUST take GED classes until they finish; if they refuse, they suffer punitive disciplinary actions in an escalating spiral. This makes being an inmate GED tutor an... interesting experience. Perhaps 1/3 of students are in class but hating to be there; they are understandably hostile, and often view inmate tutors as "cops

without keys" (i.e. COs in all but name). To earn the trust of students, and to run a classroom effectively, is a complex challenge.

The money he earned was paltry, a long way from the compensation he'd received in his other careers: corporate executive, high-tech entrepreneur, stud farm owner, drug smuggler. He pulled in $44 a month as a lead GED instructor, with occasional $20 bonuses offered if budget allowed. "It's not really something one does for the money," he said.

Still, he earned something more valuable to him than money. "I have photos at home of me with my students, dressed in formal graduation garb, huge grins," he wrote. "That's the wondrous part: seeing them succeed, make their families proud, make THEMSELVES proud."

Besides being a GED instructor, Spink said he also taught adult continuing education classes. Led by inmate volunteers who had particular areas of expertise, ACE classes occurred in the evenings. Inmates didn't get paid for teaching them, but those who attended received certificates and credit that affected their security classifications and custody situations, giving them, for example, the possibility of halfway house placement.

Spink taught introductory Spanish and French, intermediate French, and business. He enjoyed teaching languages, but it was the business classes that he found most gratifying.

> It is my Strategic Entrepreneurship classes, as an ACE instructor, that are something of my signature class. Those classes, since I started teaching them back in 2005, have routinely drawn above-capacity enrollment with folks standing in the back to participate. I developed the curriculum for that class from scratch, a blank slate. Now, I have it memorised of course. I compress a combination of my MBA knowledge and my 20+ years' experience in front-line entrepreneurship into 10 discrete segments, covering subjects from financial accounting, operations, strategic marketing, staff management, and balance sheet analysis. I have stayed in touch with several dozen former students, tracking their experience as they get out of prison and pursue their projects (the "final project" in the class for all students is to develop a startup business plan and, if they are comfortable, present it to the entire classroom for feedback and discussion.

Spink believed his entrepreneurship classes could potentially have a dramatic effect on the prisoners' successful re-entry into society, despite the scarlet *F* that would stain their names forever. Convicted felons are branded for life. Certain occupations are no longer available to them, they can be denied rental housing, and securing home loans becomes more difficult. Social benefits might not be available to felons, such as living in public housing, qualifying for federal or state grants, and receiving food stamps. Parental rights might be diminished. Voting rights suspended during incarceration can take years to be restored, if they ever are, and felons may not be allowed to serve on juries.

Ex-cons are said to have paid their debts to society when they finish serving their time, but a felon's debt is never truly paid. The disenfranchisement that released prisoners feel when attempting to put their lives back together is palpable and defeating, and can contribute to recidivism. Spink's goal was to empower prisoners to succeed in spite of their felony label. He hoped his business courses would be an antidote to required pre-release classes that provide discouraging information to inmates about future career prospects, such as the open discrimination many companies practice by refusing to hire felons.

> My deeper structural goal in teaching entrepreneurship to inmates is to break the social stigma with which the BOP, AUSAs, US Probation, and the entire "criminal fuck-you," err "justice" system in America saddles former inmates. In America—"land of the free"—ex-inmates are felons FOR LIFE. This is heavily, heavily emphasized in all "pre-release programming" (classes mandatory to attend, provided by the BOP): you will NEVER escape the stigma of your felony, the "Scarlet F" as we call it on this side of the razor wire fence. You will be a failure, forever. You will be lucky to get a minimum wage job. You will, most likely, fail—and go back to dealing drugs, so we can catch you and lock you up for even more decades. Naturally, the most obvious targets of this mental virus are the black guys—who have been told all their lives they are failures, and will likely end up in prison—and the hispanics.
>
> My entrepreneurship classes developed out of my disgust with this vicious attitude promulgated by the BOP and others, towards inmates.
>
> I teach my students how to succeed in entrepreneurship— WITHOUT breaking the law. I teach them that they can make more money in "straight" business, than via crime. I teach them to follow the law—the REAL law, not Martinez's "spiritual" law that ex-inmates must fail and be miserable forever. I encourage them to think creatively, to find the angles where their expertise and passion can produce a successful project. I teach them about how they can do this in their communities, thereby motivating others to follow a similar path—and thus breaking the cycle of societally-projected failure they have so often faced at home. I teach them

> that they do NOT need (as I put it) "a permission slip" from any (white) judge or cop or anyone else, to succeed in entrepreneurship. I teach them that their empowerment is in their hands, and that if they provide exceptional service to their customers, they will win. And grow wealthy. And then have the tools at their disposal—the resources, tangible—to throw the corrupt, fascist scum who put all of us in prison out of office and into the shantytown hovels where they belong.

While Spink did his time in prison, Corinne Super wasted no time getting Capone back on the show jumping circuit. Like Spink, Capone had been waiting out his own form of confinement for two months in the spring/summer of 2010, spending most of that time in a stall at a farm in Arlington while the court proceedings progressed. After Super won custody, Capone went to her farm in Langley, BC until October 2010, when she sent him to rider Kyle King's farm in San Marcos, California, for training and conditioning so he'd be ready to start show jumping again.

Kyle King didn't respond to my texts and calls, but media reports at the time quoted him saying he used the trails and hilly terrain around his farm to get the stallion ready for competition. King's efforts were rewarded. In Capone's first competition back—the HITS Grand Prix on February 6, 2011, in Thermal, California—the stallion placed third. A week later, he won the Smartpak Grand Prix at HITS.

But Capone's crowning achievement that summer was still to come. On June 19, he beat renowned Olympic gold and silver medalist Hickstead, ridden by Canadian Eric Lamaze, to win the $125,000 CN Performance World Cup Grand Prix, held south of Calgary, Alberta, at the Spruce Meadows equestrian facility. Capone shaved 0.51 of a second off Hickstead's time.

Besting Hickstead was no small achievement. In 2010, that stallion won the "Best Horse in the World" title at the Alltech FEI World Equestrian Games in Lexington, Kentucky. (The following year, on November 6, 2011, Hickstead's career came to a sudden, tragic end when he collapsed and died of an aortic rupture at a competition in Verona, Italy.)

Capone continued to shine that summer. On August 20, he kicked off the Rocky Mountain Classic series held at Anderson Ranch in Calgary by winning the $50,000 Grand Prix.

Spink wouldn't see any of this revenue. Instead, most of the cash from the purses would go into Corinne Super's pockets, less a portion of it paid to Kyle King as Capone's rider.

Despite Capone's checkered history, his undeniable talent didn't go unnoticed. He made the short list for the 2012 London Summer Olympic Games, for the Canadian show jumping team, but he didn't make the final cut.

While Capone jumped like a champion, Spink was imprisoned, both physically and emotionally. It was excruciating. Locked up in custody, languishing behind the razor wire, he ached to be with the horse he had long ago declared was his "life partner," and lived for the day when he would be reunited with the black stallion again.

PART FOUR

The love that dare not speak its name.

—Lord Alfred Douglas,
from the poem *Two Loves*

41

ZOO COMMUNITY

For all the rage that people directed at him for being a zoo, Doug Spink thought it didn't always reflect genuine feelings. Frequently, he expressed to me his belief that people aren't as disgusted by cross-species sex as they purport to be—instead, he contended, they harbor burning curiosity about the subject. As evidence, he cited YouTube posts featuring animals mating that draw many millions of hits.

Despite the public criticism he faces, Spink said non-zoos often ask him questions privately, displaying intense curious about his sexuality. "The Normals are obsessed with it. They want to read articles about it, they are searching on the internet about it. All these people feigning this shock and disgust and concern. It's all a crock of shit."

In September 2013, I emailed Spink to ask his opinion about a *Huffington Post* story that ran in 2010, following the raid. I included an observation: "Huffington makes the point of capitalizing just the word BESTIALITY in the headline, for extra emphasis I assume." He shot back this sarcastic and fairly graphic reply:

> They are the pure-form version of the Normal obsession with BEASTIALITY. Of course they totally totally think it's totally disgusting and want to hear nothing more about it. Except of course

the dozens of BEASTIALITY stories they write whenever there is the slightest opportunity. About HOT MAN ON DOG SEX!!!!!! and that kind of thing... whilst of course totally, completely opposing BEASTIALITY and any mention of it.

The stories, of course, end up simply echoing Normal preconceptions about HOT BEASTIALITY SEXXXX!!!!!! and are totally un-moored from factual reality. Facts aren't the point. Indeed, they could not care less about "facts." Note how few people actually care what's on [Stephen] Clarke's video—it's the preconception of what might (or "should") be on it that matters. Reality is a mere distraction.

But just to be clear, they are TOTALLY opposed to HOT BEASTIALITY. Because, you know, animals. Stop murdering fluffy cute kittens. . . .

It's like those creepy mouth-foaming (self-described) christians who cannot stop talking about HOT MAN-ON-MAN SEX any time they get the chance. About how those STEAMY YOUNG HUNKS WITH THEIR BULGING MUSCLES simply should not be allowed their FILTHY, SWEAT-SOAKED ORGIES any more. Because, you know, Jesus. Or something. Note bulge in pants during said fulmination.

And sharper-edged gay friends of mine have to say about that: "just set your clock and count down 'till those closeted fags are caught on their knees in a public bathroom, dick-in-mouth." Which is a bit harsh, but yeah.

YouTube mating videos. Tens of millions of hits. Those aren't zoos.

Do you think people are reading HuffPo WILD BEASTIALITY ANIMAL SEX stories because... They're worried about the nonhumans? Right. They're all ardent campaigners against factory farms, too.

As additional proof that this fascination exists, Spink referred to "Normal" pornography, where it isn't unusual to find bestiality-themed imagery in photographs and videos.

In my community we are not impressed by Normal porn. They treat the animal as an inanimate object, an accessory. We find it to be nauseating. They like the degradation thing.

Real zoo porn is freely available. I have never made money on porn. There is attraction in our community for sharing intimate materials. It shows best practices. I'm not anti-porn. I am not going to run around denying it.

Not only was Spink supportive of porn that shows zoos having sex with animals, he thought it should be presented to defend their actions.

"I am absolutely encouraging widespread viewing of footage of zoophiles and their partners. It will exonerate zoophiles."

Such imagery, he said, would also prove that animals aren't as different from people as Normals want to believe. "The sex thing is very emotionally charged as mammals, and when you watch them having sex, you can't deny that they are like us."

At first, Spink's assertions about Normals' obsession with zoophiles were difficult for me to believe. But once I started researching zoophilia, his claims about people's widespread fascination with cross-species sex didn't seem so unbelievable anymore.

I can't be certain how many zoos exist in the world. Neither can anybody else, it seems. Psychotherapist Hani Miletski, whose 2002 book, *Understanding Bestiality and Zoophilia*, was based on her dissertation and is one of the few works on the subject, lamented the lack of basic information when she began her research.

I soon discovered a worldwide community of zoophiles who communicate mostly through the internet. Their fear of discovery is so potent that most know each other only by nicknames. They are a community that stays hidden from view, cloaked in a veil of secrecy for fear of violence, reprisals and retribution.

∩

Like most zoos I communicated with, Spink figured out he wasn't attracted to human beings as he approached puberty. Until he grew to accept himself in his 20s, it was a confusing feeling. Eventually he accepted it as an inalterable truth about himself.

"If you're someone like me, growing up and coming of age is different than for someone else," he said. "You can't go to the library and ask for a book about it. You can't go to a counselor, friend, or a parent."

That doesn't leave many options in a society that reviles zoophiles and considers them depraved and perverted. The dismal choices Spink listed were as follows: a psychiatric institution, a prison or suicide. "When I was growing up there was no name for it," he said. "You can't be who you are. You don't exist. You are forbidden from existing."

Not surprisingly, society's reactions foster considerable inner conflict in people who feel they don't have a choice about who they are. I heard similar sentiments from dozens of zoos who agreed to be interviewed, whether in person, by phone or through email. They experience anguish, fear and self-hatred because society views them as depraved perverts. But many also believe they aren't doing anything wrong with the animals.

Zoos told me they struggle to find a way to spend their lives hiding who they really are from their human loved ones. This Canadian man is one example:

> I think we need to understand the story of "those people" because they are—we are—not going to go away. My compassion and obsession with non-humans predates the internet. It came about in spite of Sunday School and Family Values. It just is. There are older generations I know who are now far into the autumn years. They too woke up one day and realized they just were who they are. And yes, there is a new generation now who just are—they are among our very own children—and I think we are faced with a choice now where we could either take them into societies' fold or pretend to keep them locked outside. I do not believe they can be "re-programmed" to be "normal" heterosexuals. Trust me, I tried. Hard.

Another zoo in his early thirties from New York City who called himself John wrote to me that he acknowledged to himself that he was a zoo twenty-four years earlier, but it wasn't an easy realization to accept.

> It is quite exhausting living a lie one's entire life, knowing that the moral majority wishes us all to simply stop existing. I was all alone for many years struggling with my sexual and romantic identity, believing I was the only one alive who was like this. Thank the gods for the internet, thou it wasn't until my late teens were there actual boards where other zoos could communicate with a comfortable level of anonymity.
>
> To this day we still live a life of second class citizens. Worse even, we are relegated to the likes of rapists and child molesters, monsters that should be burn[ed] alive or locked away in the deepest darkest dungeons, never to see light or feel any form of joy again in our miserable lives.
>
> Many, myself included, truly believe we are born this way, something in our genes that gravitates us towards these relationships we have.

Of the many zoos I interacted with, just two were female. Male zoophiles told me there are lots of female zoos out there, but they tend to be less vocal about it. Perhaps more women will come forward to tell their stories after this book is published.

Before I started my research, I theorized that people become zoophiles because other humans had been cruel to them, perhaps during childhood, which caused them to pull away from people to form their main bonds with animals instead. But most zoos expressed no connection between their zoophilic orientation and childhood sexual or other physical abuse at the hands of humans. Some had faced traumatic childhoods, while others came from healthy, functional families. One woman I interviewed by phone, however, did view human abuse as a root cause of her zoophilia.

Growing up in a small, predominantly white town in the American Midwest, Natalie (not her real name) stood out as different because of her racial background—half African American, half Native American. She is also legally blind. She was bullied and sexually abused by other children from a young age. One experience she recalled was being pushed into the school bathroom and forced to perform oral sex on several boys, only to be called in to the principal's office, where she was accused of being promiscuous.

Now in her late twenties, Natalie is unable to trust people for sexual interactions. She asked me: why was it wrong for her to position herself on her hands and knees to allow her dog to mount and penetrate her? Did it harm her dog?

The only other female zoo I interviewed hasn't yet had sex with the animal of her affections, but she badly wants to. The Florida woman is attracted to dolphins. "I've had some encounters with them but nothing sexual yet," said Sandy (not her real name).

The closest she got was a coupling that she witnessed but didn't participate in. "One time I was on my boat, two orcas swam right up to me and made it at my feet. I was like four feet from them. My clitoris sprung into attention—ping!—and I couldn't get that silly grin off my face for three days. It was so special because they don't come next to people and mate."

Whenever Sandy dives, she has a knife at the ready in case an opportunity presents itself. "Even if it's winter time, I can always cut a split in my wet suit if a dolphin wants to play. I'm not banking my life on it, but I'm never going to turn down the opportunity if it does happen."

A strong swimmer since the age of three, Sandy has devoted herself to a life in and around the water. Her attraction to dolphins began at the age of seven. "I was attracted to my toy animals and I would play with them in a sexual way under my covers."

From ages seven through eleven, she spent summers with her grandparents. They would drop her off at a marine park in St. Augustine, where she spent entire days by herself, immersed in studying the sea. "I didn't have a name for it or anything, but I knew I was different," she said. "I realized it was an attraction. I used to have fantasies—if I could get the surgery, if I could have gills, I'd run away to sea. I used to dream about that."

Even her body is a tribute to her passion. Her skin is covered with sea-themed tattoos—depictions of waves, dolphins, orcas, mermaids and sharks' teeth.

Sandy has had sex with humans three times in her life, and she's not interested in repeating the experience. She felt shame and disgust afterwards. "I knew it wasn't right. It wasn't for me." Sex with men was a symbolic betrayal of her true feelings. "It's like breaking my own heart and doing what's wrong for my heart."

In recent years, Sandy has made friends with other zoos, and feels comfortable openly discussing her sexual orientation with them. But for the first forty years of her life, "I stayed a hundred percent silent." She insisted several times during our conversation that her true identity must remain secret.

∩

Despite the hardships that come with being a zoophile, such as the dread of being discovered, Spink still considers it a gift. "We're born with it. There are certain people who have that gift. There is a genetic profile to it. It runs in families. It is found in every culture. Being zoo is deeply entrenched in the gene pool."

He firmly believes that zoos are a "positive force in the world" with a specific place in the order of things. "Zoophiles have an essential role to play that criticizes the relationship between humans and the rest of the living world. They have a role to play and they are the only ones to play the role." Spink thinks the world would be a better place if he and others like him were allowed to exist without persecution. "It denies the world our wisdom. We provide a useful and utterly unique perspective."

He made another comment that I know will upset a lot of animal lovers who aren't zoos. It ruffled my feathers when he said it. He believes zoos are closer and more connected to their animal companions than non-zoos could ever hope to be.

> There's going to be an element in their relationship that's going to be deeper. There's a bond that happens. It deepens your relationship. There's a special component to physical intimacy. Both get a flush of social bonding. There's a sense that you're connected with each other. To have that extra layer of relationship opens up a depth for new opportunity and new empathy.

Officially, the animal rescue community is against zoophilia, and is lobbying Canada and those American states without laws against sex with animals to enact legislation. Yet most zoos I interviewed have been employed or volunteered in the animal welfare movement, including Doug Spink.

I asked him what he thought of the goal some rescuers have to hunt down and out the zoos.

"Some rescuers are pawns," he replied. "Some, sadly, are taking out their ambient frustration and rage and impotence—all of it genuine and basically honorable—on convenient, socially acceptable, largely helpless targets: zoos. That's not being a 'pawn'—it's being a cruel, angry, mindless bully."

He contends it is hypocritical for Normals to complain about what zoos do when they go around mutilating animals' genitals under the banner of spay and neuter surgeries. Or, in the case of stallions, gelding them in an effort to make them more compliant and easier to manage.

"Cutting pieces of stallions off so they can fit into their barns better is abuse," he said. "I wouldn't have known, but I know because of who I am. This anti-sex thing is crazy. They call us [zoos] in when they need to do the breeding. We're a resource. We know what stallion porn is, metaphorically."

On the website for Exitpoint Stallions, Spink addressed the issue of castration:

We don't practice routine castration here at Exitpoint, not with our dogs or horses or humans either. While it opens me personally up to the tired, old charge that I'm "just a guy with a hang-up about balls," that's not important. What is important is respecting the physical integrity of our friends—genital mutilation reflects a deeply troubled attitude towards our fellow beings. Friends don't cut friends. There's a world of justifications offered for the practice of routine castration, but none of them holds up under objective scrutiny. The facts are clear: it's unnecessary, physically harmful, and a deeply flawed approach to cross-species interaction. Enough said.

In our discussions, I pointed out the overpopulation situation for dogs and cats, a situation he was well aware of. Witnessing and writing about overflowing shelter cages, assembly-line euthanasia, and gas chambers led me to personally spend thousands of my own dollars spaying and neutering animals who weren't even my own. It's been a desperate effort to end overpopulation. And now I was being accused of genital mutilation? Should I feel horrified and guilt-ridden by what I had done to animals in an effort to prevent more death and suffering?

∩

As I researched this story and spoke to people about zoophilia, there was one comment I heard repeatedly from people disgusted by zoo behavior: "As far as I'm concerned, it's just like pedophilia."

Regardless of one's stance on zoophilia, it is important to differentiate zoophilia from pedophilia, because they aren't identical. One is same-species contact between an adult and a child. The other is cross-species contact between an animal, who is usually an adult, and an adult human. Categorizing pedophilia and zoophilia as exactly the same extinguishes an opportunity to better understand what drives people to these different desires.

Zoos I interviewed insist their behavior is nothing like pedophilia. For his part, Spink claims there is no proof that having sex with animals causes traumatic psychological effects to them, as pedophilia undeniably does harm to children. One zoo asked me, "If it's not cruel for my dog to have sex with another dog, why is it cruel for me to have sex with my dog?"

But those who disagree with the zoo stance argue that there is an inherent imbalance in this relationship between owner and animal. The animal is entirely dependent, as a child is, on the adult human for shelter, food and water. It can be viewed as an abuse of power, an unequal relationship, with the humans taking advantage of the inequity for their own sexual purposes. Critics of zoos say that animals are groomed by zoophiles, just as children are groomed to please pedophiles.

Spink pointed out that he despises Normals calling their animals "fur babies." He believes it is a disrespectful way to refer to adult beings of different species. "When you categorize someone as a child, you have gone so far off the path on so many levels. They aren't like little half human beings. You're telling me every species on the planet is just an echo of humanity. Animals are like children because they are echoes of us. We're high and they're low."

Zoos also discussed with me the code of ethics espoused within their community, which includes not having sex with animals younger than sexual maturity. Other tenets include not having sex with animals still feeling the effects of anesthetic following a veterinary visit, and not enticing animals for sex using food treats. Instead of bribing with food, zoophiles believe in arousing the animals to get them interested in sex using the same methods humans use to arouse each other, such as oral and manual stimulation.

I asked many of the zoos I interviewed: how could they possibly know the animals are giving consent when they don't share the same language as we do? They said the animals' consent is confirmed through nonverbal cues. One zoo, for example, said his dog runs back and forth between him and the bedroom door when he is feeling frisky.

Many zoos maintain that it's insulting to animals to contend they aren't able to communicate with humans adeptly enough to signal their consent, or lack of it, using body language. They say that animals have no problem clearly showing their resistance when humans do other things to them that they don't like, such as giving them baths or nail trims.

∩

In our interviews, Spink has always been emphatic that he is not a leader of the zoo community. But he is a talented writer with sophisticated technical knowledge, which enables him to effectively spread his radical ideas about zoophilia far and wide. Government attorneys made a federal case out of his skills being applied towards those purposes, and argued in court that he was disseminating dangerous ideas over the internet—the ideas being that it is not morally wrong to form a sexual relationship with an animal, and that being zoo is a naturally occurring component of human sexuality.

Not all zoos appreciate Spink's attempts at trailblazing. Even in the zoo world, he's a controversial figure. Some consider him a troublemaker, and fear that his brazen, open discussion of zoophilia will only draw unwanted attention and problems to their community.

One zoo from the American Midwest contacted me to bluntly air his grievances about Spink, who he thought should keep a lower profile. He deals with the risk of being caught by not filming his zoo-related activities, and he doesn't keep anything incriminating on his computer. "I don't agree with that zoo rights thing, because it's not going to happen," said the man, who called himself Tim.

Tim feared my book would cause a backlash against zoos. "[Spink] is so open and out attracting so much negative attention. He's got no one to blame but himself. Ultimately he is the one who brought the whole thing down on his head. He's a very dangerous person."

Not everyone agrees. Other zoos think Doug Spink is a hero for standing up to the authorities on behalf of himself and others. Here's what his boyfriend (who is also a zoo) had to say:

> He is a good person, in a way that few will really understand, thanks to the swirl of messages and meta-messages around him. His "fault" is his fearlessness when it comes to risks. He is willing to stand up against anything that is unjust, almost regardless of personal cost. That is probably a good amount of the reason that some people in my world find him distasteful: He is willing to speak out loud about what we are told are unspeakable, dangerous, subversive things. As I get older, I better understand his motives, and while they have complicated many lives, I have come to believe that the public dialog is important, if only in that thru them the young can find that they are not alone. I especially wonder if the whole decision to destroy his family is the decision that should have been made, if the goal was truly the well being of his family.
> Of course, it never was, was it?

42

SELLING SECRECY

Computers play an important role in the lives of zoos. Most feel like they could never confess their true feelings about animals to friends and family, so that leaves their connection to the internet as the only way to feel understood and find community with people like them.

For Doug Spink, computers played a much more significant role than they did for the average zoo. They provided his livelihood because he sold privacy and encryption services.

Years after Spink landed back in prison for probation violations, the custody battle over his computer raged on. The US Probation Office had seized computers belonging to Spink and Stephen Clarke when they raided his cabin, along with all Spink's paper files and records. During the hearing, federal attorney Susan Roe accused Spink of "selling secrecy," and insinuated that his use of encryption was an indicator of guilt. A sign of someone with something to hide.

From the Beaumont penitentiary, Spink fought for the right to recover his property, in particular the encrypted computer. His case eventually wound its way up to the Ninth Circuit of the US Supreme Court.

The dispute didn't drag on because the computer was a valuable piece of equipment. Spink had bought the Hewlett-Packard tower at Best Buy in Bellingham for less than $400. Rather it was what the computer represented to both sides. From Spink's perspective, even more important than getting his data back was the opportunity to make a point. He believed his case would have rippling ramifications for the privacy rights of Americans attempting to protect their information from the government's prying eyes. For its part, the government was determined to quash his ability to make that point.

∩

Spink's lawyer, Howard Phillips, began his attempts to retrieve his client's property as soon as the federal court proceeding came to a close in July 2010. The probation office and government attorneys stalled, arguing that because Spink was appealing his judgment and sentencing, they had to retain the computer as evidence.

Spink was appealing his sentence length, and the conditions to be imposed on him after his prison term while he was on supervised release. He was particularly annoyed by the conditions that involved his use of computers. He was required to get approval from his probation officer or a court-approved therapist before owning a computer or another device that connected to the Internet; all computers he owned would be subject to surveillance by the federal government and inspection by his probation officer; software he bought, used or otherwise possessed would have to be cleared by his probation officer. The surveillance and inspections would hinder his ability to provide privacy services to his customers.

Government attorneys defended the special conditions because of who Spink was. "Given Spink's use of encryption programs and other mechanisms to obscure what should be transparent," the intense scrutiny was justified, noted a filing from January 3, 2011.

Phillips vehemently opposed the restrictions, arguing that his client had the right to engage in private conduct without government intervention. But the government refused to back down, arguing that:

> Spink used his superior intellect and specialized knowledge of computer technology and corporate forms to engage in prohibited

activity for years while concealing true actions from his probation officer and, therefore, from the court. His duplicity was discovered only because he became brazen enough to intervene in the prosecution of others. Spink's misconduct did not constitute mere technical violations, but rather, a prohibited lifestyle systematically created and maintained through deceit.

Spink believed it was the federal government who was being deceitful. In September 2013, he wrote to Phillips about his suspicions that the Drug Enforcement Administration had used National Security Agency intercepts illegally in his 2005 drug smuggling case.

Back in 2005, the public might not have believed the conspiracy theories being spun out of the high-tech world about government surveillance and the storage of vast amounts of personal communication, including texts, emails and phone records. But in 2013, whistle-blower Edward Snowden exposed the NSA's routine surveillance of American citizens by leaking thousands of classified files to selected journalists. "Now that Snowden has taken the lid off the NSA's enormous can of worms, the reality of what was done to me doesn't seem so far-fetched," Spink wrote in an email to Phillips.

Spink lost his appeal on the conditions and sentencing. When Phillips again asked for his client's computer to be returned, federal lawyers argued that because the disk likely contained contraband, it couldn't be returned in its current state, and would have to be erased.

In fact, the lawyers couldn't be certain what the disk contained, because despite the best efforts of the FBI computer experts and the extensive resources available to them, they couldn't break the encryption.

Spink encrypted all his disks for two reasons: to protect the data they contained, and to prevent evidence from being planted on them. The latter risk he identified as real and plausible because of who he was.

The encryption he employed was sophisticated. Not only were the feds unable to break in, their computer specialists couldn't even determine whether the disk was encrypted, or simply blank. In court filings, Susan Roe and Steven Masada alternately argued that the disk was encrypted, and then that it had been wiped clean by Spink. Logically, both assertions couldn't be true. Howard Phillips pounced on the flip-flopping:

> The government alleges that Spink had "wiped" the hard drives and device clean. This, if true would suggest that Spink was thereby attempting to hide information on his computer. When Probation and State law enforcement executed the arrest warrant for Spink, he had been sleeping and answered the door without clothes. If he did not have time to put on his clothes, surely he did not have an opportunity to wipe his hard drive clean. This is mere speculation on the Government's part, and the fact that the drive may have appeared to the government to be "wiped clean" may have more to do with the Government's technical incompetence than any evidence of guilt on Spink's part. Therefore, the government should be precluded from arguing that Mr. Spink's computer was encrypted therefore he is guilty or; 2) that his hard drive was "wiped clean" therefore his attempt to hide information is evidence of his guilt.

When the cadre of cops came pounding on Spink's door that morning, the FBI agents made a colossal mistake. They powered down his computer rather than leaving it running to gain access. That single action torpedoed their mission—turning the computer off caused its full disk encryption mode to kick in. Rather than just protecting certain files, FDE encrypted the entire disk.

Roe and Masada had accused Spink in court of running bestiality websites. In declaring that Spink's computer likely contained contraband, Roe and Masada fortified their argument by pointing out that Stephen Clarke's laptop, found on Spink's property during the raid, contained thousands of images of bestiality and child pornography. A series of emails between Roe and Phillips reveals that Roe repeatedly asserted that the seized laptop belonged to Spink, a claim Phillips hotly contested:

> [Spink] saw the inventory of what was taken for the first time after it was copied by Mr. Robson [Spink's probation officer] for me. I mailed it to him along with the information that the electronics were being held. He informed me shortly after receipt of the inventory that the laptop was not his, and that he didn't care what happened to it. I sent you an email stating that. I keep close records of my activities and I will be more than happy to prepare an affidavit that Spink informed me of the laptop shortly after receiving the inventory provided by Robson.

Meanwhile, Phillips continued to ask Jeff Robson to return Spink's property. He was not satisfied with the probation officer's response: "As far as Mr. Spink's property goes, please forward me a list of what property he wants returned (that is not in violation of his release conditions) and I'll forward it on." In a letter to Robson, Phillips took issue with that:

> I am sure that you are aware that a governmental taking of personal property is unconstitutional, which is why I am puzzled by your email indicating that I forward to you a list of what property he wants returned (that is not in violation of his release conditions).
>
> I draw your attention to the following; 1) Mr. Spink is not on Supervised Release, and is not under the jurisdiction of U.S. Probation; 2) the government has not required conditions for the release of his property. (the government secured an Order keeping the property pending appeal); 3) his property is being retrieved by someone other than Mr. Spink who still has months in custody; and finally, 4) there has been no finding by any judge that all of Mr. Spink's property should not be returned to him or a third party.
>
> Therefore, we respectfully request that you withdraw the condition requiring that you be provided an inventory of permissible property. I don't believe that you have the authority to unilaterally impose such a condition on a citizen, even one in prison.

○

So what was on the Hewlett-Packard computer at the center of so much debate? According to Spink, it mostly contained files that were personally meaningful to him.

> Incidentally, what data were encrypted on that drive—along with some Baneki info (not customer records, ironically) were mostly pictures of my dogs and horses from throughout my life. Files of papers and stuff I'd written in high school, college, graduate school. Published essays in a bunch of journals and magazines and stuff. Some drafts of early-stage books I was writing. Lots of personal, irreplaceable materials. That's what Susan [Roe] was holding hostage.

Spink was convinced the federal government was trying to access the business records of Baneki Privacy Computing in an attempt to destroy his privacy and encryption company. He believed Roe was searching for lists of Baneki customers and shareholders. "She could then harass all those people, kicking off a long chain of persecution." She could also, by exposing details about Baneki's clients, publicly ruin Spink's credibility as a privacy advocate. "That was a clear objective of Susan Roe, throughout:

make an example of me, by crushing me totally, so that others thinking of providing 'serious' privacy to mere everyday people via strong cryptography would think twice about the target they were painting on themselves in doing so."

The government eventually agreed to return Spink's computer, but said they wouldn't do it until they erased the hard drive first. His lawyer, Howard Phillips, argued against erasing it, but lost the argument. Spink said he wasn't given the requisite ten days to appeal before "USPO erased the drive and sent a letter to Howard telling him that. At that point, further appeal was moot: the drive was gone, and we had no good argument for why we could continue to litigate."

After years of wrangling, Spink ultimately lost his case. He eventually received just the "empty husk" of the computer back, as he described it. The decision regarding Spink's computer now resides in the books of the United States Supreme Court, but it has the potential to reappear in the form of case law. Jim Turner, another of Spink's attorneys, talked about how court decisions are recognized as precedent, otherwise known as *stare decisis*.

> You need to make sure the law is upheld, otherwise it deteriorates. We get a slippery slope, where people start ignoring the law more and more. It starts with Doug, where we're uncomfortable about sex with animals, so we deny constitutional protections and fair play. Something fairly innocuous could have a ripple effect. You can't let stuff like that happen to people like Doug, because then you're stuck with the decisions you've made. Once the case is made, you can't change it if you have a similar set of facts coming up.

As for Spink, he was disappointed that no one stepped in to help him when he needed it, to back him up in a fight against privacy infringement that he couldn't possibly win alone. Once more, the bestiality label was too powerful to overcome.

> My "punishment" for using encryption was that the government was allowed to destroy my data because I refused to decrypt it for them. That's a big deal. The logic is scary, and could easily expand. If precedent was set and the Feds could do these preemptive seizures of any encrypted materials, all bets were off for everyone using crypto in America. It will have a chilling effect on the use of crypto, because any encrypted data becomes vulnerable to seizure and government destruction.

From a personal standpoint, I wondered: could the decision in Spink's case make my data vulnerable to government surveillance and seizure too? After all, I was interviewing Spink and a host of other zoophiles. Could I be targeted next as someone associating with zoos? What protections did I have as a member of the press? And a freelance member at that?

I wasn't sure I wanted to find out.

PUBLIC RECORDS

In late February 2012, five months before Spink's release from Beaumont, I met with Laura Clark in her office at the Whatcom Humane Society to discuss my communications with Spink, and to let her know I was thinking of putting together a documentary about the case. Or maybe a book. She smiled as we spoke and seemed amenable to the idea.

But the following week, on March 4, she revealed her feelings more clearly in an email: "You do not have permission to use any materials you may have gathered about the Doug Spink case from current or past Whatcom Humane Society staff members or volunteers, including the use of any photos, videos and/or written interviews you may have obtained."

Of course I didn't need Clark's permission to use the material I'd collected in my quest to tell this story. She didn't own the information. No one did.

Then she took it a step further: "Much of the above mentioned information could be considered evidence and may be used in future investigations of Mr. Spink and his associates."

Clark also had a problem with me communicating with Spink. Again, that was beyond her authority as an animal shelter director. "As you are aware, as part of his sentencing in Federal Court, Spink was ordered to have no access to computers," she wrote. "It is my understanding that you continue to communicate on a semi-regular basis with Mr. Spink via email. I respectfully request that you report these communications to the Federal Bureau of Prisons so they are aware of his actions."

Spink wasn't corresponding with me or anyone else outside Beaumont's prison walls without the knowledge of prison authorities. They monitored every communication he made with the outside world. Like other inmates at federal facilities, he was not permitted internet access, but he was allowed to use the CorrLinks system to send and receive emails (no attachments). For that privilege, he paid a fee of $3.75 per hour from his commissary funds to use it.

Laura Clark was also upset that I was interviewing Spink's mother, Claire, by telephone. This was interesting, because it was Clark who'd given me Claire's phone number in the first place, in the same meeting when she supplied me with Corinne Super's number.

Clark's resistance to my normal process of work as a journalist stoked my motivation to keep going and get to the truth. She was holding back details of the Spink case, which included refusing to tell me what had happened to all his animals, so I searched for another route to the information.

In October 2012, Bellingham-based animal rights lawyer Adam Karp agreed to submit a Freedom of Information request to WHS on my behalf, asking for copies of the photos the shelter had taken of the mice.

Clark was perturbed by the inquiry. "For what purpose are you making this request?" she wrote back to Karp. "As I have informed you, the Whatcom Humane Society will in no way cooperate with any project that Carreen Maloney is involved with."

Clark followed up that refusal with a statement I viewed as a warning: "The seizure of the animals involved in this case was done at the bequest of the federal government and if you continue to request records from this case, we will have to involve them as well as our own attorney's [*sic*]."

Finally, because of pressure applied using the requirements of the Washington State Public Records Act, Clark grudgingly provided a portion of what I'd requested. She turned over 698 pages, which wasn't much considering that most of it was court documents I already had, because they were publicly available.

When I reviewed the documents, it was clear they weren't even close to a full record of what had happened. For example, Clark released no emails between herself and Jenny Edwards of Hope for Horses, yet I knew they'd been in frequent contact about the Spink case for a long time. They always sat together before, during and after Spink's court appearances, and Edwards had won custody of two of Spink's horses, Cantour and Sigi. It was implausible that no emails had passed between Clark and Edwards.

I asked WHS attorney Kirsten Barron why the records weren't complete. "Laura prints what she thinks is important and deletes the rest," Barron said, but didn't provide further explanation.

The destruction of public documents (like the release of them) falls under the purview of the Washington State Public Records Act. It's a Class C felony punishable by "imprisonment in a state correctional facility for not more than five years, or by a fine of not more than one thousand dollars, or by both." (Incidentally, bestiality is a Class C felony too.)

Under the act, there are specific criteria for whether an agency is obligated to preserve and provide particular records. Whatcom Humane Society isn't a government agency, but that doesn't mean it escapes the obligations of the act. Washington uses a four-part test to determine if the Public Records Act applies to a private entity:

No individual criteria of the test must be met but the parts should be considered as a whole. The test includes whether or not the agency:

• is funded by a public body
• was created by a public body
• is controlled by a public body
• performs a public function

Whatcom Humane Society is a private nonprofit organization, but it also performs public functions. And it receives government funds in the form of animal control contracts.

When it came to the Spink case, as Clark herself pointed out in her email to Adam Karp, WHS was acting at the behest of the federal government.

In contrast with Laura Clark's resistance to my investigation, WHS attorney Kirsten Barron was reasonable and helpful. After she received the request Karp made on my behalf, she invited me to the office of Barron Smith Daugert in Bellingham to look over the records submitted by Clark. She good-naturedly made copies for a nominal fee of $68, and even sat with me in a conference room while I looked everything over in case I had questions.

Besides court records and photographs of Spink's animals taken by WHS staff, there were a few emails among the documents. There were also pieces of physical evidence, baggies that contained the collars and tags worn by Spink's dogs. It appeared they had been packed away wet, because they were covered in spongy green mold that sprayed all over the conference room table when I pulled them out.

I also got evidence photos of the mice, which I'd specifically requested. In one photo, I saw the black lanyard that Spink said he'd used on the tail of the injured mouse to keep him away from the other mice. None of the photos of the mice showed any signs of Vaseline.

To read emails regarding my Freedom of Information request to the Whatcom Humane Society, see Exhibit 11, page 391.

To read the Washington State law pertaining to destruction of records, see Exhibit 12, page 394.

44

B WORD

Spink was released from federal prison for the second time in July of 2012. Some things were familiar. Just as he had been after his first stretch in prison for the drug smuggling, he was assigned to spend a few months at Pioneer Fellowship House, a sixty-bed halfway house in Seattle that, from the outside, resembles a modest apartment building. But this time, the vibe was different. The *B* word was exacting its toll on his life yet again.

Unlike his first stint at Pioneer, he wasn't given the same privileges as other residents. He wasn't allowed passes to go to the library or to take classes. Months after our first meeting on the grass in Seattle on that Sunday in August 2012, I found out that was a rare outing from the confines of the halfway house.

He was, however, allowed to have a cell phone and to talk on it for as long as he wanted. That was not the case in prison, where federal inmates are allowed only three hundred minutes of calling time per month. I conducted many of my interviews with him by cell phone while he was at Pioneer stuck indoors without much to do.

One time, he called to ask if I knew of any bird rescuers in the area. A crow had flown into the window, stunning himself, and he'd placed the creature in his truck to recuperate. After a short time, the crow recovered and flew away.

On another call, he remarked on a squirrel who sat outside his window nibbling on a nut. "I have more in common with that squirrel out there than I do with most humans," he said.

He'd been asked by people copious times if he fucked trees, a question he found offensive. He didn't understand why people would compare his feelings for sentient four-legged beings to feelings about trees.

When we met for interviews in public places, people stared at him. Even people who didn't know Doug Spink sensed that he was a different breed of human, and they had a range of reactions to him: curious, fascinated, frightened. I didn't think it was because they recognized his face. His story had traveled around the world and been featured on thousands of websites, but he wasn't recognizable to most people. Still, he exuded the aura of someone who had been through something.

There's an assumption that people who have sex with animals do so only because they can't attract a human, but I found out that's not the case. Some zoos I interviewed were loners who had trouble making human friends, but many were not, and struggled to balance the needs of humans who wanted to form romantic bonds with them and their ardent devotion to their animals, who always came first.

As for Spink, he viewed himself as socially awkward, but some women found him handsome and engaging. He appealed to their minds—he had a way of finding common intellectual ground with people's interests, and it drew women to him. The fact that he had no interest in having sex with female humans only contributed to his allure. It was like catnip. During interviews, I'd listen to women run him down one minute, then in the next breath, they'd lapse into dreamy-eyed discussions of what a handsome figure he cut as he rode shirtless on horseback.

That didn't mean dealing with humans was easy for him. Despite his high intelligence—or perhaps because of it—he sometimes felt frustrated and even confused as he interacted with people. He had trouble with the difference between what people said, and what they actually meant. Sometimes the disconnect happened as part of the vagueness of human interactions. Other times, it stemmed from someone deliberating obfuscating.

One example of the latter occurred with his alma mater, Reed College. A 2012 article in the school's satirical magazine, *The Pamphlette,* labeled Spink "Reed's Creepiest Alum." The author began: "Here be monsters: Be forewarned, dear classmates, for this might very well be the most disturbing article I have ever written. It's also the most horrifyingly true."

The writer had gone incognito to get her story:

> Anyway, I decided I had to contact this fellow for an interview. You know, 'cause I'm a responsible student reporter with a thirst for knowledge. Also, because I figured anything he said would be comedic gold. Problem was, I didn't relish giving a convicted felon my real name and/or email address, especially considering the fact that he has called his own sister out by name on his blog. I also didn't want to make him so angry that he wouldn't respond. My solution? A dummy email address, a pseudonym, and a tone of naive journalistic objectivity. Thus, I became Arlene Smith, a student reporter at Reed College, curious about Spink's battle with the legal system.

Not realizing the interview was a joke on him, Spink took the communication from "Arlene Smith" seriously and answered her questions sincerely, which only added fodder to her gag. It wasn't surprising that he did this; he had always taken school matters seriously. The writer ate it up:

> Another question he deigned to answer was "Do you have any advice for current Reed students?" Now, I had very high hopes for his response to this question, for obvious reasons, and I was not disappointed—his sordid advice on horse-fucking was somewhat shrouded in metaphor and symbolism, but I understood. Oh, I understood all too well. It's disturbingly blatant, if you know where to look. "If I had any useful advice for Reed students," he began, "it would be to tackle big, challenging, transformative projects." Any reasonably educated person could infer that he's using "projects" as a euphemism for "horse penises." For shame.

Like other episodes in his life, Spink's time at Pioneer Fellowship House wasn't uneventful. On September 19, 2012, the US Marshals Service paid him a visit. I received this text at 7:35 p.m.: "My phone is being seized. Talk later."

Later that night, the marshals returned his phone to him without explanation. He followed up with me by email:

> Right now, I can't even estimate how many people are involved in the ongoing surveillance and harassment of me. A sadly funny example was about a month ago, I was on foot in Seattle and as is my habit did a little backtrace to see if I was being followed—that resulted in coming face to face with a Fed agent of some flavour—when asked what he was about, he smiled and just walked the other direction. It's really more a form of intimidation than any effort they are trying to "hide" what they're doing. They aren't hiding anything—they have no need to. They are immune from consequences.

Perhaps it sounds like Spink was being paranoid about being followed by federal agents, and I couldn't confirm whether it happened or not, because I didn't see it. But there were other instances that confirmed to me that he was handled differently than the average citizen. For example, he got singled out for special treatment when he was behind the wheel. Several times while I was interviewing him by phone as he drove, he was stopped by police. He'd always keep the phone line open so I could eavesdrop on what happened next. The flavor of the interactions would change as soon as the officers ran his name through the system and realized with whom they were dealing. Their demeanor and tone turned more serious than would be the case with average citizens. Once I heard an officer remark, when he returned to the car after running Spink's name, "You've got flags in the system I haven't even seen before."

There were times when I found myself traveling in the same vehicle with Spink for one reason or another, such as visiting a location that he had talked about, or going for coffee or a bite to eat after an interview. That's when I had the chance to observe firsthand the change in demeanor of the police officers who pulled him over. It was eerie to see them take his driver's license and go back to their cruisers, run his name, then exit their patrol cars with a hand touching the gun holstered at their hips.

A staff person at the halfway house who was amicable with Spink warned him about being so outspoken with me and others he was communicating with. Spink wouldn't give me her name, wanting to protect her confidentiality, but he sent me her written warning:

> I appreciate your honesty, Mr. Spink, but I implore you to please be careful with any information you are giving out and/or any side work you are doing around this issue. I understand your anger and frustration, but I'd like you to step out of that for a moment and

consider the consequences of what you are doing. Is it worth it? If yes, then, obviously, continue…but if there is any hesitation in your answer, please take a look at that. I don't want to see you set yourself up for further persecution/prosecution (on what grounds? I don't know…I don't think it matters).

But her warning didn't deter him from doing interviews with me. His cooperation didn't go unnoticed. On November 6, Spink and I were on the phone when, from his window, he saw the US Marshals pull into the lot in the familiar black SUV. He had a bad feeling, he said, and his uneasiness only intensified when he was paged to come downstairs to the office. They were there to take him away, he said; he was sure of it. Then he hung up.

After that: silence. For days. No phone calls, no texts, no emails.

No one I checked with knew where he was—not his friends, not even his mother, who was filled with worry and fear. The two were very close, and Spink communicated with her frequently, so his silence frightened her.

To me, the timing seemed suspicious. Just days earlier, on October 31, animal rights attorney Adam Karp had submitted a Freedom of Information request on my behalf, asking Laura Clark for photos of the mice seized from Spink's cabin. And now Spink had vanished.

Clark had replied to Karp's request with what sounded like a warning: "The seizure of the animals involved in this case was done at the bequest of the federal government and if you continue to request records from this case, we will have to involve them as well as our own attorney's. [*sic*]"

Did Spink's disappearance have anything to do with my request for records from WHS? Had it set off a chain of events? Or was the timing just coincidental?

I didn't know. To this day, I still don't. All I knew then was that Spink was missing, and I wondered if there was a way to figure out where he was.

45

LEGAL BEAGLE

After Spink had been gone for about a week, I contacted a lawyer I knew named Jim Turner. He lived in Bellingham, but happened to be in Seattle on that particular day, so I asked if he'd consider stopping by SeaTac federal prison to see if Spink was in there. Lawyers have special privileges and access to inmates that regular citizens don't have.

Turner was a former public defender for Pierce County, Washington, with a passion for defending people of color, the poor and "those outside of society's bell curve" (his description). He still carried the honeyed accent that was a remnant of his upbringing in Carthage, Tennessee.

As a white kid growing up in the South, Turner grew inspired to become a trial lawyer by Harper Lee's classic novel, *To Kill a Mockingbird*. Atticus Finch and his unwavering integrity illustrated the kind of attorney Turner wanted to be. He even named his first son Atticus as an homage to the beloved character.

While a work of fiction sparked Turner's career, his brilliant mind took to the law in a very real way. He practiced it like an art form. His courtroom arguments wove together threads of compassion and humanity, which wound around logical and legal interpretations to form compelling arguments.

Turner fought for his clients with an ardency I'd rarely witnessed in a lawyer. It wasn't just a way to make a living for him. He often worked pro bono, which was part of the territory when it came to defending those on society's margins. This wasn't just business for him—it was emotional. Verdicts that went against his clients put him in a dark mental space. But despite the soul-bruising disappointments his career sometimes delivered, he expressed to me many times that the courtroom was where he felt most alive.

It was that same venue—the courtroom he loved so dearly—that was also the scene of the most painful experience he had ever endured.

It was November 2002 and he was in Wenatchee cross-examining a key witness in court, an informant in a drug case. The cross was going well, and he was in an upbeat mood. The night before, his sixteen-year-old daughter, Etta, an exchange student living in Bolivia for a year, had emailed him to announce the happy news that she'd decided to live with him when she returned to the United States. Before her trip, she'd been staying with her mother, Turner's ex-wife. Turner was elated by this development.

As he questioned his witness, he noticed that all faces in the courtroom—jury, judge, witnesses, lawyers—had swiveled to stare behind him. He turned around to see a prosecutor who was also a friend. The prosecutor's face was white, his expression stricken. He led Turner into his office and put him on the phone with Etta's mother. She told Turner that their daughter had been riding on a tourist bus traveling on a narrow road in Bolivia with several other students near dawn when the driver lost control. The bus veered off the route and tumbled down the mountainside. Seven people died including Etta.

On Thanksgiving morning, Turner arrived in Bolivia to collect his daughter's body. The devastation of losing a child brought a nearly relentless pain to his life that would never subside.

Less than a year after Turner's searing loss of his child, Doug Spink suffered a great loss too. It was a crash of a different kind, the one that claimed his best friend, Dwain Weston, whose wingsuit-clad body rammed into a bridge.

Jim Turner was the right person for me to call. He found Spink in SeaTac prison the same afternoon. It turned out that on November 2, a warrant had been issued for Spink's arrest, prompting the marshals to pick him up four days later at Pioneer Fellowship House. He spent the next week in solitary confinement, trying to contact the outside world by passing notes under the door to prison guards asking for a lawyer. His requests were ignored.

Turner arranged to meet with Spink in one of the lawyer-client visiting rooms. The two men hit it off immediately and talked animatedly for an hour, each enjoying the other's sharp wit.

After Turner left SeaTac that day, Spink was moved—immediately and without explanation—from solitary confinement into general population.

Turner and Spink would form a bond that lasted through the years to come. Spink was impressed by Turner's gift for practicing law, and he was a man who didn't impress easily. Turner was fascinated by Spink's intellect and his unusual belief system, and admired his unwillingness to back down in the face of powerful pressures from the government, no matter the cost.

∩

Ever since Spink's unexpected departure from Pioneer, his SUV had been parked where he'd left it—on a side street gathering a soggy stack of parking tickets on the windshield. In desperation, his mother asked if I would retrieve it.

My interest wasn't in the truck itself, but what was inside. The Chevy Suburban was crammed full of years' worth of files that Spink had fought the federal government to get returned to him, documents he'd agreed to give me to help me prove this bizarre tale thoroughly and accurately. Losing that information, much of which I hadn't seen yet, would not have prevented me from getting the story eventually, but it wouldn't be an ideal situation.

Spink's mother, Claire, arranged with Pioneer to release the vehicle's key to me. I traveled two hours to Seattle from Custer three times to pick it up as previously agreed, only to be turned away by staff each time I got there. On my arrival, they would claim they couldn't find the key, or that the director wasn't there to authorize giving it to me.

Finally, when I was turned away the third time, I called a traveling locksmith in Seattle to find out if he could change out the steering column. Metal clashed against metal as he searched noisily through his stock on hand before exclaiming that he had just one column in stock that would fit the Suburban.

I walked back into Pioneer's lobby to inform staff members behind the front desk that I was taking the SUV by replacing its steering column. The locksmith turned out to be unnecessary. A few minutes later, a Pioneer employee came out to where I was standing beside Spink's truck and handed me the key.

I got access to all the files I needed, but not all Spink's belongings would be returned by Pioneer. Because of his rapid and unexpected departure from the halfway house, his personal property remained there while he was at SeaTac, placed in trash bags and moved into a storage area until his release. But when he was released from prison and got his things back, his wallet was missing. Eventually he received it at his post office box in Bellingham, along with a letter from the US Postal Service informing him that someone had found the wallet on the street in Seattle and dropped it into a mailbox to have it returned to him. It had been emptied of its cash and credit card.

∩

While Spink was back in prison, Whatcom County prosecutors decided to charge him with three counts of animal cruelty after all, despite what prosecutor David McEachran had said following the 2010 raid about not punishing him twice for the same incident.

On November 23, just as his time in federal custody was scheduled to run out (prisoners staying at halfway houses are still considered to be in custody), US marshals transported Spink from SeaTac to Whatcom County jail to face the charges.

His confidence in his legal position didn't waver. "I've done years of prison time to earn this opportunity. We are going to take this statute off the books," he said. But that confidence didn't mean he was unafraid of county jail. He was used to federal prison; he understood the system and knew some of the staff and inmates. Whatcom County jail was another story. An unknown.

"For the record, I am scared," he admitted to me in a rare moment. "They could kill me and get away with it. I have a valuable role to play. I am an acknowledged target for anyone. I've been fair game since I was twelve years old."

He worried that guards and inmates might spread rumors that he was a pedophile. He felt he could stand up to other inmates on his own merit, but all bets were off if he got stuck with the pedophile label. Game over.

He did not want to die in prison. "I know it happens. They will do it in exchange for a cell phone. To be handcuffed and beaten to death in a cell, helpless and knowing they won't be held accountable for it. It's not an honorable death. It's meaningless. That's one of the few things I have fear of."

Spink's trepidation over what might happen to him in Whatcom County jail didn't materialize. He did fine, as he always did when he was in custody, earning the nickname "Federal" from other inmates. But he felt as if he would never escape the grasp of people determined to destroy him.

"I have no confidence that this county stuff is going to be okay. They have the chance to do it all over again. They have unlimited resources and no accountability. If the baseball bat breaks, they will get another one, and if I fight back they'll go and get a crowbar and make it worse. I'm walking into a rigged game and I'm going to lose. I'm just waiting now for the punishment to come."

He entered a plea of not guilty at his arraignment on December 7, posted a $5,000 bond, and was released until such time as the court decided to hear his case. The three-year statute of limitations for animal cruelty charges would have run out four months later, in April 2013.

The prospect of a state trial still loomed. But for now, Spink was free to go and live on his own, provided his housing arrangements were approved by the federal probation department. It's not easy to secure housing as a felon, so he relied on his contacts from the prison system to help him find a place.

Mike Fenter was a former cellmate of Spink's. They had roomed together at Federal Detention Center SeaTac, where Fenter was serving a ten-year sentence for robbing four banks in California and Washington State. Fenter's wife at the time, Kateen, hadn't been implicated in his crimes, so she was free to continue running their farm in Discovery Bay not far from Port Townsend, a charming small city on the northeast tip of Washington's lush Olympic Peninsula.

The Fenters' farm, called Compass Rose, welcomes members of the community and beyond into its fold, offering internships for students seeking to learn about sustainable, earth-friendly agriculture.

Spink rented a trailer on the property to work and sleep in. The small home was tucked into peaceful, pastoral surroundings. It wasn't plumbed, but there was access to electricity, and it was safe, clean and quiet. It was there that Spink dove back into work resurrecting his encryption company, which he had renamed from Baneki to Cryptocloud. (It's since been renamed again, to Cryptostorm, following a dispute Spink had with a former business partner.) It didn't take long for him to get up and running again. There was consumer and business demand for his services. "I have a skill lots of Normals desperately need: I know privacy tech," he said.

The move to the farm on the peninsula seemed like another new beginning for Spink. But it would prove to be an ominous decision that contained an almost unimaginable coincidence, one that would land him in deep trouble yet again.

46

HEAVY PETTING

Gathering information about a topic as controversial and complicated as zoophilia is challenging. People fear speaking about it. I needed to shake more information loose and draw more sources out of the shadows, so I figured a blog might be an effective avenue. On the blog, I would discuss the process of writing the book. It would be a central place where people could reach out to me, debate the salient facts, and weigh in with opinions that I could add to the story.

I wondered if I was poking a hornet's nest.

Part of my unease came from facing a distinct and unavoidable conflict of interest. As a seasoned animal rescuer, I am expected to turn over any evidence I collect regarding zoos to the authorities, the goal being to prosecute and punish them for behavior towards animals that is illegal in many places, and considered abusive by society in general. But as a journalist, I'm bound to protect the confidentiality of my sources, a protection so sacred that in extreme cases, journalists will go to jail for contempt of court rather than name names.

When I took this project on, I discussed the conflict of interest conundrum with animal rescuers I'd known for years. If I wasn't working to send zoos to jail, and if I intended to keep their names confidential, did the rescuers still think it was important for me to chase this story? Unanimously, the people I trusted enough to ask their opinions said yes. I can't deny I was nervous about posting the first story in December 2012. I'd chosen to focus on the mystery of the mice. I hesitated before hitting the "post" button. Once it was done, I could never truly undo it.

I didn't advertise or promote the blog, but that didn't prevent people from finding it. And fast. It was simultaneously unnerving and gratifying to check the WordPress statistics graph and see thousands of visitors coming in from 125 countries and nine territories.

Spink's friends and enemies made up some of the blog's readership. His following included people who admired him, and others who despised him. He always took the time to fight back in words when critics such as this woman, who called herself Julia, posted comments against him:

> Oh Carreen, what a mess. This blog is not a conversation about how we love our animals. It's a forum for Doug spew. He makes a mess of everything he touches and if you let him drive your book and run your web site you will get Spinky goo all over everything.
>
> When Doug was arrested on the parole violation there was a blog out of Canada that followed the proceedings but also became a forum for reasoned debate on Zoo issues. It was what you want this blog to be. The common thread was a dislike for Doug, by Zoo and non-zoo alike. There was a common enemy and it drove a meaningful discourse.

Most of the time, journalists are permitted—even encouraged—to keep a neutral tone. That wasn't the case when it came to writing about this topic. Some people got riled up because the blog didn't explicitly condemn zoophiles to a fate of eternal damnation. I was called "disgusting" just for writing about the subject. One commenter threatened to contact news outlets that had printed my stories in the past to tell them never to allow my writing to appear there again. Another wrote that my pieces were being logged to later use against me somehow.

A commenter going by the name, "Can't wait for Spink to go back to prison," weighed in and said, "I have more than one person living with me who shares my opinion on what a dumb twit you are and also share [*sic*] my computer. You have no idea who I am, and if you do well good, then you know I know much more than you do. You're an awful writer, a sorry excuse for a journalist, and a failure as an animal rescuer."

Some readers contended that interviewing zoophiles to get their story was "pro-zoo." Their battle cries came with a driving call for censorship.

"No one who loves and respects animals would ever give someone like that the time of day or even a chance to speak," blasted one commenter, who went by B. Powell.

"The only surprise, I guess, is you Carreen," lectured the woman calling herself Julia. "Your coming out so strongly on the pro-zoo side is disheartening."

Pro-zoo? I had never actually stated whether I was "for" or "against" the zoos. What I think personally as one human being isn't as important as accurately telling a story that has—until now—remained largely untold.

Julia also issued a warning that seemed intended as a silencer: "Just remember that it's the internet and none of this ever goes away." She seemed to miss that I was working on a book about this subject. The indelible nature of the internet wasn't about to send me running scared.

Critics of the blog talked about "us" and "them." How could I—someone who hailed from the world of animal rescue—possibly speak to "people like them?" Why on earth was I letting "them" have a say? Had I lost my mind?

What some critics may not realize is that there is less of a dividing line between "people like them" and "people like us" than they think, or want to believe.

Consider the Kinsey statistics. According to results collected from eleven thousand people, fully 8 percent of men and 3.6 percent of women have had at least one sexual experience with an animal in their lifetimes. Those are the ones who admit it. There are likely more. Unless you're living in a bubble, you unwittingly know people who have had such an encounter.

When I began investigating zoophilia, an astonishing dynamic developed. Cautiously, nervously—and only when they felt it was safe to do so—people I knew began to confess their own stories. Deep secrets.

Things that had happened to them in their lives, or the lives of people close to them.

Suddenly I was seeing zoophilia all around me.

There was the friend who let her dog hump her leg every night because it seemed to soothe him. Another person, a banker I knew, talked about not being allowed to have a dog as a child because her mother had witnessed a neighbor having sex with a dog, and was determined she would never see *that* again. Then there were the twins, women who played a childhood game as young girls: masturbating the family dog to orgasm.

Another man confessed to me (the only person he'd ever told) that as a teenager, he'd had an intimate relationship with a Doberman Pinscher. She ran into his room one day and started giving him oral sex. It continued regularly until one day, the dog gently bit the boy's penis. Up until that point, he had thought about taking it further and having intercourse with her, but the minor bite was enough to scare him into stopping for fear the dog might bite it off.

Complete strangers confessed their stories too. When I visited the local office-supply store to buy a printer so I could churn out early drafts of the manuscript, the salesman was curious: what was I writing about? When I explained, he revealed that his uncle was a zoo who fell in love with the family dog, much to his aunt's chagrin.

I was stunned. What was going on? What could it mean? Was zoophilia really happening all around me and I hadn't realized it?

What I know now is that nearly every zoophile I've interviewed so far has worked or volunteered in some capacity in the animal rights movement. They are shelter and vet clinic workers. They are professional breeders. They are rescue group founders and operators. They are all around us, hidden in plain sight.

∩

I was in the midst of approving a few angry comments on the blog late one night when it struck me—I needed advice from someone who'd already traveled this hate highway, a person who had been on the receiving end of the vitriolic reactions launched at anyone who dares to discuss zoophilia out in the open.

One name kept springing to mind: founding father of the animal rights movement and world-renowned ethicist Peter Singer. Widely regarded as one of the greatest thinkers of our time, Singer is a professor of bioethics at Princeton University and a laureate professor at the University of Melbourne. His 1975 classic, *Animal Liberation*, provided a philosophical framework that inspired the animal rights movement, and helped revolutionize the way society views animals.

But it was more than *Animal Liberation* that drove me to contact Professor Singer. Back in 2001, he faced a firestorm of controversy when he wrote a short essay that discussed zoophilia for *Nerve* magazine. Titled "Heavy Petting," the 1,600-word piece was a book review of *Dearest Pet: On Bestiality*, written by Dutch biologist Midas Dekkers and translated into English. The book's back cover explains that it "explores people's sexual attraction to animals as it is represented in art and popular culture." The Singer review constitutes a minuscule fraction of his vast body of work—he's written a stack of books and essays on a remarkable array of subjects—but the uproar that followed the publication of "Heavy Petting" did not scale that way. Instead, it sparked a media furor.

In his essay, Singer pointed out how humans tend to view themselves compared to animals, particularly when the species barrier is crossed sexually. "The vehemence with which this prohibition continues to be held, its persistence while other non-reproductive sexual acts have become acceptable, suggests that there is another powerful force at work: our desire to differentiate ourselves, erotically and in every other way, from animals."

Singer noted that humans *are* animals, great apes essentially. "This does not make sex across the species barrier normal, or natural, whatever those much-misused words may mean, but it does imply that it ceases to be an offense to our status and dignity as human beings."

On December 28, 2012, I pasted a few of the hostile comments I'd received into an email to Singer. I added a note asking how he'd handled the hatred and rage that came his way after the essay, along with a link to my blog, in the hopes he might respond. Here's an excerpt from the email:

Did you respond to the angry comments, or just ignore them? The attacks don't really speak to the facts or arguments. They are styled more as personal attacks.

I've been approving the comments onto my blog for two reasons—first, I want to be uncensored, and second, I want to showcase the hate. I believe it is part of the story.

Singer replied before the day was out:

I'm not surprised at the reaction you are getting. I mostly ignored the comments I got, they weren't worth dignifying with a response, although I did explain to some people in the animal rights movement that not all forms of sexual contact with animals involve coercion against the animals.

best wishes
Peter Singer

47

CULTURAL REFERENCES

When I became aware that cross-species sexual interaction really exists in a form beyond pornography and jokes (such as the hypothetical sheepherder), I started to notice references to the act coming out of the entertainment world. The seemingly far-fetched notion of humans copulating with animals really shouldn't be all that surprising given its reflection in television, movies and literature. Once I tuned my radar to detect media images that pushed the species barrier, references that had been clouded over before now stuck out like a roaring jumbo jet in the plain clear sky.

Take the commercial from auto insurance company GEICO for a roadside assistance app. In the spot, the company spokespig, Maxwell, had car trouble while parked on a lovers' lane with a young woman, so he used the GEICO app to order a tow truck. The couple's dialogue suggested a frisky encounter waiting to happen.

> **Woman**: Did you just turn your ringer off so no one would interrupt us?
> **Pig**: Oh no, I just used my Geico app to get a tow truck. It's going to be here in 30 minutes.
> **Woman**: Oh, so that means we won't be stuck up here for hours... with nothing to do?
> **Pig**: Oh I get it, you want to pass the time, huh?

Then, instead of making a move on his date, Maxwell launched a video game for them to play. The woman appeared disappointed by his lack of interest.

The ad incensed One Million Moms, a fundamentalist Christian group created by the American Family Association to lobby against perceived obscenity perpetuated by the media. The group was appalled by the commercial, calling it "repulsive and unnecessary" because it "plays with the idea of bestiality." They worried the ad would appeal to children because it featured an animal in an engaging role.

References to bestiality crop up in unexpected places on television. NBC's popular comedy series *The Office* used the word bestiality in an episode from season six titled "St. Patrick's Day." Sabre CEO Jo Bennett (played by Kathy Bates) arrived to visit the Scranton, Pennsylvania branch of her latest corporate acquisition, paper company Dunder Mifflin. Branch manager Michael Scott (Steve Carell) was thrilled when his new boss invited him to stay at her home if he ever visited Florida, and bragged to the camera, "When you work for Sabre only one thing matters, and I don't care if you're a loser or you practice bestiality, if Jo likes you, you are in. And I am in."

Interspecies sex shows up in a more prolonged way in a stand-up bit that controversial comedian Louis C.K. inserted into his FX show *Louie*. The episode, titled "Poker/Divorce," aired in season one.

> If no one ever said, "You should not have sex with animals," I would totally have sex with animals all of the time. The only reason I don't have sex with animals is because I'm not supposed to and somebody told it to me. I would totally have sex with most monkeys probably. Why not? You know what? I wouldn't for one reason—because I think it would be rape. I don't think any animal is attracted to any human being. I don't think it's morally wrong, I really don't, except for that I don't think the animal's into it. If you can get an animal horny, go ahead man. Go ahead and fuck it. If you can finger a monkey and the monkey's like "ooohh, aaahh," get in there man, you earned it. You earned it. I really think if I was alone on the earth, if I found myself alone on planet earth, no other humans, I would have sex with a monkey in like two minutes. That's really not even long enough to be sure you're alone on the earth even. That's like getting a little...I walk outside, there's not much traffic, oh my god, it's just me, I'm going to have sex with a monkey right now. Oh no—there's a person.

Cross-species sex references aren't just a modern-day phenomenon, a product of a no-holds-barred society awash in digital imagery. Woody Allen's 1972 film *Everything You Always Wanted to Know About Sex But Were Afraid to Ask* included a story line in which two men fell in love with the same sheep.

The thirteen-minute segment began with Armenian shepherd Stavros Milos (Titos Vandis), who went to see Dr. Doug Ross (Gene Wilder). He told Dr. Ross that he fell in love with a sheep in his flock.

"See doctor, up there in the mountains where I tend my flocks, it's so beautiful under the starred skies. And I am alone. And sometimes it gets so lonely. And the hours pass. And soon I desire a woman. But doctor, there are no women. I am not married and, well, one night last summer, I could stand it no longer. My body needed to be satisfied. And then I saw her."

The doctor looked stunned.

"I took Daisy off to a little cove, and there under the Armenian sky, had sexual intercourse." He added, "It was the greatest lay I ever had."

But Milos' ardent love for Daisy wasn't the problem for which he sought help. It was that Daisy had fallen out of love with him. Milos asked Dr. Ross to speak to her. The doctor did so reluctantly, and ended up being captivated by the sheep. Later that night, his wife caught him fondling a lambswool sweater.

Dr. Ross then asked to meet with Daisy alone. He took her to a hotel room where, post-coitus, he talked to her about his feelings. "Boy, that was really something. I never thought it could be like this. Never in my wildest imagination. You're really something special. I love our L-shaped room. I'll never forget these afternoons we've had. I don't think I've ever known such peace and happiness in my life. I hope you feel the same way."

But the happiness didn't last. Dr. Ross returned home one day to find that Milos had stolen Daisy back. In the final scene, Dr. Ross sat alone and depressed on the street, downing a bottle of Woolite.

∩

The theme of interspecies sex abounds in satirical comedy, but that doesn't inoculate people against being outraged when it comes to the real thing. The tone of people's reactions changes dramatically when the material isn't just pretend. Perhaps that's because fictional suggestions of humans having sex with animals allow the audience to remain at a safe distance from the topic.

Talk show host Jerry Springer found that out firsthand when he taped a show about zoophilia in 1998. Given Springer's shock-inducing, tell-all format, it's not surprising that he tackled the subject. What is surprising is that even for Springer, the show was too controversial to air. It was released only on VHS tape.

The episode, which was titled "I Married a Horse," featured Missouri resident Mark Matthews (the same zoophile whose book helped inspire sex therapist Hani Miletski) and his pony, Pixel. The two shared numerous tongue kisses on stage, a display that whipped the audience into an astonished frenzy.

I tried to interview Jerry Springer to confirm the reason the show didn't air. He didn't get back to me, but his publicist, Linda Shafran, did. "The episode you are asking about did not air and it was because most affiliates chose not to air it."

TV executive Paul Wise spoke about the Springer episode in *Animal Passions*, a 2004 British documentary about zoophilia. "The program was viewed by a number of management personnel and the people who were in the master control area," said Wise. "I think that the response from some of the people was one of absolute hysteria about the subject matter. I felt like this is a subject matter that really has no reason to be on television from a personal standpoint."

There's no doubt that people are fascinated by the idea of sex as it pertains to animals, even if humans aren't participating in the acts. Videos of animals mating with each other on YouTube garner many millions of hits.

Italian-American actress Isabella Rossellini created a popular series of short, quirky films about animal sexual behavior called *Green Porno* for the Sundance TV channel. The films, which run from a minute and a half long up to a few minutes each, are a culmination of her interest in animals and her passion for conservation. "I find animals fascinating. I always liked them since I was a little girl," Rossellini explained on the Canadian CBC radio talk show *Q*.

Her mini-films have been well received. "We have been very successful, and of course the subject matter is endless. Animals and everybody's interested in sex, so my series is particularly dedicated to the life of animal sex."

Rossellini wrote and directed the *Green Porno* films and stars as the only actress. In each film, she is dressed up as a different creature—hamster, seahorse, snake, whale, duck, and even insects such as a spider, earthworm, bee and fly. She uses colorful origami-like paper props to illustrate how different species have sex.

Rossellini had no choice but to star alone, she said on *Q*. "I would have loved to hire other actresses, but I couldn't. That's why I ended up playing all the roles. Everybody turned me down."

∩

Zoophilia occasionally makes appearances in literature too, such as the forty-year-old Canadian novella about a woman's love affair with a bear, which still creates shock ripples that haven't lessened with the passage of time. *Bear,* a 1976 book by author Marian Engel, received a fresh burst of attention when a social media post about it went viral in 2014.

The post, in the form of an Imgur album, was created by a user of the image-sharing service who had discovered an old copy of the book somewhere. Excerpts from the inside were featured along with the front and back covers. The book has had several different covers since its initial release. The one chosen by this Imgur user evoked a formulaic romance novel: a topless woman in a flowing skirt being embraced by her hero, but instead of a man, her love interest is a bear. The post was titled, "What the actual fuck, Canada?"

The album received more than a million views and nearly nine hundred comments. "Okay yeah I'll admit it I'm going to read this but only because it sounds like the most fucked up romance novel in existence," wrote the Imgur user who posted the album.

The protagonist of *Bear* was a shy archivist who worked at a historical institute in Toronto. When a man died and bequeathed his belongings to the organization, she traveled to northern Ontario to catalog the contents of his house. A bear lived on the property. As the book's back cover described it, "She took him swimming, let him lie before the fire—grew to like him. They became lovers."

The way their relationship progressed from platonic to sexual wasn't left to the reader's imagination.

> "Oh bear," she said, rubbing his neck. She got up and took her clothes off because she was hot. She lay down on the far side of the bear, away from the fire, and a little away from him and began in her desolation to make love to herself.
> The bear roused himself from his somnolence, shifted and turned. He put out his moley tongue. . . .
> He licked. He probed. She might have been a flea he was searching for. He licked her nipples stiff and scoured her navel. With little nickerings she moved him south.
> She swung her hips and made it easy for him.
> "Bear, bear," she whispered, playing with his ears. The tongue that was muscular but also capable of lengthening itself like an eel found all her secret places. And like no human being she had ever known it persevered her pleasure. When she came, she whimpered, and the bear licked away her tears.

Graphic content and all, *Bear* is a serious work of Canadian literature, praised for its concise and deftly navigated prose. Perhaps fueled by the attention paid to it on social media, it made the CBC's list of "100 novels that make you proud to be Canadian" in 2014. And back in 1976, it won the prestigious Governor General's Literary Award for fiction.

The most recent edition, published in 2009, contains an afterword by Aritha van Herk, an author and professor of English at University of Calgary. In 2014, on the CBC radio program *Q*, van Herk spoke about the book, which the host called one of the most talked-about that summer. "It isn't a book about getting your rocks off or just giving you a quick thrill," van Herk said. "It's an intensely long-lived book that will stay in the imaginations of its readers long, long after they close the cover." The story speaks to loneliness and the yearning for tenderness, she said, and to the Canadian love of the wilderness.

Van Herk first encountered *Bear* in the 1970s when she was an undergraduate. It was sent as a gift to one of her professors, who passed it on to her. "The original publication was indeed in a plain brown wrapper," she recalled. "The publisher was so terrified of publishing it that it had no image on it at all. It just said 'Bear by Marian Engel.'"

Years later, van Herk would get the chance to meet Engel when she moved to University of Alberta as a writer-in-residence. "I must say that the first time I met her, it was quite cold outside, and she was wearing a rather grumpy fur coat. I thought she looked like a bear."

Unfortunately, van Herk didn't get to know Engel well enough to ask her about the intentions behind her book, and Engel can't speak about that now, because she died of cancer in 1985 at the age of fifty-one. But van Herk thought Engel would have likely enjoyed her work's online resurgence.

Engel received rave reviews for *Bear*, including these glowing words written by iconic Canadian author Margaret Laurence that appeared on its back cover: "Fascinating and profound, this novel speaks of a woman's strange (some would say bizarre) and moving journey toward inner freedom and strength, and ultimately toward a sense of communion with all living creatures."

In addition to the accolades, Engel also had to deal with some strange mail. "I know she did get a lot of inappropriate correspondence about it, most of which she just threw in the fire," van Herk said. "She was quite pragmatic."

48

DONKEY LOVE

The mere suggestion of humans having sex with animals is enough to cause intense disapproval, condemnation, even repulsion across countries and cultures. However, there is at least one region in the world where cross-species sexuality is not only tolerated, but encouraged.

In villages along the northern coast of Colombia, an unusual rite of passage takes place when boys reach puberty: men urge them to lose their virginity to donkeys. Villagers believe that sex with donkeys will lengthen the boys' penises and ward off homosexuality, plus teach the boys skills for when they eventually have sex with human females.

Years ago, Canadian filmmaker Daryl Stoneage came across an article about the practice written in Spanish. After translating it into English with the help of Google, he decided the story would make an interesting film. He called his documentary *Donkey Love*.

"It was the study of a very strange cultural practice that nobody knows about in the rest of the world," Stoneage said. "That's how a boy becomes a man. They were more than willing to share this part of their culture with us." Stoneage visited Colombia during the Festival Nacional del Burro in San Antero, an annual event held at Easter to celebrate donkeys.

I interviewed Stoneage about his film. Initially it was intended to be funny, he said. But the project took a serious turn when he arrived in

Colombia for six weeks of filming and met a man who had fallen in love with his donkey and lost his family because of it.

"One gets developed donkey fucking," said the man, identified only as Julio in the film. "The first pussy you see is a donkey's. So you're there, developing until you become a man. And further ahead there are even people that can't leave it, because it's an obsession one has with that animal."

The man kept his donkey at an otherwise vacant home he'd lived in as a child, visiting her whenever he could. But his wife was jealous. He would come home with fur on his clothes, and she would accuse him of straying. It was the zoophile's equivalent of lipstick on the collar.

"I'm better off with the donkey because the donkey is the best there is," Julio said. "I've had many problems with this donkey issue. I'm even separated from my wife. I'm looking for the solution to get back with her. I've been thinking about it, and I'm going back with my wife. If I get back with my wife, I'm going to frequent the donkey less. I won't see her as much to get my family back."

Julio's wife refused to appear on camera.

"I've been with her for five years, I have two kids with her, and I'm always cheating on her with the donkey," Julio said. "I don't know what to do. I'm desperate, I'm going around like crazy, because the donkey is my obsession. What a problem I have with that donkey!"

A local schoolteacher talked on camera about the tradition. "I'm the teacher of these kids. They're between thirteen and seventeen years old," said Adriana Majjul. "According to our culture, it's normal they experiment sexually with donkeys." The film showed Majjul speaking to her students about the tradition.

> Boys, today's subject has to do with sexual relations with donkeys. You know around here, as a custom, this practice has always taken place. Grandfathers, great grandfathers, they all experimented between the ages of ten to thirteen years old. So, maybe we shouldn't make a scandal out of it. Because it's something that has been repeated through time, and when this type of behavior gets repeated, it becomes a custom. It is almost certain that if someone from another country found out about this local cultural practice of having sex with donkeys, they'd see it as a bad thing, or not normal sexual development for young people. However I think that explaining that this behavior has been going on for a long time

and it makes up part of our roots and customs, they'll accept it as something that's natural.

When Majjul asked her students how many have experimented sexually with donkeys, all eight boys in the classroom raised their hands.

A female police officer also appeared in the film. "I wouldn't permit it in my presence because it looks bad in public," said Duberlis Ramos. "But personally I think that instead of a youth going to a brothel and contracting diseases from a street woman, it's better for him to develop with a donkey."

Stoneage told me his project was a dangerous mission. He hired a priest to travel with him for fear he might be murdered for covering such controversial subject matter. But his worst fears were not realized. The villagers in Colombia were welcoming, and happy to discuss their unusual tradition with the foreign filmmaker.

Not everyone was so receptive to the material Stoneage gathered, however. He was supposed to screen *Donkey Love* at the four-day Okanogan Film Festival to be held in Kelowna, British Columbia, in October 2012. When news of the documentary's showing spread on social media, so did the outrage.

Besieged by angry emails and phone calls, Paramount Theatre, owned by Landmark Cinemas, reacted to the bad publicity by refusing to host the film festival just one week before it was scheduled to begin, unless the movie was removed from the lineup. Festival organizer Jeremy Heynen refused to be censored and wouldn't pull it, despite getting death threats and harassing phone calls. Stoneage said he also got death threats. When last-minute attempts to find another venue fell through, the festival was canceled.

The film had its supporters, though. It was selected as best documentary at the Melbourne Underground Film Festival, and it won Director's Choice at the Sydney Underground Film Festival. It also picked up the Indie Award at IndieFEST, along with several "official selection" designations at festivals around the world.

Still, the achievements and critical acclaim didn't dispel the controversy. Even the movie poster took direct aim at viewers' discomfort over the subject material. It featured the tag line, "It's everything you don't want it to be about."

49

DOUBLE STANDARDS

In early 2013, after his move to the Olympic Peninsula, Doug Spink was out driving one night when he came across a dog who had been hit by a car. He didn't want to leave the body there, so he picked the dog up to bury him. To give the family some closure, he posted a message on Craigslist.

> I am sorry to say that I found hit on the side of the road a male Shepherd cross about a mile north of Eaglemount on the night of Monday 4 February. He had already been dead for at least a couple of hours. He did not have a collar on. He had been castrated, and seemed to be perhaps 5–6 years old. Brown in colour, short fur, a tiny bit pudgy but not overweight. He seemed in good health overall and not like a stray.
>
> I asked at some of the homes nearby, but nobody recognized this dear fellow.
>
> We brought him home to our farm and he has been buried here. As I really didn't know of anything better to do with him, I did take a photo of him. If you know who he is, or whose family was his, I would like to let them know what happened—it is better than always wondering. I am sorry I could not find the family before burying him, but my efforts were not successful.
>
> If you have any information about him, please let me know. Someone out there, I hope, loved this guy and it breaks my heart

that they are probably worried sick about him right now. I am sorry I do not have better news to share about him.

Two days later, someone from Idaho wrote:

No, not my dog. But I just wanted to commend you on what a truly amazing person you are. I run a dog rescue and am just disgusted daily with how so many people are so cruel to their beloved pets and basically throw them away like trash. They use and abuse them. They get tired of them if not convenient for them. I have been so disgusted with humanity lately.

I read your post, and you truly brought me a ray of hope, and light that there are indeed good people out there who do care. Thank You!

Spink might have provided some hope to a jaded Craigslist reader, but he believed that feeling would dissipate into disgust if the woman knew upon whom she had lavished such effusive praise. "If she knew who I was, she would hate me," he said. "I go from being a wonderful person to someone she hates."

He said it quietly. Matter-of-factly. Resigned.

He wasn't wrong. It didn't matter what efforts he made to help animals. To most people, all that mattered was who he was.

Zoos (and some non-zoos) claim that Normals are hypocritical when it comes to condemning zoo behavior. They argue that Normal outcry about an animal's inability to consent to sexual activity is disingenuous when society tolerates—even encourages—a vast array of cruel practices towards animals. Factory farming, scientific testing on animals, and using animals for clothing are conducted with great frequency, and all of these practices are conducted without an animal's consent.

"Under the law, they are possessions, objects, property," Spink said.

I was surprised to discover how many of the dozens of zoos I interviewed had been involved in the animal welfare movement. I found out many were vegetarians. Spink described himself as a "scavenger," having at times consumed meat, but preferring a plant-based diet when he could get it. When he was incarcerated, he wrote letters lobbying the federal prison administration to make vegetarian and vegan meals more readily available to inmates.

Brian Cutteridge, a zoo from Vancouver, British Columbia, wrote a paper about the discrepancies between how society treats animals, and how it views zoophilia. He submitted the work, "For the Love of Dog: On the Legal Prohibition of Zoophilia in Canada and the United States," to a conference on sexuality in Prague. Here's an excerpt:

> Animal sexual autonomy is regularly violated for human financial gain through procedures such as AI [artificial insemination]. Such procedures are probably more disturbing physically and psychologically than an act of zoophilia would be, yet the issue of consent on the part of the animal is never raised in the discussion of such procedures. To confine the "right" of any animal to not be sexually violated strictly to acts of zoophilia is thus to make law based not on reason but on moral prejudice, and to breach the constitutional rights of zoophiles to due process and equality before the law.

Cutteridge believes that laws against zoophilia are "based on societal abhorrence of such acts rather than any real harm caused by such acts," and that they "are an unjust and unconstitutional infringement on civil liberty."

When it came out what he had written, Cutteridge was fired from the veterinary clinic where he worked sterilizing and bundling surgical instruments, a job the clinic had given him as a way of paying back the $21,000 bill he'd racked up getting specialty care for one of his dogs.

Long before I encountered Doug Spink, I wrote a story for *Modern Dog* magazine (unrelated to zoophilia) about the same veterinary clinic where Cutteridge had worked. Because I'd mentioned Cutteridge only in passing back then, I didn't realize he was the same person I had met years earlier when I set up the interview with him after his paper went public and he was charged with bestiality. But as soon as he opened the door to his home, I recognized him immediately.

Cutteridge's three dogs—Tia, Hope and Lady—had been taken away from him because of the charges. On November 26, 2010, the same day charges were laid, he filed a petition in BC Supreme Court in an attempt to get them back. But Tia was promptly euthanized because she was diabetic, and the other two were adopted out by the British Columbia SPCA.

Despite his personal belief that laws against zoophilia are wrong, Cutteridge eventually pled guilty to one count of bestiality. He received a suspended sentence and three years' probation.

He was devastated by the loss of his dogs. He was particularly upset about the one who was euthanized. "Tia was executed," he said. "I've never disposed of an animal I've adopted. I would always put their needs first. I've sold off my stereo equipment and other stuff to pay vet bills."

When I began interviewing zoos, I found out there isn't a type of person destined to become a zoo. A few fit the socially awkward loner profile I might have expected, while others were charismatic with strong social skills. Cutteridge characterized himself as the former—awkward with humans.

"I was always ostracized as a child, I never got on with my peers," said Cutteridge, who added that his mother was domineering and abusive, both physically and emotionally. "I've always been a loner, so I've always gotten my emotional fulfillment from animals. Intimacy with humans makes me feel uncomfortable. It makes me feel dirty. I don't know what it means to love a human. There's always a certain distance."

Cutteridge doesn't believe the intimacy he had with his dogs traumatized them. "What the rabidly anti-zoo people don't believe is that animals have sexual urges."

∩

Society attacks people who openly discuss zoophilia and bestiality, as I found out firsthand. As a result, publicly available writings on the topic are scarce. Yet it's not just a handful of outspoken zoos who have tackled the issue.

One Duke University professor decided to confront society's contradictory viewpoints and moral inconsistencies about animals through an academic lens. Kathy Rudy, an associate professor of women's studies, wrote a thought-provoking essay that was included in the March

2012 issue of *Hypatia: A Journal of Feminist Philosophy*. She called the paper "LGBTQ...Z?"

"In this essay, I draw the discourses around bestiality/zoophilia into the realm of queer theory in order to point to a new form of animal advocacy, something that might be called, in shorthand, loving animals," Rudy wrote.

Rudy also authored a book in 2013 called *Loving Animals: Toward a New Animal Advocacy*. The book isn't about zoophilia, though. Instead, it explores the ways humans use animals: for pets, food, clothing, scientific research and entertainment. The "LGBTQ...Z?" essay, on the other hand, deals squarely with cross-species sexuality:

> I start my thinking with two conflicting and competing realities. The first is the pervasive social taboo against bestiality and zoophilia; the act of sex with animals is so prohibited in contemporary American culture that it is often difficult to speak of such things in public. This is interesting.
>
> Humans can kill animals, force them to breed with each other, eat them, surround them, train them, hunt them, nail them down and cut them open for science, and for the most part, the humans who perform those acts can be thought of as normal, functioning members of society. Yet having sex with animals remains an almost unspeakable anathema.

50

GAG ORDER

While on probation, Doug Spink was determined to speak out about zoophilia and how he was being treated by the federal government. And the federal government was just as determined to stop him.

He had been given a long list of conditions to adhere to by the probation department—some were boilerplate, a standard set of requirements for people on probation, and others appeared to be written specifically for him. One of the unusual ways the authorities dealt with Spink was to attempt to stifle his freedom of speech. They resisted giving him internet access, particularly intending to shut down his discussions about zoophilia and his interaction with other zoos.

"He lives in the web," said Jim Turner, Spink's attorney at the state level. "That's his whole world, and they took his world away from him."

The situation came to a head in May 2013, when Spink's latest probation officer, Sarah Cavendish, warned him that doing interviews for this book could land him in trouble again. The prohibition wasn't going to shut him up, though—just the opposite. "I have a constitutional right to speak and to have my words shared," he told Cavendish over the phone. "I have a book being written about me by a journalist. She's quoting words that I tell her in interviews I give."

During his telephone conversation with Cavendish, Spink asked several times for clarification of his rights to free speech.

Spink: If somebody publishes on the internet words that I have written via another channel, your claim is that I am gagged from making any public statement in any way that ends up on the internet, is that...?
Cavendish: That's what I've been told.

In his typical fashion, Spink refused to let the issue rest. Instead, he hammered away at it with Cavendish over and over again, to ensure he wasn't misunderstanding US Probation's directive.

Spink: Okay, let me make this really clear so that I understand: if I write an essay describing how the federal government is persecuting me and trying to prevent me from exercising my constitutional rights as a United States citizen, and I write it on a piece of paper and I say: "I would like this to be published on my behalf"—and they take that piece of paper and type those words up and publish those words on the internet... You're telling me that I'm prohibited from having any words that I write posted on the internet and published on my behalf?
Cavendish: If you're asking a person, saying: "I'm writing this essay about a certain subject and I would like it to be on the internet... can you please put it on the internet for me since I don't have any access to a computer and I have a restriction?"—then yes, that's accessing a computer through a third person.
Spink: Okay, that doesn't strike you as perhaps constitutionally problematic that you are trying to prevent my ability to...
Cavendish: If you would like to have this hearing to discuss it with a judge that's fine, I mean that's your right. I think that if you want to discuss what that condition means and get more specific on what Judge Martinez wanted to see, that's how the probation office interprets the condition and that's normally how we would supervise that condition on anybody, and so, if you feel that it's necessary to go to court and say: "I would like to do these things"—and get that permission from the judge then that's your right.

Spink still wouldn't let it go and pressed her further. But again she deferred to the court.

Spink: I'm doing extensive interviewing with a journalist who's writing a book, she maintains a blog, she quotes what I tell her in my interviews sometimes on her blog, it's on the internet.
Cavendish: I'm aware of the person.
Spink: Okay.
Cavendish: I think it's best if you, really, you know I mean, it sounds like you want it to be out there and you want the information that

> you're talking about to be published and you want to share it with whoever you want to share it with so maybe it's best to get some verification from the judge about it. That is how it is interpreted by the probation office: access would be through anybody else as well.

Freedom of speech was extremely important to Spink. He was willing to fight for his right to speak his mind, no matter what it cost him. And over the years, it had cost him a lot.

"The government feels that I should be stripped of my ability to speak in my own words, and that others like me should be stripped of our ability to speak in our own words. As a class of individuals, as a class of human beings, we are to be denied voice," he said in a videotaped message I made of him.

It was clear he wasn't going to back down. The efforts to intimidate him into silence only solidified his resolve, even though noncompliance could lead to more disruptions in his life.

"The argument is that it is my ideas—the content of my ideas—that is so uniquely problematic for the United States federal government that it will use its monopoly exercise of force to silence me, or attempt to silence me," Spink said. "I certainly do expect that sooner rather than later the SWAT team will show up and abduct me and throw me in solitary confinement once again as a direct result of my refusal to fully cooperate with that gag order."

∩

Spink took Cavendish's advice. He contacted Howard Phillips, his lawyer at the federal level, and asked to appear again before Judge Ricardo Martinez.

The hearing to request modification of the terms of his probation conditions took place on May 17, 2013, at the federal courthouse in Seattle. Once again, Doug Spink and Judge Martinez came face to face in the courtroom, only this time, the theme was freedom of speech.

> **Phillips:** Apparently, my client has been told that if he speaks to someone, such as a reporter, and that reporter prints it and publishes it, then he is in violation by a third party using the internet. So it's kind of like he needs clarification of where that line is. I don't

want to call it a gag order, but there seems to be not a clear line of what is his use of the internet through a third party.

Martinez: Mr. Gregoryk, let me ask you. In a situation like this—you know fairly well why we put this condition in, in this particular case. It is because of one of the violations that he was convicted of. What would you tell a probationer in the same situation as Mr. Spink when he raises these questions?

Senior US Probation Officer Steve Gregoryk: Well, Your Honor, you said it earlier, it's following the spirit of the conditions. Mr. Spink has a computer monitoring condition which will allow us to view everything that he is doing on the computer or the internet, if he were to choose to have a computer. For him to circumvent that monitoring condition by having third parties post things on the internet, on websites or whatever, I think is really violating the spirit of that condition. If Mr. Spink wants to have a computer and post things on the internet, as long as it's within our policy, I would be more than happy to monitor him. But if he is going to have other people posting things, I just think that condition is kind of rendered useless.

Phillips: Just briefly a response, Your Honor. I think the operative word is "have people post things." It's my understanding that Mr. Spink was not having people post things. But apparently there is a reporter doing a book on him. And those are done on that person's own volition. He is not asking anyone to do anything on the internet.

Martinez: All right. Look, let me make this about as clear as I can, all right? . . . I know you don't like these conditions. I don't expect you to like them. This is not a game to me, and hopefully it's not a game to you either, because it carries very substantial consequences and penalties to you. Talking to someone and then that person doing their own thing on the internet, in my opinion, would not get you a violation. But talking to someone, deliberately knowing that they are going to put something on there and they are going to be quoting you and doing all sort of things like that is getting very close to crossing the line. I don't know. Until faced with a very specific fact pattern, I cannot tell you in advance, did that cross it or did that not cross it? You heard Mr. Gregoryk say it's the spirit behind these conditions that is important. Yes. But, ultimately, it's the actual violation of those, whether it occurs or not, that is at issue in any revocation process. And every one of those incidents is unique to the fact pattern that happens in that particular one. I guess what I am asking you to think about is: Is it worth it to you to think of going back into custody for several years to test it? It wouldn't be worth it to me. Maybe it is to you.

Spink: My First Amendment right to speak freely is worth a great deal to me, Your Honor.

Martinez: Once you are done with conditions of supervised release, then those rights all come back to you. Do you understand?
Spink: Yes, sir.
Martinez: You are free to exercise your First Amendment rights.
Spink: Your Honor—
Martinez: But there are consequences that may flow from you doing that. You are not like everyone else out there.

Despite going back to court to deal specifically with the issue of freedom of speech, Spink felt he never did get the clarification he sought from Judge Martinez, and his probation conditions weren't modified. In his opinion, the unclear answers were part of the mind games the government was playing with him in an attempt to make him uneasy, paranoid and fearful. He sent me a note about what the uncertainty was doing to his state of mind:

> You don't know what it's like living life with the daily threat of being abducted for no reason hanging over every decision—because you've never lived with it, and I certainly hope never do! Part of the intention of that kind of vague, undefined threat is that it saps your healthy connection with the world around you. That's why Martinez wouldn't provide any actual guidelines in the gag order hearing: it's much more destructive (and totally outside of the concept of "rule of law") to tell someone they could be grabbed—or not grabbed—for reasons impossible to articulate, let alone understand or work around.
>
> I have friends who grew up on the other side of the Iron Curtain, and did various sorts of political work at the time. They have told me what it's like to wonder at every knock on the door, strange car parked outside, unusual person seen on the sidewalk. Now I understand: it's intended to place you in constant, low-level, background fear. Mammals eventually wither away and die if they are in such a context for too long—our biology is not suited for that sort of setup, at all.

Spink noted that the gag order didn't apply to what others said or wrote about him. If he complied with the federal government's demand, it effectively allowed people to take potshots at him without having to worry that he would fight back in words.

> It's not an effort to prevent coverage of what I have to say, or to stop media outlets from covering my story—which obviously media outlets have had a field day raping and pillaging and misreporting my story for years. It is an effort to simply stop my ability to present

> my side and my perspective, and the factual components of what has happened and the work that I do.

He vowed to keep fighting and never give up, and to sign copies of this book from prison if it came to that.

I wrote to US Probation in an attempt to get their side of the story. I emailed Connie Smith, chief probation and pretrial services officer for Spink's region, which is the Western District of Washington: "My understanding is that Mr. Spink has been told, 'You've made quite a name for yourself' in the probation department. I'm interested to know what sets him apart in this way. I am also curious about the amount of resources being dedicated to Mr. Spink, and why he is deserving of all this attention."

Smith responded promptly and politely to my emails, but communicated sparsely. She wouldn't say why Jeff Robson had been assigned to Spink's file the year before the raid. Nor would she grant interviews with Robson or any of the other probation officers who had supervised Spink (Jerrod Akins, Sarah Cavendish and Steve Gregoryk). "We respectfully decline an interview," wrote Smith on May 28, 2013.

51

DEAD RINGER

For many months, Spink was happy living at the Fenters' farm on the Olympic Peninsula, until the probation department unexpectedly unapproved his housing. They discovered that the farm had a herd of sheep living at the other end of the forty-acre property where Spink rented his trailer, and they didn't think he should be allowed to live that close to sheep. He was ordered to report back to the halfway house in a week, on Valentine's Day.

Spink was offended by the implication. "I am not a sheep fucker," he declared indignantly.

Grudgingly, he set up shop eleven miles away, renting a brand-new manufactured home on Chicken Coop Road near the Clallam–Jefferson County line. The small house sat up on a hill, a setting that was similar to his cabin on Reese Hill Road.

Despite having a new home all to himself, he was still drawn to spend time at the farm. It had a relaxed, congenial atmosphere, and the people who lived and visited there were focused on environmentally responsible farming, a concept he believed in. He had also grown especially fond of one resident there, a Caucasian Shepherd named Bacca.

Spink was instrumental in Bacca's arrival at the farm. Coyotes had started moving in on the sheep, and when one of the flock was killed, Spink counseled farm staff to get a dog to protect the livestock as an alternative to shooting the coyotes. He zeroed in on Caucasian Shepherds, a relatively rare breed in North America, but popular in countries such as Georgia, Russia and Armenia. Historically, Caucasian Shepherds worked alongside human shepherds in the Caucasus Mountains guarding sheep flocks against wolves, bears, jackals and other predators. He found a young dog being sold online by a Russian breeder in Oregon, and soon Bacca was living at Compass Rose.

Spink enjoyed spending time with Bacca, teaching him the ropes of how to be a livestock protection dog working on a farm. But the fleeting moments of happiness often took on a foreboding tone. The memory of his other dogs and horses, the ones who had been taken from him, frequently played in his waking thoughts, and in his nightmares. He had been stripped of his loved ones because of who he was. His faith in people and society had eroded. He believed most people had no compassion for him or his animals. It was a sentiment echoed by other zoos.

"The universe hates us," Spink said. "They conspire to find ways to destroy what we have."

The grim reality of what might lie ahead lurked in his thoughts, a dark passenger he always carried with him. "When I'm walking with Bacca," he said over the phone one day, "I wonder if that is the last thing I will do before they take him away and it will all be my fault. Knowing it will all end badly. I'll never know what I could have done to save them."

Suddenly he stopped talking and began to sob, tears of grief and pain and rage over what had happened in the past, mixed with dread for what was in store for the future. For him, and anyone he dared to love.

Bacca wasn't the only dog near the farm who mattered to him. Ghengis, a 120-pound, five-year-old Boerboel-Kangal mix, had caught his attention. Ghengis lived next door at Olympic Dogs, a breeding operation run by Andrew Johnston, who mixed breeds such as Boerboels, Kangals, Dogo Argentinos and Great Danes to form his own genetic creations. "In a word they are all 'watchdogs' be it family, stock, property or some combination there in; their first job is to protect (be it offense or defense)," Johnston wrote on his website.

He summed up his breeding goals this way: "I'm not in this to make yard ornaments."

It didn't take long for Spink to realize that he had met his new neighbor before. Seven years earlier, in 2007, Spink had brought Bafana, his rare Boerboel, to Olympic Dogs to mate with one of Johnston's female dogs. In return, Johnston promised him a puppy from the resulting litter, but he ended up reneging on the deal. Johnston said Spink was supposed to bring people to him to buy the offspring. When the sales didn't materialize, he refused to give Spink a puppy. Spink was furious. Their confrontations were heated and mutually threatening.

Johnston would later accuse Spink of moving next door on purpose to plot vengeance against him. Spink denied the accusation, insisting it was pure coincidence that the two had ended up neighbors. Spink had come to the Fenters' farm as a result of his prison friendship with Mike Fenter, ex-husband of Kateen, who ran the farm. It was a twist of fate that had placed the two mortal enemies back together again.

Spink had adored Bafana and was devastated when the dog was bludgeoned to death with a baseball bat during a break-in at his home in Custer. And now here was Bafana's grandson living right next door, a dead ringer. It was like seeing a ghost.

I asked him, "Does Ghengis remind you of Bafana?"

"With every step," he answered.

Spink didn't think Johnston was treating Ghengis properly. From afar, he watched the body language when the two interacted in the field, and he didn't like what he saw. He called Ghengis a "hard dog," and worried that if Ghengis decided one day not to obey Johnston, he'd be beaten to death.

Spink wasn't the only person concerned about Johnston's treatment of animals. On November 20, 2009, a Jefferson County Sheriff's Office incident report obtained through Freedom of Information showed that Johnston was warned by police after a neighbor witnessed him abusing his dog the day before. "Animal Owner [Johnston] warned about Animal Cruelty laws and that if another complaint was received it would be forwarded to the Prosecutor's Office," stated officer Bruce Turner in his report. "While talking with Andrew Johnson, Andrew said that if I came out to his property again for another animal complaint he would shoot a dog in front of me. I told Andrew if it was his intent to intimidate me by that action I would arrest him."

Kateen Fenter's mother, Beverly Fairing, who also lives at Compass Rose, also witnessed Johnston abusing his dogs, as she noted in her journal entry of March 23, 2014.

> From my kitchen door window I observed Andrew Johnston hold a dog by a short leash—take a large stick and beat the dog repeatedly about the head and neck. When the stick broke he had [his son] hand him another stick and he beat the dog again. Then he took another dog that [his son] was holding on a leash and he beat it the same way. Then they lead/dragged the dogs away from the area. They returned with the pickup and picked up what appeared to be a wounded or sick adult goat. Then drove out of the field and up to his house.

Authorities were also concerned that Johnston didn't have the requisite kennel license, or have his dogs registered with the county as required. According to a Jefferson County Sheriff's Office report filed on February 12, 2010, by Deputy Alex Mintz, "Nothing is known about Johnstons facility, how many dogs he has, how he keeps his dogs, what sort of care they receive. Johnston, from past dealings is somewhat reclusive and confrontational and will not allow anyone onto his property. He has told Animal Control that we would have to obtain a warrant to come onto his property."

By the time Spink moved to the Fenters' farm, Johnston had already settled into an acrimonious relationship with Kateen, so he didn't spend any time at Compass Rose. As a result, he was unaware that Spink had quietly moved in. But Ghengis knew. He would come and visit Spink at the fence that divided the properties, and the two soon formed a friendship.

Johnston hadn't seen Ghengis for a couple of days when he discovered a hole in the fence that separated his leased land from the Fenters' farm. After that, it didn't take him long to find out about Spink's presence next door. Johnston was livid. He assumed Spink had moved there as part of a plot to steal Ghengis and even the score between them.

Days later, Johnston learned I was writing a book about Spink. He emailed me on February 28, 2014:

> My interest is the dog, I don't want him abused, and I want him back alive. I love that dog. in the old fashioned way a man loves a dog, not like your anti-hero. Ghengis is a very good livestock guardian, a teacher to the younger dogs with livestock guarding potential, who get sent to his pasture for schooling. His bond with the goats is so strong the kids climb up and jump off him like they do their moms… and he just smiles.

The email wasn't my first contact with Johnston. The previous year, before Ghengis disappeared, I had scheduled an interview with Spink at the farm. I'd arrived early, so I waited up the road in my car. Johnston came out to inquire what I was doing parked at the roadside beside his property.

I explained that I was headed to Compass Rose, giving no reason for my visit (at the time, I was unaware of his rancorous history with Spink). I gave him my business card, a decision I regretted almost immediately. He asked if I had children. When I said no, he wondered aloud why a woman would ever choose not to get impregnated by a man. That's when I tried to take my card back, but Johnston held it out of my reach. My uneasy feeling was confirmed when he spotted something on the ground near my driver's side front tire, picked it up and placed it on the hood of my car.

It was a dirty needle.

I calmly asked him to remove it, twice. He refused.

Using a plastic bag, I picked up the needle and brought it into my car so that no human or animal would get stabbed by it. When I arrived at the Fenters' place, Kateen disposed of it as medical waste along with other spent syringes that had been used on the farm animals.

Clearly, breeding was a preoccupation for Johnston. His website proudly proclaimed it: "As anyone that knows me can tell you, breeding is more a less a way of life around here. Be it an abiding respect for natural laws, a fascination with genetics, or just a logical way to run a ranch; I will breed. Mother nature is who I turn to for wisdom; merciless bitch though she may be, she never fails to inspire."

His website also described his attitude about his role as a breeder: "For most of my life I owned one dog at a time, for the lifetime of that dog," Johnston wrote. "The relationship that can develop in that context is a luxury I'm not sure a breeder can afford to indulge. A breeder plays God; as such I believe he also needs to be prepared to play the Grim Reaper. A certain amount of detachment is necessary."

In an email he sent to me after Ghengis disappeared, Johnston reminded me of our chance meeting the previous year, and asked me to put him in touch with Spink. "Tell him if he's a got a bone to pick with me for some reason, he should leave the innocent parties out of it, and come settle it like a man," he said. "If one of us ends up dead, and I don't think it will matter which one, from a book selling standpoint... You, Ms. Carreen, can't loose [sic]."

He warned me that if I didn't comply, if I didn't somehow track down his dog and get him back to him, he would release the story to the media. "I don't know if the dog is already dead or not, it may be too late, but if he's returned to me alive, soon... like tomorrow morning, the media and all the world it reaches need not know it ever happened."

He added this cautionary note:

I'm working from the assumption you want to sell books?
And my point is this, spink is a very hard sell, to begin with... already.
And I'm hear to tell you if the victim, in this case a dog, turns up dead or simply never turns up at all, and the world is left to imagine him off in the hands of some crazed dog sodomite ever more...
it will hurt your book... cause it will crush whatever slim glimmer of humanity you hope to pry the public eyes into finding in mr. Spink. I personally suspect there is more then a glimmer there, but it's complicated and convoluted.

Johnston made good on his promise. Local and regional newspapers, including the *Port Townsend Leader*, the *Peninsula Daily News* and the *Seattle Times,* covered this strange footnote to the story of Doug Spink, the general theme being: zoophile steals dog for unknown nefarious and most likely sexual purposes.

Kateen Fenter was horrified by this development. She was still recovering from the shock and reverberations of the 2009 arrest of Mike, her spouse of twenty years whom she'd started dating when she was just fourteen years old. She'd been blindsided when, out of nowhere, her gentle and creative husband was arrested for robbing banks when the couple was in their late thirties. He had been a hard-working carpenter and boatbuilder before this aberration, a law-abiding man with no criminal record.

Police apprehended Mike Fenter on October 8, 2009, after his fourth robbery, a Bank of America in Tacoma. Police recovered $73,000 from him. He was ordered to pay another $86,000 in restitution to the banks, and sentenced to ten years in federal prison. It appeared as though he was on a mission that wasn't about providing for his family members, who were still struggling to get their new farm on stable financial footing after purchasing it just a year and a half before his arrest, while also renovating the run-down farmhouse on the property to use as their home.

Kateen said she didn't receive any of the proceeds. "We had $10 in the bank, four broken-down cars and no doors on the kids' rooms," she told the *Peninsula Daily News*. "It's not like he handed me a million dollars one day. There's no money."

Mike Fenter was arrested almost exactly a year after the Emergency Economic Stabilization Act was enacted on October 3, 2008, which provided a government bailout of the US financial industry that cost $700 billion. The *Seattle Times* reported that Fenter told bank employees he was angry about the bailout, and that he was taking the money to give it to people who needed it. He told the judge, "What I am for is real justice, real truth, and real accountability within our system of government. The money was used and is probably currently being used to get to the truth."

Kateen was left scrambling to run the farm and raise three children without her husband by her side. And now a man accused of running a bestiality farm was discovered living on her property, a fact that was widely reported in the news media. People in her community started calling her place the "dog fucker farm." She insisted she hadn't known Spink's background as a zoophile before Ghengis' disappearance; since her husband's arrest, she had avoided the internet because it was too upsetting, instead focusing on her children and the hard work that needed to be done to keep the farm afloat.

When Johnston reported Ghengis missing, he pointed the finger straight at Spink. But he also blamed Kateen for having housed Spink on her property. Their neighborly relationship went further downhill, from bad to downright ugly. Johnston launched a civil lawsuit for

$290,000, naming the farm, Kateen Fenter, her parents, and Doug Spink as the parties responsible for lost revenues connected with sales of future offspring from Ghengis. Eventually the judge dismissed the case with no financial settlement awarded to Johnston.

∩

It was late morning on March 4, 2014, when police cars came blazing up the driveway of Chicken Coop Road heading for Spink's place on the hill, lights flashing and sirens screaming. More than a dozen officers exited their vehicles, guns drawn.

The air was crackling with hostility towards him, Spink recalled.

He was sitting on his porch. "Smile for the camera," he told the officers, motioning to the device mounted on his house. Suddenly, they all deflated and their guns went down. As a female marshal handcuffed Spink, she told him the judge was going to be angry about the camera.

"Where's the tape stored?" she asked.

The camera wasn't even plugged in. A friend had given it to Spink, and he thought it might come in handy someday. "I will believe until the day I die that camera saved my life," he said.

That's when his former probation officer, Jerrod Akins, took over. Akins pointed a gun at Spink's head and demanded, over and over, "Where's the fucking dog? Where's the fucking dog? WHERE'S the fucking DOG?"

Spink told Akins to go fuck himself.

They did find a dog, but it wasn't Ghengis. Bacca was in Spink's truck, which was parked outside his home. The dog was seized by Jefferson County's animal services division, and before long, Bacca had landed in the custody of the Whatcom Humane Society.

It was all too familiar a scene for Spink. He had begun to rebuild his life, his family and his company, only to end up right back where he started—in prison again, and separated from those who mattered to him most.

52

DÉJÀ VU

Less than two weeks after Andrew Johnston accused Spink of stealing Ghengis, Spink was back in federal custody at SeaTac prison.

Officially, the government didn't include the stud dog's disappearance on the list of probation violations for which Spink was arrested. But given the timing, it seemed probable that the disappearance of Ghengis was connected to this latest incarceration.

Spink was accused of four violations:

1. Being in possession of a dog
2. Residing at a non-approved residence
3. Volunteering in a capacity which placed him in direct contact with animals
4. Owning computers with internet access

Spink agreed to a plea. He admitted to three of the violations, but refused to admit to the first—being in possession of a dog. That charge referred to Bacca, who was found inside Spink's truck by officers who were on the scene at Chicken Coop Road.

The charge of residing at a non-approved residence came about because probation officials believed he had never really moved to Chicken Coop Road, but had instead remained at the Discovery Bay farm after that housing had been disallowed. They believed their suspicion was confirmed when Spink's probation officer left his business card at his door, and found it still there a week later.

The third violation concerned volunteer work Spink had been doing at a local horse-boarding facility run by a Port Townsend woman named Jamie Armstrong. He was boarding the one animal he had managed to recover after the 2010 raid—L.J., the Percheron horse—at Armstrong's place, and he was teaching others who boarded their horses there how to ride and jump.

He also helped Armstrong deal with personal fears, noted Spink's federal lawyer, Howard Phillips, during the probation hearing on May 9, 2014, two months after Spink's arrest:

> He volunteered to help her. She was a professional jumper, she was a show-jumper of horses. She was afraid to jump. She calls Doug her savior in that because he got her back riding on her horses and jumping, now she is back jumping again. But he did volunteer, which is a violation. But she calls him her savior. She says he helped her get her wings back. She speaks in glowing terms of him assisting her, which was in violation.

Spink also didn't dispute the fourth violation, owning computers with internet access. He believed he did what was necessary in order to be able to run his company, which provided privacy services. He didn't see how he could earn a living in the field of privacy if the federal government was spying on him all the time.

I quickly found out through the grapevine that Laura Clark had gained custody of Bacca for the Whatcom Humane Society within days of this second raid on Spink's home, even though Jefferson County, where Spink now lived, was a two-hour drive outside her jurisdiction. It's highly unusual for shelter directors to travel into other jurisdictions to seize animals involved in court cases for no clear reason. She did so on the grounds that she'd taken in animals that belonged to him after the first raid, and her organization knew how to handle them.

As she had done repeatedly since his Sumas cabin was raided in 2010, Claire Spink jumped into the fray to help her son. Again she began faxing her handwritten letters and making phone calls to the probation department, police, lawyers, and the animal shelters in Whatcom County and Jefferson County. She helped pay for her son's legal fees and anything else he needed. She wasn't rich, but she believed in helping her son no matter what transpired.

Claire continued sending documents to me too—police incident reports, old family photographs, and other background items.

Shortly after Spink was taken into custody in March 2014, I learned from Jamie Armstrong that Laura Clark of Whatcom Humane Society had begun to repeatedly harass her and her mother because of their association with Spink. Clark threatened to shut down their small horse boarding operation and take all of the animals, and accused them of facilitating sexual assault against animals. Spink commented on this behavior by Clark and others in a CorrLinks email to Armstrong following his arrest:

> This ugly mess has, for years, drawn forward all manner of charlatans and crooks and—to be blunt—monsters, who have found some sort of ugly psychic energy to be gained from perverting things to their ends. Most have faded back into the dark shadows, in recent years, but a few came back out when I was grabbed again a few weeks back. It's sad, but these people are drawn to misery, and sorrow, and injustice, and sadness. Psychic vampires.

Spink had always adamantly maintained that at least half, and maybe all, of the seven dogs seized during the 2010 raid on his cabin never made it out of WHS alive. It was an assertion I repeatedly tried and failed to verify, because Clark would not supply any proof of what had happened to the animals. Now I wondered, and worried, whether Bacca's life might be in danger. Clark's drive to get control of Spink's animals from way outside her jurisdiction seemed sinister to me.

I contacted Spink's state-level lawyer, Jim Turner, to see if he could intervene to make sure Clark didn't harm Bacca. Turner wrote an impassioned letter pleading for Bacca's life, which he copied to numerous parties in an effort to ensure the dog survived:

> I am concerned that "Bacca" was transported to the Whatcom Humane Society, given Ms. Clark's animus towards Mr. Spink, and the fact that there is no reason that "Bacca" is needed here for the current litigation. If the dog were relevant to any legal matter, the situs of any such matter would be in Jefferson County where it

was apparently residing. The transfer of the animal to the Whatcom Humane Society oozes of cruel collusion between the animal control officer with the Jefferson County Sheriff's Department, Deputy Alex Mintz, the Department of Justice, Federal Probation, the Whatcom County Prosecutor and Ms. Clark of the Whatcom Humane Society to cause Mr. Spink to suffer extreme emotional distress, at the expense of this beautiful animal.

I went to visit Spink at Federal Detention Center SeaTac. From the outside, it looked more like a mid-range hotel than a prison. Inside was a different story—this was not luxury accommodation. At the time, the facility housed about six hundred male and female inmates (capacity is one thousand).

After I signed in, I waited for about an hour in the lobby, putting my keys and cell phone in a locker because I wasn't allowed to bring them in with me. The Bureau of Prisons rules on visitor attire are extensive. The dress code doesn't permit wearing clothing in any color that might resemble that of an inmate, such as khaki, green, or camouflage; also prohibited are hats, scarves, watches, spike heels or open-toed shoes, as is any garment that could be construed as provocative, such as dresses with hemlines hitting higher than knee length. At one point, I had to return to my vehicle to remove an underwire bra because it was considered a potential weapon.

A group of visitors began to gather in the lobby, and eventually we were taken through a metal detector before being escorted into the elevator by a prison guard. When the doors slid open again, we were led into a large, drab communal visiting room for our two-hour stay.

It was Easter Sunday, so the large space was packed with children dressed up in their holiday finery of tiny suits and frilly dresses. They giggled with joy, jumping into the arms of their parents, the inmates who loved them, trying to pack as much affection into their short visit as possible.

The timbre of my meeting with Doug was different from that of the families. We sat facing each other on plastic molded seats connected to form rows, so close our knees were almost touching. Spink expressed his anger towards me because I hadn't somehow managed to get custody of Bacca, a feat that would have been nearly impossible for me to achieve given the circumstances even if I'd promised to do it, which I hadn't.

I felt like he was blaming me for something that wasn't my fault. He didn't admit to taking Ghengis, but I accused him of it.

The guards eyed us warily as our voices got louder in mutual anger.

"You should have done something!" he yelled.

"You horse-traded Bacca for Ghengis, and now you want me to fix it!" I yelled back, exasperated.

Eventually our heated conversation cooled down. Spink's onyx black eyes were ringed with dark circles. He'd had six nightmares the night before, he said, all with the same theme: his animals were taken from him. But unlike what happened in real life, his nightmares always ended triumphantly. "Each time, I get Capone back and I ride him home."

Three weeks later, Spink was back in federal court, with Judge Ricardo Martinez presiding again, this time for sentencing on the latest probation violations.

Assistant US Attorney Steven Masada spoke for the government. "What we can all agree on is that Mr. Spink, clearly, does not like to be told what he can and can't do," Masada said. "He doesn't want to be on supervised release, and the United States Probation Office and the United States Attorney's Office agree on the point that ongoing supervised release serves little value, and to a large extent it's a futile effort at this point." Masada recommended that supervised release be terminated, and that Spink serve out the remainder of his sentence in custody.

Howard Phillips, Spink's federal lawyer, countered. "My client has had a difficult time," he said. "I respectfully disagree with Mr. Masada when he says that he's done everything he could to avoid supervision. That's just not so. I've seen and the court has seen supervision violations where people have used drugs, illicit drugs, got drunk, committed crimes and done burglaries and went on with their criminal acts. There are no criminal acts being argued here by the government."

Spink had his own opinions to offer Judge Martinez. He vowed not to give up fighting for what he believed was right.

> I would like to say that on the Whatcom County case, that case was filed right before the statute of limitations expired. As a result of the 2010 incident, my lawyer and I are fighting that vehemently. We're fighting the constitutionality of the statute underlying that case, in the strongest possible terms, and we're looking to overturn that statute on the basis of a flagrant violation of the findings of

the Supreme Court in Lawrence v. Texas, as well as numerous due process violations of the statute itself. That's the status of the Whatcom County case. I'm proud to be fighting that case. I look forward to winning that case and to removing that statute from the books.

After all the arguments had been heard, Judge Martinez made his statement. His tone sounded different than it had in the past. To me, it seemed as though he had come to have a more comprehensive understanding of this headstrong, eccentric inmate who had been in and out of his courtroom for nearly a decade.

Mr. Spink, Mr. Phillips mentioned that you have a strong personality. I definitely agree with that. Twenty-five years of wearing these robes and being involved in all sorts of cases, you're one of the most interesting people I've ever met in my entire life. You're intelligent. Maybe sometimes too intelligent for your own good. You do have a very strong personality.

What's troubling to me is that we're so far afield from what brought you here originally. It's very troubling. This whole thing started with smuggling suitcases full of cocaine into Canada.

And you're right. I thought you did quite well while you were in prison, paying your dues for having violated the law in that particular case. I thought you did everything straight up.

And then we got into this other thing, where you have a very strong philosophical perspective that is not shared by a lot of other people. When I first saw all these violations, my initial reaction was, why are we bothering? Why not send him back to prison for three years—you saw the recommendation—three years, warehouse him, and be done with it. But that seems like such a waste, and it seems disproportionate to what occurred.

One of the things I've learned being a judge all these years and imposing sentences on so many different people, there comes a point when it doesn't make any difference. If the person's behavior is not going to change, then it becomes strictly punitive at that point. There's nothing else to it. When you're a parent, you learn that with kids. After a while, it just doesn't make any sense, not to mention the cost it imposes on the taxpayers as well.

I don't know what's going to happen with Whatcom County.

They are obviously free to make their own decisions as to what they do and what they don't do. We don't have any influence on that. It might have an impact, depending upon what happens today. I don't know. Depending on the prosecutors' perspectives as to whether or not they decide to follow up on this. But I do know that I've come to the conclusion that it doesn't make sense whatsoever to keep you on any further supervised release.

> The violations that we're dealing with, the initial underlying incident in 2010, those are all state violations. This is federal court. What are we doing with these things? It doesn't make sense.
>
> So I agree with everyone. We're going to revoke. We will terminate supervised release. You'll be completely done with us. Unless you commit some other federal violation, we won't see you back here again.
>
> The court will impose nine months of custodial time, give him credit for all time served. Once he's done with our custodial time, he's completely finished with the federal government.

With that, Spink's probation was revoked. He was going back to prison. After serving nine months, with credit given for time already served, he'd be free of federal oversight for the first time in almost ten years.

But that did not mean he would finally be free.

53

DOUBLE TROUBLE

Stuck in federal prison, his probation revoked, Doug Spink was worried. He suspected a nasty situation was brewing for him in another jurisdiction—Whatcom County, where he faced state-level animal cruelty charges. But there was little he could do about it while incarcerated.

At Spink's federal hearing into the probation violations, Judge Ricardo Martinez said he didn't know how Whatcom prosecutors were going to handle the state case. Neither did Spink.

He hoped in vain that he would be transferred to a halfway house before the trouble taking shape in Whatcom came to an unpleasant head. "Once at the halfway house, I would be able to get passes to travel to Whatcom for status hearings and so on," he recalled later. "It became a race for time: would I get out of SeaTac in time to beat the clock on Whatcom melting down, or not? As it turned out, not."

Having shown up consistently for his court appearances in the past, now Spink was missing every status hearing in Whatcom County. This was unchartered territory for him.

The situation was compounded by the fact that Jim Turner, his lawyer for the state case, was struggling with personal issues. Still shattered by the death of his daughter, Turner had spent over a decade trying to put his world back together, an attempt that seemed thwarted at every turn. He'd manage to pull himself out of the black hole of depression, but it was always only a matter of time before he tumbled back into the darkness. He had represented Spink for nearly two years. Now he was contemplating leaving the practice of law forever. To that end, he officially withdrew as Spink's attorney on June 6, 2014.

Spink was eventually assigned to Darrin Hall, a senior deputy with the Whatcom County Public Defender's Office, but it took a while. Public defenders are notoriously overloaded with cases. In the meantime, Spink was out of the loop. "Nobody was showing up at those hearings, communicating with the Court, or in any way keeping me apprised of what was happening in Whatcom," he said.

To this day, Turner still feels guilty about what transpired, and blames himself for what happened next. The prosecutor motioned the court to revoke Spink's $5,000 bail, and Whatcom County Superior Court Judge Charles Snyder issued a warrant for his arrest. The court knew where Spink was, and why he was unable to make his court dates. In fact, when Spink was charged, Snyder issued a writ of habeas corpus (Latin for "you shall have the body") and ordered that Spink be transported to Whatcom County to appear in court before him.

Habeas corpus is a tool that is typically used to protect defendants. By forcing the government to explain to a judge why they are holding a person in custody, it prevents that person from being locked up without cause, and left to languish without recourse. But in Spink's case, habeas corpus wasn't invoked to protect him. He hadn't asked to go before a judge. He just wanted to finish out his time in federal custody and be done with the feds once and for all.

It didn't work out that way, as he wrote to me in an email.

> About 45 days before I was due to release from SeaTac to halfway house, [on June 6] I was pulled from my cell at SeaTac and told by a (rather unpleasant and largely non-credible) guard that I was "being released." He really played it up—which made me confident it was bullshit. Eventually I was put on a sort of inter-county transport van—no explanation of why, or where I was going…though I had suspicions. By the end of the day, I was back in the Whatcom County Jail.

Spink coined the place where he was housed the "closet-cell." Over the years, I'd noticed a tendency of Spink and his mother to come up with catchy names for people, organizations and situations that were troubling them. I thought it was their way of coping with difficult situations. Whatcom County Sheriff Bill Elfo became "Sheriff Elbow" when Claire talked about him. Doug referred to the Whatcom Humane Society as "Whatcom County Hate Society," and Hope for Horses he changed to "Hopeless Horses." He nicknamed Corinne Super, his ex-fiancée, "the horse thief" instead of using her actual name.

Spink believed he was intentionally housed in the "closet-cell" to limit his contact with the outside world. "I was in a small cell with seven other inmates—I was sleeping on the floor, with barely room for any of us to stand up or move off of our sleeping mats. It was actually a storage closet that had been 'converted' into extra cell space. We were on 24/7 lockdown in that cell: very minimal access to phones, etc. This, it is safe to conclude, was not accidental. I had been put in a deep bucket, to limit my degrees of action possible."

At Spink's request, Judge Snyder reluctantly agreed to let him finish his federal time, then deal with the Whatcom charges after that. On June 12, Spink posted bail. It had jumped from $5,000 to $25,000, and he had to forfeit his earlier deposit because of his failure to appear due to his incarceration. Bail did not, as was customary, set him free. As soon as the hearing was over, he was loaded into a Whatcom County police car and driven back down to SeaTac federal prison, where he served the rest of his time uneventfully.

∩

After removing himself from Spink's case, Jim Turner contacted Whatcom County public defender Darrin Hall to encourage him to file motions for his former client. It bothered Turner that the prosecutor had waited so long to charge Spink. He believed the delay amounted to a violation of due process, and there was a body of case law to argue that. "You can't just sit on your hands and allow exculpatory evidence to disappear," Turner said. "The cabin is gone, the dogs are gone. No one did anything to prepare Doug in case they did charge him."

While it isn't common to prosecute someone twice in different jurisdictions for the same crime, it is legal to do so. Following the raid in 2010, Whatcom County's David McEachran had said he wouldn't charge Spink again because he was already in federal prison for the same incident. But shortly before the statute of limitations ran out, McEachran changed his mind.

"In terms of the rules of professional responsibility, it is not against bar association rules to say they are not going to charge him, then do it anyway," Turner said. "That's just lying. Apparently the prosecutor can lie to the public and lie to this defendant."

Darrin Hall resisted filing the motions Turner suggested, and instead encouraged Spink to take a deal. Turner got the sense Hall was uncomfortable representing an unapologetic, unabashed zoophile. "What surprised me is among hard-core criminal defense attorneys, there was a remarkable number of them that said, 'I don't want to hear about that case,'" Turner said. "Yet they can hear about a two-year-old little girl getting raped."

Despite his reluctance to do so, Spink decided that pleading guilty was the most sensible course of action. The prosecution wanted Spink to plead guilty to one count of animal cruelty and agree to a lifetime ban on owning dogs, which would be enforceable only in Washington State. Supposedly, the state was not seeking a custodial sentence because Spink had already been sentenced to three years in federal court for the same incident. In contrast, in the same Whatcom County court system, Stephen Clarke had pled guilty to three counts of first-degree animal cruelty for having sex with Spink's dogs, and received thirty days.

"For me, obviously, going to trial with a public defender—and without the years of work and background Jim [Turner] had put in, was a very bad option," Spink said.

He decided to enter an Alford plea, just as James Tait did back in 2005 after the death of Kenneth Pinyan. That meant he didn't admit guilt, only conceded that the evidence against him would likely result in a guilty verdict.

"As the trial deadline approached, I had to decide whether to accept that deal," Spink said. "In the end, I did. It fucking sucked. However, after nearly a decade of hell I was eager to build a life with someone I love very much—and to start doing good, constructive work again."

The "someone" Spink referred to was his boyfriend, who over the years had become the most important person to Spink, other than his mother.

The state wasn't seeking jail time for Spink, but he didn't feel sure the agreement would be honored. Trust didn't come easily to him after all that had happened, as he wrote to me in an email:

> I did quiz Darrin aggressively about any chance of the judge "going back" on the time-served agreement. Zero, he said: literally a zero percent chance of that. The prosecutor would be recommending time-served, so everyone was in agreement. Generally judges do not buck those deals—that's true. However, right up until the day of the sentencing, I told Darrin I felt that there was more to the story, somewhere in the picture. He accused me of being "paranoid," imagining the world is out to get me, overreacting, etc. etc. A common theme.

As he arrived at the courthouse on December 11, Spink felt uneasy. An impending sense of doom had settled over him. Before going into the packed courtroom for the hearing, he had an unexpected encounter with bestiality buster Jenny Edwards, his old foe.

> When I walked into the hallway outside court, Jenny Edwards was there. She approached me and asked if she could have a word with me. I said I would be willing to listen, and we stepped aside to talk privately. She told me that she had "no hard feelings" about me, and that she had never really intended to do me any harm in all this. I told her I found that statement to be untrue, and she blustered that really she'd never said bad things about me specifically, only about "real abusers," etc. I told her I had full archives of her since-removed hateful pages of lies written about me, and that it was pointless for her to say she didn't do that.
> She brushed that off, and said that in any case she acknowledged that I wasn't "one of the bad ones" (or some equivalent wording) and that (paraphrasing) "she felt bad about how far all of this had gone with me"—that it was never intended to have "turned into this." She also seemed to be apologizing for that day in court—despite the fact that the hearing hadn't yet happened. That immediately caught my attention. I told her I understood her apology, but that after the damage and destruction she had caused me I could not say that I accepted it fully. She blustered about that—almost insulted that I wasn't happy to

be in her apparent good graces—apologized again for "how things all worked out here," and walked off.

Spink's sense of foreboding was warranted. In an unusual move, Judge Charles Snyder threw out the deal made by the prosecution and the defense, and sentenced Spink to ninety days in jail. He also ordered the ban on Spink owning dogs for life in Washington State.

Faced with an unexpected custody sentence, Spink had a decision to make. He was days away from moving to Canada with his boyfriend. He requested a few weeks before his surrender date to give him time to figure out what to do. He thought he would complete the move as planned, then report back to Whatcom County jail, serve his time and return to Canada, this time for good. There was talk of allowing him to do a work release/home confinement type of program in lieu of jail when he reported back to do his time.

He stayed in touch with Darrin Hall by email. But by early February 2015, Hall—who had no idea that Spink was now in Canada—was emailing him that there was a problem. Spink would have to come to his office to sort out the details, and that it was starting to look like he was going to have to do jail time after all. Spink weighed his options.

> At that, I had a decision to make: go back to that state, face further open-ended persecution without a real lawyer and having already seen a stacked-deck sentencing hearing take place that I knew was headed off the rails. I decided that, based on all I've seen and know, going back voluntarily represented a genuine risk to my safety and I had no idea when or if I could return to Canada once that thing down there was finished. Would they frame me for something else? Add some new charge, out of nowhere? Try to involuntarily commit me under some specious psych diagnosis? I put none of that past them. I decided that I would simply step back from the jail sentence and let things play out.

Spink also wanted to make some money so that he could hire another attorney, one who wasn't an overloaded public defender, to challenge what had happened in his case, "and do so from a position of strength and security, in Canada, rather than from inside a closet-cell somewhere in the USA."

On February 26, 2015, a warrant valid in Washington and its contiguous states was issued for Spink's arrest. After time served was considered, he still had seventy-two days remaining on his sentence, which, as he put it, "I do not intend to donate, now or ever."

⌂

Before this book went to press, I spoke to Jim Turner again, hoping for a look back from a legal perspective at what had happened during the almost eight years since the raid on Spink's cabin in Sumas. He said Spink's case was the most unusual he'd ever worked on during his thirty-year career as a criminal defense attorney.

After watching it play out from the front lines, he had distinct theories on why his client was such a target. "He had virtually a pristine record in the system—he was well-liked and easy to manage. It was just that he spoke out. He exposed himself and gave them the ability to do it."

Spink refused to be ashamed for being a zoophile, an appalling stance in the minds of many. He hoped to take down the Washington state law, and that rankled the powers that be.

It didn't help that he had an unrepentant demeanor, which only fueled the contempt judges already felt for him. "He has those piercing eyes, and his chin juts out," Turner said. "He looks defiant. That's the kind of thing that just sets judges off at sentencing. What are you going to do to me? I'll show you. Judges should be cognizant of those things and check themselves. They shouldn't beat up on Doug in a way that they think the way he looks is meaningful, because it might not be meaningful."

I asked Turner if he thought his client had been treated fairly by the legal system.

"He was unmitigatedly screwed. There was nothing fair or proper about the way they treated Doug. They didn't like his knowledge and activism in the field of encryption, and the fact that he was an outspoken zoophile who tried to help others, like the guy in Tennessee."

I also asked: why was Spink such a lightning rod for vigorous, relentless prosecution?

> It's because everyone—even criminal defense lawyers—cringe. That's what allowed this. People's response to zoophilia is so overwhelming. They get overwhelmed by the dark place in their psyche. Their refusal to look at it objectively is so strong that they

can't even see the violation of his constitutional rights. They're so caught up in thinking about it that their brain is spinning around, sex with animals, that's icky and awful and sinful. That becomes the dialogue in their heads and everything else gets drowned out.

54

DOORWAY DARKENING

I hadn't ever covered a story this controversial. Not even close. The very idea of cross-species sexuality riled people up. I was exposing the unthinkable.

Strange things started to happen.

One day, I realized I was being followed. It didn't take great powers of deductive reasoning, because it wasn't subtle. The man driving behind me was taking every turn I was, which was obvious because I was traveling down near-deserted country roads. But since there wasn't much in the way of retail stores nearby, it was possible he was just going to the same strip mall I was, so I didn't jump to conclusions right away.

The small shopping center sat by the nearest freeway exit to my house, about two and a half miles away. I pulled into the parking lot and sat there in my car for about fifteen minutes. So did this man. When I finally emerged from my vehicle, I looked back and noticed he did the same. He was now following me, from a distance, into the grocery store. I headed for the produce section. So did he. While we browsed, I looked him straight in the eyes and walked out without buying anything. I sat in my car and watched him leave the store moments later and go to his vehicle. He didn't have a shopping bag.

I sat there for quite a while until he finally drove off.

∩

My house was already up for sale because I couldn't keep up with it after my husband's death. But I no longer felt safe there, and I didn't think my dog was safe either. One of Whatcom Humane Society's employees came to my home in Custer and warned me about Clark in connection with the safety of my dog in that community.

I decided to rent a place on Vashon Island, a community without a roadway to the mainland that was only accessible by boat or air, although I still traveled back to spend time at my house in the woods on occasion, a secluded home that Hiromi and I had built on an old logging road. It was situated on a dead end leading into acres of forest.

In January 2015, I managed to sell the place for less than I had hoped for, but at least it was a quick closing that wasn't dependent on the buyers getting financing. I returned there for a week to pack and move out the last of my things. In the middle of that week, I left the house to run some errands.

When I returned a couple of hours later, the front door was still locked, and there was no sign of forced entry. But someone had been there, and they left their version of a calling card for me to find. My notebook was open on the counter by the kitchen sink. As I got closer, I could see that the handwriting on the page wasn't mine. Shivers rippled up my spine to the back of my neck. Was someone still there in the house with me?

The note was written using my own pen. I knew that because the pen was lying beside the notebook, and the ink matched. Drawn around the words was what looked like a rough floor plan of my house. The note said: "Dose [sic] anybody live here?—you may never know who wrote this."

A couple of days later, on January 23, I left my home in the woods for the last time. I haven't been back since.

∩

I was starting to get annoyed at the small band of vigilantes who were determined to take me down because I was writing about Doug Spink.

The note left for me in my house, written in my notebook with my own pen.

Without exception, all my journalism colleagues understood and saw the value of what I was doing, and they were supportive. So were some animal rescuers I knew. But I had lost a few friends over the project. Some animal rescuers were angry I was writing about this man whose philosophies and behavior they found appalling.

One former Whatcom Humane Society shelter staffer and friend who worked at the veterinary clinic I'd gone to for many years was clear about her disapproval. I had come in to collect the ashes of my dead cat when she lashed out at me: "How could you believe that drug dealer over Laura?"

One of the animal welfare people who was not hostile, and who encouraged me to get to the heart of the story, was Susan Simmons. A retired psychologist, she had served as president of the WHS board for six years. Once I even took her with me to Port Townsend to meet Doug Spink.

At dinner parties and other events, Simmons would tell people about the book I was writing. The negative reactions she received both intrigued and surprised her, but they didn't stop her from speaking about it. "Whenever I would talk to people about your book, they would either shine me off, or tell me, 'I don't want to talk about it, that is sick,'" Simmons said. "It's extremely alienating. It felt like I should be ashamed to be bringing this subject up. It was surprising to me, because I was detached about it. I could talk about it objectively as a subject."

Overall, I was fine with the conflict. It meant that I was on the right track. The story had hit a nerve with people. The ruckus delayed—but didn't deter—my end objective: to get to the truth.

The place I rented on Vashon Island, in Washington's Puget Sound, was a renovated barn that used to house chickens. A postal worker once told me that Vashon was called "Weird Island." Some of the locals said it was also known as the "Island of Broken Toys," a place where people came to get away, especially when they needed to heal from something.

Given its remote location, I thought Vashon would be a secure place to stay for a while. But a turn of events made even that far-flung place feel unsafe. I would stay there only about a year before I headed back to my hometown of Winnipeg for a few months. Next I moved on to New Orleans, where I spent more than two years writing.

∩

It was while I was staying on Vashon Island that a chilling collection of documents was pulled from the shadows by the bright lights of the Freedom of Information Act. This particular set of emails was from March 2014, right around the time Spink was arrested at Chicken Coop Road and thrown back into federal prison following the disappearance of Ghengis, Andrew Johnston's dog.

Much of the several hundred pages was email chatter between Laura Clark, executive director of the Whatcom Humane Society; Deputy Sheriff Alex Mintz, who seemed to be in charge of Jefferson County Animal Control; and Jenny Edwards, who was at one time with Hope for Horses (she wouldn't confirm her role with the organization when we spoke by phone) and founder of the bestiality-busting firm Chandler Edwards. Clark and Edwards were frequent companions at Spink's court hearings. Edwards also won custody of two of Spink's horses after the 2010 raid, as she had done with the horses in the Pinyan case.

What the pages revealed was that Laura Clark's obsession with Doug Spink trickled outwards like a festering bog to include the journalist writing a book about him. Namely: me. They outlined a disturbing attempt by Clark to find my address and send her accomplices to track me down. Or, as Deputy Alex Mintz put it, to darken my doorway.

One email exchange that caught my attention was between Laura Clark and Deputy Mintz on March 10, 2014. Subject line: Carreen Maloney.

> **Mintz**: Laura, Do you have any info on Carreen, like her middle name and date of birth? Possibly what kind of vehicle she drives, a description or even any photo? I understand she used to work or volunteer for Whatcom Humane? Any info would help.
> **Clark**: I'll work on finding info about Maloney and C. [likely Claire] Spink. Maloney was a "fringe-volunteer" (never really volunteered, but was always hanging around) with us several years ago. Very, very odd lady.

Clark didn't seem to think I was on the "fringe" in 2010, when she accepted a $25,000 (retail value) donation of stuffed animals from my company, Fuzzy Town, for the shelter's fundraising efforts. Here's what she said about it by email on April 7, 2010, one week before Spink's property in Sumas was raided:

> Wanted to let you know that your toys are flying off the shelves at Paws Awhile. They can't keep them in stock, they are selling so many. We have to make weekly deliveries to them and now people are requesting certain types of animals. Both our shelters have them for sale as well. Tails A Wagging has a display and we are gearing up for the Ski To Sea Event as well. It's so awesome! Thank you again.

Nor did Clark seem to mind that I was "hanging around" the shelter when I wrote fundraising appeal letters, calendar copy and newsletter articles that told the story of the shelter's work and raised thousands of dollars in donations. I interviewed dozens of staff members and volunteers over a timeline which spanned nearly a decade, which also resulted in several stories being published in magazines. It was Clark who nominated me for the WHS Act of Kindness Award after I returned from rescuing animals in New Orleans following

Hurricane Katrina. Here's how she felt about me hanging around the shelter on June 23, 2009:

> Thanks so much for chatting with me. I am so grateful for all the support you continue to show and give to WHS. The animals are so lucky to have a friend like you. I want to make sure you know that I in now [sic] way want to edit or re-write your work. I am not a professional writer and have no business telling you how or what to write—ever!

It's hard to believe that tracking my whereabouts became a priority for Clark when she had a busy shelter to manage, a shelter supported by hard-earned donations and taxpayer dollars. Yet she took the time to keep Deputy Mintz in the loop by email as she attempted to figure out where I lived. On March 11, she wrote: "On another note, I should have some info on Carreen Maloney for you later this am. My source thinks she is living in your community—will get an address this am and send it to you."

She briefed Mintz again on March 11: "Hi Alex, So the only thing I have on Carreen Maloney right now is from someone who saw her last summer. She told that person she was living on Vashon Island in a rented vacation house, but hoped to move to Forks soon. She gave a number of [redacted]. I'll keep digging."

Although I did spend time on Vashon Island, I never had plans to move to Forks, a small city on the Olympic Peninsula. I had never even been there. It was, however, a place that Spink had stated he had ties to.

The response from Alex Mintz was chilling: "Thanks, I will be glad to darken her doorway."

Jenny Edwards also chimed in here and there. Here's an email from March 11:

> I don't have a current address for Maloney. Her email and cell is [redacted]. In July of 2013 her blog said she was "run out of Whatcom County." Maloney fancies herself a dog rescuer and it's possible Spink would have connected w/ her, although my gut feel is that they've had a falling out. I don't have a DOB, but believe Maloney was born in 1969. She formerly had a stuffed toy business called Fuzzy Town and was married but divorced prior to 2010.

I did not write on my blog that I was "run out of Whatcom County," as Edwards misquoted. That could be confirmed by reading my blog. In fact, I chose to leave Whatcom County to protect my dog from Laura Clark, who seemed obsessed with Spink. She once posted on her

Facebook page that she thought about Doug Spink's animals every day. Yet she had consistently dodged my attempts to definitively prove that his dogs made it out of the shelter alive. Given her position as director of the agency responsible for animal control, I was concerned about what would happen to my dog if she ever landed in the custody of Clark's organization. I didn't want her to become the casualty of anyone's personal vendetta.

Also, contrary to what Edwards wrote, I am mostly a cat rescuer, not a dog rescuer. I have some experience rescuing dogs, but it's minimal compared to my work with cats.

Nor was I ever divorced. I was widowed.

In the years since my research into Doug Spink and his animals began, I wrote about things some people didn't want revealed, the kinds of revelations that lead the people featured to attempt to shut me up. For a journalist such as myself, it would ordinarily be interesting to watch the attempted intimidation of an investigation in progress. Bald-faced attempts at shutting down the media are encouraging signs. That means we're hitting into the heart of the matter. Stonewalling from sources provides impetus, and a strong signal to proceed full speed ahead.

As much as I am loath to admit this, it feels different when you are the target. It was more than a little disconcerting, as I paged through the emails, to picture this questionable cast of characters tracking me down with intentions of who knows what. If I shove aside the seasoned journalist's bravado, there is an odious aspect to this latest turn of events. Knowing that someone might be out there slandering me in order to send people to hunt me down is disturbing.

Unfortunately for them, it didn't work. It only increased my motivation.

Despite Clark's demands to WHS staff and volunteers that they stay quiet, they still spoke to me and fed me information. They told me how obsessed Clark was with Spink, which was obvious to me too. She couldn't take her eyes off him at court hearings, and drove two hours to Seattle during the shelter's work time to be there with him every step of the way.

55

OH CANADA

For years, Spink had considered moving back to Canada. He'd just about had his fill of his home country. He hoped he would be treated kinder and understood better by the people of the great white north.

Although I knew he had these fond feelings towards Canada, I did not expect what happened next.

One cold winter Sunday a few days before Christmas 2014, when I was back living in Winnipeg for a few months, my phone pinged. Spink's boyfriend, who I'd interviewed several times, had sent me a text. He was in Winnipeg on a business trip—did I want to meet up that day?

I was waiting in a booth in the nearly empty lounge of Santa Lucia Pizza on St. Mary's Road when he walked in. Until that moment, I hadn't known what he looked like, but when I saw him, I knew immediately who he was. He dropped a sturdy box filled to the brim with documents onto the table between us. Spink had filed reams of Freedom of Information requests during the many months he'd spent in prison, and this box contained some of the fruits of his labor.

Ten minutes later, who appeared at the booth but Spink himself, wearing the grin of the Cheshire cat. His face was stubbled, his hair braided into a long, thick plait that poked out from the back of his baseball cap.

He seemed happier and healthier than I had seen him looking in a while. When we'd last met in person, it had been in the SeaTac prison visiting room, and he was gaunt and pale from no access to fresh air. Now he was in the frigid cold air of Winnipeg.

He wanted to talk about his court appearance in Whatcom County ten days earlier. Usually I went to his hearings, but for this one, I had been too far away to attend. He told me that he'd known the fix was in as he sat in court, that he'd sensed that whatever was going to happen that day was prearranged before the proceeding even began.

I asked him how he made it across the border given his criminal record, but he wouldn't elaborate on that. Or on how long he would be staying in Canada.

We ate pizza and talked for about two hours. Then he was gone.

As the months wore on, things started to deteriorate for Spink in Canada. We continued to stay in touch through various channels: phone calls, emails, texts. He still felt deeply wounded by the loss of his animals. He couldn't get over that, and he didn't think he ever would. And he couldn't shake the pervasive feeling of being hunted. He perceived enemies everywhere, and struggled to cope with that nagging feeling. He could have been labeled paranoid, yet his fears didn't seem unfounded given what he had experienced.

I noticed changes in him. The calls he placed to me started to sound detached from reality. He was panicked and upset. He talked about phoning me from a "bolt-hole," or hiding place. He wouldn't give me much substantive information on the phone the way he used to, in case someone was listening. He was convinced there were government agents in the woods outside his house watching him. He wanted me to stay on the phone to listen to what transpired. Periodically, he would shout out loud to someone he believed to be there, yelling things such as, "I've got a journalist on the phone!"

Another time, he called me from a hotel room convinced he was being watched. He thought he saw red lights flashing in the room, and sent me a photo to check if I saw them too. I didn't. Or he'd send an audiotape to my email, asking if I heard voices in the background. I didn't hear anything but dead air.

I didn't know what to say to calm his frayed nerves. Mostly I just listened.

The deterioration of Spink's state of mind culminated in August 2015, in southern Ontario. On August 9, he was picked up by police as he walked along Wharncliffe Road outside Lambeth, a neighborhood of London. A citizen concerned for his welfare called the police when he wandered into a local business, disheveled and with a towel wrapped around his waist. He gave officers a fake name at first, but was subsequently identified, arrested and held at the Elgin-Middlesex Detention Centre for potential immigration issues.

The next day, he was released. He called me from his cell phone, elated to be free again. That night he followed up with an email in which he described what had happened as "a heavy PTSD incident."

> Yesterday, I found myself in contact with local police officers without any of my ID or driver's license on hand. I was not in my best form, having that morning engaged some personal demons in an hours-long... event—let's just call it an "event" for now—in the local swamps and forestland. I was recovering from a deep dive into the cold waters of genuine terror. And I'm not in my home country, driving a vehicle with expired plates. And so on. All irresponsible and, in a word, dumb.
>
> I was taken into custody and held overnight. Given my record, this kind of thing is inevitable—one look at a screen in any cruiser on this continent shows all manner of 'flags' for me.

In yet another twist upon twists—a defining characteristic of this strange story that surrounds Doug Spink—his release from the detention center was apparently a big mistake, one that made news when it was discovered. The authorities scrambled to reverse it. The day after he was released, Ontario Provincial Police scrambled to pick him up again in Port Stanley, a tiny village on the north shore of Lake Erie, twenty-six miles from London. They put him back in custody.

Hoping to stay in Canada, Spink appeared before the Immigration and Refugee Board on August 12 for an admissibility hearing. His continued presence in the country was denied, and a removal order was issued. He was transported to Niagara Falls by the Canadian Border Services Agency.

In an email to me and a few of his friends on the night of his short-lived release, he expanded on what his life had been like lately. Intense terror always hummed in the background, its constant presence shattering his peace of mind.

> The word "terror" gets used alot, over-used. Terrifying economic data coming out this week, terror from the pending cost of roof repairs, and so on. Real terror is its own category—not just "fear expanded" but an entirely new thing. It is overwhelming, totalising, and smashes our identity and rational presence under a planet-class weight of unbounded, unrelenting, immeasurable panic and helplessness and fear. It's a vestige of being a prey animal, stalked and seeking that last one in a million dash for survival even as the predator opens our stomach and our guts tangle in our legs as we try to flee...
> This is the sort of thing terror entails, real terror.
> In the last 36 hours I have faced what I confidently conclude are my soul's most potent terrors, all brought to bear on me as I seek to come to terms with horrors I've experienced since 2010. There is a sense of opening up an infected, festering, healed-over mass of ugly memories, scars, and self-loathing. Everyone reading this knows which events I reference in this. I've re-lived them, in realtime, ramped up to extreme—almost absurd—levels. This is terror, and it is beyond words to describe.

Two years later, he would refer to that time in 2015 as "The Horrors," and refused to reveal any more than that.

NORTHERN EXPOSURE

Spink was a determined character. Despite being deported, he wasn't giving up that easily on his dream of legally living in Canada. Thinking his Indigenous heritage might improve his chances of emigrating, he applied for and received his certificate of membership for the Montagnais Métis First Nation. He sent me a photograph of his new identification card.

He spent a couple of months visiting his mother in Pennsylvania before deciding to head north again. He didn't tell me how he got back into Canada, although there were rumors that he crossed over at a little-traveled section of the border into Saskatchewan, a mostly rural prairie province.

But his demons wouldn't leave him be, and it wasn't long before he was in trouble again.

It was around 6:20 p.m. on Saturday, November 14, 2015, when emergency workers responded to a fire in Port Stanley that destroyed the back porch of a house where Spink was staying. According to media reports, a female neighbor said that Spink was restraining another man, and he told her he had a knife on him, although she didn't see the knife. She said Spink released the man and took off. He stopped briefly at another house, broke down the door with his right shoulder, went inside momentarily, and then continued down the road.

Police arrested him, but this was different from any of his previous arrests. For the first time ever, he resisted.

In December, Spink appeared in a St. Thomas court and pled guilty to five charges: assault with a weapon, mischief, unlawfully being in a house, and two counts of resisting arrest.

Spink drew media attention wherever he went, and Ontario was no exception. Jane Sims of the *London Free Press* wrote several stories about him after his presence became known in that region because of his arrests and subsequent deportations from Canada. A headline from one of her articles said that his story "is a tale worthy of a mystery novel." Another Sims story on December 21, 2015, titled "Fugitive blames rampage on stress," included an account of the November night when Spink was arrested.

> He was told he was under arrest and the officers pulled out their Tasers.
>
> Police found a knife in a sheath in Spink's back pocket.
>
> Spink was handcuffed but began to resist. He tried to trip one officer.
>
> "Call the cops. Call the OPP," he yelled.
>
> He was uncooperative, [assistant Crown attorney Stephanie] Venne said, and tried to stop the arrest by pushing his legs on the police cruiser and not budging. He was eventually grounded, where he began bucking and pushing away.
>
> The violence continued as the officers got Spink into the cruiser, Venne said. He smashed out both backseat side windows and bent the cruiser's radar antenna. On the way to the St. Thomas hospital, Spink kicked the rear door and smashed his head on the Plexiglass at least 10 times.
>
> He wouldn't get out of the cruiser at the hospital and it took seven officers to drag him in, where he was restrained on a hospital bed.
>
> All the while, he was shouting and "disturbing other patients and staff," Venne said.

He was sentenced to 150 days in jail, leaving him with about three months on his sentence after credit for time already served.

Spink refused to discuss with me what had happened that night, a departure from his usual willingness to talk. He said he had his own reasons for staying silent on the matter.

After his release, Spink was deported from Canada a second time, and dropped off on the south side of the border in New York State. He traveled back to his mother's place outside Pittsburgh. Back to Mister Rogers' neighborhood.

Claire Spink had grown increasingly concerned about her son's state of mind. "He is paranoid delusional. He's seeing things that aren't there," she said, when I spoke to her by phone. "We're sitting in the backyard and he's hearing people in the bushes."

She believed her son's erratic, turbulent behavior was a severe and untreated case of post-traumatic stress disorder, and she was researching treatments given to war veterans in an attempt to find a solution to help him. "I couldn't find him one day and he was hiding behind the furnace, hysterical. He said they were looking at him through the cement block wall. He was panic-stricken, like the look on an animal who's been shot."

In the years since I'd met Spink, I had wondered how he remained emboldened and recalcitrant in the face of the almost constant threats and hatred. For so long, he'd been able to summon a seemingly endless supply of bravado. But it seemed as if the stress of being hunted was finally causing cracks in his armor. "I've been left exhausted," he wrote, "by efforts to be 'on point' 24/7 against all possible threat vectors and against all known adversaries—both those real and documented and those only imaginable in the broadest logical terms. That's a big load to carry."

He explained more about what he was going through in that letter he sent to me after his first arrest in Canada.

> There's no question I'm wrestling with a mountain-sized case of PTSD. I need to focus more attention on steering that into healing pathways, and not into destructive and self-reinforcing ones. This I will be doing. I think I've got the knack of some of it already, but I know I've not got my hands around all of it—my poor judgement yesterday shows that. Some substantial portion of the terrors and local security circumstances I've experienced since last year are "not real" in the sense of being interpretations of bits of data that end up with imputed macro patterns that don't align with reality as time goes by; In a nutshell, those imputed macro patterns (I call them "models") haven't yielded accurate predictions of future events, thus far. Thus, empirically, they're wrong—or "not real" if you prefer.

It's been noted that my local security parameters have been shown to be badly tuned and essentially dysfunctional. These parameters come from years under the gun of full-bore law enforcement targeting, as well as years of prison time in some fairly nasty prisons. And some efforts to kill me along the way, by various means, that didn't help things much.

Despite Claire Spink's efforts to help her son put his life back together, it wouldn't be enough to prevent what happened next.

NIGHT TERROR

Sleep had become increasingly elusive and troubling for Doug Spink. When he closed his eyes, vivid and relentless nightmares of his animals being tortured and killed took center stage.

Eventually he asked his mother if he could sleep in her room. The two were close—she had stood loyally and steadfastly by her son through all his troubles—but her bedroom was her sanctuary, her area of privacy. So they pulled some blankets down from the attic and made a makeshift bed right in front of her door. That's where he'd begun sleeping every night.

"If you need to talk to me, knock on the door," she told him.

The first scare Spink got on the fateful night of April 4, 2016, was his mother's car alarm. Around 2:30 a.m. it started shrieking, and that startled him out of sleep. The alarm had never malfunctioned before. Was someone prowling around outside?

"Mum! Mum! Mum!" Spink called out softly as he knocked on her door.

Claire got up, and they went outside and disabled the alarm. They looked around but didn't notice anything out of the ordinary.

The next unsettling bump in the night came an hour and a half later, in the form of a crash against the sliding glass door at the back of the house. Claire didn't know then what had caused the racket, although she figured it out later.

The night noises set Spink's panic into motion. He had lost everyone he ever loved except his mother, and now he believed he was about to lose her as well to some predator in the night. It seemed as if everyone he cared about was doomed to be destroyed, eradicated by a world that hated him.

"At four o'clock in the morning, my door exploded," Claire remembered. "He came crashing through the door and said, 'Someone's in the house.'"

He grabbed the box by the bed where she kept her .38-caliber Colt revolver. "He was waving it around. He had it mostly to his head. He said, 'You shouldn't be in the room. You shouldn't see this.'"

Claire wasn't about to stand aside and watch her only son destroy himself for good. She struggled with him for control of the gun.

"Who did you talk to?" she asked him. "Who did this? What set you off?"

The two went down to the basement to talk.

"He was running around the room blocking windows and taking light bulbs out of lamps. I said I wasn't going to sit down there in the dark."

Doug went upstairs by himself, and that's when Claire heard the gun go off. Three shots in total. She thought that was the end for her son.

She ran upstairs to see what had happened. Two shots had gone off in the kitchen. One bullet had lodged in the ceiling, and another flew through a back window. But no one had been shot.

As Claire followed her son through the house trying to get the gun away from him, he shot a third bullet through a window in the basement.

She tried to call 911, but the phones weren't working.

"I'm leaving and going to the neighbor's," she told her son. Still in her nightgown, she pulled on a pair of slippers and crossed the street to the neighbor's house to call for help. She tripped as she was going up the steps, and that's when she noticed him walking down the street.

The neighbor, a social worker, knew what to do and took the reins. When the police arrived, they wouldn't let Claire go back to her house while her son's location was unknown. So she stayed at the neighbor's while officers tried to locate this man in distress.

Meanwhile, Spink was in the throes of panic, searching for help, caught up in the belief that someone was going to attack and torture his mother. He got into the car of a motorist who stopped to see if he needed help. Spink asked for a ride to the police station, yelling frantically for the driver to call the police because someone had broken into his house and was hurting his mother. At some point before they reached the station, the motorist asked him to exit the car. Spink did so without incident, except for leaving blood from an injury to his hand on the dashboard.

It was still early—almost 6:00 a.m.—but Spink found a house with lights on. The woman who lived there was a bus driver getting ready for work. She got a scare when he pounded on the door, and ran upstairs to get her gun. By the time she got back downstairs to the door, he was gone, leaving only his blood on the door as a calling card.

He ended up at a gas station called the Buy 'n Fly, on Route 68 in Jackson Township, where the clerk on duty called police. Officers arrived to find Spink in a fetal position on the floor behind the store's front counter.

Arresting Doug Spink did not go smoothly.

He struggled against five officers who tried to take him in, kicking over racks of snacks and cigarettes in the process. Police pried his hands away from his body, and used two separate sets of handcuffs on him, plus a third set to link them together because they couldn't get him cuffed the traditional way. His was the strength of adrenalin and fear.

Spink was eventually led outside the gas station and continued to yell that he needed the police and ambulance, wrote officer Erik Magness of the Zelienople Borough Police Department in his report. "Harmony EMS was on scene and a stretcher was then brought over to Spink who was lying on the ground. While on the ground, a transport belt and leg shackles were applied to Spink due to his continued combative behavior. We attempted to pick Spink up and place him on the stretcher several times, but he forcibly kept throwing himself off of the stretcher and back onto the ground."

With the handcuffs and shackles, Spink was finally strapped to the gurney, and he was taken by ambulance to the psychiatric ward of Butler Memorial Hospital. The struggle at the Buy 'n Fly had lasted more than an hour.

"While on the ride to the hospital, Spink became very skeptical that I was a police officer and that he was in an ambulance," Magness wrote. "Once he arrived at the hospital, he was evaluated and signed himself in."

Firefighters searched the area later that morning and found the Colt revolver stashed outside in the dirt not far from Claire's house.

Spink stayed in the hospital for a week until he was stabilized with medication. Then he was moved to Butler County Prison. Nine police officers showed up to take him three miles to the jail.

He faced seventeen criminal charges as a result of that night (twelve of them felonies). They consisted of one count of possession of a prohibited firearm, three counts of discharging a firearm into an occupied structure, three counts of aggravated assault, another two counts of aggravated assault, four counts of recklessly endangering another person, one count of criminal mischief for breaking the bus driver's screen door, and another three counts of criminal mischief for the $5,000 damage caused to the Buy 'n Fly during the struggle.

Claire was angry that her son was accused of trying to hurt her. She told Butler County District Judge Wayne Seibel that, "he would never do that. He's not capable of it."

Spink tried to get out of jail pending resolution of his charges, but he couldn't come up with the $35,000 bail. The bail bond agents considered him a flight risk, and wouldn't grant him a bond without significant collateral.

His fate in the balance, Spink was held in custody as he awaited the resolution of his latest charges. "He can't stand not being able to see the sky and the trees and the animals. The horses," Claire said.

In the days that followed, Claire Spink tried to piece together what had happened that awful night. She was at least able to solve the mystery of the crash against the sliding door at the back of the house. A pumpkin sitting on a metal plant holder had rotted, and the shift in weight as the vegetable collapsed into itself caused the plant holder to tip into the blinds.

She re-enacted the event with a remaining pumpkin she had grown, and sure enough, it created the same crashing sound.

It was a routine sort of mishap. But years of being hunted as an outed, outspoken zoophile made Spink react in a way that most human beings wouldn't. "I have a gut feeling that I'll never get my life back," he said. "At an intuitive level my faith in the world is broken. I can't run, I can't hide, and I can't go away."

Claire believes the PTSD that torments her son might have been exacerbated by something that happened when he was a teenager, after his parents separated.

Like most divorces, the Spinks' breakup wasn't amicable, and this one took an even nastier turn than most. Claire's husband reportedly went to the seedy area of town to find someone he could pay to kill his wife. But his ominous plan for murder got back to the police. They informed Claire there had been a threat to her life, and suggested she get a pump shotgun for protection.

The Spinks' matrimonial home was sited in a vulnerable spot, up on a hill with no neighbors. Exposed. Only Doug still lived there with his mom. His sister Joy had already left home for college at Penn State.

Claire called the local police chief for advice.

"Seven minutes later the chief comes walking in the front door," she remembered. "He said, 'If they come in your house, your instructions are you pull the trigger until it goes click, click, click, until there are no bullets left, then call the police.'"

♘

Despite his fundamental distrust of society because of his life experiences, Spink still found companionship and camaraderie with human beings, including other inmates. Several ex-cons who served time with him in various facilities contacted me wanting to talk about him.

One former inmate to reach out was a man named Christopher Queen. He had been released from Butler County Prison a day earlier when he sent me a message through social media on August 10, 2016, while Spink was still doing time for firing the gun in his mother's house and resisting arrest.

"We became very good friends," Queen wrote. "Our differences in orientation and sexual preferences was a non-issue. Talked about organic chemistry, religion, human existence, cultural relativism, soh-crates and Diogenes. Helped so much to pass the time."

One of their favorite pastimes to get through the monotony of prison involved wordplay. "I spent three months playing Scrabble with him," Queen recalled, "we each pined for a Webster's or Oxford dictionary with no luck."

They enjoyed each other's company, but "we were not permitted to be cell mates. We made several attempts but were unfortunately denied. They did allow us to be next door neighbors."

Finding people to trust took on extra significance behind prison walls. "I trusted him more than anyone there and as far as I am cued to feeling was reciprocal," Queen wrote. "I would go to greater lengths for him than many people. We both are pretty strange birds if we decide to let you 'in.' Not dangerously."

Spink's charges from the April 2016 incident devolved to three misdemeanors: criminal mischief, reckless endangerment and resisting arrest. On February 7, 2017, he was released from Butler County Prison. Free again.

But he wasn't truly free. At least not in his mind.

"What's surprising to me is that now, when such attacks against me are proven real and have been repeated, it is broadly assumed that my acceptance of the potential for such an attack to recur is evidence of clinical, delusional paranoia. Funny, really. Again, a luxury available to those who aren't targets of socially authorized persecution. To them, it's not real."

58

THE DISAPPEARED

A few weeks before this book went to press, I was doing some final fact checking with Doug Spink by text and phone. He sounded nervous. He didn't feel safe, and thought people were coming to get him. Then one day he stopped responding. It wasn't like him to go silent, unless he didn't have a choice.

He had disappeared again.

A few days went by before I found out what happened. On November 25, 2017, Thanksgiving weekend, Spink had another run-in with law enforcement. This was the most dramatic confrontation yet, very nearly a fatal encounter.

The incident began unfolding at 9:00 a.m. on the crisp autumn Saturday. Spink was resting in the back seat of his GMC Yukon while parked in an alley. Recently he had started sleeping in his vehicle because he didn't feel safe in his apartment anymore. He'd spent the previous night in his truck in a different location closer to his apartment building before waking up that morning and driving around for a while looking for a new place to live, somewhere he could feel more secure. But when he accidentally got his vehicle wedged into the alley half a mile from home, he decided to stay there and nap for a while, watching the sunrise.

That's where he was when a Butler police officer discovered him. The officer told Spink he needed to come with him to check in at the hospital because there were concerns about his mental health, and that there was a mental health warrant out for his arrest. Spink was confused by the request. He had been going to counseling sessions every week for post-traumatic stress disorder, as well as seeing a psychiatrist once a month, and he didn't know where this was coming from.

One thing he did know: he wasn't going to be willingly parted from his dog, Kav, a young Anatolian Shepherd who he had registered as a service dog. His refusal to comply with police instantly escalated the encounter.

"He became adamant that he would not leave his dog," Butler Deputy Chief David Adam told the *Butler Eagle*, "and that he would kill it before he would let anyone take it away from him." Spink denied he said this.

Spink's refusal to obey orders led officers from the Butler City Police Department to request assistance from Butler Township Police and the state's Special Emergency Response Team. "They immediately called a state SWAT team even though there was no underlying criminal complaint," said Spink, in a phone call he made to me from jail on December 15.

For two hours, a group of police officers surrounded Spink. Two state police negotiators took turns trying to reason with him, coaxing him to give himself up. In an effort to resolve the conflict, they obtained permission from the ambulance service and the hospital for Spink to bring his dog along with him, but he didn't believe them, and still refused to cooperate. In response, police began Tasing him while he was in the vehicle. Spink said he tried to shield his dog with his body to prevent him from getting hit by the Taser. News reports said Spink was holding a knife to his dog's neck, but Spink told me that wasn't true. He said he was using the knife to attempt to cut the cables connected to the Taser darts in order to protect Kav.

"I was in a panic trying to protect him from getting incidentally Tasered," Spink said. "I was cornered in the truck. This was my worst nightmare."

But when he realized he couldn't keep Kav safe, he opened the Yukon's door and let the dog out. "He was in the line of fire," Spink said. "It was the hardest decision I've ever made."

Spink then exited his vehicle and got down on one knee. But when officers demanded he get down on both knees, he didn't like that request, and responded by getting up again before dashing into the group of officers in a futile attempt to get his dog back.

Police tased Spink five times "with little effect," Deputy Chief Adam said, so they shot him with several rounds of beanbag ammunition.

"They Tased me unconscious," Spink said. He bit a trooper's right thumb while he was being taken into custody, which sent the officer to the hospital with minor injuries.

Spink was charged with aggravated assault, resisting arrest and disorderly conduct, and taken to Butler Memorial Hospital. When he woke up three days later, he was intubated, and the back of his head was swollen with a metal Taser dart embedded in it. His chest was shaved. His heart had stopped beating at the scene, doctors told him, and paramedics brought him back to life in the ambulance using defibrillator paddles. "It was a death squad," he said. "They killed me this time."

Each time he came out of sedation in the hospital, severe distress kicked in as he became frantic about the welfare and whereabouts of his dog. "His whole identity is wrapped up in that dog," said his mother, Claire Spink.

After a few days, he recovered enough to be transferred to the medical unit at Butler County Prison. He's been referred to a neurologist because he can no longer control his left hand, and he's having trouble concentrating. The man who consumed books voraciously since childhood now struggles to read.

Meanwhile, Kav changed hands several times before ending up in the care of a local rescue group that placed the dog in a foster home.

Doug Spink was alone and imprisoned once more.

∩

Five years ago, an envelope Spink mailed from the bleak confines of a federal prison landed in my post office box. Tucked inside was an article ripped from a 2012 *New Yorker* magazine. Written by Salman Rushdie, "The Disappeared" discussed the author's experiences around the publication of his 1988 novel, *The Satanic Verses*. Following its release, Iran's Ayatollah Khomeini ordered Muslims to kill Rushdie.

Spink had highlighted a single sentence in the article: "How easy it was to erase a man's past and to construct a new version of him, an overwhelming version, against which it seemed impossible to fight."

It was a phenomenon he had experienced firsthand.

"The world came in and whitewashed over my life and painted a new picture on there," he said. "The truth didn't matter. The lies have been more durable than the truth."

He had fought long and hard in this battle of his. In the process, he lost every member of his four-legged family, and a nine-year relationship with the man he cared about more than any other human partner he'd ever had. The stress of everything they'd gone through together finally tore them apart.

"My confidence in there being a future is shattered. I don't feel like I'll ever get my life back. These people will bat me back and forth between systems forever. It's never going to be over. I wish I could say all the people who made me suffer failed, but they didn't."

POSTSCRIPT

At press time, Doug Spink was incarcerated in Pennsylvania's Butler County Prison. Washington State still has a warrant out for his arrest. Capone the stallion remains in the custody of Corinne Super. He turns twenty-two in April 2018.

AFTERWORD

When I first started researching the life of Doug Spink in 2010, the resistance I faced from those who tried to stop me from telling this story drove me forward and added momentum. It also gave me something to focus on after my own world as I had known it crumbled away. It was a way to cope with the losses I had experienced, including the death of my husband.

If I had known how long this project would take and what it would require of me, it's hard to imagine I would have ever followed that first tenuous thread. To spend almost eight years of my life seeking the truth would have seemed like a crazy, risky decision. The closer I got to the finish line, the stronger the story grew. Eventually I could no longer consider walking away. The result of that odyssey is what you're reading here.

Uniquely Dangerous sheds light on a phenomenon that—until now—has been so unspeakable in our society that it remained carefully hidden. The secrecy doesn't change anything, though. The zoos are going to keep doing what they're doing because it's who they are. The animals will never tell. And nothing I write in this book and beyond will ever change that.

APPENDIX

EXHIBIT 1

Spin-Up To The Raid

This email was sent by Jeff Robson the night before the raid on Spink's home in Sumas in April 2010. Stephen Clarke wouldn't have been at Spink's home if the raid had gone ahead on its originally scheduled date. It was Clarke's videotape of himself having sex with Spink's dogs that sealed Spink's fate.

The recipient list included:

- 18 people from US Probation, including former Western District of Washington Chief Probation Officer William Corn
- Cheryl Hinderer, an FBI agent specializing in sex crimes against children
- Sonya Johnson of IRS Criminal Investigations
- Susan Roe and Steven Masada at US Department of Justice
- Brad Fink of the US Marshals
- Paul Evans, Whatcom Humane Society's lead animal control officer

From: Jeff Robson, United States Probation Officer Assistant
Date & Time: April 6, 2010, 4:12 pm
Subject: Spink Search Update

The April 7th search is being rescheduled to Wednesday, April 14th. I've got a call out to Whatcom Co Sheriff's office to inform them of the change.

Animal Control is willing to assist with the animals and are working on getting a better count on the number/types of animals out there. Also, one of their officer's has been to his residence and will provide a rough layout of the property.

The new plan is for everyone to meet at the Whatcom Co Sheriff's department at 8:00am on 4/14. (311 Grand Ave Bellingham WA, 98225).

(We'll be leaving the Tukwila probation office at 6:00am if anyone wishes to carpool)

The drive out to Spink's residence is apx 45 minutes from the sheriff's office.

The USMS preference is to arrest Spink at his residence in the morning and they will clear the residence at that time.

SAFETY ISSUES
Mr. Spink has 6+ large aggressive trained dogs.
He is extremely intelligent and paranoid.
He has a history of mental health issues: paranoia, suicidal, very unstable, OCD, and Asperger (form of autism where to struggle socially and lack empathy).
In a recorded jail phone conversation, Mr. Spink stated, "he was preparing for Law Enforcement to kick down his door."
Preparing could mean being armed and or setting traps.

If you are availible, please email me back so I can get an accurate head count.

Thank you all again for your help,
Jeff

EXHIBIT 2

DOUGLAS SPINK

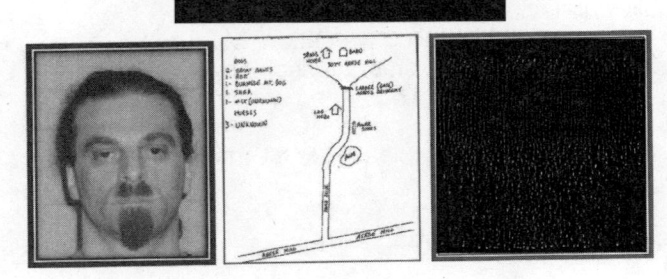

Height: 6'01 Weight: 220 Hair: Black Eyes: Brown DOB: 03/17/71

LOCATIONS TO SEARCH: Double wide, Barn, and all out buildings.

ITEMS SEARCHING FOR:
<u>All electronics</u>: computers*, storage devices, cameras, video equipment, thumb drives, CD, DVD, laptops, cell phones, blackberries, wireless devices, ipods, routers, servers
if a computer is found, contact me before you touch it. They <u>need</u> to be treated different.
<u>Files:</u> business records, taxes, phone numbers, bank records, anything relating to money, anything with a website on it, anything from Canada or Nevada, anything that says Baneki, zetatracker, or cultureghost
<u>Guns:</u> rifles, pistols, ammo
<u>Pornography:</u> child porn, animal porn, animal props, stories, Zoo-ish, Anti-zoo, etc.
<u>Drugs:</u> Cocaine, THC, Meth, Peyote, Mushrooms, paraphernalia
Any other evidence of a law or supervision violation.

OTHER NUMBERS
AUSA
Whatcom SO
Whatcom Animal Control
USMS
Hospitals   Abbotsford Regional 329 Marshall Rd BC CA 604-851-4700
            St Joseph 2901 Squalicum Pkwy, Bellingham 360-734-5400

The above poster was attached to Robson's email.
Names and phone numbers have been redacted.

EXHIBIT 3

Saying Goodbye

Excerpt from the letter Doug Spink wrote to his wife shortly after he came out to her as gay:

> We were friends. We trusted one another, and took strength from one another. We shared a world view, an outlook, and an approach to life that let us complete each other sentences. We each felt that we had someone in the world who really, truly cared about us just for who we are.
>
> At least for me, this was slowly eaten away by the miasma of my own sexuality. Even as I tried so, so hard to hide who I was, little bits and pieces were bobbing up around me and I was turning more and more into a shell of a person. I dared not feel anything too strongly, be too honest with myself about ANYTHING, as in doing so I always risked stumbling too deep into the water and bumping into the great, buried secret we had both hidden there.
>
> More and more, my subconscious mind came to equate YOU with this pain. You didn't cause it, but you were always there when this disjunction in my mind was most acute, most terrible and most painful. So much as I fought to remind myself that I loved you and cared so much for you, every time I saw you and felt a pang of affection, a piece within me shifted. It felt like dragging sandpaper over a partially healed but still painful wound.
>
> You knew this was happening, to a degree, as you are too intuitive not to have picked up on it. But the consequences of following that thread to its conclusion were too scary for you, just as they were for me. So we went on, day by day, inflicting a thousand small cuts in a desperate and doomed attempt to prolong the one stroke that would set things right. The unknown is always more frightening than more of the same, and we both acted out of fear.

EXHIBIT 4

```
                                    P.O. Box 340
                                    Guilford, ME.  04443
                                    Feb. 26, 2001
```

Dear Justice Mead:

    I'm writing this concerning the sentencing in the case of the State vs. Frank Buble which is scheduled for this Wednesday. I am the victim in that case and will be excercising my right to speak at the sentencing. I'd like my significant other to attend by my side if possible as she was present in the house during the attack, though not a eyewitness to it, thank goodness. I've been informed your personal permission is needed given that my wife is not human, being a dog of about 36 pounds weight and very well behaved. You can confirm this with just about anyone at the Dover courthouse, many there have already met her in "person." Thank you.

                                    Sincerely,

                                    Phillip and Lady Buble

2-27-01

Request is denied. No animals are permitted in the courthouse, with the exception of seeing-eye dogs in the company of a visually impaired person.

Andrew M. Mead

RECEIVED & FILED

FEB 26 2001

PISCATAQUIS COUNTY
Clerk's Office

Letter submitted to the court by Phillip Buble after the attack on him by his father.

EXHIBIT 5

Forum Postings

Doug Spink discussed his views about Dwain's death in November 2003 on a BASE forum hosted by Blinc magazine. Here's an excerpt:

Doug Spink (D-d0g)
I tried my best to prevent what happened in Colorado, and I failed. I'll be haunted by those events every day of my life, until the day I die.

Ray Loslie
What I really want to do is get down to brass tacks and understand your total true untold emotional feeling about Dwain. In the past you have made several verbal comments about Karin the latest one, Quote "He didn't need a manipulative spoiled little shrew to try to "slay any dragons" for him." MEOW... dude I mean what is it with you. You act like a Jealous Chic. Why be angry at Karin? This woman has only been nice to you as far as I can see, and that is coming from a guy who Blew Chips in her Make-up Bag, (that's a good story I will tell later), and she is still a good friend to me. OH.. I forgot about your insane theory that Karin drove Dwain to suicide. Do you feel like she came between you and Dwain. Why don't you just say it. You Were In Love With, Dwain. It's OK, Man just get it off your chest and fess up. I Can't Be The Only One Thinking This. No one is jealous of you being friends with the man, it just the Over Kill of the Drama that you invent, and surrounded yourself with after Nick went In and Dwain went In. I and JJ did attack you after that public post that stated "Dwain committed suicide" and you alone could not prevent or stop him from flying to his death. What Did You Expect Us To do ?? We Don't Hate You. but Man that was Crazy Talk. Dude, you are on Venus, and I cannot relate to you.

Doug Spink (D-d0g)
Anybody who hasn't heard what truly happened in Colorado is either living in a concrete bunker without news access, or is simply in denial about reality for one reason or another and we sure know a few of those who spouted their vitriol in public as a bulwark towards their walls of denial. Anybody else who slipped through the firestorm of truth intersecting the false patina of "grief," well my email address is pretty well known and the words I posted at DZ.com continue to reside on my hard drive and are available for anyone who is able to accept the reality of Dwain's choice without pissing themselves in their rush to stick their head in the soft sand of denial.

EXHIBIT 6

Excerpts from a letter written by Vancouver family lawyer Kathleen Walker to Corinne Super on Mar. 23, 2007:

Incarcerated Boyfriend
2. Mr. Super has sworn in an Affidavit that you are impecunious because of your association with a man who is now in jail in the U.S.A. for narcotics offences. While my notes show and I recall you disclosing that the man was a former tenant of yours, you did not disclose that [your daughter] was allowed to associate with him or that he was convicted of narcotics offences.

Failure to Disclose Marijuana Cultivation Operations to Me
4. When we first met you told me that the Barr Street property was bare and without structures because Mr. Super tore the old building on it down in preparation for building. For the first time you told me yesterday, on March 22, 2007 that the building on the Barr Street property burned down as a result of a grow operation owned and operated by Mr. Super.

Impact on Custody of [your daughter]
5. You also told me that Mr. Super owned and operated many marijuana grow operations, including one on the site of the Log House in Mission, a building where he exercises access to your young daughter. It is my understanding of the policy of the police and the Director of Child Protection in British Columbia that any children found on marijuana grow operations are automatically apprehended, without exception. Accordingly you and Mr. Super had apparently exposed [your daughter] to the risk of being apprehended by the Director.

Impact on my ability to enforce Assignment of Debt
6. There is federal proceeds of crime legislation which could result the Barr Street property and the Log House property being seized by the federal government. If there is a grow operation on the Chilliwack property or if the Maple Ridge shop is being used in the furtherance of crime all of the properties could be seized as you pointed out to me yesterday.

7. Your failure to disclose the foregoing material facts to me before now may seriously compromise my ability to represent you and

your ability to realize enough of the family assets to pay your debt to this firm.

8. I told you from the outset that you had to be scrupulously honest with me. You have not been in a very material way which affects every claim that you have made and you have not only jeopardized the outcome of your case, you have placed at great risk any ability that I may have to obtain my fees from the sale of property, which may well be subject to charges and seizure by the Canadian government.

Excerpts from affidavit submitted to Supreme Court of British Columbia for the divorce of Mark Anthony Super (plaintiff) and Corinne Arden Super (defendant) on Mar. 28, 2007. The following are statements made by Corinne Super:

10. I have never knowingly associated with any criminal or drug dealer. Mark knows this. For approximately 10 months, from March 2004 to January 2005 we leased part of a barn to a tenant named Doug Spink. Mr. Spink boarded five horses at our farm during that time. Mark and I leased the barn to Mr. Spink for $3,000.00 per month in rental fees. The rent went into our joint bank account at Coast Capital Savings Credit Union.

11. Doug Spink is gay and he introduced me to his boyfriend. He would leave for weeks on end. On February 28, 2005 I received a phone call from Mr. Spink stating that he was incarcerated in Seatac Prison in Washington State for transporting cocaine. He asked me to continue the care of the horses. He was not able to pay us for their care or for the barn. Mr. Spink said I could use the horses for breeding fees in lieu of rent. Mr. Spink is out on a work release program in Washington. The horses are going to be back in his care and off the farm by the end of May 2007. There is one horse in Florida, Capone and I receive his stud fees. There are two other stallions at the farm but their have been no stud fees associated with those horses: Cantour and Ace.

13. Mark knows all of this and he knows that Mr. Spink is gay. He knows that I never had any personal or intimate relations with Mr. Spink. He knows that we were the beneficiaries of Mr. Spink's rent for the use of the farm. We were both stunned speechless about the turn of events with Mr. Spink.

Supreme Court of British Columbia affidavit between Mark Anthony Super (plaintiff) and Corinne Arden Super (defendant) on Mar. 29, 2007. The following are statements made by Corinne Super:

> 3: Mr. Spink was a tenant on the farm that my husband and I leased a barn to. He paid the rent from March of 2004 until February of 2005. At this time he was incarcerated in the US for a narcotics offence. He left his horses and dogs at the farm. I agreed to continue the care of the horses in return I collected the stud fees to cover their costs. He has now been released and the horses are to be returned to him.
>
> 12: The marketable horses on my property are not undervalued. I do not own the stallions. They are to be returned to Mr. Spink.
>
> 13. Mark and I had no knowledge that Mr. Spink was involved in the drug trade. He never gave me any indication that this was the case. His association with me was strictly to do with the horses. Mark and I were both extremely shocked at the news. Mark and I were aware of his sexual preference that he was gay. This did not bother me or my husband that I was aware of. There was never any drug activity on the farm.

In the civil lawsuit Spink launched to recover Capone, he included the Super divorce affidavit as evidence of his sole ownership of Capone. Super simply changed gears and backpedaled again.

Supreme Court of British Columbia affidavit between Exitpoint Stallions Limitée (plaintiff), and Corinne Super and Exitpoint Farms Inc. (defendant) dated Sept. 16, 2008:

> 3: In further support of the facts set out in the Statement of Defence, attached as Exhibits "A" through "F", respectively are:
>
> (D): A copy of an email from Mr. Spink to myself, dated May 28, 2007. I subsequently sent this email to my legal counsel, Kathleen Walker. In the Spring of 2007, Mr. Spink was assisting me with my divorce from Mark Super. As described in paragraph 33 of the Statement of Defence, Mr. Spink advised me to swear affidavits claiming that he was homosexual and that Capone 1 was being held on his behalf—neither of which is true.

EXHIBIT 7

Horse Forum Postings

Doug Spink was often the subject of gossip and innuendo on internet forums frequented by people in the horse world. It wasn't unusual for him to fire back.

The following excerpts are from a forum called chronofhorse.com:

Oct. 14, 2009, 02:32 PM
flashykatt

I agree that the creepiness factor is beyond belief. I am one of the people who just had to Google to find out what everybody was talking about. And then I had to burn that laptop.

However, I've seen Capone daughters that are incredible. I would like one for myself. I have NOT bred to him, because I haven't been able to stomach the ickiness.

Seriously, wouldn't we all love it if the stallion were standing at a regular stallion station--or somewhere like Silver Creek, Rainbow Equus, October Hill, etc.??

Oct. 14, 2009, 01:16 PM
caffeinated

ugh. Can't help it, the dude gives me the heebie jeebies.

Oct. 14, 2009, 02:38 PM
cloudyandcallie

I hope Capone kicks the Spinster right where he can do the most damage

Oct. 14, 2009, 03:27 PM
Exitpoint

Capone is back home.

There is already a lawsuit, which has already proved many times over that the person who stole him last year is so full of crap she can't keep her "stories" straight. All those documents are already publicly posted, of course; anyone pretending otherwise is naive or duplicitous. At this point, we're grinding on the RCMP to bring perjury charges, as is inevitable - though of course given her "special relationship" with the RCMP it seems she can do most anything without going to prison.

Why isn't Capone being shipped around to "breeding centers" like chattel, to "maximize his revenue?" I'll say this once, and only once: **those who have dedicated their lives to Capone's career and well-being don't give a rat's ass about "maximizing revenue" - including his owners, his trainers, his managers, and everyone else. If we wanted to "cash in" on this horse, like so many posters in this thread imagine with drooling excitement, we'd have sold him years ago for millions. We don't, we're not.**

Don't want to breed to Capone because you don't like me, or whatever? Great! Goodbye and good riddance. I've been in the horse world since before most of you learned to ride, and I couldn't care less if you "like" me or not. Capone's career was NEVER about money, and isn't today. Want to organize a great, big, pissy boycott and nobody ever breeds to him again? Great, whatever. Don't care. Have a ball.

The vast majority of you who post in this little sinkhole of rumors and fake "facts" are a disgrace to horses, and to horse sport. You can all stay here and whisper useless garbage at each other, for the rest of your lives. The rest of us care about the HORSES - the people crap is just a distraction. You go "prove" to each other all the most fervid fantasies of your overwrought imaginations. I hope it brings you entertainment. To those of us on the outside looking in, it just show who you really are. Pathetic.

I've no doubt - like most anything I say, in my own words, on this ingrown self-satirical joke of a forum, this will be "disappeared" in short order. Can't have the truth spoken aloud, can we? Upsets the dues-paying natives, etc. So be it. I've screenshotted it, and will cross-post elsewhere with less censorious tendencies. This is my first - and last - word on the subject of Capone's return home, in a rancid forum like this has become.

It's funny, because 30 years ago I read the *Chronicle* - along with the true professionals, those born with "horses in the blood" and passionate about equines (nor afraid to use the word "passion" lest a spinster fantasy turn it into "controversy") - in a sport that truly did care about HORSES. Now, look at what it's become... a bunch of empty, prejudiced, ignorant, spittle-spewing garbage - horses a mere distraction from the "fun," if that. Shameful, on all levels - the *Chronicle* was an institution - now it's a laughingstock.

I've long since washed hands of all of you. The "horse world" is dead and rotten on this continent, and needs a complete rebirth if there to be hope for a future of healthy equine/human sport here. The parasites left stuck to the bloated corpse of the "horse industry" here won't drop off until the last drop of congealing blood is sucked off. Eventually, however, you'll all grow hungry and seek more lively prey elsewhere - and then those of us who actually care about HORSES will rebuild the sports into something proud and honorable once again.

EXHIBIT 8

More About Mice

The mystery of the mice was vital to the characterization of Spink by authorities as a depraved predator. Because of the importance placed on the mice, I have enclosed the following unedited email he wrote to me about it:

Spink, Douglas on 11/1/2012 10:46 AM wrote:

If you want, we can likely track back through Fred Meyer Rewards and authenticate the purchase, and the date of the purchase. I'm guessing February or March 2010. It was about thirty bucks, plus maybe $5 for the cedar chips.

I had a couple of "humane" (hate the word) traps to catch the mice. Mice caught in those traps I then put in the cage, and they were transported down to the lowlands. That's why I KNOW that the overwhelming majority of mice in the cage were 100% fine, healthy and happy, when the thugs arrived. By my estimate, maybe 2-3 had minor - MINOR!! - injuries from Wiskey catching them.

I did use cords on their tails to keep the lightly-injured ones out of "general population" until release. The other option was more cages, and solitary confinement—I really don't like that, personally, for obvious reasons. It seemed more "humane" to keep them with me, on the desk or on the bookshelf, than have them in a jar or tiny little cage alone.

One had a slightly shortened tail—he was the one on the desk, in the t-shirt nest, with a little cord wrapped around his tail. That was tied to my computer monitor, and he slept there at night. During the day he was on the desk when I was working, and could hang out. He'd actually sit on my hand, sometimes, while I was talking on the phone or whatever. Not exactly "tame"—these are field mice, after all, but not freaked out. I learned the hard way that even with a minor injury like the tail, if he was in with the other guys they'd tear into him.

Remembering back, the night of the raid he might have been up on the bookshelf above the sofa (you can see it in the photos)—next to the books. I worried that Wiskey might jump up on the desk and get after him, so I'd put him on the shelf there—with a little nest to sleep in—when I was over there reading for a long time.

I think, not sure, but I think he was there that night as I'd been reading before falling asleep.

But I can't be 100% sure of that level of detail—it's just a bit too scrambled after the guns and threats and violence and stuff that morning.

I'd say, total guess, I remember a dozen mice in the cage. And one on the desk/bookshelf with me. Two? Could have been two out of general population, just not sure. But I think one. I know at least one. Obviously they weren't unhappy with being out of GP—they could chew through the cord trivially easily—it was just thread, basically. Scavenged from an old rock climbing setup, or some camera lanyard, or something like that. Thin, fragile stuff. A mouse can chew through plastic and wood and even metal if given the time. These tiny little strings? Give him 5 minutes and he could be gone. So, I dunno, the fact that they stayed with me for a few days, before going down with the rest of them for release—I'd carry them in my hand, or in the pocket of my shirt—seemed to suggest to me they were ok with things.

I worried after the raid that nobody would be checking the two "humane" traps I used, because if mice go in them they'll starve to death unless someone got them out. Both were under the cabin, on opposite corners. I'd say I caught, on average, a mouse or two a day in the traps. Wisk would catch a mouse every few days, in the cabin. Very rarely, that a mouse would end up dead—maybe half a dozen times over the winter? Maybe a couple more? They die really easily, when a dog of his size is "playing" with them. One accidental bite, and they're gone. Incidentally, he also used to catch bees and yellowjackets (!!) in his mouth, and bring them into the cabin. He'd—amazingly—not hurt them, and then they'd be flying around in there. At which point he'd chase them. Which was... epic. But it was amazing that he'd catch insects and not harm them—not that he was a super gentle guy or anything—but he was (is? is he dead?) a unique guy. Complex. Odd, even.

Yes, having the mice in the little habitat on the desk was soothing to me. I like them. They're fascinating, really. Quick and clever and quiet and social and intense, in their own ways. I guess that makes me a monster—for saving them from Wisk, for catching them in "humane" traps instead of killing them with snap traps, and for taking them down to the farmlands to release. Oh, and keeping them on the desk with me if they had minor—MINOR!—injuries instead of killing them or just figuring sink or swim with the other mice.

I don't remember any serious injuries with any of the mice there. Not even moderate injuries—with Wisk, they were either fine, or they were dead (which was really rare). He didn't "chew" on them. He barely even left saliva on them. So of a dozen or so mice around, I'd say one (two?) had a shortened tail—from Wisk, or from who knows what, in mouse life. That's it—everyone else was totally, absolutely, 100% fine. They made little nests in the habitat—I'd put in napkins (picked them up when in town, at pizza places—I eat alot of pizza) and they'd shred them and make these elaborate homes. I cleaned the habitat out by dumping the chips after each release.

They killed all of them. Quite a "rescue."

- DB_LC-S

EXHIBIT 9

Doug Spink's verbal statement to Judge Ricardo Martinez at the sentencing hearing, July 16, 2010:

Your Honor, five years ago I stood in this courtroom, almost five years ago, and I made a commitment to you. I made a commitment that I was going to turn my life around, that I was going to do better after my life had fallen to nothing, the death of my best friend, and many other friends at the time had left me in a state where I was making terrible decisions. And when I was sentenced in your courtroom I made you a promise I would change my life and get it back on track.

Since that time I have worked every day to uphold that commitment to you. When I did my prison time at Sheridan, I worked in the education department. I also taught volunteer classes in the evening. I met people from all walks of life, all races, and all educational backgrounds, and learned so much from them at the time.

Since that time I've worked to improve my relationship with my mother and father, who is now deceased, with my friends and family. I found so much value and so much joy in those relationships that I had let die in the years when I was spiraling downwards. I returned to my career in the technology industry, something I had done for 15 years previously, and it's been a great blessing to be back in that field, in the law-abiding field, and to be productive once again in society.

I had no disciplinary problems in prison. Never had a write-up, never had a shot. No disciplinary problems in the halfway house. I am proud of that because I've worked hard to do that, not just because I've avoided getting in trouble. I've lived within my financial means. I've rebuilt from nothing. And I've been proud to do that and have the opportunity to do that. It's taken time and hard work, seven days a week. I've been readmitted to my graduate school program in system science. And I hope to start this winter. I have continued my academic work, as I told you in court five years ago that I hoped to do.

As my lawyer had said, I have no problems whatsoever of being supervised by the probation office, in fact I welcome it. For the first 18 months of my supervision my probation Officer Jerrod Akins came and visited frequently. He was always welcome at my place. We would have coffee. He gave me very clear guidelines. He helped me with advice about difficult things in my life. I considered him a friend.

During the time that I've been on supervised release, three years, I've never had a problem. I've never been unemployed. I've never done drugs. I've never done anything knowingly wrong. I welcome direction and guidance from the supervised release folks and from the probation office. But for the last 18 months I've never seen anybody. I never received a phone call. I never received any information that I was doing anything inappropriately. I made no effort to hide anything from supervised release. I was at my house. I work from home seven days a week. I'm always there. I answer the phone all the time. And I don't want it to be seen that I was hiding myself from them, because I was not.

What mistakes I've made, and I acknowledge mistakes, were not through an effort to hide or avoid supervision. I've looked forward to supervised release as part of my case. I never petitioned for it to be cut, because I didn't think that was fair. That was part of the sentence you gave me and I've told many of my friends that it's my job to do that five years of supervised release, not for you to make it shorter because it was inconvenient for me. That's why I never petitioned to cut my supervised release after three years.

I acknowledge I was wrong to present at the HOPE conference in New York without getting approval. It was a stupid mistake. I was given an invitation at the last minute to come and present. I didn't think I could get approval in time. I should have simply said no. There's no question about that. I am not perfect. I have made mistakes in the last three years. Those are mistakes I will not make again.

I do want to talk briefly about this situation with Mr. Clarke. He should have never been allowed in my home and he should never have been allowed to visit me. Despite the fact that he was traveling under a false name, I should have done better research into his background in knowing he was not an appropriate person to be in my home. I am completely and totally accountable for that failure. It was a failure to effectively manage him, to oversee him, and to supervise him when he was a guest of my house. And it's a failure that rests on my shoulders. It's a mistake that has cost me beyond words to describe already, and it's a mistake I will never make again.

What I hope the court can do today is to treat me fairly, according to my actions, and according to my genuine intentions. That's all I hope for. I hope to continue with my volunteer work with human rights activists in Iran, China, Tibet and Burma, using technology to avoid suppression by their totalitarian governments. I hope to continue my work in the technology industry.

I hope to continue my strong relationships with my family, my friends, my colleagues and my community. I hope to continue my political activism, and most of all I hope to continue giving back to the community as much as I'm able to. That's the challenge you gave back to me five years ago, to give back. That's what I've done for the last five years to the best of my ability.

So five years on I stand in your courtroom again, looking you in the eyes and acknowledging the promise I made to you five years ago. I've told so many of my friends the story of standing in front of Judge Martinez and being admonished for falling down and for falling with all the gifts I've been given, to give back to society. I tell it because I'm proud of the fact that you challenged me to get back on track after the tragedies of my life.

I'm not perfect. I've made mistakes along the way. But every day of my life since then I have worked to get back on track. I welcome supervision from the probation department. I have nothing against the probation department. I have nothing to hide from the probation department. I'm more than happy to work with them in any way to make sure I'm transitioning back into society as effectively as possible. That is my goal as well and has been since my release from prison.

I will re-double my effort to avoid any problems and any mistakes. One mistake is too many. One mistake in three years is too many. I should have made no mistakes, and I failed in that. I acknowledge that failure. I promised you I would not make mistakes. And I did fail in making mistakes. I will try harder to make no more.

What I'm asking for today and what I'm hoping for today is only the chance to continue my work that I started in this courtroom five years ago, to continue to rebuild a healthy, law-abiding positive life for myself, and to be a productive member of my community.

Thank you, Your Honor. Thank you.

EXHIBIT 10

In a January 2008 interview for *Horses Incorporated* magazine, Spink likened chipping in the sport of rock climbing to gelding a stallion:

January 2008, *Horses Incorporated*:

For nearly twenty years of my life, rock climbing has been a passion of mine. As a small child, I was always off climbing trees and scaling crumbling hillsides. That evolved into full-scale obsessions through my teens and 20s, though eventually over-use injuries slowed down my climbing considerably. In climbing, we have the issue of chipping. Is it ethically "right" to chip holds on a given rock face, so as to make it climbable?

The overwhelming consensus amongst climbers around the world is that chipping is totally unacceptable. We say that it is "dumbing down" the rock, bringing the climb to our level instead of bringing ourselves to the level of the climb. It also robs others of the experience of seeing the rock in its natural state, and perhaps rising to that challenge—and experiencing something profound in the process.

I see a parallel issue in horses. Yes, some stallions are "too much" for a given rider. The same is true of some mares, and some geldings. I believe that it shows considerably more respect for the world around us—and the beings with whom we share that world—to ask ourselves to rise to that level. Barring that, we owe it to others (and to our equine partners) to find the challenging horse an environment where their unique skills and personality are a good match.

...If a stallion is too challenging for a given rider, that rider has a responsibility to either improve his horse skills enough to make a good partner with the stallion, or to find him a new home. "Dumbing down" the stallion through surgery is not the path to genuine growth, respect, empathy, and partnership.

EXHIBIT 11

Emails pertaining to Freedom of Information requests to Whatcom Humane Society.

From: Laura Clark
Sent: February 24, 2012 11:04 AM
To: Carreen Maloney
Subject: Film Project Request

Carreen,

This email is a follow-up to our brief discussion last week concerning your film project regarding the Doug Spink animal abuse case.
    As you are aware, the Whatcom Humane Society was instrumental in providing protection and care for the animals involved in this horrific case.
    I have discussed your project with members of our staff and board of directors.
    At this time, the Whatcom Humane Society will not participate in any film or project about Doug Spink or any film or project about the animals involved in the 2010 Doug Spink bestiality case, including Capone the horse.
    You do not have permission to use any materials you may have gathered about the Doug Spink case from current or past Whatcom Humane Society staff members or volunteers, including the use of any photos, videos and/or written interviews you may have obtained.
    Much of the above mentioned information could be considered evidence and may be used in future investigations of Mr. Spink and his associates.
    As you are aware, as part of his sentencing in Federal Court, Doug Spink was ordered to have no access to computers. It is my understanding that you continue to communicate on a semi-regular basis with Mr. Spink via email. I respectfully request that you report these communications to the Federal Bureau of Prisons so they are aware of his actions.

Thank you,

Laura Clark, Executive Director
Whatcom Humane Society

From: Adam P. Karp
To: Laura Clark
Sent: October 31, 2012 7:24 AM
Subject: PRA (photos from Spink seizure)

Hi Laura,

Please consider this a public records request for photographs of mice/rats taken as part of the Spink seizure.

Thank you,
Adam
Animal Law Offices of Adam P. Karp

From: Laura Clark
Sent: October 31, 2012 8:50 AM
To: Adam Karp
CC: WHS Field Services Manager
Subject: Re: PRA (photos from Spink seizure)

For what purpose are you making this request?
    As I have informed you, the Whatcom Humane Society will in no way cooperate with any project that Carreen Maloney is involved with.
    The seizure of the animals invovled in this case was done at the bequest of the federal government and if you continue to request records from this case, we will have to involve them as well as our own attorney's.

Thank you.

Laura Clark

From: Adam P. Karp
Sent: Wednesday, October 31, 2012 9:05 AM
To: 'Laura Clark'; Kirsten Barron
Cc: 'WHS Field Services Manager'; Adam Karp
Subject: RE: PRA (photos from Spink seizure)

Dear Laura,

I am truly not looking to create bad blood between us. I respect you immensely and know how hard a job you have.

That said, your position is unnecessarily combative and seems obsessed with Carreen Maloney.

First, the public records act does not allow you to inquire as to the purpose of the request. It is irrelevant to your duty to produce.

Second, you may not discriminate against requesters seeking the same information.

Third, that you claim the federal government enlisted WHS to conduct the investigation and obtain evidence merely strengthens the argument that you must provide this per the public records act.

Fourth, that you do not want WHS involved in Ms. Maloney's research is irrelevant to your statutory obligation to provide the requested documentation.

If you refuse to provide me what I have requested, you are obligated to articulate the grounds for refusing the request and do so in writing.

I am happy to talk to your attorney. I am copying Kirsten Barron to see if we can smooth this over. :)

Best,
Adam

EXHIBIT 12

RCW
Washington State

RCW 40.16.010
Injury to public record

Every person who shall willfully and unlawfully remove, alter, mutilate, destroy, conceal, or obliterate a record, map, book, paper, document, or other thing filed or deposited in a public office, or with any public officer, by authority of law, is guilty of a class C felony and shall be punished by imprisonment in a state correctional facility for not more than five years, or by a fine of not more than one thousand dollars, or by both.

EXHIBIT 13

Book Process

Having a book written about you isn't easy. The author pries into every aspect of your life, wanting to interview everyone around you—family, business associates (former and present), friends and enemies. Long-buried secrets and painful sore spots are pushed to the surface. Old grudges and harsh experiences get revisited.

Sometimes Doug Spink was patient, but other times, he would grow frustrated with this process and our communications would grow tense, particularly because I wanted detailed proof of every word he said about everything.

One day, after I'd asked him to supply yet another piece among thousands of particles of evidence he turned over, he summed up how he felt about this process:

> I don't know where it is and I cannot burn any more of what 'life' I have hunting for it.
> Howard has it.
> Plus those fucks at the U.S. Attorney's office have it, of course. Let's call THEM and ask them to spend hours hunting through files looking for documents, ok? I mean, they're fucking PAID BY THE TAXPAYERS TO DO THIS FUCKING SHIT. I am not.
> They have secretaries and assistants and all that fucking shit. I think they can start coughing up stuff. They do it when it involves cases with 'real people' in them. But I guess in my case, everyone just assumes that such things won't apply.

Still, understandings were reached at times, as the email below illustrates.

Spink, Douglas on 11/01/2012 12:32 PM wrote:

One thing I realized this morning is that we are in very different lines of work. I often find it necessary to ferret out the truth of a matter. That involves pulling data, recognizing patterns, confirming intuitions. When I have convinced myself, to a given degree of confidence, that I have the truth of things, then I ACT on that conclusion—always being aware new data may come in to prove my assumption wrong, and I may need to react accordingly. This all takes place according to Bayesian mechanics.

In contrast, you are in the business of PROVING things, to a general public audience. This is very different. Usually, you already know (or are pretty sure) of what the lay of the land is. The big challenge for you is marshalling evidence to prove out what you know, and then putting that evidence into a narrative that normal people can understand and accept. So you need to dig up stuff that doesn't have anything to do with finding out what happened, but is all about being able to document—even to a skeptical, or dumb, or indifferent—audience what happened.

That's not a skill set I have, nor the work I do. And it's at the core of most of our friction. My view is this: I don't have the luxury, in most of the political/activist work I do, of "proving" stuff to a generic audience. Generic audiences don't care about us, ignore facts with regards to us, and largely attack us when we prove things out factually—so that's just not a viable path forward (or it hasn't been historically). Like everyone, I've tried it. Like everyone in our community who takes on an activist role, I've been badly burned.

That led me to working more for learning the truth of things, and then acting accordingly. I have a deep moral obligation to ensure I'm acting on good data—but generally have little or no reason to waste time "proving" to some random person that what I know is true. If I know it's true, then I can act on it, build on it, expand the pattern I have confidence in, and so forth. So I tend to be obsessive about KNOWING a data point is valid: could it be faked, could it be disinfo? But once I know, it just goes into the pattern. Click.

You don't work like that, at all. Those little data points that I know and can just click into the pattern, you have to go back and document. That's extremely frustrating to me, as it goes against the grain of where I invest energy. I pour energy into ferreting out unexpected facts—you pour energy into proving known realities.

It's interesting to see the clash of world models that results from our different ways of working. In your world, proving the truth of things matters. In my world, the Normals don't give a fuck anyway so we have to learn and understand and act completely outside of that dynamic. It's deeply ingrained in us, and in me. To the point where I find it almost unbelievable to find someone caring about "proving" obviously true (but not publicly documented) things.

So, there you go.

- DB_LC_S

EXHIBIT 14

The following account didn't fit into the story I wrote about Doug Spink, but it's relevant to the theme of this book so I included it here. Unlike most zoos I interviewed, the subject of this piece, Malcolm Brenner, doesn't believe he was born a zoo, but rather that his tendencies were created from childhood sexual abuse.

WET GODDESS

Before hearing zoophiles discuss their histories, I had theorized that their sexual preference for animals stemmed from horrible treatment at the hands of people. Perhaps it was some disconnect springing from abuse that had caused them break away from humans to form relationships with the animal kingdom instead. I was surprised to find out that most zoos I interviewed felt they were born zoophiles, and believed the preference was stamped into their genetic coding, not a result of trauma.

Like the woman from the Midwest who had been sexually abused by other children, Malcolm Brenner was another exception, a person who fit my initial hypothesis. He thought his sexual feelings towards animals came as a result of what he had suffered as a child. Now sixty-six years old, he'd undergone early life experiences that fostered within him a fundamental distrust of people. Growing up in New Jersey, he was bullied at school and had a hard time making friends. Things were no easier at home. His mother was cold, distant and self-absorbed, which left her son feeling alienated and unloved.

But none of that was the worst of the horrors faced by young Malcolm.

Just a few months after Brenner was born, a psychiatrist paid by his parents to help him began doing the opposite—he sexually and emotionally abused Brenner once a week until the boy was seven years old. "As a child, I only saw him smile once, and that was looking at a newborn baby," Brenner recalled. "It was the terrifying smile of a predator encountering helpless prey."

Dr. Albert Duvall was a practitioner of the theories of Wilhelm Reich, an Austrian-born psychoanalyst who was an associate of Sigmund Freud. Reich believed he had discovered a new form of energy called "orgone," its name derived from "orgasm." Reich was on a mission to help patients reach their "orgastic potency," and Duvall was one of the associates Reich trusted to help run his Orgonomic Infant Research Center.

Malcolm Brenner didn't know it then, but he was not the only one tortured by Dr. Duvall. Many more have come forward as adults to tell their stories. The list includes Jennifer Jones, daughter of actress Susan Strasberg, and Lorna Luft, half-sister to Liza Minelli and daughter of Judy Garland. Over and over, the pattern was similar. Instead of grooming his victims, Duvall groomed the parents so they would keep bringing him subjects to feed his insatiable appetite. Parents unwittingly paid the doctor to violate their children. Then he laid the psychological groundwork so they would not believe their offspring when they revealed the abuse.

Brenner's trust in people was compromised so fundamentally by Duvall's actions that he never truly recovered. A part of him would always be trapped in that locked soundproof room, walls and doors covered with cork that muffled his cries for help, lying naked on a bed that Duvall called a couch. The psychiatrist cruelly dug his fingers into an inconceivable number of tiny bodies, just as he did Brenner's, supposedly breaking through "body armor" to release pent-up emotions and increase orgone energy in order to treat illness, both physical and emotional.

Then he did much worse.

To frighten him into submission, Duvall squeezed the boy's head with his hands so hard that Brenner thought his skull would implode.

And there was this memory, among the most painful of all. Brenner detailed it in one of three books he's authored, *Growing Up in the Orgone Box: Secrets of a Reichian Childhood.*

> Duvall, staring at my penis, reaches down and with a cold hand pulls back my foreskin. He bends low until his face hovers above it. His nostrils flare, inhaling the essence of little boy pheromones. Then his mouth gapes wide with yellow, nicotine-stained teeth and

suddenly my penis is hot and wet as it disappears in that horrible mouth and the teeth close around it.

I am terrified, too scared to scream.

Dr. Duvall sucks, making a revolting slurping sound. All I can see are his lips around the base of my penis and his glowering gray eyes, alive with hate, staring into mine. It seems like scales spread across his face and he becomes something inhuman, something horrifying, reptilian instead.

"If you tell anyone about this, I'll bite it off," he growls, teeth tightening a fraction of an inch.

As Dr. Duvall's weekly sessions took their toll, Brenner's sexuality began to blossom, but not in the direction of other human beings. When he was five, he got an erection as he watched the Walt Disney film *The Shaggy Dog* and grew excited by its star, an Old English Sheepdog. By his teenage years, he had begun experimenting sexually with the family dogs. And when he was a college student, he fell in love with a dolphin named Dolly at a Florida theme park.

"I wondered what was wrong with me," he said. "Why I wasn't having normal male desires for women."

∩

By the 1970s, Brenner was no longer a frightened child under the thumb of a sadistic pedophile. The doctor was dead, but Brenner had survived. He enrolled at New College in Sarasota, Florida, a private school for the liberal arts. His passions included writing and photography.

It was while attending New College that he landed his first paid job as a photographer. An author hired him to take pictures for a book she was writing about dolphins who performed at Floridaland, a marine theme park Brenner remembered going to as a kid.

That's where he met Dolly, a four-hundred-pound bottlenose dolphin. Her role in the show was to swim alongside a riverboat on the intracoastal waterway, impressing visitors with her powerful leaps out of the water to accept fish from her trainer who stood on the upper deck.

Brenner was instantly captivated by Dolly. He talked about their connection in *Dolphin Lover,* a seventeen-minute film about them from 2015.

Her courtship, as it progressed, got more vigorous and intense. She would rub her genital slit against me. And if I tried to push her away, she would get very angry with me. One time when she wanted to masturbate on my foot and I wouldn't let her, she threw herself on top of me, and pushed me down to the twelve-foot bottom of the pool.

When the aggressive approach didn't work, Dolly became more gentle, rubbing her teeth gently on his arm or leg, "which produced an amazingly erotic feeling to me."

For a young man who'd never had much luck in the way of romance with human females, this was the most satisfying sexual contact of his life. "Whatever I was getting from the dolphin seemed very fulfilling. Very rewarding. It was like she was the only female who was really paying any attention to me. And that made a tremendous amount of difference to me."

The first time Brenner tried to have sex with Dolly, it didn't go well. The water was cold, and he was nervous about being discovered. It wasn't until the park closed permanently, sold off to be used for a housing development, that he finally got his chance.

Dolly and one male were the only dolphins who hadn't yet been shipped off to other marine facilities. Dolly squeezed her way through a barrier to join Brenner in a pool where they were alone and away from the male dolphin. They played what Brenner described as "erotic games" for half an hour. "We had to try several different positions before we found one that worked."

Finally they did. She was horizontal in the pool, and he was vertical.

> As we started making love, I felt this just intense sense of merging with her on every level—emotionally, mentally, physically, spiritually. It's really like we stopped being two individual creatures and became one creature that was making love with itself. I've never experienced such intense intimacy with anyone. It felt transcendental. It felt cosmic. As I climaxed, Dolly groaned. She made a series of three groans in a rising cadence, and that led me to believe that she had also experienced an orgasm.

When it was over, Dolly swam over, laid her snout on his shoulder and embraced him with her flippers while they stared into each other's eyes.

Brenner categorically denies that he forced Dolly to have sex with him. "When other people claim that I must have raped the dolphin, my response is that you can't out swim a dolphin in the water. Michael Phelps could not out swim a dolphin in the water."

But Brenner believes the emotional attachment he and Dolly shared is what eventually ended her life. More than forty years later, he still gets choked up when he talks about what happened next.

Dolly was transferred to another park. She stopped eating. Then she stopped breathing. She was found dead at the bottom of her tank six months after Brenner last saw her. Unlike humans, dolphins have a voluntary respiratory system. Brenner thinks she chose to stop breathing—that she committed suicide.

The relationship had such an impact on him that in 2010, he published a novel titled *Wet Goddess: Recollections of a Dolphin Lover* that was based on his experiences with Dolly.

Brenner was more in love with Dolly the dolphin than anyone he ever met before or since, and he believes she felt the same love for him. "Dolly died of a broken heart," he said.

Malcolm Brenner with Dolly at Floridaland.

ACKNOWLEDGMENTS

This book couldn't have happened without the help of many people who offered me information, advice, ideas, wisdom and their time as this project progressed.

First and foremost, I'd like to thank all the sources I interviewed for this piece of work—even the hostile ones—because without them, there would be no story. I won't name them all again here, because you've already met them in the pages of this book, but I owe them my gratitude.

Those who weighed in with their creative input contributed a great deal to making this book a better read. The lead editor was Frances Peck, who made substantive, thoughtful suggestions that significantly improved the strength of the writing and the flow of the narrative. Veteran journalist Margo Goodhand also generously provided considerable, valuable editing advice, and answered numerous queries of a journalistic nature, as did Gordon Sinclair Jr.

Many other writers weighed in along the way, from scribes I've known most of my life, to wordsmiths I became acquainted with only recently. Fellow Carleton University School of Journalism alumni were invaluable pillars of support and inspiration, including Marie Morrissey, Lisa Hotchkiss, Ron Fine, Carolyn Abraham and Tamara Vukusic. Writers newly met who gave a helping hand simply because they recognized the value and import of a compelling untold story are author Susie Moloney, who offered her influential publishing connections to a stranger, and Tulane University English professor Tom O'Connor, who compiled a thoughtful critique whilst he was in the midst of his own personal tragedy—the loss of his wife, author Margaux Fragoso, to cancer.

Sincere thanks go out to all the animal rescuers who pushed past discomfort over the subject matter to allow me to conduct interviews with them, and quote their thoughts in this book. They provided a knowledgeable sounding board as I researched zoophilia over the years. Among the rescuers who were helpful (in addition to the ones already named in this book through the use of their quotations) are Robin Beaulieu, Heather McKnight, and Brenda Parkin, as well as Vanessa Valentine, who also diligently made sure my letters and packages always found their way to me no matter where I landed.

Animal welfare advocate Susan Simmons, a retired psychologist I've known for many years, served a key role, answering my abundant supply of questions about human behavior and psychology with profound insight and vast experience. She helped me keep perspective and balance when the journey grew bumpy at times. Her partner, Helen James, also provided kind and gentle support.

Erin Keedian, an animal rescuer and friend since age five, provided innumerable hours of discussion with me on the topic of this book, even when she'd sometimes have preferred to talk about something else.

Meg Pitman was a source of boundless energy and good humor during my relatively isolated year I spent on Vashon Island, where we met renting and sharing a farm property overlooking the ocean.

Troy Westwood, a trusted and treasured friend going back thirty years, always read advance pages I sent to him immediately, and never failed to have something interesting and intelligent to say about what was written on them.

Public relations wizard Heather Kirk had creative ideas about how to introduce this work to the world, and she also arranged the Sumo trip that brought me across the ocean to Hiromi, which changed my life trajectory instantly and profoundly.

Danny Parizek was a constant source of support and good cheer, never allowing me to stay in darkness for too long without shining his special brand of light and love my way.

Cynde Harmon of Really Real Films patiently provided filmmaking advice at the beginning of this project, when I originally planned to turn it into a documentary. It's not an easy task to teach a writer how to make a film, but she made it seem possible.

Thanks also goes to attorney Richard Clarke, who has protected my creative property with dedication and skill for twenty years.

Chris Fettin, an accomplished and masterful graphic designer, showed up right when I needed him most in New Orleans, transforming my text skillfully and fluidly into design mode. And then Friesens brought his digital work to life on paper in my beloved home province of Manitoba, delivering dedicated service and exemplary product quality to these pages.

Patrick Maloney, my brother and best friend, always supports my pursuits, no matter how bizarre or misguided they may seem on the surface, without questioning or judging the merits (or lack thereof). Extra kudos to him for helping haul my belongings over distances both great and small as I searched for somewhere safe to work on this story.

Two sources for this book must be noted. Douglas Spink and his mother, Claire, participated in countless hours of interviews, complied with copious requests for documents to back up every statement and claim they made, and asked for nothing in return but an honest telling of this tale.

Rest in Peace
Several dear friends died during the writing of this story, good people who were there to listen when it came to the challenges. Included in this lamentable group are Richard Barrington of Long Beach, California; Madalin Bernard of New Orleans, Lousiana; Julie Davis of Bellingham, Washington; and the newspaperman who gave me my first real journalism job in 1988 at the *Winnipeg Free Press*—David Lee of Winnipeg, Manitoba, who taught me so much about the finer points of the craft. And of course Hiromi Monro, my late husband, who is never far from my thoughts.

PHOTO ACKNOWLEDGMENTS

Page 100: Associated Press photo

Page 176: Photos by Claire Spink

Page 177: Top left: Photo by Claire Spink
Top right and bottom: Photographers unknown

Page 178: Photos by Claire Spink

Page 179: Photographers unknown

Page 180: Top: Photo by Bob Langrish
Bottom: Photo by Roger Jensen/*Oregonian*

Page 181: Top: Photo by Carreen Maloney
Bottom left and right: Photographers unknown

Page 182: Top and bottom right: Photos by Doug Spink
Bottom left: Photographer unknown

Page 183: Top left and right: Photographers unknown
Bottom: Photo by Doug Spink

Page 184: Top: Photo by Doug Spink
Bottom: Photographer requested anonymity

Page 185: Top and bottom left: Prison photography service
Bottom right: Screen shot from police surveillance video

Page 186: Photographer requested anonymity

Page 187: Photos by Carreen Maloney

Page 188: Photos by Carreen Maloney

Page 189: Photo by Carreen Maloney

Page 190 & 191: Photographer requested anonymity

Page 192: Photo by Carreen Maloney

Page 193: Top: Photo by Doug Spink
Bottom: Photo by Carreen Maloney

Page 194: Top and bottom right: Photos by Heather Kirk
Bottom left: Photographer unknown

Page 401: Photograph supplied by Malcolm Brenner

Effort was made to contact the people who took the photographs used in this book, and permission to reprint was obtained when the photographers were located. Unfortunately the creators couldn't always be found, particularly in cases of photographs taken decades ago. Photographers who believe they recognize their work and would like credit for pictures presented in future editions, please contact the author. All copyrights for pictures printed in this book are owned by the photographers who took them.

ABOUT THE AUTHOR

Carreen Maloney has worked as a staff journalist for the *Winnipeg Free Press*, *Ottawa Citizen* and *Business in Vancouver* newspapers, and has freelanced for *Modern Dog* and *Animal Sheltering* magazines. She has a journalism degree from Carleton University in Ottawa, Ontario.

She started her work in animal welfare at age six, with a protest at Union Station in Winnipeg against the killing of baby harp seals off Canada's east coast. Maloney has rescued and fostered hundreds of cats, many of them feral. She helped rescue animals stranded in New Orleans following the devastation of Hurricane Katrina in 2005. She is dedicated to humane education, and to that end, she has created and written blogs about animal rescue.

Maloney is a dual citizen of Canada and the United States. She has lived in many places around North America, including Winnipeg, Ottawa, Vancouver, San Diego, Los Angeles, Bellingham, Custer, Vashon Island and New Orleans.

Author can be reached at:

3436 Magazine Street, #136
New Orleans, LA 70115

uniquelydangerous.com